DIETITIANS OF CANADA

Simply Great Food

250 quick, easy & delicious recipes

Patricia Chuey, MSc, RD, Eileen Campbell
and Mary Sue Waisman, MSc, RD

Robert
ROSE

Library and Archives Canada Cataloguing in Publication
Chuey, Patricia, 1967-
    Simply great food : 250 quick, easy & delicious recipes / Patricia Chuey, Eileen Campbell,
Mary Sue Waisman.

At head of title: Dietitians of Canada.
Includes index.
ISBN-13: 978-0-7788-0155-9
ISBN-10: 0-7788-0155-1

    1. Cookery. 2. Nutrition. I. Campbell, Eileen, date II. Waisman, Mary Sue (Mary Suzanne),
1957– III. Dietitians of Canada IV. Title.

TX714.C478 2007   641.5'63   C2006-905903-9

Disclaimer
The recipes in this book have been carefully tested by our kitchen and our tasters. To the best of our
knowledge, they are safe and nutritious for ordinary use and users. For those people with food or other
allergies, or who have special food requirements or health issues, please read the suggested contents of
each recipe carefully and determine whether or not they may create a problem for you. All recipes are
used at the risk of the consumer.
    We cannot be responsible for any hazards, loss or damage that may occur as a result of any recipe use.
    For those with special needs, allergies, requirements or health problems, in the event of any doubt,
please contact your medical adviser prior to the use of any recipe.

Design & Production: PageWave Graphics Inc.
Editors: Judith Finlayson and Sue Sumeraj
Proofreader: Sheila Wawanash
Indexer: Gillian Watts
Photography: Colin Erricson
Food Styling: Kate Bush
Prop Styling: Charlene Erricson

Cover image: Chicken in Butter Sauce (page 172)

We acknowledge the financial support of the Government of Canada through the Book Publishing
Industry Development Program (BPIDP) for our publishing activities.

Published by Robert Rose Inc.
120 Eglinton Avenue East, Suite 800, Toronto, Ontario, Canada M4P 1E2
Tel: (416) 322-6552 Fax: (416) 322-6936

Printed in Canada
1 2 3 4 5 6 7 8 9 CP 15 14 13 12 11 10 09 08 07

Contents

Acknowledgments

Few great works can be achieved alone — most of the time it's a group effort, and *Simply Great Food* is no exception. Talented authors, a distinguished expert Review Committee, dedicated staff and supportive sponsors have joined to make this cookbook a success.

Sincere thanks go to the authors: Patricia Chuey, RD, for creating the innovative nutrition text and Chef Eileen Campbell for both her culinary expertise and her significant contributions to the editorial content. Hats off to Donna Bottrell, RD, who was a great help to Eileen, testing each and every recipe.

Thanks also go to Caroline Dubeau, Manager, Public Service Initiatives and Regional Development at Dietitians of Canada, for her vision for this book; to Mary Sue Waisman for coordinating the effort and keeping the group focused; and to Helen Haresign, Vice-President Development, Dietitians of Canada, for her guidance. A special thanks to the members of the Review Committee for volunteering their time to review the text and ensure the accuracy of the content. Dietitians of Canada members who participated on the Review Committee include:

Heather McColl, British Columbia
Wendy Shah, Alberta
Heidi Bates, Alberta
Carol Schnittjer, Manitoba
Marcia Cooper, Ontario
Linda Ross Stringer, Ontario
Christina Blais, Quebec
Laurie Barker Jackman, Nova Scotia
Bonnie Conrad, Nova Scotia

Dietitians of Canada (DC) gratefully acknowledges the Nutrition Month® 2007 Official Sponsors for their generous contribution in the development of this book:

• Compass Group Canada
• Dairy Farmers of Canada
• General Mills Canada Corporation

Our advice, disseminated through DC products and services, is based on sound science and the professional expertise and experience of our members. Materials are written by dietitians, then reviewed by dietitians with experience in that topic area. DC maintains full editorial control of materials.

Dietitians of Canada makes a point of being transparent regarding sources of revenue. We do this through acknowledgments on our website, on specific educational tools and resources and at meetings. However, the acknowledgment is not an endorsement of the products or services of the contractor, sponsor or advertiser. Dietitians of Canada does not endorse or promote any commercial products or services.

We also want to thank our publisher, Robert Rose Inc., and in particular Bob Dees and Marian Jarkovich. Thanks, too, to editors Judith Finlayson and Sue Sumeraj for their editorial support; to the staff at PageWave Graphics — Andrew Smith, Joseph Gisini, Kevin Cockburn and Daniella Zanchetta — for their expert contribution to the design and production of this book; to food stylist Kate Bush; to prop stylist Charlene Erricson; and to Colin Erricson for his fabulous photographs.

Last, but certainly not least, thanks to all the Canadians who generously shared their recipes and tips for this book. Without your contributions, *Simply Great Food* would not exist!

About Dietitians of Canada

Dietitians of Canada
Les diététistes du Canada

Dietitians of Canada (DC) is the national voice of dietitians, your trusted source of food and nutrition information. DC represents more than 5,500 dietitians committed to improving the health of Canadians through food and nutrition.

Dietitians are the ideal source of current, reliable nutrition advice. If you need information on healthy eating, contact a registered dietitian. To find a registered dietitian in your community, contact your local department of public health, community health center or hospital. You can also find registered dietitians who work in private practice on Dietitians of Canada's award-winning website, **www.dietitians.ca**, or by calling the Consulting Dietitians Network at 1-888-901-7776.

Nutrition Month® Encourages Canadians to Eat Well, Live Well!

March is Nutrition Month® across Canada. In celebration of healthy eating, dietitians across Canada unite to organize events and communications to reinforce the importance of nutrition in achieving health and well-being. Nutrition Month® celebrated its 25th anniversary in 2006. The campaign has been growing since the early 1980s and is now one of the most recognized social marketing campaigns in Canada.

Nutrition Month® stimulates nutrition-related activities in communities across Canada, which helps you find dietitians, your best source of reliable nutrition information.

Watch for this logo to identify Nutrition Month® activities in your community:

eat well   live well
manger mieux   c'est meilleur
TM/MD Dietitians of Canada
Les diététistes du Canada

Foreword

From time to time, we all need to reflect on what's important in our daily lives. In our fast-paced world, where time is one of our most precious commodities, many of us find it difficult to eat well and even more difficult to get into the kitchen and cook. But there's good reason to do both! Cooking can be creative, fun and easy. It can also produce delicious, healthy food that your family will enjoy and reap many benefits from.

Simply Great Food is a compilation of 250 recipes submitted by dietitians and consumers who are looking for ways to make healthy eating quick, easy and delicious. But it's more than just a cookbook. In addition to recipes that will help you create tasty food, this book provides you with up-to-date nutrition information and an abundance of ideas to support you in making cooking and healthy eating a regular part of your everyday life.

This book represents the fifth cookbook from Dietitians of Canada. Following on the successes of *Eat Well, Live Well*; *Healthy Pleasures*; *Great Food Fast*; and *Cook Great Food*, *Simply Great Food* is destined to become a household treasure. Each recipe is accompanied by a nutritional analysis outlining the nutrients per serving: calories, protein, fat, carbohydrate, fiber, calcium, sodium and iron. In addition, the recipes have been analyzed to help people with diabetes use them in menu planning (see page 328). Helpful tips and menu suggestions prepared by the authors and professional dietitians also accompany many of the recipes. Every page contains useful information that will help you cook and eat well.

Dietitians continue to be the most trusted source of nutrition information for Canadians. They are health professionals, working in health care, industry, government and education, who play a major role in helping Canadians enjoy a healthy lifestyle through food and nutrition. They influence the development and promotion of consumer products and services, and manage quality food service operations. In addition, they provide advice to decision-makers that will have an impact on healthy eating choices where you live, work, play and learn. Visit Dietitians of Canada's award-winning website, **www.dietitians.ca**, for a wealth of current and practical information on food and nutrition — everything from how to read food labels to what foods to eat if you have a chronic illness.

In *Simply Great Food*, Dietitians of Canada provides you with solutions to everyday nutrition challenges. It is our hope that, in thumbing through this book, you'll realize:

- getting into the kitchen and preparing healthy meals is easy;
- involving your partner, spouse, friends and/or family in the experience of cooking and eating is fun; and
- taking the time to enjoy a meal with family and friends is one of life's great pleasures.

Enjoy this cookbook and use it every day!

Mary Sue Waisman,
Registered Dietitian, Professional Chef
and lover of all things food-related

Introduction

Pause for a moment and imagine this scenario. You arrive home after a busy day at work or running around with the kids, or both. Everyone is hungry, including you. You want to put a delicious, wholesome meal on the table, and you need to do it fast! A smile comes to your face as you open your well-organized fridge. You did some preparation last night, and a container of washed and sliced carrots, red and yellow peppers and cucumbers is ready. You pop the top off a great-tasting, nutritious dip and pour refreshing fruit spritzers, and everyone enjoys an energizing nibble. The snack boosts your family's energy and buys you time while, like the finest chef in town, you work your magic to quickly throw together a dinner such as Sticky Mango Chicken Salad (page 156) or Tasty Fish Cakes (page 205), just two of the recipes in this book that can be completed in short order. The kids help, everyone loves the meal, and it fits into your partner's cholesterol-lowering diet.

It's not a dream. It's possible. *Simply Great Food* can help make it happen by providing you with the tools you need to create meals and snacks your family will love, in time frames that fit your busy schedule.

In *Simply Great Food*, we give you a quick review of the basics of healthy eating, then show you simple solutions for turning this knowledge into action. The book is divided into the following sections:

- "Let's Eat!" which provides nutrition advice from registered dietitians and reviews the basic principles for eating well.
- "Easy Food Solutions," which shows you how to plan meals and organize your kitchen so you can prepare delicious recipes at a moment's notice. You'll also find grocery shopping know-how and information on keeping food safe, as well as tips to make cooking an enjoyable experience.
- 250 delicious, user-friendly recipes, with accompanying nutrient information.

Boxed information, which answers frequently asked questions about nutrition and food, as well as tips for overcoming barriers to healthy eating, are highlighted throughout the book.

In addition, all the recipes have been analyzed according to the "Beyond the Basics: Meal Planning for Healthy Eating, Diabetes Prevention and Management" system. If you have diabetes, refer to the Canadian Diabetes Association (CDA) Food Choice Values listed with each recipe to see how it fits with your menu plan.

The best part is, all of the recipes have been chef- and family-tested, so we're confident that you will enjoy them!

Let's Eat!

Did you feel good when you read the title of this section? While we need to eat to provide our bodies with energy and nutrients, for most people eating is also a social experience. We go "out to lunch" with the girls, invite friends over for "a bite to eat" after work on a Friday night, plan elaborate meals for special occasions such as birthdays and weddings, bring chicken soup to friends when they're not feeling well and make funny shapes out of vegetables for children. Many fond memories come from sharing food with others.

Healthy eating means paying attention to what and how much we eat. From a physical perspective, our bodies need food for a variety of important reasons. Food provides energy (calories) and nutrients, which keep our bones strong, muscles moving and organs functioning. Along with physical activity, eating well helps us achieve a healthy weight, keep blood cholesterol levels on target and reduce the risk for certain diseases, such as diabetes. Healthy eating also keeps us energized so we can enjoy an active life!

Canada's Food Guide

One of the best ways to make sure you get the right amount and type of food is to become familiar with Canada's Food Guide. The guide translates scientific advice into actual food choices that will help us get enough of the nutrients our bodies need. It outlines the *kinds* of foods we need to eat to stay healthy, and also provides information on *how much* to choose daily from the following four key food groups:

- **Vegetables and Fruit**
- **Grain Products**
- **Milk Products**
- **Meat and Alternatives**

Recommendations vary for children, men, women and pregnant or breastfeeding women. The Food Guide shows us how to get all the different nutrients our body needs by choosing a variety of foods from all food groups. You can view the Food Guide online at **www.healthcanada.gc.ca/foodguide** or **www.santecanada.gc.ca/guidealimentaire**.

nutrient contribution from foods

Your body needs over 50 different nutrients. Every food is unique in terms of the nutrients it offers. Because no single food provides all of our daily nutrient needs, we need to consume food from all of the food groups to ensure that we get all the nutrients we need.

Our Top **5** Tips for Healthy Eating

Today, everyone has an opinion about what, when, where and how we should eat to stay healthy. The problem is, much of this information conflicts, so it can be difficult to know what's right. The best way to start is to build your approach around basic information that has stood the test of time. Here are our top five tips for healthy eating:

1. Make eating a satisfying and pleasurable experience.
2. Achieve balance by choosing foods from all four food groups.
3. Be adventurous — eat a variety of foods, prepared in new and different ways.
4. Be sensible about how much you eat and how often.
5. Make quality food choices.

1. Make Eating a Satisfying and Pleasurable Experience

Take time to enjoy the experience of planning and preparing meals. You'll get a great sense of accomplishment from selecting the menu and preparing the shopping list, and from cooking delicious and nutritious meals for your family and friends. Include your children in food preparation and cleanup to teach them about cooperation and sharing responsibilities, as well as food skills.

Sitting around the table as a family is a relaxing and enjoyable experience, and it provides an opportunity to connect with your loved ones and discover what's going on in their lives. You'll hear about everyone's day and make plans for future activities. Plus, you'll be able to be a positive role model for your kids by demonstrating healthy food choices and portion sizes. You'll learn what foods your family likes and dislikes, which will help you identify new foods to balance your overall eating habits.

Other important benefits of having dinner together include:

- Better nutrition. Families who frequently gather at the table have better nutrition than those who eat together less often.
- Improved emotional health. When families eat together regularly, children are more likely to do well in school and are less likely to engage in risky behaviors such as abusing alcohol, smoking and using drugs.

Take the Eating Together Challenge

In the past, families ate together every day. If that's not part of your family's routine, challenge yourself to bring everyone together as often as possible — even if it can't be every night.

What Healthy Eating Means to Me

"To me, healthy eating is ultimately peace of mind with food — ending my day knowing I made reasonable choices, fed my family well and did the best I could to apply what I know about eating healthy. Feeling energized and choosing not to diet is also a big part of it."

— Liz, stay-at-home mom, Saskatchewan

2. Achieve Balance by Choosing Foods from All Four Food Groups

Balance is another cornerstone of healthy eating. When putting meals and snacks together, we need to include a variety of foods from all four food groups to ensure we get the full range of nutrients we need. Think of it as a simple puzzle — when you put all the pieces together on the table, the picture is balanced and complete.

Achieve balance by trying to have at least three of the four food groups in Canada's Food Guide at each meal. When snacking, make an effort to have foods from two groups at each snack. This approach will help ensure that your body gets the nutrients it needs every day. The following examples show how choosing foods from the various food groups can help you achieve balance in your meals:

	instead of...	go for better balance...
Breakfast:	½ grapefruit Toast	½ grapefruit Toast with peanut butter Glass of milk
Lunch:	Grilled vegetable salad on a bed of spinach with balsamic vinaigrette	Same vegetable salad topped with shredded Cheddar cheese or leftover salmon or chicken breast Slice of multigrain bread
Dinner:	Spaghetti with vegetable sauce	Red and green bell pepper strips Spaghetti with vegetable and meat/lentil sauce, topped with grated Parmesan Fresh fruit such as cherries or orange slices

Take the Balanced Meal Challenge

Write down the foods you ate in your last three or four meals. (If you're having trouble remembering what you ate, think about where you were, what you were doing, who you were with and what time it was.) Did your meals include foods from at least three or all four of the food groups? If so, great job! If not, think about what foods you might add to improve the balance.

a matter of balance

Enjoying foods from all four food groups doesn't mean eating equal amounts of each. Emphasize grains, vegetables and fruit.

What Healthy Eating Means to Me

"Healthy eating means that you eat foods from all of the food groups and try not to eat very much candy."

— Taylor, grade 3 student, Alberta

3. Be Adventurous — Eat a Variety of Foods, Prepared in New and Different Ways

"Variety is the spice of life," as the saying goes. When it comes to food and nutrition, choosing a variety of foods means you'll get a variety of nutrients. Challenge yourself to try new foods and to prepare foods in new ways. Experimenting with different flavors, aromas and textures will stimulate your senses.

We can all fall into a rut from time to time, making the same foods over and over again. Sure enough, we're soon bored and looking for something new. Make a conscious effort to try one new food or recipe each week. Check with the kids — maybe they've seen a new food eaten by a friend at school. Ask them to find out more about it and have them help you prepare it at home.

What Healthy Eating Means to Me

"Shopping weekly for healthy food, involving my family in the kitchen, taking time to enjoy home-cooked meals — these are a big part of healthy eating for me."

— Anne, grade 2 teacher and mom, Nova Scotia

Take the Variety Challenge

Start by preparing a new recipe from this cookbook every week — preferably one that features an ingredient you haven't had before. Take your taste buds on a culinary journey by trying Chicken in Butter Sauce (page 172), Vegetable Quinoa Salad (page 153) or Sweet Chili Tofu Stir-Fry (page 226). You'll soon have many new favorites.

break the barrier: Healthy Eating Is Expensive

Many factors affect access to healthy food. If time-saving is the main goal, grabbing ready-to-go healthy foods at your grocery store can, at times, cost more, and ordering in or eating out is generally more expensive. However, when you have time to plan, many healthy choices, such as bulk whole grains, bulk or canned legumes, eggs, pasta, rice, powdered milk and fresh in-season produce, are inexpensive. Many healthy frozen and canned goods go on sale regularly. Knowing the regular prices can help you identify a good deal. To feed your family at least a couple of times at a moderate price, plan on making extra when you're preparing meals.

4. Be Sensible About How Much You Eat and How Often

Eating sensibly means paying attention to both how much and how often you eat. Different people need different amounts of food, depending on age, body size, activity level and whether they are male or female.

The best way to monitor your intake is to pay attention to portion sizes. For help figuring out how much you're eating, check out **www.dietitians.ca/eatracker**.

Here are some tips to help you manage how much you eat:

- Avoid the temptation to fill your plate with large portions. Start small; if you're still hungry, you can always go back for more.

- Leave serving bowls in the kitchen. If they aren't on the table, it will be more difficult to reach for extra servings.

- Cook less food.

- When cooking with measuring tools, make mental notes about what different measurements and serving sizes look like.

- Relax, eat more slowly and enjoy your food.

- Forget about cleaning your plate. Pay attention to your body's signals. Stop eating once you feel full and satisfied.

- Save leftovers — they can be useful ingredients for the next day's meal.

Take the HALT Challenge

Sometimes we use food to satisfy feelings other than hunger. The next time you're thinking about eating, take a moment to figure out whether you are truly hungry. You might instead be experiencing emotions that are triggering your desire to eat. HALT stands for "hungry, angry, lonely or tired." Say it out loud before you reach for a snack. Which are you feeling? If it's not hunger, food is not the solution.

break the barrier: I Don't Have Time to Cook Healthy Meals

Healthy eating and cooking may be easier than you think. They do, however, take a little planning. Use all the tools and recipes in this book to help ease your load.

5. Make Quality Food Choices

Making quality food choices means emphasizing nutrient-rich choices, fiber and whole grains, and limiting salt, fat, sugar, alcohol, caffeine and items that do not belong to a food group, such as sweets, greasy snack foods, soft drinks and rich desserts. The following tips will help you make the best choices.

Vegetables and Fruit
Fresh, frozen and canned varieties are all quality choices.

- When choosing frozen vegetables and fruit, look for those with minimal added salt, sugar or sauces.
- Choose canned varieties that have been packed in water or juice, without added sugar or salt.
- Look for fresh fruits and vegetables that are deeply colored, such as bright orange or dark green.
- Although juice is a healthy choice, choose whole fruits and vegetables more often for additional fiber. When choosing fruit juice, be sure that the label says 100% fruit juice. Fruit drinks, beverages, punches or cocktails often contain added sugar and only a small amount of real fruit juice.

Grain Products
- Choose whole-grain breads and cereals more often. Check the label to ensure that a whole grain is at the top of the ingredient list.
- Choose whole wheat pasta or couscous and brown or wild rice more often than refined products.
- Limit the amount of spread you use on bread and bread products, and avoid rich sauces on pasta.

Milk Products (and alternatives to milk)
- Check the %MF (milk fat) or %BF (butter fat) on milk, yogurt and cheese. Make lower-fat choices more often.

- If choosing a soy beverage, make sure the label says it is fortified.

Meat and Alternatives
- Choose lean cuts of meat, such as chicken, turkey, sirloin steak or pork tenderloin, and trim fat from meat when possible.
- Choose lean or extra-lean ground beef and drain off any extra fat in the pan after cooking.
- Remove the skin from chicken and other poultry after cooking.
- Eat all types of fish and seafood, and include fish rich in omega-3 fatty acids, such as salmon, herring, mackerel, rainbow trout or sardines in your meals. (For more on the benefits of omega-3 fatty acids, see page 20.)
- Use lower-fat cooking methods, such as grilling, steaming or baking, instead of frying.
- Eat legumes (beans, peas and lentils) regularly.
- Enjoy meat alternatives that are higher in fat, such as nuts and seeds, in moderate amounts.
- Limit meat, poultry or fish products that are breaded, coated with batters or deep-fried.

Other Foods
- There are many foods in the marketplace that do not fit into the four food groups: higher-fat snack foods, rich pastries, jams/jellies and other sweets, soft drinks, spreads and dressings. When eating foods that aren't known for their nutritional value, choose wisely and think about quality. Read labels and select snacks that are lower in fat (especially trans fat, hydrogenated fat and saturated fat), as well as salt and sugar.

being vegetarian

People decide to become vegetarian for different reasons. Eating vegetarian means more than just cutting out meat. There are many vegetarian eating styles. Some people are semi-vegetarian, occasionally choosing to eat meat. Lacto-ovo-vegetarians eat milk products and eggs, while lacto-vegetarians eat milk products but not eggs. In the vegan approach, no foods of animal origin are consumed.

The more foods you restrict, the more planning you'll need to do to ensure that your vegetarian menu provides all the nutrients you need to stay healthy. If you eliminate foods from some animal sources (a source of high-quality protein), you'll need to replace them with good plant sources of protein, such as legumes (beans, peas, lentils), nuts and seeds and soy products such as tofu. Nutrients that could be at risk include iron, zinc, calcium, essential fatty acids and vitamin B_{12}, so alternative sources of these nutrients need to be in place. In more restrictive vegetarian styles (vegan, in particular), vitamin or mineral supplements may be needed, especially vitamin B_{12}. Unless it's fortified, no plant food contains a sufficient amount of this vitamin.

As with all approaches to healthy eating, if you choose to follow a vegetarian approach, keep "Our Top 5 Tips for Healthy Eating" firmly in mind (see page 9). For further information, see our Vegetarian Food Guide at **www.dietitians.ca/resources/resourcesearch.asp?fn=view&contentid=2701**.

Food and Energy

Food provides our body with calories — energy, or fuel, that gets us going and keeps us running. The number of calories you need varies based on age, body size, gender and activity level. Babies, children and teens in active growth phases have higher calorie needs per pound (kg) of body weight than adults. Generally speaking, as adults age, energy needs decrease. This is why someone who is 50 years old and hasn't changed his or her eating habits may start to gain unwanted weight.

When your energy or fuel starts running low, your body sends hunger cues to encourage you to eat. Hunger is a powerful instinct, and it doesn't go away if ignored. Getting ravenously hungry can interfere with the best plans to eat well. If you're too hungry, you may be tempted to eat whatever is at hand, and overeat as well. To avoid becoming over-hungry,

- Stay energized. Eat every three to four hours to provide your body with a steady supply of fuel.

- Eat smaller amounts more often. This works well for many people and is a good strategy for eating healthier, as it's nearly impossible to meet all of our nutrient requirements in just one or two meals a day.

- Don't skip meals or snacks; if you do, you will likely feel extra hungry and may overeat.

- Understand which hunger cues are real. Try to distinguish between "wanting" something to eat because it looks good or you're bored and really feeling hungry.

Maintaining a Healthy Weight

If you consume too many calories and don't get enough physical activity, you'll likely gain weight. Through lifelong healthy eating and daily physical activity, not only will you be able to better control your weight, but you will reap many other health benefits. Make health, not appearance, your weight management goal. Find physical activities you enjoy enough to do regularly, from walking and dancing to kicking the ball around with the kids. Being active helps you use up any extra energy you have eaten as calories and will keep you energized. You'll feel good about yourself and will set a positive example for your children. Canada's Physical Activity Guide (**www.phac-aspc.gc.ca/ pau-uap/paguide/index.html**) provides more specific guidelines on how much, how often and what types of exercise are best for overall health.

Two easy measurements — body mass index (BMI) and waist circumference (WC) — can help you determine whether you are at a healthy weight and assess your risk of developing health problems associated with overweight or underweight. For more information, go to **www.hc-sc.gc.ca/fn-an/nutrition/weights-poids/guide-ld-adult/ qa-qr-pub_e.html**.

If you are concerned about your weight, consult a registered dietitian for sound advice on how to improve your eating habits (see page 28 for information on how to find one).

break the barrier:
I Hate Grocery Shopping

Everyone gets tired of grocery shopping. To ease your frustration, choose a time when the store is quiet, shop when you're full and bring a list. Focus on all the time a well-stocked kitchen will save you! You'll save money on eating out, too. Try shopping at your local farmer's market — it feels like a fun outing.

EATracker Pulls It All Together

Now that you've read a little more about healthy eating, it's time to see how you're doing. Are your food and activity choices on track? Use the Dietitians of Canada EATracker tool (**www.dietitians.ca/eatracker**) to get personalized feedback on your calorie, nutrient and food group intakes.

Nutrients in Food

The food we eat contains various kinds of nutrients that work together to give us energy and keep our bodies functioning well:

- The macronutrients — carbohydrate, protein and fat —are known as the "energy nutrients" because they provide us with calories.
- The micronutrients — vitamins and minerals — promote normal growth and development, help release energy from food and keep us healthy by fighting infection and protecting against cell damage.

The Macronutrients: Carbohydrate, Protein and Fat

Carbohydrate, protein and fat, along with alcohol, are a source of calories for your body. Gram for gram, fat supplies more calories than protein or carbohydrate:

- Carbohydrate provides 4 calories per gram.
- Protein provides 4 calories per gram.
- Fat provides 9 calories per gram.

The Dietary Reference Intakes (DRI), published by the U.S. Institute of Medicine, National Academy of Sciences, recommend the desirable percentage of calories from these different sources:

- **Protein:** 10% to 35% of total calories
- **Fat:** 20% to 35% of total calories (for adults over 18)
- **Carbohydrate:** 45% to 65% of total calories

Use the EATracker tool at **www.dietitians.ca/eatracker** to see how your calories measure up.

carbohydrate

Carbohydrates are your body's main source of fuel. Foods rich in carbohydrates should provide at least half of the energy (or calories) your body needs. Carbohydrate-containing foods include starches (potatoes, rice, bread, pasta) and sugars (both naturally occurring sugars such as honey and molasses, as well as those found in vegetables, fruit and milk, and refined sugars and sweets such as syrups, jams and jelly, soft drinks, candies and sweet desserts).

Nutrient-dense carbohydrates (meaning they provide a rich mix of vitamins, minerals and dietary fiber in addition to calories) come primarily from whole grains, vegetables, fruits and legumes. These foods are also the best sources of phytonutrients (see page 26), the benefits of which scientists are just beginning to study. Healthy eating emphasizes nutrient-dense carbohydrate choices.

A Closer Look at Dietary Fiber

In addition to nutrients, many carbohydrate-rich foods — in particular, whole grains, legumes, fruits, vegetables, nuts and seeds — supply dietary fiber. Fiber is found only in plants, and it plays a significant role in keeping us healthy. Our bodies cannot digest fiber and, oddly enough, that's where the benefit comes from. Experts continue to discuss the best way to describe the different types of fiber and their health benefits.

Insoluble fiber, also known as roughage, aids digestion. It does not dissolve in water, but absorbs it and bulks up in your gut. The bulk prevents constipation and moves waste through the gut more quickly. Therefore, insoluble fiber promotes regularity and shortens the time that any potentially harmful chemicals are in contact with your gut. Just make sure you drink lots of water to help this fiber do its job well. Insoluble fiber is found in whole grains such as wheat bran, corn bran and flaxseed. Eating the skins of fruit and root vegetables is another good way to add insoluble fiber to your meal plan.

Soluble fiber does dissolve in water. Increasing your intake of foods high in soluble fiber may help control blood cholesterol and can help people with diabetes control blood sugar levels. Soluble fiber is found in legumes, oat bran, barley, fruits such as apples and vegetables such as okra and eggplant.

Fiber may also play a role in achieving and maintaining a healthy body weight. Fiber-rich foods often take longer to chew, and the bulk makes you feel full longer. These foods are also typically lower in fat.

Because most foods contain a mix of fibers, adding a variety of fiber-rich foods to your meals and snacks is a healthy eating strategy. Despite its benefits, many Canadians eat less than half the daily recommended amount of fiber. Adult women should aim for 25 grams each day, while men should aim for about 38 grams. Women over 50 should aim for 21 grams, and men over 50 should aim for 30 grams. For children over the age of two, a simple rule of thumb is the child's age plus five equals the grams of fiber needed daily. To ensure that you get enough fiber, emphasize whole grains, vegetables, fruits and legumes in your daily choices.

whole grains

Whole grains are those that are minimally processed, leaving most of their components intact and thereby retaining most of the nutrition. A whole grain contains all three parts of the grain: the bran, the endosperm and the germ. The bran (outer coating) provides fiber, B vitamins and the minerals zinc and magnesium; the germ contains B vitamins; and the endosperm contains some protein, carbohydrate and a few more B vitamins.

When grains are refined or highly processed (such as for white flour, pasta and rice) the bran and germ (and most of their nutrients) are stripped away, leaving only the endosperm. Although refined grains are enriched with vitamins and minerals, they are still not as nutrient-rich as whole grains, and they contain far less fiber.

To identify whole grains, look for the word "whole" on ingredient lists. For example, "whole wheat flour" is made from whole-grain wheat. Flour identified simply as "wheat flour" is made from refined wheat.

As often as possible, choose whole-grain Grain Products. To get started, try Mediterranean Lentil and Rice Salad (page 155), Greek Kamut Salad (page 154), Vegetable Quinoa Salad (page 153), Greens and Grains Gratin (page 214) and Big-Batch Mediterranean Bulgur Meatloaf (page 195).

How Can I Eat More Fiber?

Eating more fiber can be as simple as making a few changes to your daily food choices. One good way to start is to read the Nutrition Facts table on food packages. Two grams of fiber is a "source" of fiber; 4 grams is a "high source"; and 6 grams is a "very high source." Here are some of our favorite tips:

- If your favorite cereal is low in fiber, top it with a higher-fiber cereal or fresh fruit.
- Aim to eat at least five servings of vegetables and fruits (fresh, frozen or canned) every day.
- Add wheat bran, oat bran, rolled oats, wheat germ, ground flaxseed, nuts or seeds to baked goods.
- Add drained, rinsed canned black beans, kidney beans or chickpeas to salads, soups or stews.
- Instead of a "meat and potatoes" meal, enjoy a savory bowl of chili made with beans, lentils and a variety of vegetables. Use canned legumes rather than dried to save time and make preparation easier.
- Choose whole-grain breads that contain at least 2 grams of fiber per slice, such as whole wheat, oatmeal, rye and pumpernickel.
- Adapt recipes to use a combination of whole wheat and white flour. You can replace up to half of the all-purpose flour called for with whole wheat flour without making other adjustments to the recipe.
- Try whole grains such as wheat berries, bulgur, kamut, amaranth and quinoa.
- Snack on fruits and nuts more often, and enjoy lower-fiber foods such as cookies, cakes and muffins less often.
- For a tasty snack, add bran, ground flaxseed or whole-grain cereal to yogurt and enjoy with fresh fruit.

What About Low-Carb Diets?

Low-carbohydrate/high-protein diets, which were popular in the recent past, have left many people short on necessary carbohydrates. Foods containing carbohydrates have important vitamins and minerals such as calcium, vitamin C, folate, potassium and magnesium that may not be as available in other types of foods. Cutting out carbohydrates puts you at risk for vitamin and mineral deficiencies. Some carbohydrate-containing foods are also important sources of fiber.

Standing the test of time for the best nutrition and healthy weight is a pattern of eating that provides mostly carbohydrate, moderate fat and enough protein to build and repair body tissue. By following Canada's Food Guide, you improve the odds that you will get the right proportions of the macronutrients, as well as all the other essential nutrients. Healthy eating, along with daily physical activity and feeling good about yourself, is the key to vitality and a healthy weight.

Adding Fiber to Your Meal Plan

The chart below shows how small changes in what you eat can make a big difference in your fiber intake. One word of caution: increase the amount you eat gradually, so your body can adjust. A gradual approach will minimize undesirable side effects such as gas, cramps or diarrhea.

Meal	Low-fiber menu	High-fiber menu	Very high-fiber menu
Breakfast	• crispy rice cereal with milk • orange juice	• oatmeal with ground flaxseed • fresh or frozen berries • milk	• yogurt topped with whole-grain bran cereal, chopped banana, raisins and ground flaxseed
Snack	• rice cakes with cheese	• rye crackers with cheese • fresh fruit	• almonds • fresh fruit
Lunch	• tuna with iceberg lettuce on white bread • cantaloupe slices • vanilla yogurt • water	• tuna with tomato slices and romaine lettuce on whole wheat bread • carrot sticks and dip • vanilla yogurt • water	• tuna salad (tuna, red and green bell peppers, celery and green onion) with romaine lettuce on whole wheat bread • carrot sticks and dip • vanilla yogurt with raspberries • water
Snack	• chocolate chip muffin • apple juice	• blueberry bran muffin • fresh apple, peel on	• blueberry bran muffin • fresh apple, peel on
Dinner	• white pasta with cream sauce • grilled chicken • salad of iceberg lettuce • chocolate cake	• whole wheat pasta with tomato sauce • grilled chicken • small slice of cake with mixed fruit salad	• whole wheat pasta with tomato sauce, red and green bell peppers, broccoli and onions • grilled chicken • fruit crisp

protein

As well as providing calories, protein supplies the building blocks (amino acids) we need to grow and to maintain and repair body tissues. It's important to consume protein every day, as our skin and organs are constantly making new cells. Protein is digested more slowly than carbohydrate, so including a source of protein at a meal keeps you feeling full longer and can help with appetite control.

The richest sources of protein are meat, fish, chicken, meat alternatives such as eggs, nuts, legumes and soy foods, and milk products. Protein-rich foods are important sources of iron and zinc and also supply magnesium and B vitamins. However, you need only a couple of servings a day and should keep portions in line with Canada's Food Guide.

fat

We all need to eat some fat. Fat is a great source of energy (or calories), providing more than twice as much as either protein or carbohydrate. It also adds flavor and texture to many foods, making them more appetizing.

Fat is made of building blocks called fatty acids. Some of these fatty acids are essential (for example, linoleic and linolenic acids), which means your body cannot make them. Consequently, they must come from food. Your body also needs fat so it can absorb the fat-soluble vitamins A, D, E and K.

Fat in food has become a very complex and confusing area of nutrition, so let's come to "terms" with it. Terms such as "monounsaturated," "saturated," "omega-3 fatty acids" and "trans" describe the chemical structure of the fat. Fats act differently in your body depending on their structure.

The consistent bottom-line message is that eating too much saturated and trans fats can increase our risk for heart disease or stroke. Trans fats that result from the process of partial hydrogenation raise "bad" cholesterol and lower "good" cholesterol levels in your blood. Because there are no known health benefits from this type of trans fat and because of the risks it poses to our health, many Canadian manufacturers are working to remove trans fats from their products. (For more information on "good" and "bad" cholesterol, visit **www.dietitians.ca/public/content/eat_well_live_well/english/faqs_tips_facts/faqs/index.asp?fn=view&id=1314**.)

Another important message is that healthy unsaturated fats, when used to replace saturated and trans fats, can help protect us from heart disease and stroke. Healthy unsaturated fats include monounsaturated fats and the essential polyunsaturated fats linoleic (omega-6) and linolenic (omega-3) fatty acids. Ongoing research suggests that some omega-3 fatty acids (docosahexanoic acid, or DHA, and eicosapentahoic acid, or EPA) may have additional health benefits, including improvement of immune and inflammatory disorders.

The nutrition information on food labels gives you information on total fat, as well as saturated fat and trans fat. Saturated fat and trans fat have one combined % Daily Value in the Nutrition Facts table.

break the barrier: Cooking Leaves a Mess in the Kitchen

Yes, it can. But you can keep the mess to a minimum by:
- keeping the kitchen organized and choosing simple recipes like the ones in this book
- making foods that can be prepared in advance
- getting family members to help
- cleaning as you go, instead of leaving it all until after the meal

Making Healthy Fat Choices

Here are some general tips that will help you make healthy fat choices:

- Limit the total amount of fat you eat.
- Choose food products with a lower amount of fat per serving as listed on the Nutrition Facts table on the food label; it is not necessary to always buy "fat-free" products. And remember, "low-fat" and "fat free" are not always lower-calorie choices.
- Keep all fat portion sizes sensible.
- Choose oils that are a source of unsaturated fat, such as olive, canola, corn, safflower and soybean.
- Use little or no added fat when preparing and serving foods.
- Enjoy small portions of nuts and seeds.

More specifically, you can reduce your intake of saturated fat by:

- trimming fat off meat;
- choosing lean meat with words such as "round" or "loin" in its name;
- buying lean or extra-lean ground beef;
- removing skin from poultry;
- limiting processed meats such as bologna, wieners, bacon, sausages and pepperoni;
- choosing skim, 1% or 2% milk, lower-fat yogurt and cheeses with less than 20% MF;
- limiting use of butter, lard, shortening, hard or hydrogenated margarine, gravy, sour cream, table (18%) cream and whipping (35%) cream;
- checking the ingredient list on food labels and limiting foods containing hydrogenated vegetable oil, shortening, coconut oil, palm oil, palm kernel oil or cocoa butter. These ingredients are often found in commercial baked goods, crackers, chocolate bars, specialty coffees and non-dairy creamers and whipped toppings.

Reduce trans fats by:

- buying foods with zero trans fat or with the fewest grams of trans fat per serving listed on the Nutrition Facts table;
- avoiding or limiting foods made with partially hydrogenated vegetable oil, such as commercial baked goods, crackers, cookies, biscuits, pies, waffles, snack foods and deep-fried fast foods.

Choose foods with monounsaturated fat by:

- using olive, canola or peanut oil in cooking and baking;
- choosing salad dressings and soft non-hydrogenated margarines made with olive, canola or peanut oil;
- snacking on nuts such as almonds and pecans;
- sprinkling slivered or chopped nuts and seeds, such as pine nuts and sesame seeds, over cooked vegetables or salads;
- spreading peanut butter or another nut butter, such as almond, on toast or bagels instead of butter;
- tossing slices of avocado onto a salad.

Increase omega-3 fatty acids by:

- enjoying two fish meals a week using fresh, canned or unbattered frozen fish;
- choosing fish high in omega-3 fatty acids such as salmon, sardines, tuna, herring, mackerel and rainbow trout (shellfish, such as shrimp, are also a good source of omega-3 fatty acids);
- sprinkling ground flaxseed, wheat germ, chopped walnuts or pumpkin seeds on cereal, yogurt and salads, and using them in baking;
- using canola oil in cooking and baking;
- choosing salad dressings and non-hydrogenated margarines made with canola or soy bean oil;
- considering the option of using foods fortified with omega-3 fatty acids.

Although sorting out the facts on fat is important for good health, you still need to achieve balance by eating a variety of foods, containing a wide range of nutrients.

The Micronutrients: Vitamins and Minerals

Your body needs vitamins and minerals only in small amounts, so they are often called the micronutrients.

The word "vitamin" comes from the Latin for "vital to life." These important nutrients promote normal growth and development, help release energy from food, fight infection, protect against damage to cells and generally keep us healthy.

Some vitamins are water soluble, which means they are not stored in the body. Your body uses what it needs and releases excess amounts in your urine, making it necessary to consume these vitamins daily.

Vitamin C and the B vitamins (thiamin, riboflavin, niacin, B_6, B_{12}, biotin, folate and pantothenic acid) are water-soluble vitamins. Others are fat soluble. These vitamins are stored in the body, but you need to eat a certain amount of fat to ensure that they are properly absorbed. Vitamins A, D, E and K are fat-soluble vitamins.

Minerals help regulate fluid balance, muscle contractions and nerve impulses. They also play an important role in forming and maintaining healthy blood cells, bones and teeth.

The following tables show the different functions of some important vitamins and minerals and list food sources for them.

Functions and Food Sources of Vitamins

Vitamin	Functions in the body	Some food sources
Vitamin A	• aids in normal bone and tooth development • aids in night vision • helps maintain the health of the skin and membranes	dark orange vegetables such as carrots, sweet potatoes and pumpkin, cantaloupe, pink grapefruit, tomatoes and tomato products, broccoli and dark green leafy vegetables including spinach, beet greens, Swiss chard and kale
Vitamin C	• helps in the development and maintenance of bones, cartilage and teeth • helps heal cuts and wounds and keep gums healthy • acts as an antioxidant • aids in iron absorption	oranges and orange juice, grapefruit and grapefruit juice, kiwifruit, strawberries, red, yellow and green bell peppers, broccoli, Brussels sprouts, potatoes and tomatoes
Vitamin D	• helps the body absorb and use calcium and phosphorus • plays a role in bone and tooth formation and maintenance	fish liver oils, fish (salmon, mackerel, sardine, tuna), fortified milk and margarine
Vitamin E	• protects the fat in body tissues from oxidation	sunflower seeds, nuts, vegetable oils, papaya, peanut butter, avocados, sweet potatoes and wheat germ
Vitamin K	• plays an important role in blood clotting	dark green vegetables such as spinach, kale and broccoli, cabbage, asparagus, cauliflower, strawberries, beef liver, lentils, dried soybeans, canola oil and soybean oil
Thiamin (vitamin B_1)	• releases energy from carbohydrates • aids in normal growth	whole-grain and enriched breads, cereals and pasta, pork products, green peas, dried beans (kidney, navy, soybeans), lentils and nuts

Functions and Food Sources of Vitamins (continued)

Vitamin	Functions in the body	Some food sources
Riboflavin (vitamin B$_2$)	• plays a role in energy metabolism and tissue formation • is involved in the metabolism of other B vitamins	milk, cheese and other milk products, meat, eggs, nuts, green peas, cooked spinach, beans (navy, soybeans), lentils and whole-grain and enriched breads, cereals and pasta
Niacin (vitamin B$_3$)	• plays a role in energy metabolism • aids in normal growth and development	meat, fish, poultry, milk, cheese, peanuts, peanut butter, beans (kidney, navy, soybeans, chickpeas), corn, green peas and whole-grain and enriched breads, cereals and pasta
Pyridoxin (vitamin B$_6$)	• aids in energy metabolism and tissue formation	meat, fish, poultry, organ meats, whole-grain and enriched cereals, beans (kidney, navy, soybeans, chickpeas), lentils, potatoes, bananas and watermelon
Cobalamin (vitamin B$_{12}$)	• aids in red blood cell formation	animal products such as meat, fish, poultry, eggs, milk, cheese and milk products (some foods, such as soy and rice beverages and soy-based meat substitutes, are fortified with B$_{12}$)
Folacin	• aids in red blood cell formation • has an essential role in making new cells	liver, cooked beans (kidney, navy, soybeans, chickpeas), lentils, asparagus, cooked spinach, romaine lettuce, Brussels sprouts, beets, broccoli, corn, green peas, oranges and orange juice, canned pineapple juice, honeydew melon, cantaloupe, sunflower seeds, nuts, peanut butter, wheat germ and enriched bread, cereals and pasta

Functions and Food Sources of Minerals

Mineral	Functions in the body	Some food sources
Calcium	• helps build and maintain strong bones and teeth • plays a role in controlling blood pressure and heart functions	milk, cheese, yogurt, calcium-fortified beverages (soy, rice and orange juice), canned salmon and sardines with bones, tofu containing calcium sulfate (bok choy and kale also provide calcium, but in smaller amounts)
Fluoride	• plays a key role in protecting teeth from decay • helps form strong bones and teeth	fluoridated water and foods grown or cooked in it, canned fish with bones
Iodine	• aids in the normal function of the thyroid gland	iodized salt
Iron	• aids in red blood cell formation	**heme iron:** clams, oysters, beef, poultry, pork, veal, lamb and fish (see page 180) **non-heme iron:** eggs, cooked beans (white beans, soybeans, lentils, chickpeas), sesame and squash seeds, iron-enriched breakfast cereals, tofu, enriched egg noodles and pasta, dried apricots, nuts, bread, oatmeal, wheat germ, dried raisins, baked potatoes and blackstrap molasses

Functions and Food Sources of Minerals *(continued)*

Mineral	Functions in the body	Some food sources
Magnesium	• plays a major role in bone development • aids in energy metabolism and tissue formation • helps maintain normal muscle and nerve function	cooked beans and lentils, nuts and seeds, peanut butter, green leafy vegetables, brown rice, oat bran (smaller amounts are found in most food groups, including grain products, milk products and meat)
Phosphorus	• aids in building and maintaining bones and teeth • helps generate and regulate energy in the body • is involved in cell growth and repair	fish (halibut, salmon, sardines and salmon with bones), cooked beans, lentils, milk, cheese, yogurt, almonds, meat, poultry, cottage cheese, peanut butter, green peas, tofu containing calcium sulfate
Zinc	• aids in energy metabolism and tissue formation	oysters, veal and pork liver, beef, turkey, beans, wheat germ, brown rice, yogurt, milk

calcium

Healthy adult women ages 19 to 50 need 1,000 mg of calcium per day. To help meet this requirement:

• Have three servings per day of milk products that supply 250 to 300 mg of calcium each. These include 1 cup (250 mL) of milk, ¾ cup (175 g) of yogurt or 1½ ounces (45 g) of cheese.

• Eat a variety of snacks that supply calcium, such as yogurt, cheese, dried figs or almonds.

• Make your next coffee a latte (steamed milk with a shot of espresso).

• Savor hot chocolate made with milk or fortified chocolate soy beverage when you crave chocolate.

• Eat dark green vegetables such as broccoli, kale and bok choy regularly. Try our Simple Stir-Fried Kale (page 260) or Stir-fried Chinese Greens (page 259).

• Make salmon salad sandwiches with canned salmon, bones and all. Mashed well, the bones aren't noticeable.

• When baking muffins or making cream soups or mashed potatoes, replace regular milk with evaporated skim milk straight from the can, or add a few tablespoons of skim milk powder to the recipe.

• Make soups with milk rather than water.

• Enjoy desserts rich in milk products, such as bread pudding, custard or milk pudding, frozen yogurt, yogurt and fruit parfaits.

milk alternatives

Milk is a great source not only of high-quality protein, calcium, riboflavin and vitamins B_{12} and D, but also of other essential nutrients. If you dislike milk or can't drink it due to an allergy or intolerance, some fortified beverages, including soy and rice beverages, are an acceptable substitute. Check the label to make sure the beverage has been fortified to provide nutrients similar to those found in milk.

Healthy Bones Need Vitamin D

Vitamin D helps you use calcium to build strong bones, but getting enough of this vitamin can be a challenge. Adults up to age 50 need 200 IU (international units) of vitamin D each day; those between 50 and 70 need 400 IU; and people older than 70 need 600 IU. Fish such as herring, mackerel, salmon, tuna and sardines contain vitamin D. Eggs are another source, and milk and margarine are fortified with it.

We also get vitamin D from exposure to sunlight. Being in the sun for 15 minutes a day can help you meet your vitamin D needs in the summer, but this won't be enough in the winter or if you're wearing sunscreen. And it is not advisable to be in the sun without sunscreen because of the risk of skin cancer.

Some people may need to take a vitamin D supplement. Most daily multivitamin supplements provide 400 IU, which, combined with wise food choices, should provide enough vitamin D for most people.

Can I Drink Milk if I Have Lactose Intolerance?

Most people with lactose intolerance can still drink some milk, particularly if it is taken in small amounts or as part of a meal. Some people find milk that has been heated is easier to digest, for instance a latte (steamed milk with espresso) or hot chocolate made of milk. Lactose-reduced milks are also available and work well for many people.

What About Supplements?

While supplements will never replace all the nourishment found in food, there are some situations in which you may need to consider taking supplemental vitamins and minerals:

- If you're a woman of child-bearing age, take a multivitamin that contains 400 μg of folic acid. If you become pregnant, folic acid reduces the risk that your baby will have neural tube defects.

- If you're a vegan, you will likely need to supplement with vitamin B_{12}, since it is found only in foods from animals and fortified soy foods. If you are not getting enough iron and calcium from plant sources, consider using a supplement containing these nutrients. For more detailed information, see the Vegetarian Food Guide at **www.dietitians.ca/resources/resource search.asp?fn=view&contentid=2701**.

- If you're over 50, you may have trouble absorbing vitamin B_{12} and, as a result, may not be getting enough from food sources. To prevent a deficiency and the onset of anemia, a supplement may be needed. Talk to your doctor for guidance.

- If you've been diagnosed with osteoporosis or struggle to get enough calcium, take calcium with vitamin D as prescribed by your doctor and/or recommended by a dietitian. If possible, maintain an active lifestyle that includes weight-bearing exercise, which is important for bone health.

- If you're a constant dieter or a very picky eater, restrict what you eat or are often too busy to eat, consider taking a daily multivitamin/mineral supplement. Just be aware that it won't help you feel more energetic if you aren't getting enough calories.

- If you're on medications, talk to your doctor or pharmacist about whether they might affect your nutritional status. Some medications reduce the absorption of certain nutrients, increasing your requirements, so you might need a supplement.

Phytonutrients

Phytonutrients (meaning "plant nutrients") is the name for hundreds of chemicals that occur naturally in plant foods such as grains, vegetables and fruit. Recent research suggests they offer some protection to health. Phytonutrients include phytoestrogens such as isoflavones and antioxidants such as carotenoids.

Antioxidants

Vitamins C and E and beta carotene, the plant form of vitamin A, act as antioxidants in the body, as does the mineral selenium. Antioxidants help counter the adverse effects of free radicals, which are formed when cells oxidize. Free radicals can damage cells and are believed to play a role in the development of heart disease, cancer, cataracts and some deterioration associated with aging. This continues to be an area of active research.

kaleidoscope eating

To eat more phytonutrients, aim for a rainbow of colorful produce, as well as whole grains. For instance, bright red vegetables and fruits, such as beets, tomatoes, red peppers, cranberries and cherries, contain lycopene and/or anthocyanins. Several studies suggest that eating foods rich in lycopene is associated with a lower risk of prostate cancer and cardiovascular disease. Anthocyanins may help to reduce the risk of cancer.

Water, Water, Everywhere

Because our bodies are nearly 70% water, we need to drink a lot of fluid to stay hydrated. Drinking enough fluid is important for circulation, temperature control, digestion, keeping blood pressure regular, muscle contractions and replacing lost fluids. Even the simple act of breathing uses up fluid, which needs to be replaced. By the time you feel thirsty, you may already be on the way to dehydration.

Headaches, fatigue, dark-colored urine and muscle cramps may be signals that you're not getting enough fluid. Fluid requirements are 11 cups (2.75 L) a day for women and 15 cups (3.75 L) for men. This can come from a variety of sources, including water, juice, milk, soup broth, juicy fruits and vegetables and other beverages. Kids and older people generally need less water, while pregnant and breastfeeding women need more.

Water and Exercise

You need to drink additional water to maintain fluid balance when you're exercising, because you lose water when you sweat. Aim to drink $1\frac{1}{2}$ to $2\frac{1}{2}$ cups (400 to 600 mL) two to three hours before exercise and another $\frac{3}{4}$ to $1\frac{1}{2}$ cups (150 to 350 mL) 15 minutes before. While you're exercising, drink $\frac{3}{4}$ to $1\frac{1}{2}$ cups (150 to 350 mL) every 15 to 20 minutes. And don't forget to drink plenty of water after you're finished.

Salt

Canadians have developed quite an appetite for salt. In some cases, sodium intake is double what it should be. Most of the sodium we consume (about 77%) comes from processed foods and restaurant meals. If you significantly reduce your intake of processed foods, you will dramatically reduce the amount of salt in your diet.

Food labels include a Nutrition Facts table that lists the amount of sodium in a serving. Read labels and check the sodium count on the foods you are considering. Foods with less than 5% DV (Daily Value) are considered low in salt. A healthy person should try to keep sodium intake to less than 2,400 mg per day. People with high blood pressure and specific health concerns should consume even less.

Here are a few quick tips to help you eat less salt:

- Make food at home rather than eating out. Restaurant food is often much saltier than homemade versions.
- Try reducing or eliminating the salt in recipes (this won't usually work in baking, where salt may be needed to make dough rise).
- Rinse canned foods that contain added salt, such as legumes or vegetables.
- Enjoy sodium-reduced or "no salt added" canned soups and broths, vegetables and tomato juice.
- Limit salted snack foods such as chips, crackers, popcorn and nuts. Buy unsalted nuts, seeds or crackers.
- Use only small portions of condiments such as ketchup, soy sauce, salsa, commercial salad dressings and pickles.
- Limit instant packaged foods, especially those with salty powder or sauce packets.
- Choose fresh meats instead of processed, cured or smoked meats such as sausage, wieners, ham, bacon and pepperoni. Limit smoked fish and seafood.
- Keep salt in the kitchen, not on the table, where it will be easy to sprinkle on food. Out of sight, out of mind.
- Learn to enjoy the wonderful flavors that ingredients such as fresh lemon or lime juice and fresh herbs can add to food.
- Watch out for seasonings that contain salt, such as seasoning salt or garlic and celery salt.

Where's the Sodium?

- 77% comes from processed foods and restaurant meals.
- 12% comes from salt added at the table and when cooking.
- 11% comes from foods in their natural form.

What Healthy Eating Means to Me

"It's hard to define healthy eating. I guess it's about eating lots of fruits and vegetables. I also try to read labels and buy foods that are lower in fat — and salt, too. I find drinking enough water helps me feel better too."

— Sandeep, hairstyling student, Ontario

Where Can I Find Trusted Nutrition Information?

Visit **www.dietitians.ca/eatwell** for updates on current nutrition issues, and fun and interactive tools the whole family can use to asses their food intake, plan meals and test their nutrition knowledge.

Canada's dietitians are ready to support you in your ongoing quest to stay healthy. Here are the best ways to locate a credible nutrition expert in your area:

- Head to **www.dietitians.ca/find** for a list of consulting dietitians across the country.
- Look in the Yellow Pages, under "Dietitians and Nutritionists." Remember that "nutritionist" is not a protected term in all areas. When calling potential counselors, ask if they are registered dietitians.
- Check the Blue Pages for your local health department. Most have community or public health dietitians who can help you or can connect you to the right people.
- Ask at your local grocery store — some stores have a dietitian on staff.

When looking online for health and nutrition information, make sure the websites you're looking at are reliable and have accurate information. An excellent starting point is the Canadian Health Network: **www.canadian-health-network.ca**.

---

break the barrier: I Can't Control My Weight Because Unhealthy Food Is Everywhere

It's easier to make healthier food choices if we create environments that support healthy eating where we live, work and play.

At home
- Stock your cupboards and fridge with healthy food choices. When you need a "grab and go" meal or snack, it will be at your fingertips.

At work
- Look into making changes to the vending machines in your workplace to ensure that they are stocked with healthy food options.
- Create a "good food box" and fill it with healthy choices, such as dried fruit mix with nuts, rice crackers and canned or fresh fruit.

At restaurants
- Get to know healthy cooking methods and ask questions about menu items and how they are prepared.
- Large portion sizes encourage us to eat more food than we really need. Take part of a meal away for another day. We should no longer feel a need to "clean the plate."

Easy Food Solutions

Get ready to have fun in the kitchen, and invite the whole family to join in. In this section of the book, we will show you five simple steps for turning everything you know about healthy eating into action:

1. **Make meal planning easy.** Learn how a little planning goes a long way toward helping you put delicious meals on the table with ease.
2. **Give your kitchen a makeover.** Get your kitchen and pantry set up so you always have healthy ingredients on hand to make delicious recipes at a moment's notice.
3. **Be savvy about grocery shopping.** Understand the latest nutrition information on food labels and simplify grocery shopping.
4. **Cook with ease.** Discover how to make cooking easy and enjoyable with tips from a professional chef.
5. **Keep food safe.** Find out about food safety and preventing foodborne illness, from preparation to cleanup to storage.

1. Make Meal Planning Easy

There are four ways you can make it easier to plan healthy meals: use the information included with the recipes in this book; involve your family in meal planning; plan ahead; and try some of our easy food solutions.

Use the Information Accompanying the Recipes

The information that accompanies each of the recipes will help you plan nutritious meals. We've paid particular attention to making recipe and meal preparation convenient and less stressful. For instance,

- Many recipes include menu suggestions or serving ideas, to make it easier for you to round out the meal.
- "Big-Batch" recipes can be prepared in quantity and divided for several future meals.
- Our helpful tips and sidebars give you additional information on ingredients, equipment and techniques to help you make dinner in short order.

- Some recipes have ideas for variations, in case you want to change an ingredient.
- "Freezer Friendly" recipes can be made ahead and quickly defrosted when there's no time to cook.
- "Slow-Cooked" recipes and "Slow Cooker Friendly" soups can cook all day while you're away from the kitchen, so dinner will be ready when you walk in the door.
- "Kid Approved" recipes have been tested by children and given the thumbs-up.
- Every recipe has a nutrient analysis that identifies the amount of calories, fat, carbohydrate, protein, fiber, sodium and key nutrients provided. When you are deciding what recipes to prepare, you can use these numbers to help you control some nutrients and maximize your intake of others.

Involve Your Family in Meal Planning

Involving your family in meal planning is a key way to make sure they'll enjoy the nutritious meals being prepared. Once you've determined what foods your family likes, you can make sure you always have the right ingredients on hand. Here are six ways to get your family involved in planning meals:

1. Sit down as a family and brainstorm about favorite foods. Divide a blank piece of paper into five columns. At the top of each, write the food groups: Vegetables and Fruit, Grain Products, Milk Products, Meat and Alternatives and foods that don't fit into any group. Place family favorites in the appropriate columns. With this list in mind, talk about combinations for meals. Keep the list posted on the fridge and use it to think about foods you can put together to make healthy meals and snacks. These ideas can really help on nights when you draw a blank about what to make for dinner.

2. Make a habit of talking to your kids about what they like to eat. Try to have these conversations when they're feeling good — for instance, on the way to soccer practice or just after dinner, before cleanup starts.

3. Try new foods and experiment with recipes. Enhancing your family's culinary resources will add zest to healthy eating. Begin by having all family members flip through this book and other cookbooks, jotting down recipes (with page numbers) that seem interesting or new.

4. Encourage older children to become involved in meal planning and preparation. Giving kids responsibility for planning and preparing some or all of a meal at least one night a week will help them develop valuable life skills. Tell them they can invite friends over to share the work and turn it into a fun event.

5. Plan a cooking "date" with your partner. On weekends or evenings when the kids are busy, use your time together to spark a little adventure and romance around food. Shop together at a local market or specialty food store for ingredients for a new recipe. Light some candles and enjoy a glass of wine while you work together to prepare a special dinner.

6. Discover "Let's Make a Meal" at **www.dietitians.ca/eatwell**. This interactive tool is an easy way to plan nutritious meals and snacks. Adults and kids can have fun while learning about healthy eating.

Plan Ahead

When you don't have any time constraints, going on a trip without a map can be a fabulous adventure. But when time is of the essence, a little planning can speed you to your destination. Getting a meal ready is almost like going on a trip — having a plan will help you put a delicious meal on the table quickly and easily.

What Healthy Eating Means to Me

"Healthy eating… hmmm. I think about it a lot. I know it's good for me. I guess I try to eat lots of fruits and vegetables. I try to set a good example for the kids."

— Jacquie, writer and swim coach, Quebec

Planned Extras

When you're investing time in cooking a meal, why not get the most out of your investment by making more food than you need for that one meal? The extra can be saved for another meal within the next couple of days. Rather than "leftovers," we call this intentional surplus "planned extras."

Many dishes, such as soups and stews, actually improve after a day in the fridge, as the flavors blend and mellow.

The table below will give you some ideas on how you can plan for extras. Look for more planned extras within the recipes.

Great planned extras	Suggestions for the second meal
Cook an extra chicken breast.	Cut into strips and use as a topping for a salad with vinaigrette dressing.
Roast a whole chicken.	Use in Chicken and Corn Chowder (page 128), Mango Chicken Wraps (page 74), BBQ Chicken Salad Sandwiches (page 69) or Caribbean Chicken and Pineapple Pizza (page 252).
Cook beef brisket in a slow cooker.	Slice and use for beef sandwiches or add little cubes to a chunky vegetable soup.
Grill extra portions of salmon.	Make Tasty Fish Cakes (page 205).
Bake a lean ham.	Make Ham and Pineapple Pizza (page 253).
Cook a double batch of brown rice.	Make Pineapple Vegetable Rice (page 274) with shrimp.
Roast an extra batch of vegetables.	Add to tomato sauce for a great pasta topper or use in a frittata or as a pizza topping.
Double the recipe when making dinner.	Pack for lunch the next day.

break the barrier: Everyone in the Family Wants Something Different

We all have different tastes, but sometimes we have to give and take a little. Talk with your family about the cost and practical barriers to making many different meals every night. Instead, allow family members to pick their favorites for a certain night of the week. To appeal to different tastes, choose recipes that can be self-assembled, such as make-your-own pizzas, salads or wraps with a variety of toppings.

Storing Leftover Rice

To store cooked rice safely, place in uncovered shallow containers and let cool until no longer steaming. Cover and refrigerate at or below 40°F (4°C) for no more than 2 days. Foodborne illness can occur when people consume food contaminated with *Bacillus cereus* bacteria, which can be present in rice. If temperature conditions permit, the bacteria can multiply and produce toxins that may make you sick. *Bacillus cereus* can multiply quickly in cooked rice that isn't cooled properly. Brief reheating (such as stir-frying) will not destroy the toxin.

Food Solutions

In this section, you'll find some of our favorite tried-and-true methods for easy meal solutions.

Menus at Your Fingertips

Consider posting these menu ideas on your refrigerator for help and inspiration.

Weeknight menus

- **Soup night:** Hungarian Goulash Soup (page 131, made the day before and reheated) whole wheat rolls, Pears in Tosca Sauce (page 298)
- **Soup and salad:** Cream of Broccoli Soup (page 115), Sticky Mango Chicken Salad (page 156), Big-Batch Multigrain Bread (page 280)
- **Low cost 1:** Hamburger Noodle Casserole (page 240), raw veggie sticks, Soft Apple Cinnamon Cookies (page 316)
- **Low cost 2:** Kitchen Sink Frittata (page 63), Fruity Slaw (page 147), Baked Granola Apples (page 296)
- **Breakfast for dinner:** Greek Scrambled Eggs (page 58), Garden Patch Spinach Salad (page 141), Orange Cranberry Muffins (page 291, baked on the weekend)
- **Kid-friendly:** Chicken Parmesan Strips (page 171), Sweet-and-Sour Sauce (page 110), Oven-Baked Potato Wedges (page 271), Fruity Slaw (page 147), Pink Strawberry Wiggles (page 325)
- **Fast Friday:** Easy Pasta with Beans (page 235), bag Caesar salad, Carrot Cake (page 305)
- **Mexico olé:** Easy Salsa Chicken (page 167), brown rice cooked with vegetable juice instead of water, corn kernels, Dessert Nachos (page 300)
- **Indian-themed:** Chicken in Butter Sauce (page 172), Basmati Rice Pulau (page 275), green beans, Mango Lassi (page 85)
- **Thai-themed:** Stir-Fried Chicken with Mango and Cashews (page 170), steamed jasmine rice, Asian Carrot Cucumber Pickle (page 145)
- **Moroccan-themed:** Moroccan Lamb Tagine (page 198), Couscous with Currants and Carrots (page 273), orange slices drizzled with honey, mint tea
- **Gone Fishing:** Salmon in a Parcel (page 206), Spinach Spaghettini (page 272), frozen mixed vegetables

Weekend menus

- **Special family dinner:** Stuffed Roast Pork (page 194), Oven-Roasted Lemon Potatoes (page 269), Ginger Carrots (page 257), Lemon Blueberry Panna Cotta (page 299)
- **Comfort meal for family and friends:** Lemon-Thyme Roast Chicken (page 164), Baked Springtime Risotto (page 277), Big-Batch Oven-Roasted Ratatouille (page 266), Apple, Pear and Cranberry Crisp (page 302)

Menus for entertaining

- **Brunch:** Crustless Zucchini Quiche (page 62), Spring Vegetable Salad (page 139), Big-Batch Multigrain Bread (page 280) and/or Pumpkin Spice Nut Bread (page 283), fresh fruit salad, Peanut Butter Flaxseed Cookies (page 317)

- **Fusion dinner party:** Easy Tomato Basil Bruschetta (page 96), Broiled Cilantro Ginger Salmon (page 207), Black Bean Salsa (page 106), Steamed Asian Vegetable Medley (page 263), Chocolate Fondue (page 311) with fresh fruit chunks

- **Mediterranean dinner party:** Snow Pea and Bell Pepper Salad (page 140), Chicken Stuffed with Mushrooms and Cheese (page 169), Spinach Spaghettini (page 272), Balsamic Strawberry Sauce (page 297) over frozen yogurt

- **Cocktail party:** Antipasto Platter (page 98), Grilled Cilantro Shrimp Skewers (page 97), Lightened-Up Guacamole and Chips (page 102), fresh vegetable sticks and whole wheat pita wedges with Spicy Hummus (page 104)

Super-Quick Dinners

For those nights when following a recipe just won't happen, try these simple dinner ideas that are quick and easy to prepare.

Salads
- Mixed vegetable salad topped with canned tuna or salmon, served with a whole-grain roll
- Black bean and corn salad topped with grated cheese
- Leftover meat or chicken on mixed greens with a glass of milk

Sandwiches and wraps
- Ham and low-fat cheese sandwich on whole-grain bread with mustard, served with raw vegetables on the side
- A soft tortilla wrapped around leftover meat and vegetables

Eggs
- Scrambled eggs with chopped vegetables, served with a slice of whole-grain bread and a glass of milk
- Frittata served with whole-grain toast (see Kitchen Sink Frittata, page 63, for inspiration)

Leftover rice
- Fried rice with chopped vegetables, meat pieces and/or tofu and egg
- Pineapple Vegetable Rice (page 274) with leftover chicken or shrimp added

Pasta
- Pasta topped with a meaty tomato sauce
- Pasta tossed with pesto
- Pasta topped with a mixture of prepared tomato sauce, canned tuna and parsley

"Fast Food" at Home

If your family feels they need a fast-food fix from time to time, make your own "fast food" at home using nutritious recipes from this book:

- Chicken Parmesan Strips (page 171) served with any of our great dips and raw veggie sticks
- Tasty Meatballs in Tomato Sauce (page 189) served on whole wheat submarine buns with a green salad
- Turkey Apple Burgers (variation, page 179) served on multigrain buns and loaded with fresh vegetable toppings
- Any of our great pizzas, such as Grilled Veggie Pizza (page 249) or Caribbean Chicken and Pineapple Pizza (page 252)
- Lightened-Up Guacamole and Chips (page 102), Black Bean Salsa (page 106), Pineapple Salsa (page 105), Veggie Quesadillas (page 221), Sweet Potato and Bean Wraps (page 76), Open-Faced Grilled Bean and Cheese Tortillas (page 223) or Bean Burritos (page 222)

big-batch recipes

Weekends can be a great time to prepare big batches of food that can be refrigerated or frozen for later use. Get together with family, friends or neighbors and share the work. Divide the prepared dishes so everyone can benefit from planning ahead. Check out our Big-Batch recipes, which are scattered throughout the book (look for the words "Big-Batch" in the title of the recipe).

What Healthy Eating Means to Me

"Healthy eating means real food, making my own meals as often as I can, not eating on the run, knowing where all the food came from."

— Brian, business consultant, British Columbia

❄ FREEZER FRIENDLY

Many recipes can be doubled or tripled and frozen in meal-sized containers that can be quickly defrosted on nights when there is no time to cook. Avoid freezing dishes that contain mushrooms or cooked cubes of potatoes, as their quality is affected by freezing. (Mashed potatoes are fine to freeze.) Always freeze cooked food in airtight plastic containers or freezer bags. Look for the "Freezer Friendly" symbol on recipes throughout the book.

○ SLOW COOKER FRIENDLY

A slow cooker is a great time-saving kitchen appliance that can help you have a hot dinner on the table without much fuss. All you have to do is load the slow cooker with ingredients in the morning, turn it on and go about your business for the day. The key is that the food cooks slowly, at a safe but low temperature, for a long period of time. By the time you get home, your meal is fully cooked and ready to enjoy. Many of our recipes can be cooked this way, and some were specifically tested with this cooking method. Look for the "Slow Cooker Friendly" symbol on recipes in the Soups chapter; in other chapters, look for the words "Slow-Cooked" in the recipe title.

2. Give Your Kitchen a Makeover

To pull together tasty, healthy meals and snacks in short order, you need a kitchen that's ready for action and fully stocked. If it's disorganized, you're more likely to order in or eat out. Not only is this more expensive and likely less healthy, it can actually take longer than making a meal yourself. You also miss out on all the rewards that come from making a meal at home — the delicious aromas wafting through the house, the satisfaction of knowing your family ate a nutritious meal and the great leftovers that make future meal preparation a breeze.

Here are some steps for getting your kitchen in tip-top shape:

Organize your fridge

- Throw out any expired items, old condiments that won't be used and leftovers that have been in there for more than 4 days.
- Get rid of limp or wilted vegetables and fruit. Take some time to semi-prep the remainder. (Semi-prep means to get the items ready to be used — for example, peel the carrots, wash the lettuce and store them for easy use.)
- Stock up on nutritious beverages, such as milk and 100% fruit or vegetable juice.
- Place ready-to-go healthy items near the front for easy access.

Organize your shelves and drawers

- Keep enough canned and packaged goods that fit the needs of your family and donate extras to a local food bank.
- Designate a shelf or drawer for plastic containers. Keep lids in one container and stack the bottoms in another.
- Assign a drawer to aluminum foil, plastic bags and related items so you can find them quickly.

Get Your Family to Help

The whole family can help organize the kitchen. Ask your kids for tips on what would make it easier for them to pack their own lunches. Encourage family members to write items on the grocery list when they use the last ingredient or notice that the supply is getting low.

What Healthy Eating Means to Me

"Having a good supply of healthy food on hand at all times and cooking most of our meals at home are big parts of healthy eating in our household."

— James, retail store manager and dad, Northwest Territories

3. Be Savvy About Grocery Shopping

Knowing what you want before you go shopping can save you time and money and prevent you from making impulse purchases that might be less nutritious or not get used. Keep a notepad in your kitchen (a magnetic pad for your fridge works well) and jot down items as they run low. With a list in hand, you're far less likely to forget anything. Once you're at the store, use the information on food labels to help you make the best choices.

Organize Your Shopping List

Sort the items on your list by the departments in the store: Produce, Meat, Bakery, Dairy, and so on. It will save you backtracking time.

Putting Groceries Away

When you get home from shopping, take some time to put your groceries away in an orderly way. Don't cancel out all the work you did to get the kitchen organized! As you're unloading, wash and semi-prep vegetables (see page 35) so they will be ready when you need them, and separate large packages of meat into meal-sized portions and date them before putting them into the freezer.

Keep Healthy Meals Affordable

Eating well doesn't have to be expensive. Many nutritious foods, such as bulk beans and grains, large packages of oatmeal and brown rice, in-season fresh produce, eggs, legumes, powdered milk and sale-priced frozen or canned fruits, vegetables and fish, are inexpensive. Here are some tips for keeping your grocery bills down:

- Make a list and stick to it to prevent or reduce impulse purchases.
- Read flyers and look for weekly specials. Plan your menus around them or use them to stock your freezer.
- Use discount coupons, but make sure they are for products you will actually use. If you don't need it, a sale item is actually an added expense, not a savings.
- If freezer space allows, buy meat and bread on sale and freeze for later use.
- If you have extra shelf space, stock up on staples such as canned beans or fish when they are on sale.
- Buy lots of in-season vegetables and fruit when they are most affordable and freeze for later use. Blueberries, strawberries, raspberries, peaches, apricots and rhubarb freeze well.
- Check best-before dates to make sure the product won't expire before you use it up.
- Buy bigger packages of products you will use. You can then repackage into smaller amounts and freeze. But don't buy bigger packages just because they are cheaper. If having a lot of extra food will cause you to overindulge, or if you end up throwing food out, the sale price won't be a bargain.
- Compare the cost per serving listed on shelf tags to ensure that you're buying the most economical size.

Use Convenience Food to Your Advantage

When shopping, keep an eye out for nutritious time savers. These products sometimes cost a bit more, but they can be worth it. Here are some of our favorites:

- Washed and ready-to-eat produce can make short work of prep time. Most grocery stores carry a good selection of salad mixes, vegetable platters with dip and chopped vegetables for stir-fries, among other items.
- Rotisserie-cooked chicken is often the perfect way to jumpstart a meal.
- Precut fresh meat for stews or stir-fries saves time at home. You can also ask meat department staff to cut meat or fish any way you want it.
- Frozen precut vegetables are nutritious, and the prep work is done, so you can just add them to soups, stews and stir-fries.
- Canned fruit in its own juice is a great start to a fruit salad, among other uses.
- Peeled and cored pineapple makes a healthy dessert or a refreshing snack. You can also put it on the grill for a delicious accompaniment to barbecued meats.
- Shredded cheese can make quick work of pasta dishes and is great for sprinkling on salads, pizzas and wraps.
- Frozen, partially baked bread can be popped into the oven for a fresh baked treat.
- Frozen pizza dough or prepared crusts make homemade pizza an easy option.
- Prepared tomato sauce can be enriched with vegetables and meat at home.
- Prepared soup can be used as a base; boost flavor and nutrition by adding vegetables, pasta or rice at home.

Take Your Family Shopping

Getting your family involved in grocery shopping can save time and effort and ensure that everyone gets to eat some of their favorite foods.

- When a family member says, "We have nothing to eat," encourage him or her to add a couple of healthy items to the grocery list.
- Minimize stress by choosing a shopping time that works for everyone. The job will be extra challenging if you're rushed or hungry.
- Ask your kids to help you find healthy foods that offer good value for the price. Have them review key information on the Nutrition Facts table (see page 38) and compare different package sizes and prices.
- Encourage kids to choose a healthy item they have never eaten before, such as an exotic fruit or an uncommon vegetable.
- Ask if your store has a grocery tour program and attend as a family. Some stores offer educational school tours and cooking classes for kids.

Crack the Code on Food Labels

Nutrition labelling is now mandatory on most food packages. Labelling helps you know the nutritional value of foods; compare the nutritional content of products more easily; manage special diets better; and increase or decrease your intake of a particular nutrient.

The Nutrition Facts table on food labels has a standardized format and must include information on serving size, calories, total, saturated and trans fats, cholesterol, sodium, carbohydrate, sugars and fiber, protein, vitamin A, vitamin C, calcium and iron.

Use the Nutrition Facts table to choose foods with the least amount of saturated and trans fat. If a product is labelled trans fat–free, look at the Nutrition Facts table for the total fat content — the food might still be high in fat overall. Also, check the Nutrition Facts table for sodium. You might be surprised at how high the sodium content can be in foods that don't even taste salty.

Be sure to check the serving size that the nutrition information is based on. The serving size is not a recommended amount, but rather a reference amount for the nutrient information. The % Daily Value shows at a glance if there is a lot or a little of a nutrient in the specified amount of food.

The Nutrition Facts Table

Nutrition Facts	
Per 125 mL (87 g)	
Amount	**% Daily Value**
Calories 80	
Fat 0.5 g	1 %
Saturated 0 g + Trans 0 g	0 %
Cholesterol 0 mg	
Sodium 0 mg	0 %
Carbohydrate 18 g	6 %
Fibre 2 g	8 %
Sugars 2 g	
Protein 3 g	

Vitamin A	2 %	Vitamin C	10 %
Calcium	0 %	Iron	2 %

ingredient list

In addition to looking at the Nutrition Facts table, check the ingredient list to get a clear picture of what you will be eating. Ingredients are listed by weight, from the highest to the lowest. Use this list if you want to avoid certain ingredients because of allergies, special diets or other reasons.

To learn more about label reading, visit **www.healthyeatingisinstore.ca** and **www.healthcanada.ca/ nutritionlabelling**.

Nutrition Claims

Two types of nutrition claims may appear on food labels:

- **Nutrient Content Claims:** These appear on the front of the package and highlight if a food is high or low in certain nutrients such as sodium, fat or fiber. Examples are "High source of fiber" and "Excellent source of calcium."

- **Health Claims:** These describe the potential health benefits of a food or nutrient. Health claims are restricted to four health conditions: heart disease, certain types of cancer, osteoporosis and high blood pressure. "A healthy diet rich in a variety of vegetables and fruit may help reduce the risk of some types of cancer" is an example of a health claim. Claims relating to dental caries or cavities may also appear on foods such as sugar-free gum or candies.

4. Cook with Ease

Many little tips and tricks can make cooking easier. Being aware of them can save you time and effort.

Know How Much to Cook

Every recipe in this book indicates the number of servings it will yield, based on average healthy portions. Before starting to cook, check the number of servings. If the recipe makes more than you need, you can use the remainder as planned extras. If it makes less, consider doubling it.

If you're making a meal without using a recipe, try to estimate visually how many people the food will serve. Use the following table as a guide.

Item	Average portion per person
Side salad	1 cup (250 mL)
Main-dish salad	2 cups (500 mL) or more
Soup (as an appetizer)	1 cup (250 mL)
Soup (as an entrée)	2 cups (500 mL)
Protein (meat, fish, poultry)	2 to 4 oz (60 to 125 g), depending on other ingredients to be added
Whole chicken or turkey	8 oz (250 g) raw
Vegetarian casserole	1 cup (250 mL)
Pasta	½ cup (125 mL) uncooked
Vegetable side dish	1 cup (250 mL)

Add Taste, Not Fat or Salt

You can add zing to your meals without adding fat or salt by using herbs and spices to flavor foods. For instance, a sprinkling of finely chopped dill makes a fillet of grilled fish spring to life; so too a dollop of mustard or horseradish on a slice of beef. You can also create your own salt-free spice mixture. Use it to add some quick flavor to steamed vegetables or to sprinkle over pasta or rice.

What Healthy Eating Means to Me

"Healthy eating is about feeling good — not being on a diet, but instead making quality food choices that leave me energized and able to be active."

— Melanie, runner, doctor and mom, Manitoba

Make Recipes Healthier

The recipes in *Simply Great Food* are dietitian-approved and healthy. But when following a recipe from another source, you might have an opportunity to modify it to make it healthier. Even small changes can sometimes create big savings in fat, sugar or calories. There are also a few simple ways to add fiber to your favorite recipes. Many of these tips will also boost the nutritional value of your meals:

Reduce fat and calories

- Use two egg whites instead of a whole egg. This works best in pancakes, muffins or scrambled eggs.
- Use lower-fat yogurt instead of sour cream in dips, dressings and baked products.
- Use skim or 1% milk instead of whole milk. Use evaporated skim or 1% milk instead of higher-fat milk or cream.
- Reduce the amount of oil called for in baking recipes by up to a third and replace it with an equal amount of unsweetened applesauce or prune purée (baby food).
- Bake or broil meats and vegetables rather than frying.
- Try using broth rather than oil or butter to sauté meat or vegetables.
- Use a smaller quantity of stronger-tasting cheese to replace milder cheese. For example, substitute Parmesan, aged Cheddar or Asiago for mozzarella or brick.
- Drain fat after browning ground meats, or substitute ground chicken, turkey or vegetarian ground round for beef, pork or lamb.
- Substitute vegetables for some of the meat. If a stew calls for 2 lbs (1 kg) of beef, use 1½ lbs (750 g) and make up the difference with extra vegetables or legumes.
- Cook turkey stuffing in a separate dish outside the bird so it won't soak up fat in the cooking process.
- Skim fat off gravy with a gravy separator or, better still, chill the gravy. The fat will rise to the surface and harden, making it easier to skim off. You can then reheat the gravy before serving.
- Season vegetables with lemon juice, herbs and vinegar instead of butter or margarine.
- Add salsa and plain yogurt to a baked potato instead of butter and sour cream.
- Make sundaes with frozen yogurt and fruit instead of ice cream and chocolate sauce.

Reduce sugar

- Reduce sugar by a third in recipes such as cookies, muffins, squares and quick breads.
- Use canned fruits packed in their own juice instead of syrup.
- Use extra cinnamon, nutmeg or cloves (just add a little, to taste) instead of extra sugar.

Increase fiber

- Add ground flaxseed, wheat bran or oatmeal to homemade breads.
- Substitute ground flaxseed for up to a quarter of the fat or flour called for in a baking recipe.
- When making muffins, cookies, bars or quick breads, replace up to half of the white flour with whole wheat flour.
- Choose brown rice instead of white rice.
- Choose whole wheat pasta instead of white pasta.

Get Your Family Involved in Cooking

Family members can take part in all aspects of meal preparation, from setting the table to cooking to cleaning. Older kids can help with just about anything, as long as you teach them how to use knives and kitchen gadgets safely; younger children can do simple tasks with ingredients you've already prepared. Here are some tips on how family members can help in the kitchen:

- Keep the menu for the week on the fridge and the evening's recipe on the counter. Whoever gets home first can get the meal started.
- Kids of all ages can help set the table. Preschoolers will have fun carrying unbreakable placemats, utensils and plastic cups to the table.
- Invite kids to read recipes and help collect the ingredients and utensils needed to make them.
- Let kids as young as two or three help scrub potatoes or tear lettuce leaves for a salad. When they are a little older, they can help measure, mix and stir ingredients that are not on the stove.
- Kids of any age can help measure ingredients. They can also help stir and scoop — all under supervision, of course.
- Let your kids help prepare their own sandwiches and wraps: spreading ingredients, adding toppings, rolling, choosing their own condiments.
- If you don't mind kids standing on a chair beside you at the stove, they can add ingredients to the saucepan, stir soups and stews or just be there to watch what you are doing.
- Ask your children to taste your recipe and tell you what they think of it — do they like the taste, color, texture and so on? If they don't like it, ask why.
- Older kids can be responsible for at least part of the meal — a vegetable platter with dip, a salad or even dessert.
- Just about everyone can help with cleanup. Find ways to make the task more fun. See who can do it the fastest on different nights, play favorite music or reward kids for involvement. Make a chart and give kids points towards a prize for every time they help make meals, clear the table, wash dishes, sweep the floor or take out the trash.

All of these activities will help teach your children that sharing meal preparation and cleanup is part of being a family.

5. Keep Food Safe

Studies indicate that a significant number of cases of microbial foodborne illness could be prevented if food is handled properly. When you're cooking, there are four simple, yet important steps recommended by FightBAC! that you can take to eliminate harmful bacteria and greatly reduce the risk of food poisoning:

1. **Clean.** Before, during and after cooking, wash your hands and all surfaces that come in contact with food; wash them well and often.
2. **Chill.** Return foods to the fridge or freezer promptly after using.
3. **Separate.** Keep raw meat, poultry and seafood and their juices separate from one another and from other foods. Don't use tools or dishes that touched raw meat for cooked meat or other foods.
4. **Cook.** Cook foods to a safe internal temperature. Use a digital food thermometer to check doneness. Visit **www.canfightbac.org/cpcfse/en/cookwell/charts** for more information.

You can find more food safety information at **www.canfightbac.org**.

Store and Reheat Leftovers Carefully

To keep food safe to eat and as tasty as possible, it must be stored and reheated properly. The general rule of thumb regarding leftovers is "if in doubt, throw it out." But here are some tips that will keep you from being in doubt:

Refrigerating leftovers

- Refrigerate leftovers within 2 hours of preparation. Very hot items should be cooled at room temperature for about 30 minutes before being refrigerated. Frequent stirring helps the food cool faster.
- Never remove a large pot of food (such as soup, stew or pasta sauce) from the stove and place it in the refrigerator. Large masses of food can take hours or days to chill properly, and a slow cooling process provides an ideal environment for the growth of harmful bacteria. Instead, divide the food into meal-sized portions and pack it into airtight containers.
- Debone large pieces of meat or poultry and divide them into smaller portions before storing.
- Always put leftovers in clean containers, and never mix them with fresh food.
- Use covered shallow containers or resealable plastic bags. Food will cool faster in these containers, which have a large flat surface. If using bags, be sure to close them securely.
- Place containers on wire refrigerator shelves to allow air to flow across the bottom, cooling food twice as fast as it would sitting on a solid shelf.
- Do not overcrowd your refrigerator. Leave airspace around containers to allow circulation of cold air, which will help ensure rapid, even cooling.
- Date leftovers to ensure that they are not stored too long; eat leftovers — even those that have been previously frozen — within 3 days.

Freezing leftovers

- Let foods cool completely in the refrigerator before packing them for the freezer.
- Pack foods in meal-sized portions and leave some headspace in containers — most foods expand as they freeze. Squeeze out any excess air from wraps and bags.
- Use containers or wrap designed for freezer use and seal airtight.
- Don't overstuff the freezer. Cold air needs to circulate above and beneath food.

Defrosting leftovers

- Food can safely be defrosted in the refrigerator, under cold running water or in the microwave. If you defrost food in the microwave, cook it immediately. Do not thaw perishable food at room temperature, as this encourages the growth of bacteria that may cause foodborne illness.
- Thaw packages on a plate to prevent leaks.

Reheating leftovers

Reheat foods as quickly as possible to prevent bacterial growth, which can cause foodborne illness:

- In a 350°F (180°C) oven, reheat solid leftovers, such as chicken pieces or meatloaf, to at least 165°F (74°C).
- Reheat soups, sauces and gravies to a rolling boil over high heat.
- When reheating leftovers in a microwave, follow the manufacturer's instructions on timing for each type of food.
- If leftovers are uneaten after they have been reheated, discard them.

For more information on food safety, visit **www.inspection.gc.ca** and visit the consumer centre.

Storage Times for Prepared Foods

Product	Refrigerator (40°F/4°C)	Freezer (0°F/−17°C)
Soups and stews	up to 3 days	up to 6 months
Cooked meat, meatloaf and meat casseroles	up to 4 days	up to 3 months
Gravy and meat broth	up to 2 days	up to 3 months
Cooked poultry casseroles	up to 4 days	up to 4 months
Chicken pieces, plain	up to 4 days	up to 1 month
Chicken pieces, in sauce	up to 2 days	up to 6 months
Pizza	up to 4 days	up to 2 months
Cooked fish	up to 4 days	up to 6 months
Cooked shellfish	up to 4 days	up to 3 months
Combination dishes (such as lasagna)	up to 4 days	up to 6 months

Storage Times for Baked Goods

Baked goods should be wrapped tightly in plastic wrap and/or aluminum foil and placed in an airtight bag or container. Frozen baked goods can be thawed at room temperature.

Product	Room temperature (72°F/22°C)	Freezer (0°F/−17°C)
Biscuits, coffee cake, fruit bread	up to 5 days	up to 3 months
Muffins	up to 5 days	up to 12 months
Cooked pancakes	not recommended; refrigerate for up to 2 days	up to 1 month
Cookies, baked	up to 3 weeks	up to 6 months
Cookies, unbaked	not recommended	up to 6 months
Bars and squares	up to 1 week	up to 6 months
Bread (no preservatives)	up to 3 days	up to 3 months
Cake (not frosted)	up to 3 days	up to 3 months

Breakfast and Brunch

Eating breakfast is a great way to get the body up and running. It sets the tone for making good choices all day and helps in weight control. Kids perform better in school when they eat breakfast. For a special weekend treat, try serving brunch. It's a great way to offer a variety of foods and beverages that you may not have time to make every day. In addition to the recipes in this chapter, experiment with some of our delicious smoothies and baked goods.

no cooking necessary

Don't skip breakfast just because you're in a hurry and don't have time to cook. There are lots of speedy ways to get the nutrition you need first thing in the day:

- Enjoy a handful of nuts and a banana along with your latte.

- Savor some leftover fruit salad, topped with yogurt and a sprinkle of your favorite whole-grain cereal.

- Have the kids assemble breakfast parfaits before they go to bed. Layer vanilla yogurt, fresh berries and granola in a glass. Cover and place in the fridge. In the morning, open the fridge and enjoy!

- Scoop some Big-Batch Seed and Nut Granola (page 47) into a bowl and add cold milk.

- Enjoy a hearty, homemade muffin such as Triple B Health Muffins (page 287) with a piece of cheese and some fruit. In fact, any of our muffin or quick bread recipes can be baked and frozen for a quick breakfast.

- If you need to eat breakfast in the car, prepare a sandwich on whole wheat bread and cut it into quarters. Include a bunch of grapes or cut fruit in a plastic container.

time-saving breakfast solutions

- Keep ready-to-serve whole-grain cereals in the cupboard.

- Keep a variety of breads, bagels, whole-grain muffins, tortillas and English muffins in the freezer.

- Make a large fruit salad at least once a week. Use canned fruit packed in juice for a quick and easy base, then add some fresh fruits, such as chopped peaches, pears, kiwis and fresh berries in season.

- Have cut-up fruit ready in the fridge. Add milk and pop in the blender for a quick smoothie.

- Always keep yogurt and milk on hand for cereals, fruit and smoothies.

- Make a quick muesli by pouring milk over rolled oats. Refrigerate overnight. In the morning, top with yogurt and fresh fruit.

- Bake a large batch of healthful muffins at the beginning of the week and freeze them. Take some out before going to bed and defrost in the refrigerator.

- Make pancakes or waffles on Sunday morning and freeze the leftovers. Pop them in the toaster during the week for a quick treat.

- Hard-boil some eggs when you're making dinner and refrigerate until breakfast. Serve with multigrain toast and fruit.

- Set the table for breakfast before going to bed — or, better yet, have the kids do it! They can put out boxes of their favorite whole-grain cereals so they'll be ready to go.

Caffeine and Your Health

Caffeine, a natural compound found in more than 60 plants, is a component of coffee, tea and chocolate and is used to make cola and many of the new "energy" drinks. Caffeine is also added to certain medications to improve how they work. Caffeine is a known stimulant and can increase alertness and reduce feelings of fatigue. It can temporarily raise your blood pressure, heart rate and breathing rate. However, when caffeinated foods and beverages are consumed in moderation, as part of a healthy meal plan, they are not harmful to your health.

Health Canada has stated that caffeine in the following amounts is safe:

Population Group	Maximum Safe Caffeine Intake (mg/day)*
Adults	400 to 450 mg
Pregnant and breastfeeding women	300 mg
Children, 10–12 years old	85 mg
Children, 7–9 years old	52.5 mg
Children, 4–6 years old	45 mg

*There is about 150 mg of caffeine in a cup (250 mL) of coffee and about 40 mg in a comparable quantity of tea.

(Source: www.hc-sc.gc.ca/iyh-vsv/food-aliment/caffeine_e.html)

Butter or Margarine?

We spend a lot of time debating which spread is better, butter or margarine. The bottom line is that both are high in fat. They each supply 4 grams of fat per teaspoon (5 mL), which translates into 36 calories. Butter contains cholesterol and saturated fat. Margarine is cholesterol-free, but hydrogenated margarine contains saturated fat and trans fat. Non-hydrogenated margarine is usually made with canola or olive oil, both of which are high in unsaturated fats. Whatever you choose, remember to spread it thinly.

Sandra Gabriele,
Dietitian, ON

This hearty breakfast is Sandra's version of muesli, a traditional Swiss breakfast cereal.

TIP
If you're using frozen berries, thaw them in the fridge overnight and drain liquid before adding to the yogurt mixture.

Apple Berry Muesli

• *Preparation time: 10 minutes*

2 cups	quick-cooking rolled oats	500 mL
2 cups	low-fat plain yogurt	500 mL
1 cup	milk	250 mL
3 tbsp	granulated sugar or liquid honey	45 mL
2	large apples, cored	2
	Juice of $\frac{1}{2}$ lemon	
1 cup	chopped berries	250 mL
	Raisins and nuts (optional)	

1. In a medium bowl, combine oats, yogurt, milk and sugar. Set aside.

2. Grate apples, leaving the skin on. Sprinkle with lemon juice to prevent browning. Add apples and berries to yogurt mixture. Gently mix together. Refrigerate overnight. Serve topped with raisins and/or nuts, if desired.

> **SERVING IDEA:** On a cold or damp day, serve with a warm cup of cocoa or a latte.

Make-Your-Own Breakfast Cereal

To banish those breakfast blahs, try making your own nutritious cereal. It's a nice comfort food, a great energy source and a perfect start to any morning. It's also an excellent recipe for the young chefs in your household. You can involve your family in creating their own breakfast cereal blend from start to finish, including the bulk food shopping, where they choose a variety of grains. Your children will love being involved in selecting the ingredients for their custom breakfast.

Diabetes Food Choice Values Per Serving	
2	Carbohydrates
$\frac{1}{2}$	Meat & Alternatives

NUTRIENTS Per Serving		
Calories: 201	Carbohydrate: 36.1 g	Calcium: 164 mg
Fat: 3.3 g	Fiber: 3.6 g	Iron: 1.3 mg
Sodium: 58 mg	Protein: 8.1 g	

High in: Calcium, vitamin B_{12}, magnesium and zinc
A source of: Dietary fiber

Big-Batch Seed and Nut Granola

MAKES 20 SERVINGS

Eileen Campbell

This "good for you" granola keeps well in an airtight container for up to 1 month. It is great as a filling for Baked Granola Apples (page 296) or as a topper for Yogurt with Berries and Granola (see box, below).

- *Preparation time: 10 minutes / Cooking time: 30 minutes*
- *Preheat oven to 275°F (140°C)*
- *2 baking sheets*

½ cup	pure maple syrup	125 mL
2 tbsp	vegetable oil	25 mL
2 tbsp	liquid honey	25 mL
1 tsp	vanilla	5 mL
2¾ cups	quick-cooking rolled oats	675 mL
½ cup	sunflower seeds	125 mL
½ cup	pumpkin seeds	125 mL
½ cup	sliced almonds	125 mL
¼ cup	sesame seeds	50 mL
2 tbsp	ground flaxseed	25 mL
¾ cup	dried fruit (raisins, blueberries, cranberries or cherries)	175 mL
¾ cup	unsweetened flaked coconut	175 mL

1. In a large bowl, combine maple syrup, oil, honey and vanilla. Add oats, sunflower seeds, pumpkin seeds, almonds, sesame seeds and flaxseed. Mix well. Spread mixture evenly on baking sheets.

2. Bake in preheated oven for 15 minutes. Add dried fruit and coconut; mix well. Bake for 15 minutes or until lightly browned. Let cool on a clean baking sheet before storing.

SERVING IDEA: This health-packed granola would be great on top of your favorite yogurt or simply served with milk.

Yogurt with Berries and Granola

For each serving, layer low-fat vanilla yogurt, fresh berries and granola in a pretty glass. Assemble in the evening, cover and place on a tray in the fridge. Better yet, give your kids a selection of fruits and yogurt flavors and have them assemble these for the whole family. In the morning, open the fridge and enjoy!

NUTRIENTS Per Serving		
Calories: 193	Carbohydrate: 22.6 g	Calcium: 34 mg
Fat: 10.3 g	Fiber: 3.2 g	Iron: 1.9 mg
Sodium: 6 mg	Protein: 5.0 g	

Very high in: Magnesium • **High in:** Zinc
A source of: Dietary fiber

Diabetes Food Choice Values Per Serving	
1½	Carbohydrates
½	Meat & Alternatives
1½	Fats

Konnie Kranenburg, AB

Konnie concocted this recipe in the 1980s, when she was competing in triathlons and needed to have an energetic start to her day. Twenty years later, she still eats it every day. You can store it in an airtight container for up to 3 months.

TIPS

Look for 9-grain cereal in the bulk food store or the bulk food section of your grocery store.

To toast wheat germ, heat a skillet over medium heat, add wheat germ and toast gently, shaking occasionally to ensure even toasting, for about 4 minutes or until fragrant.

Big-Batch Power Porridge

• *Preparation time: 10 minutes / Cooking time: 5 minutes*

6 cups	large-flake old-fashioned rolled oats	1.5 L
1 cup	9-grain cereal (such as Red River)	250 mL
¾ cup	wheat germ, toasted (see tip, at left)	175 mL
½ cup	oat bran	125 mL
½ cup	raisins or dried cranberries	125 mL
½ cup	sunflower seeds	125 mL

1. In a large bowl, combine oats, 9-grain cereal, wheat germ, oat bran, raisins and sunflower seeds. Store in a large covered container at room temperature for up to 1 week or in the refrigerator for up to 3 months.

2. To prepare 1 serving, bring 1 cup (250 mL) water to a boil in a small saucepan. Add ½ cup (125 mL) porridge mixture; stir and reduce heat to low. Cook, stirring occasionally, for about 5 minutes or until thickened.

 **✓ KID APPROVED**

SERVING IDEA: Add brown sugar and warmed milk; also delicious with a handful of blueberries.

Diabetes Food Choice Values Per Serving	
2	Carbohydrates
1	Fat

NUTRIENTS Per Serving		
Calories: 201	Carbohydrate: 33.4 g	Calcium: 26 mg
Fat: 5.1 g	Fiber: 5.3 g	Iron: 2.6 mg
Sodium: 4 mg	Protein: 8.5 g	

Very high in: Thiamine and magnesium
High in: Dietary fiber, iron and zinc

Better-than-Instant Oatmeal

MAKES 4 SERVINGS

Lisa Diamond, Dietitian, BC

• *Preparation time: 5 minutes / Cooking time: 10 to 15 minutes*

3 cups	milk or soy beverage	750 mL
1 cup	quick-cooking rolled oats	250 mL
2 tbsp	packed brown sugar or pure maple syrup	25 mL
1 tbsp	ground flaxseed	15 mL
2 tsp	wheat germ, toasted (see tip, page 48)	10 mL
1 tsp	margarine or butter	5 mL
½ tsp	ground cinnamon (optional)	2 mL
Pinch	salt	Pinch
⅓ cup	raisins or dried cranberries (optional)	75 mL
	Toasted chopped almonds, walnuts or pecans (optional)	

Lisa's kids used to love instant oatmeal. In an effort to provide them with something healthier, she developed this recipe. Now they ask for "Mommy oatmeal" and gobble it up.

TIPS
When using margarine, choose a non-hydrogenated version to limit consumption of trans fats.

Children like this oatmeal best when the optional ingredients are added.

1. In a large saucepan, over medium-low heat, combine milk, oats, brown sugar, flaxseed, wheat germ, margarine, cinnamon (if using) and salt. Cook, stirring often, for 10 to 15 minutes or until thick and bubbly. Remove from heat and add raisins (if using); let stand for 2 minutes. Serve topped with nuts, if desired.

✓ **KID APPROVED**

SERVING IDEA: This homemade oatmeal tastes delicious with an orange on the side. The night before, segment the orange to ease the morning rush.

NUTRIENTS Per Serving		
Calories: 230	Carbohydrate: 32.1 g	Calcium: 236 mg
Fat: 6.9 g	Fiber: 2.7 g	Iron: 1.4 mg
Sodium: 165 mg	Protein: 10.3 g	

Very high in: Magnesium • **High in:** Calcium, riboflavin and zinc
A source of: Dietary fiber

Diabetes Food Choice Values Per Serving	
2	Carbohydrates
1	Fat

Easy Breakfast Cookies

Lisa Haber, Dietitian, AB

Cookies for breakfast — what a unique way to ensure the whole family gets a healthy start to the day! Include your children in the preparation of any recipe, and they will be more likely to try the end result. Plus, cooking together provides some fun one-on-one time with Mom or Dad.

VARIATIONS

Substitute your favorite dried fruits for the raisins.

Experiment by adding nuts and seeds, making the cookies a little bit different every time.

For added fiber and less fat, replace the vegetable oil with ¼ cup (50 mL) of puréed fruit or cooked puréed white beans or red lentils.

- *Preparation time: 15 minutes / Cooking time: 15 to 20 minutes*
- *Preheat oven to 325°F (160°C)*
- *Baking sheet, lined with parchment paper*

1 ½ cups	whole wheat flour	375 mL
1 tsp	baking soda	5 mL
1 tsp	baking powder	5 mL
¼ tsp	salt	1 mL
¾ cup	lightly packed brown sugar	175 mL
½ cup	butter	125 mL
¼ cup	vegetable oil	50 mL
¼ cup	olive oil	50 mL
2	eggs	2
¼ cup	flaxseed (ground or whole)	50 mL
1 tsp	vanilla	5 mL
2 ½ cups	9-grain cereal (see tip, page 48)	625 mL
¾ cup	unsweetened flaked coconut	175 mL
½ cup	raisins or dried cranberries	125 mL

1. In a small bowl, combine flour, baking soda, baking powder and salt.
2. In a large bowl, using an electric mixer, cream sugar, butter, vegetable oil and olive oil until smooth. Beat in eggs, flaxseed and vanilla. Stir in flour mixture until combined. Stir in 9-grain cereal, coconut and raisins.
3. Drop dough by tablespoonfuls (15 mL), about 2 inches (5 cm) apart, onto prepared baking sheet. Flatten with a fork.
4. Bake in preheated oven for 15 to 20 minutes or until browned. Let cool on baking sheet on a wire rack for 10 minutes, then remove to rack to cool completely.

❄ FREEZER FRIENDLY
✓ KID APPROVED

Diabetes Food Choice Values Per Serving	
1	Carbohydrate
1 ½	Fats

NUTRIENTS Per Serving		
Calories: 138	Carbohydrate: 15.8 g	Calcium: 19 mg
Fat: 7.9 g	Fiber: 2.5 g	Iron: 0.8 mg
Sodium: 100 mg	Protein: 2.5 g	
A source of: Dietary fiber		

Buttermilk Pancakes

MAKES 10 PANCAKES (1 PER SERVING)

Eileen Campbell

• *Preparation time: 10 minutes / Cooking time: 15 minutes*

¾ cup	whole wheat flour	175 mL
¼ cup	wheat germ	50 mL
1 tsp	baking soda	5 mL
¼ tsp	salt	1 mL
1	egg, lightly beaten	1
1 cup	buttermilk	250 mL
2 tbsp	vegetable oil	25 mL
	Vegetable cooking spray	

This easy pancake recipe has more fiber than commercial mixes, giving you a delicious, healthful breakfast option.

1. In a small bowl, combine flour, wheat germ, baking soda and salt.

2. In large bowl, whisk together egg, buttermilk and oil. Stir in flour mixture until combined.

3. Heat a griddle or large nonstick skillet over medium-high heat. Spray lightly with vegetable cooking spray. For each pancake, pour ¼ cup (50 mL) batter onto griddle and cook until bubbly around the edges, about 2 minutes. Flip and cook until golden brown, about 2 minutes. Transfer to a plate and keep warm in a low oven. Repeat with remaining batter, spraying griddle with vegetable cooking spray and adjusting heat between batches as needed.

VARIATION
Add 1 cup (250 mL) berries to the batter. Toss berries in a small amount of flour to prevent them from bleeding into the batter.

❄ **FREEZER FRIENDLY**
✓ **KID APPROVED**

NUTRIENTS Per Serving		
Calories: 83	Carbohydrate: 9.2 g	Calcium: 35 mg
Fat: 4.0 g	Fiber: 1.5 g	Iron: 0.6 mg
Sodium: 216 mg	Protein: 3.3 g	

Diabetes Food Choice Values Per Serving	
½	Carbohydrate
1	Fat

Oatmeal Pancakes

Jorie Janzen, MB

These tasty pancakes are so easy to make. Maple syrup or mixed berries on the side will make this a kid favorite.

• *Preparation time: 5 minutes / Cooking time: 12 to 15 minutes*

6	egg whites	6
1 cup	old-fashioned rolled oats	250 mL
1 cup	fat-free cottage cheese	250 mL
2 tsp	granulated sugar	10 mL
1 tsp	ground cinnamon (optional)	5 mL
1 tsp	vanilla	5 mL
	Vegetable cooking spray	

1. In blender, on medium speed, blend egg whites, oats, cottage cheese, sugar, cinnamon (if using) and vanilla until smooth.

2. Heat a griddle or large nonstick skillet over medium-low heat. Spray lightly with vegetable cooking spray. For each pancake, pour $1/4$ cup (50 mL) batter onto griddle and cook until bubbly around the edges, about 2 minutes. Flip and cook until golden brown, about 2 minutes. Transfer to a plate and keep warm in a low oven. Repeat with remaining batter, spraying griddle with vegetable cooking spray and adjusting heat between batches as needed.

❄ **FREEZER FRIENDLY**
✓ **KID APPROVED**

SERVING IDEA: These pancakes taste great topped with fresh berries and a dollop of your favorite yogurt.

Diabetes Food Choice Values Per Serving

$1/2$	Carbohydrate
$1/2$	Meat & Alternatives

NUTRIENTS Per Serving

Calories: 58	Carbohydrate: 6.5 g	Calcium: 11 mg
Fat: 0.7 g	Fiber: 0.7 g	Iron: 0.4 mg
Sodium: 62 mg	Protein: 6.1 g	

Catherine's Healthy Cornmeal Pancakes

MAKES 12 LARGE PANCAKES (1 PER SERVING)

Ellen Lakusiak, Dietitian, ON

If your family doesn't like squash, and they ask why the pancakes are so yellow, tell them it's the cornmeal. Once they have tasted them, they won't care what's in them.

- **Preparation time: 15 minutes / Cooking time: 30 minutes**

1 cup	whole wheat flour	250 mL
1 cup	all-purpose flour	250 mL
1 cup	cornmeal	250 mL
1/4 cup	granulated sugar	50 mL
1 tsp	baking soda	5 mL
1 tsp	baking powder	5 mL
2	eggs	2
1 1/2 cups	buttermilk (approx.)	375 mL
1 cup	butternut squash purée	250 mL
3 tbsp	vegetable oil	45 mL
1 tsp	vanilla	5 mL
	Vegetable cooking spray	
1 cup	fresh or frozen fruit (see tip, at right)	250 mL

1. In a large bowl, combine whole wheat flour, all-purpose flour, cornmeal, sugar, baking soda and baking powder.

2. In a medium bowl, whisk eggs, 1 1/2 cups (375 mL) of the buttermilk, squash purée, oil and vanilla. Whisk into flour mixture. If mixture appears too thick, add up to 1/2 cup (125 mL) buttermilk to thin.

3. Heat a griddle or large nonstick skillet over medium-high heat. Spray lightly with vegetable cooking spray. For each pancake, pour 1/2 cup (125 mL) batter onto griddle and cook until bubbly around the edges, about 3 minutes. Flip and cook until golden brown, about 3 minutes. Transfer to a plate and keep warm in a low oven. Repeat with remaining batter, spraying griddle with vegetable cooking spray and adjusting heat between batches as needed.

4. Top each pancake with 1 to 2 tbsp (15 to 25 mL) fruit.

❄ FREEZER FRIENDLY
✓ KID APPROVED

TIPS

Freeze leftover squash in 1-cup (250 mL) containers and thaw one in the microwave just before adding to pancake batter.

Choose your favorite fruit for this recipe. Berries and chopped peaches work well.

Cooked pancakes freeze well in plastic bags and can be reheated in the toaster for a quick breakfast.

Ellen packs cooked pancakes as a healthy lunchbox item for her family. All they have to do is reheat in a microwave or toaster at work or school.

VARIATION

Substitute mashed sweet potatoes for the squash purée.

NUTRIENTS Per Serving		
Calories: 198	Carbohydrate: 33.0 g	Calcium: 66 mg
Fat: 5.2 g	Fiber: 3.0 g	Iron: 1.3 mg
Sodium: 174 mg	Protein: 5.7 g	

Very high in: Riboflavin and folate • **High in:** Vitamin A
A source of: Dietary fiber

Diabetes Food Choice Values Per Serving	
2	Carbohydrates
1	Fat

Claudette Mayer-Lanthier, QC

Claudette invented this recipe for a quick and nourishing breakfast, full of fiber and great flavor. To get the benefits of flaxseed, it should be ground, but whole seeds add great crunch.

TIP
Muesli, multigrain or whole wheat pitas are great healthy options for this recipe.

Quick Breakfast Fruit Pita

● *Preparation time: 5 minutes*

½	banana, crushed	½
1 tbsp	flaxseed (ground or whole)	15 mL
1 tsp	pumpkin seeds	5 mL
1	6-inch (15 cm) pita	1
1	strawberry, hulled and thinly sliced	1

1. In a small bowl, combine banana, flaxseed and pumpkin seeds.
2. Toast pita and cut open. Stuff with banana mixture and place slices of strawberry on top. Eat while still warm from the toaster.

✓ **KID APPROVED**

Diabetes Food Choice Values Per Serving	
3	Carbohydrates
½	Meat & Alternatives
1½	Fats

NUTRIENTS Per Serving		
Calories: 348	Carbohydrate: 54.4 g	Calcium: 128 mg
Fat: 11.0 g	Fiber: 8.6 g	Iron: 3.3 mg
Sodium: 329 mg	Protein: 11.1 g	

Very high in: Dietary fiber, thiamine, niacin, folate and magnesium
High in: Iron, riboflavin, vitamin B$_6$ and zinc

Double Cheese, Apple and Maple Bagels

MAKES 4 SERVINGS

Dairy Farmers of Canada

Try this unusual combination for breakfast instead of your usual bagel sandwich.

VARIATION
For a change of taste, substitute Havarti and Oka cheeses.

• *Preparation time: 2 minutes / Cooking time: 5 minutes*
• *Preheat broiler*

2	bagels, halved	2
¼ cup	unsweetened applesauce	50 mL
4 oz	Canadian Cheddar cheese, cut into slices	125 g
2 oz	Canadian Brie cheese, cut into slices	60 g
4 tsp	pure maple syrup	20 mL

1. Toast bagel halves; spread each with 1 tbsp (15 mL) applesauce. Top each with one-quarter of the Cheddar and the Brie.

2. Broil until the cheese melts, about 5 minutes.

3. Drizzle each half with 1 tsp (5 mL) maple syrup.

> **SERVING IDEA:** Serve each half-bagel with a bowl of fruit salad on the side.

NUTRIENTS Per Serving		
Calories: 283	Carbohydrate: 25.6 g	Calcium: 262 mg
Fat: 13.9 g	Fiber: 1.0 g	Iron: 1.6 mg
Sodium: 455 mg	Protein: 13.8 g	

High in: Calcium, riboflavin, niacin, folate, vitamin B_{12} and zinc

Diabetes Food Choice Values Per Serving
1½ Carbohydrates
1½ Meat & Alternatives
1½ Fats

Vrinda Walker, BC

Whether you are vegetarian, vegan or just trying to eat less meat, these sandwiches are a great addition to your weekly breakfast menu (and kids love them)! This dish is vegan if you use soy products.

TIPS

For added nutrition, choose whole wheat, multigrain or whole wheat raisin English muffins.

When using margarine, choose a non-hydrogenated version to limit consumption of trans fats.

Tofu English Muffins

• Preparation time: 3 minutes / Cooking time: 5 to 7 minutes

8 oz	medium tofu	250 g
2 tbsp	reduced-sodium soy sauce	25 mL
	Vegetable cooking spray	
¼ tsp	ground turmeric (optional)	1 mL
	Salt and freshly ground black pepper (optional)	
4	slices soy ham or back bacon	4
4	English muffins, halved	4
4 tsp	margarine	20 mL
4 tsp	ketchup	20 mL
4	slices (each 1 oz/30 g) soy cheese (or Cheddar, Swiss, Jack or provolone)	4

1. Break up tofu into chunks that resemble the texture of scrambled eggs.

2. In a small bowl, combine tofu and soy sauce.

3. Heat a large skillet over medium-high heat. Spray with vegetable cooking spray. Sprinkle turmeric (if using) into skillet and cook for a few seconds (this will give the tofu the yellow color of scrambled eggs). Add tofu mixture; cook, stirring occasionally, for 5 to 7 minutes or until edges of tofu are golden-brown. Season to taste with salt and pepper, if desired.

4. During the last couple of minutes of cooking the tofu, clear some space in the skillet and spray lightly with vegetable cooking spray. Add soy ham and cook, turning once, until lightly browned, about 1 minute per side.

5. Meanwhile, toast muffins. Spread each muffin bottom with 1 tsp (5 mL) margarine and each muffin top with 1 tsp (5 mL) ketchup. On each muffin bottom, place one-quarter of the scrambled tofu, 1 slice of soy cheese and 1 slice of soy ham. Top with muffin tops.

✓ KID APPROVED

Diabetes Food Choice Values Per Serving	
2	Carbohydrates
1½	Meat & Alternatives
½	Fat

NUTRIENTS Per Serving		
Calories: 272	Carbohydrate: 32.2 g	Calcium: 243 mg
Fat: 10.3 g	Fiber: 5.0 g	Iron: 2.5 mg
Sodium: 1,173 mg	Protein: 16.9 g	

Very high in: Folate and magnesium • **High in:** Dietary fiber, calcium, iron, thiamine, niacin and zinc

Egg Cup Delight

- *Preparation time: 10 minutes / Cooking time: 12 to 15 minutes*
- *Preheat oven to 350°F (180°C)*
- *Muffin tin, 4 cups lightly greased*

4	slices deli meat, preferably ham (8 if sliced very thin)	4
3	mushrooms, thinly sliced	3
¼	bell pepper (any color), diced	¼
	A few leaves of spinach, chopped	
1 cup	shredded Cheddar, Swiss, feta or Gouda cheese	250 mL
4	eggs	4
1 tbsp	freshly grated Parmesan cheese (optional)	15 mL
Pinch	salt	Pinch

1. Line the 4 prepared muffin cups with deli meat. Add about 2 tsp (10 mL) vegetables (mushrooms, bell pepper and spinach) on top of the meat in each cup. Add ¼ cup (50 mL) cheese on top of the vegetables in each cup. Crack 1 egg into each cup and prick yolk with a fork. Sprinkle each egg with Parmesan (if using) and salt.

2. Bake in preheated oven for 12 to 15 minutes or until egg is cooked to desired texture. To remove from pan, slide a spoon around the underside of the deli meat and lift out.

 **KID APPROVED**

> **SERVING IDEA:** Serve with hearty whole-grain bread and a fruit salad.

MAKES 4 SERVINGS

Heidi Piovoso and Kristyn Hall, Dietitians, AB

The two dietitians who created this simple recipe have had many positive comments on its presentation — one person said it was as pretty as a flower on the plate! Kids can easily help with the preparation — with supervision, of course.

NUTRIENTS Per Serving		
Calories: 225	Carbohydrate: 2.6 g	Calcium: 246 mg
Fat: 15.2 g	Fiber: 0.5 g	Iron: 1.5 mg
Sodium: 570 mg	Protein: 18.8 g	

Very high in: Vitamin A, thiamine, riboflavin, niacin and vitamin B_{12} • **High in:** Calcium, folate and zinc

Diabetes Food Choice Values Per Serving	
3	Meat & Alternatives

Greek Scrambled Eggs

Eileen Campbell

This easygoing egg dish works well for breakfast, brunch or even dinner. Tzatziki and feta cheese give it Greek flair.

TIP
To avoid sloppy eggs, make sure you dry the peppers and artichokes well!

VARIATIONS
For Italian scrambled eggs, substitute diced tomatoes and fresh basil for the artichoke hearts and part-skim mozzarella cheese for the feta.

For French scrambled eggs, substitute chopped chives for the dill and Brie cheese for the feta.

Create your own ethnic specialty scrambled eggs!

• *Preparation time: 10 minutes / Cooking time: 4 to 5 minutes*

8	eggs	8
1/4 cup	tzatziki (store-bought or see recipe, opposite)	50 mL
2	green onions, chopped	2
2	roasted red bell peppers, diced	2
1 cup	chopped drained canned artichoke hearts	250 mL
1/2 cup	crumbled feta cheese	125 mL
1 tbsp	chopped fresh dill	15 mL
1/2 tsp	freshly ground black pepper	2 mL
2 tbsp	vegetable oil	25 mL

1. In large bowl, whisk eggs and tzatziki. Stir in green onions, red peppers, artichoke hearts, feta, dill and pepper until well combined.

2. In a large nonstick skillet, heat oil over medium heat. Pour in egg mixture; cook, stirring constantly with a wooden spoon, for 4 to 5 minutes or until eggs form soft, thick curds.

SERVING IDEAS: Serve with a whole wheat pita or a thick slice of Italian wheat bread.

Breakfast for Dinner: Serve with Garden Patch Spinach Salad (page 141) and Orange Cranberry Muffins (page 291). When you need a speedy meal, serve with a bag salad, fruit and homemade cookies from the freezer.

Diabetes Food Choice Values Per Serving

1 1/2 Meat & Alternatives
1 1/2 Fats

NUTRIENTS Per Serving

Calories: 203	Carbohydrate: 7.3 g	Calcium: 124 mg
Fat: 14.6 g	Fiber: 1.9 g	Iron: 1.5 mg
Sodium: 271 mg	Protein: 11.8 g	

Very high in: Vitamin C, folate and vitamin B$_{12}$
High in: Vitamin A, riboflavin and niacin

Tzatziki

MAKES 1½ CUPS (375 ML) (1 tbsp/ 15 mL PER SERVING)

Eileen Campbell

2 cups	plain yogurt	500 mL
½ cup	grated cucumber, drained	125 mL
2	cloves garlic, pressed	2

1. Line a sieve with cheesecloth and set over a bowl. Pour in yogurt, refrigerate and let drip for at least 1 hour or for up to 3 hours, until yogurt is thickened. Discard the liquid in the bowl (or add to smoothies or milk shakes).

2. In a small bowl, combine yogurt cheese, cucumber and garlic. Cover tightly with plastic wrap and refrigerate for at least half an hour or until ready to serve.

Tzatziki is a Greek yogurt and cucumber dip that can be found in the dairy section of most grocery stores. If you can't find it, make your own from this simple recipe.

NUTRIENTS Per Serving		
Calories: 11	Carbohydrate: 1.1 g	Calcium: 33 mg
Fat: 0.3 g	Fiber: 0.0 g	Iron: 1.5 mg
Sodium: 9 mg	Protein: 1.0 g	

Diabetes Food Choice Values Per Serving

1 Extra

Cynthia Mannion, AB

In this simple but tasty breakfast, the combination of sweet raisins and savory eggs is delightful! These scrambled eggs would be great for a weekend brunch.

TIPS

When using margarine, choose a non-hydrogenated version to limit consumption of trans fats.

To tell if an egg is fresh, place it (in its shell) in a bowl of tap water. If the egg is fresh, it will lie flat on the bottom. If not, it will rise to the surface and bob.

Cheesy Scrambled Eggs

• *Preparation time: 5 minutes / Cooking time: 3 minutes*

	Vegetable cooking spray	
4	eggs	4
¼ cup	milk	50 mL
2	green onions, finely chopped	2
1 tbsp	freshly grated Parmesan cheese	15 mL
4	slices raisin bread	4
	Butter or margarine	

1. Heat a medium nonstick skillet over medium heat. Spray with vegetable cooking spray.

2. Meanwhile, in a small bowl, whisk eggs and milk. Pour into skillet and cook, stirring constantly, for 2 minutes. Add green onions and cook, stirring constantly, until eggs form soft, thick curds, about 1 minute.

3. Divide scrambled eggs among 4 plates and sprinkle with Parmesan.

4. Toast raisin bread and spread lightly with butter. Cut into wedges and place around eggs.

 ✓ **KID APPROVED**

SERVING IDEA: Serve with a glass of 100% fruit juice.

Diabetes Food Choice Values Per Serving	
1	Carbohydrate
1	Meat & Alternatives
1	Fat

NUTRIENTS Per Serving		
Calories: 166	Carbohydrate: 15.5 g	Calcium: 83 mg
Fat: 7.3 g	Fiber: 1.3 g	Iron: 1.5 mg
Sodium: 195 mg	Protein: 9.5 g	

Very high in: Vitamin B$_{12}$ • **High in:** Riboflavin and folate

Sweet Potato Omelet

• Preparation time: 6 minutes / Cooking time: 4 minutes

2	eggs	2
1 cup	shredded peeled sweet potatoes	250 mL
½ cup	chopped onion	125 mL
1	clove garlic, chopped	1
1 tsp	salt or soy sauce	5 mL
1 tbsp	vegetable oil	15 mL

1. In a small bowl, beat eggs with a fork. Stir in sweet potatoes, onion, garlic and salt until well combined.
2. Heat a medium skillet over medium-high heat. Add oil and swirl to coat the pan. Pour in egg mixture; cook, turning once, until lightly browned on both sides, about 2 minutes per side.

✓ **KID APPROVED**

SERVING IDEA: For a great start to your day, serve with a piece of fruit and a glass of milk.

Nena Wirth, Dietitian, ON

This delicious and unusual omelet is reminiscent of potato pancakes. Your tummy will be smiling!

TIP
To flip the omelet, put a plate over the skillet and turn it out. Flip over into the skillet to cook the other side.

VARIATION
Substitute sliced green beans, chopped bean sprouts, diced bell pepper, diced mushrooms or any combination of your favorite vegetables for the sweet potatoes.

NUTRIENTS Per Serving		
Calories: 193	Carbohydrate: 14.6 g	Calcium: 52 mg
Fat: 11.9 g	Fiber: 2.0 g	Iron: 1.1 mg
Sodium: 364 mg	Protein: 7.4 g	

Very high in: Vitamin A and vitamin B_{12} • **High in:** Folate
A source of: Dietary fiber

Diabetes Food Choice Values Per Serving	
½	Carbohydrate
1	Meat & Alternatives
1	Fat

Erna Braun, MB

Even without a pastry crust, this quiche is so delicious!

TIP
To ensure that you don't wind up with a soggy quiche, read the note on zucchini on page 63.

VARIATION
Blanched broccoli could be substituted for the zucchini, and ham could be added.

SERVING IDEAS:
This makes a perfect brunch dish accompanied by a green salad and whole wheat dinner rolls, with Pears in Tosca Sauce (page 298) to finish.

When you have the gang over for brunch, serve with Spring Vegetable Salad (page 139), Big-Batch Multigrain Bread (page 280) and/or Pumpkin Spice Nut Bread (page 283), a fresh fruit salad and Peanut Butter Flaxseed Cookies (page 317).

Crustless Zucchini Quiche

- *Preparation time: 15 minutes / Cooking time: 45 to 55 minutes*
- *Preheat oven to 350°F (180°C)*
- *9-inch (23 cm) deep-dish pie plate, greased*

	Vegetable cooking spray	
1 cup	chopped onion	250 mL
5	eggs	5
1½ cups	skim milk	375 mL
2½ cups	grated zucchini, drained	625 mL
2 cups	chopped red bell peppers	500 mL
3 tbsp	all-purpose flour	45 mL
2 tsp	baking powder	10 mL
1 tsp	salt	5 mL
½ tsp	freshly ground black pepper	2 mL
Pinch	cayenne pepper	Pinch
2 cups	shredded light Cheddar cheese	500 mL
¼ cup	dry bread crumbs	50 mL

1. Heat a small frying over medium-high heat. Spray with vegetable cooking spray. Sauté onion until just softened, about 5 minutes.
2. In a large bowl, beat eggs and milk. Stir in onion, zucchini and red peppers.
3. In a small bowl, combine flour, baking powder, salt, black pepper and cayenne. Stir in cheese until thoroughly coated. Add to egg mixture along with bread crumbs. Pour mixture into prepared pie plate and smooth top.
4. Bake in preheated oven for 40 to 50 minutes or until top is lightly browned and puffed and a knife inserted in the center comes out clean.

✓ **KID APPROVED**

Diabetes Food Choice Values Per Serving

½	Carbohydrate
1½	Meat & Alternatives

NUTRIENTS Per Serving		
Calories: 214	Carbohydrate: 18.2 g	Calcium: 323 mg
Fat: 7.5 g	Fiber: 2.0 g	Iron: 1.6 mg
Sodium: 826 mg	Protein: 18.3 g	

Very high in: Vitamin A, vitamin C, calcium, riboflavin, folate and vitamin B_{12} • **High in:** Niacin and zinc • **A source of:** Dietary fiber

Kitchen Sink Frittata

- **Preparation time: 10 minutes / Cooking time: 25 to 35 minutes**
- Preheat oven to 350°F (180°C)
- 8-cup (2 L) baking dish, greased

6	eggs	6
1/2 cup	milk	125 mL
1/4 tsp	salt	1 mL
1/4 tsp	freshly ground black pepper	1 mL
1 tbsp	vegetable oil	15 mL
1/2 cup	diced onion	125 mL
1	sweet potato, peeled and shredded	1
1	tomato, diced	1
2 cups	cooked chopped vegetables (see tip, at right)	500 mL
1 cup	shredded reduced-fat cheese (see tip, at right)	250 mL

1. In a small bowl, whisk eggs and milk. Add salt and pepper. Set aside.

2. In a large skillet, heat oil over medium heat. Sauté onion until softened, about 5 minutes. Stir in sweet potato, tomato and cooked vegetables.

3. Transfer vegetable mixture to prepared baking dish. Pour in egg mixture and top with cheese.

4. Bake in preheated oven for 20 to 30 minutes or until topping is golden and puffed and a knife inserted in the center comes out clean.

✓ **KID APPROVED**

> **SERVING IDEA:** For a low-cost dinner, serve with Fruity Slaw (page 147) and finish the meal with Baked Granola Apples (page 296).

MAKES 6 SERVINGS

Eileen Campbell

This easy and flavorful brunch recipe uses both leftover and fresh vegetables.

TIPS
This is a good way to use up leftover cooked vegetables. Try using any one or a combination of: mushrooms, broccoli, rapini, fennel, spinach, green peas, zucchini, green onions, red, green or yellow bell pepper, bok choy, kale, corn, asparagus or green beans.

Choose a full-flavored cheese such as old Cheddar, Gruyere, feta or Pepper Jack. The stronger the flavor of the cheese, the less you need to use to get great taste.

If Using Zucchini
Because zucchini contains a lot of moisture, adding it directly to this egg dish would result in a very soggy frittata. Drain grated zucchini well in a colander and squeeze in a clean tea towel to remove as much moisture as possible before mixing with the eggs.

When adding zucchini to baked goods, though, do not drain, as the moisture is what helps replace some of the fat content and keep baked goods moist.

NUTRIENTS Per Serving		
Calories: 183	Carbohydrate: 12.6 g	Calcium: 145 mg
Fat: 9.2 g	Fiber: 2.1 g	Iron: 1.3 mg
Sodium: 288 mg	Protein: 13.0 g	

Very high in: Vitamin A and vitamin B_{12} • **High in:** Vitamin C, riboflavin, niacin and folate • **A source of:** Dietary fiber

Diabetes Food Choice Values Per Serving	
1/2	Carbohydrate
1 1/2	Meat & Alternatives
1/2	Fat

Lorna Smith, ON

This delicious frittata has European flair.

VARIATIONS

Substitute Cheddar or Swiss cheese for the feta.

If your family does not like olives, replace them with diced red bell pepper.

Frittata with Cheese, Tomato and Basil

- **Preparation time: 10 minutes / Cooking time: 7 to 10 minutes**
- *Preheat broiler*
- *Ovenproof skillet*

10	eggs	10
1/4 cup	milk	50 mL
3	plum tomatoes, finely chopped	3
3	green onions, finely chopped	3
3/4 cup	crumbled light feta cheese	175 mL
1/3 cup	finely chopped fresh basil	75 mL
1/2 tsp	salt	2 mL
1/4 tsp	freshly ground black pepper	1 mL
2 tbsp	vegetable oil	25 mL
1/3 cup	thinly sliced pitted black olives	75 mL
3 tbsp	freshly grated Parmesan cheese	45 mL

1. In a large bowl, whisk eggs and milk. Stir in tomatoes, green onions, feta, basil, salt and pepper.

2. Heat ovenproof skillet over medium-high heat. Add oil and swirl to coat pan. Pour in egg mixture, without stirring. Cook, lifting sides occasionally to let uncooked egg run underneath, until eggs start to set and sides and bottom begin to brown, about 5 minutes. Sprinkle with olives and Parmesan cheese.

3. Place skillet under preheated broiler and cook for 2 to 5 minutes or until eggs start to puff and brown and a knife inserted in the center comes out clean.

4. Using a flexible spatula, loosen edges and bottom of frittata. Slide onto a warm plate. Slice into 6 wedges and serve warm or at room temperature.

Diabetes Food Choice Values Per Serving	
2	Meat & Alternatives
2	Fats

NUTRIENTS Per Serving		
Calories: 232	Carbohydrate: 3.5 g	Calcium: 188 mg
Fat: 17.1 g	Fiber: 0.9 g	Iron: 1.5 mg
Sodium: 596 mg	Protein: 16.0 g	

Very high in: Vitamin B_{12} • **High in:** Vitamin A, calcium, riboflavin and folate

Catherine's Healthy
Cornmeal Pancakes (page 53)

Greek Scrambled Eggs (page 58)

Thai Chicken
Muffaletta (page 70)

Mango Chicken Wraps (page 74)

Spinach Tortilla Pie

MAKES 6 SERVINGS

Maureen Falkiner, BC

The combination of spinach and nutmeg is delicious with ricotta and eggs in this quiche-like pie. Great for brunch or a light supper.

TIP
Although nutmeg that is purchased ground retains fragrance, flavor and taste better than some other spices, for this recipe we recommend using whole nutmeg and grating fresh to get the full impact of this warm, aromatic spice. Grind it using a special nutmeg grater, or use the finest blade of a box grater. If you use purchased ground nutmeg instead, reduce the amount by half. Freshly grated is more fluffy and takes up less volume to get the same flavor.

- **Preparation time: 10 to 15 minutes / Cooking time: 50 to 55 minutes**
- Preheat oven to 350°F (180°C)
- 9-inch (23 cm) deep-dish glass pie plate, greased

1 tsp	vegetable oil	5 mL
1	onion, chopped	1
1	package (10 oz/300 g) fresh baby spinach	1
3	eggs, beaten	3
2 cups	ricotta cheese	500 mL
1/2 tsp	freshly grated nutmeg	2 mL
1/2 tsp	salt	2 mL
1/2 tsp	freshly ground black pepper	2 mL
3	6-inch (15 cm) whole wheat flour tortillas	3
1/3 cup	freshly grated Parmesan cheese	75 mL

1. In a medium skillet, heat oil over medium-high heat. Sauté onion until lightly browned, about 5 minutes. Add spinach, cover and steam, stirring occasionally to prevent burning, until wilted, about 3 minutes. Transfer mixture to a colander to remove any liquid.

2. In a medium bowl, combine spinach mixture, eggs, ricotta cheese, nutmeg, salt and pepper.

3. Place 1 tortilla in prepared pie plate. Top with one-third of the spinach and egg mixture. Repeat twice, ending with filling on top. Sprinkle with Parmesan cheese.

4. Bake in preheated oven for 40 to 45 minutes or until eggs are set, top is lightly browned and puffed and a knife inserted in the center comes out clean.

SERVING IDEA: Add Roasted Vegetables (page 264) and a side salad for a delicious dinner.

NUTRIENTS Per Serving		
Calories: 263	Carbohydrate: 15.6 g	Calcium: 330 mg
Fat: 15.9 g	Fiber: 2.3 g	Iron: 2.7 mg
Sodium: 503 mg	Protein: 17.5 g	

Very high in: Vitamin A, calcium, riboflavin, folate and magnesium
High in: Iron, niacin, vitamin B_{12} and zinc • **A source of:** Dietary fiber

Diabetes Food Choice Values Per Serving	
1/2	Carbohydrate
2	Meat & Alternatives
1	Fat

Lunches and Snacks

Since lunch can contribute up to one-third of your nutritional intake for the day, you want to plan it wisely. It can be as easy as a sandwich with a piece of fresh fruit and a glass of milk, or you can try some of the creative, yet simple lunch ideas in this chapter. Snacks offer a great chance to get nutrients you might miss in your daily meals. Eating small quantities of nutritious foods throughout the day can also boost your energy and help keep you productive.

simply great lunches

Between grade 1 and the end of high school, a student may eat more than 2,400 lunches at school. Creating tasty, nutritious lunches is a challenge for many parents, but with some planning and a few ideas, you can put together a lunch that not only tastes great, but also packs a nutritional punch. Aim to include at least one food from three of the four food groups and follow these simple steps:

1. **Start with a grain:** bagel, pita bread, tortilla, pasta/noodles, rice, muffin, crackers

2. **Add a protein on top, in between or on the side:** hard-boiled egg, canned tuna or salmon, leftover chicken or turkey, canned beans, cheese, hummus

3. **Add veggies and fruits for crunch:** cucumber, peppers, lettuce, cauliflower, broccoli, carrots, apple, orange, pear, grapes, strawberries

4. **Quench their thirst:** milk, yogurt or fruit shake, 100% fruit or vegetable juice, water

5. **Finish with a kid-pleasing addition:** yogurt (for eating or for dipping fruits or vegetables), homemade cookies, pudding, canned unsweetened fruit, squares (date, rice cereal, wheat puff), raisins

Great Packed Lunches, No Recipe Required

A recipe is often not necessary for a nutritious bagged lunch. Here are some simple ideas you or your children can put together. Do the prep the night before if you can, so you won't have to rush in the morning. Use your imagination, and encourage your children to think outside the box.

- Roll a slice of lean ham and a leaf of lettuce around a stick of cheese and a strip of red pepper for a simple bread-free sandwich.
- Stuff a pita with a salad mixture such as Couscous Salad (page 150), or roll it in a whole wheat tortilla.
- Create new versions of our Veggie Sandwich (page 72) by varying the cream cheese and the toppings.
- Make sandwiches with your favorite meats and cheeses on multigrain bread. Surprise your children by cutting sandwiches into interesting shapes using cookie cutters.
- Add chopped veggies and cubes of cheese to leftover cooked pasta. Top with your favorite salad dressing and toss.
- Pack leftover cooked chicken with dipping sauces such as Mango Mint Mojo (page 109) or Peach Salsa (variation, page 105) and raw veggies.
- Spread hummus or Tzatziki (page 59) on a pita and top with leaf lettuce and grated carrot. Roll up and wrap in plastic wrap.
- Ladle leftover soup into an insulated container and pack with a savory muffin or quick bread.
- Pour a smoothie into an insulated cup to go.

Get the Gear

Invest in a collection of insulated containers, lunch bags or boxes, reusable drink bottles, napkins and cutlery. Organize everything into one spot in the kitchen to speed up prep time. When packing meals to go, food safety is always a concern. Be sure to use insulated containers to keep hot foods piping hot and cold packs or frozen juice boxes to ensure that cold foods stay well chilled.

Snacks Kids Will Love

Healthy snacks can really add to nutrient intake, especially for kids, who may need to eat more often because their stomachs are smaller. You can encourage your kids to eat healthy snacks by asking them to make a list of their favorite fruits and vegetables. Add their choices to your grocery list.

Here are some other great snacks kids will enjoy:

- homemade frozen fruit juice pops or yogurt-banana pops — check out Fruit Frenzy Pops (page 327) and Chocolate Surprise Pudding Pops (page 326)
- cheese slices or cubes
- bread sticks with dip (kids love dip!)
- unsweetened fruit cups or applesauce
- homemade parfait made with yogurt, fruit and granola
- whole-grain cereal
- smoothies made with yogurt, fruit and/or juice
- sandwiches cut into fun shapes
- anything they can eat with a toothpick, such as cherry tomatoes, grapes or ham or cheese cubes (just be sure they're old enough to manage toothpicks safely)
- Oven-Baked Potato Wedges (page 271)
- Veggie Pizza with Three Cheeses (page 250)
- healthy homemade muffins (such as Banana Applesauce Muffins, page 286) and cookies (such as Charlie and Emma's Favorite Carrot Cookies, page 318)
- apple wedges with peanut butter
- celery with cheese

dealing with the munchies

If you have a burning desire to nibble away on sweet or salty foods, it's important to identify potential causes so you can move beyond them. Some of the habits and lifestyle choices that can lead to food cravings include:

- skipping breakfast
- eating irregularly and missing meals or snacks
- dieting
- omitting an entire food group from your meal plan, or limiting foods from it
- avoiding your favorite foods for weeks
- keeping sugary, salty or fatty snack foods within easy reach

You might also be experiencing cravings simply because you've had a stressful day.

Once you know the causes of your cravings, you can take preventive measures. When a case of the munchies hits:

- Think about why you're hungry. Is the cause physical or emotional? If it's emotional, realize that eating won't fill the void. Try listening to your favorite feel-good song or calling an old friend instead.
- Ask yourself if you're bored or using eating as a distraction to procrastinate. Keep a list of distractions that aren't food-related on the fridge.
- Pour yourself a glass of water — it may stave off hunger. It is also possible that you're thirsty, not hungry.
- Give yourself permission to eat the food you're craving, but delay for several minutes. Sometimes a bit of time reduces the intensity of the craving.
- If you're really hungry, pin down exactly what you want to eat. Decide if you want something sweet, salty, crunchy, creamy, savory, hot, cold. Once you've made your choice, portion out a controlled amount.
- Most important, no guilt allowed! If eating what you want makes you feel guilty, it's just not worth it. Aim to eat realistic portions, be aware of why you choose certain foods at certain times and leave it at that.

Monkey See, Monkey Do

Be a positive role model for your kids: If they see you eating healthy snacks on a regular basis, they'll be more likely to make healthy choices themselves.

BBQ Chicken Salad Sandwiches

MAKES 6 SERVINGS

Robin Coverett, AB

Here's a pleasing change from the usual mayonnaise-based chicken salad.

TIPS
Robin often grills a few extra chicken breasts for planned extras when she barbecues. Keep cooked chicken wrapped tight in the refrigerator for up to 2 days and combine it with the other ingredients as needed for a quick sandwich.

If you baste the chicken with the barbecue sauce while cooking, it makes the salad even better.

- **Preparation time: 30 minutes / Cooking time: 16 minutes / Chilling time: 15 minutes**
- *Preheat barbecue to medium*

3	boneless skinless chicken breasts (12 oz/375 g total)	3
2 tsp	no-salt-added Italian seasoning, divided	10 mL
4	stalks celery, chopped	4
1	yellow bell pepper, diced	1
1	green bell pepper, diced	1
½ cup	barbecue sauce or Zesty Sauce (page 111)	125 mL
2 tbsp	light mayonnaise	25 mL
Pinch	cayenne pepper (or to taste)	Pinch
12	slices multigrain bread (or 6 whole wheat pitas)	12

1. Season chicken breasts with 1 tsp (5 mL) of the Italian seasoning. Place on preheated barbecue and cook, turning once, for 8 minutes per side or until chicken is no longer pink inside and has reached an internal temperature of 170°F (77°C).

2. Cool chicken and coarsely chop. In a large bowl, combine chicken, celery, yellow pepper, green pepper, barbecue sauce, mayonnaise, cayenne and the remaining Italian seasoning. Cover and refrigerate for at least 15 minutes or for up to 12 hours to allow flavors to meld.

3. Toast bread. Spread chicken salad evenly on 6 slices of toast and top with the other 6 slices (or stuff into pitas).

✓ **KID APPROVED**

SERVING IDEA: Balance the meal with a glass of milk or fruit-flavored yogurt. Finish with pineapple rings for dessert.

NUTRIENTS Per Serving

Calories: 347	Carbohydrate: 48.6 g	Calcium: 107 mg
Fat: 6.6 g	Fiber: 7.0 g	Iron: 4.0 mg
Sodium: 700 mg	Protein: 25.2 g	

Very high in: Dietary fiber, vitamin C, iron, thiamine, niacin, vitamin B_6, folate and magnesium • **High in:** Riboflavin and zinc

Diabetes Food Choice Values Per Serving

2½	Carbohydrates
2	Meat & Alternatives

Thai Chicken Muffaletta

Compass Group Canada

A new twist on the familiar New Orleans sandwich, which usually contains high-fat cold cuts, cheeses and olive salad, this version offers lean chicken and great-tasting crisp vegetables, with Thai sauce for added flavor.

TIPS

For the Thai red curry sauce, we used Sharwood's, a coconut milk–based sauce. Make sure not to buy curry paste.

If making in advance, wrap tightly in plastic wrap and refrigerate for up to 2 hours.

• **Preparation time: 15 minutes / Marinating time: 4 hours / Cooking time: 10 to 15 minutes**

1/3 cup	bottled Thai red curry sauce, divided	75 mL
8 oz	boneless skinless chicken breasts	250 g
2 tbsp	light mayonnaise	25 mL
1	round loaf sourdough bread (7 inches/17.5 cm in diameter)	1
6	leaves Chinese cabbage, core removed	6
1/2	English cucumber, peeled and sliced	1/2
1	small red onion, thinly sliced	1
1	carrot, grated	1
2 tbsp	chopped fresh cilantro	25 mL

1. Place chicken breasts in a shallow dish and brush with 1/4 cup (50 mL) of the Thai sauce. Cover and refrigerate for at least 4 hours or for up to 12 hours. Preheat broiler.

2. Remove chicken from marinade and discard marinade. Broil for 10 to 15 minutes or until chicken is no longer pink inside and has reached an internal temperature of 170°F (77°C). Let cool and cut into strips.

3. In a small bowl, combine the remaining Thai sauce and mayonnaise.

4. Slice bread horizontally through the middle. Remove about 1 1/2 cups (375 mL) of the crumb from inside the top half to make a hollow, being careful not to break the crust. Spread Thai mayonnaise on the bottom half, then layer on Chinese cabbage, cucumber, red onion, chicken strips, carrot and cilantro. Replace top half of bread and press down. Cut into 8 wedges.

> **SERVING IDEA:** Finish the meal with Fruit Gazpacho (page 301).

Diabetes Food Choice Values Per Serving	
2 1/2	Carbohydrates
1	Meat & Alternatives
1/2	Fat

NUTRIENTS Per Serving		
Calories: 287	Carbohydrate: 44.6 g	Calcium: 80 g
Fat: 5.8 g	Fiber: 3.4 g	Iron: 2.3 mg
Sodium: 515 mg	Protein: 13.9 g	
Very high in: Thiamine, niacin and folate		
A source of: Dietary fiber, vitamin A, riboflavin and iron		

Ham and Cheese Quesadillas

MAKES 8 SERVINGS

Schneider Foods, a division of Maple Leaf Consumer Foods Inc.

Your kids will love these quesadillas and the yummy dipping sauce for lunch or dinner.

- *Preparation time: 5 minutes / Cooking time: 10 to 12 minutes*
- *Preheat oven to 350°F (180°C)*
- *Baking sheet, lined with parchment paper*

1 cup	shredded Cheddar cheese	250 mL
8	6-inch (15 cm) flour tortillas	8
6	slices fat-free smoked ham, chopped	6
¼ cup	salsa	50 mL

Dipping Sauce

½ cup	light mayonnaise	125 mL
2 tbsp	low-fat sour cream	25 mL
2 tsp	finely chopped fresh cilantro	10 mL
2 tsp	finely chopped green onion	10 mL
2 tsp	grated lime zest	10 mL
2 tsp	freshly squeezed lime juice	10 mL

1. Sprinkle ½ cup (125 mL) of the cheese evenly over 4 tortillas. Sprinkle ham on top and drizzle each tortilla with 1 tbsp (15 mL) salsa. Top with the remaining cheese. Cover with the other 4 tortillas. Place on prepared baking sheet.

2. Bake in preheated oven for 10 to 12 minutes or until cheese is melted and tortillas are heated through. Let cool for a few minutes, then cut each tortilla into 4 to 6 wedges.

3. *Meanwhile, prepare the dipping sauce:* In a small bowl, combine mayonnaise, sour cream, cilantro, green onion, lime zest and lime juice.

4. Serve 2 to 3 wedges per person, with dipping sauce on the side.

> **SERVING IDEA:** Serve with raw veggies and Fruity Slaw (page 147). The dipping sauce will work great with the veggies, too!

NUTRIENTS Per Serving		
Calories: 232	Carbohydrate: 21.4 g	Calcium: 127 mg
Fat: 12.4 g	Fiber: 1.3 g	Iron: 1.3 mg
Sodium: 537 mg	Protein: 9.1 g	
Very high in: Thiamine and folate		

Diabetes Food Choice Values Per Serving	
1	Carbohydrate
1	Meat & Alternatives
2	Fats

Veggie Sandwich

MAKES 1 SERVING

Patricia Wright,
Dietitian, ON

This snack is quick and fun to make and is good any time of the day.

TIP
Keep washed lettuce in the fridge, along with a few carrot slivers, so kids can make this sandwich on their own when they are hungry.

Diabetes Food Choice Values Per Serving

½	Fat

• *Preparation time: 5 minutes*

1	piece red leaf lettuce (or lettuce of your choice)	1
1 tsp	cream cheese	5 mL
1	baby carrot, cut into 4 slivers	1

1. Wash lettuce and pat dry. Spread cream cheese on lettuce. Place carrot slivers up the middle of the lettuce on top of the cream cheese. Roll up lettuce.

✓ **KID APPROVED**

NUTRIENTS Per Serving

Calories: 22	Carbohydrate: 1.2 g	Calcium: 10 mg
Fat: 1.7 g	Fiber: 0.3 g	Iron: 0.3 mg
Sodium: 25 mg	Protein: 0.6 g	

High in: Vitamin A

Fruit Wrap

MAKES 1 SERVING

Lisa Zappitelli, Dietitian, MB

This is a quick, healthy breakfast or lunch snack for kids and adults. Don't overdo the yogurt, or it will drip out the sides!

Diabetes Food Choice Values Per Serving

3½	Carbohydrates

• *Preparation time: 5 minutes*

¼ cup	yogurt (any flavor)	50 mL
1	10-inch (25 cm) whole wheat tortilla	1
3	strawberries, sliced	3
½	small banana, sliced	½
2 tbsp	low-fat granola (optional)	25 mL

1. Spread yogurt up the middle of the tortilla. Place strawberry slices, banana slices and granola (if using) on top of the yogurt. Roll up tortilla.

✓ **KID APPROVED**

NUTRIENTS Per Serving

Calories: 236	Carbohydrate: 57.2 g	Calcium: 99 mg
Fat: 2.0 g	Fiber: 4.7 g	Iron: 1.5 mg
Sodium: 308 mg	Protein: 8.0 g	

Very high in: Magnesium • **High in:** Dietary fiber, vitamin C, thiamine, vitamin B_6 and folate

Grilled Fruit Wraps

• *Preparation time: 15 minutes / Cooking time: 6 minutes*
• *Two 6-inch (15 cm) metal skewers, or wooden skewers, soaked*

¾ cup	fruit chunks	175 mL
	Vegetable cooking spray	
½ cup	ricotta cheese	125 mL
1	10-inch (25 cm) multigrain or whole wheat tortilla	1

1. Thread fruit chunks onto skewers and spray lightly with vegetable cooking spray.

2. Heat a nonstick skillet over medium heat. Cook fruit skewers, turning occasionally, until brown on each side.

3. Spread ricotta cheese on tortilla. Remove fruit from skewers and place up the middle of tortilla. Fold in the sides of the tortilla, then fold the bottom up over the filling and roll until tight.

4. In the same skillet, grill filled tortilla, turning once, until brown and crispy, about 3 minutes per side. Cut in half and serve hot or cold.

✓ KID APPROVED

The Healthy Lunches to Go Tour

Imagine packed lunches that are healthy and easy to make, and that even your kids will enjoy. It may sound too good to be true, but it's not. Take the Canadian Health Network's Healthy Lunches to Go Tour and find out how fast and easy it can be to pack healthy and delicious lunches for the whole family. This short tour offers nutrition information and tips, including how to read nutrition labels and what ingredients to watch out for. It also addresses some of the obstacles we all face in making healthy lunches part of our daily routine and suggests simple steps for dealing with them. You'll find the tour at **www.canadian-health-network.ca**.

Kayla, Kylie and Lindsay (Students of the W. Ross MacDonald School), ON

Use your favorite fruit for these wraps. For the taste test, we used mango and pineapple chunks... delicious!

TIP
Do not mix different types of fruit on the skewers — each has a different cooking time.

VARIATIONS
Mix grilled fruit with the ice cream of your choice.

Use your favorite yogurt instead of the ricotta.

NUTRIENTS Per Serving		
(based on equal amounts of fresh mango and pineapple)		
Calories: 222	Carbohydrate: 26.6 g	Calcium: 175 mg
Fat: 8.4 g	Fiber: 3.0 g	Iron: 0.4 mg
Sodium: 293 mg	Protein: 10.4 g	
A source of: Dietary fiber and calcium		

Diabetes Food Choice Values Per Serving	
1 ½	Carbohydrates
1	Meat & Alternatives
1	Fat

Donna Bottrell,
Dietitian, ON

*This is a favorite on
grilled sandwich night
at Donna's house.
You can use leftover
cooked chicken from
Lemon-Thyme Roast
Chicken (page 164)
or purchase a cooked
chicken from the
grocery store.*

TIP

Serve cold or heat on a
preheated sandwich grill
to crisp up the tortilla.
This is also good grilled
on sliced bread or panini.

VARIATION

Replace the mango with
pineapple.

Mango Chicken Wraps

• *Preparation time: 10 minutes*

1/4 cup	light mayonnaise	50 mL
1/4 cup	mango chutney	50 mL
4	10-inch (25 cm) multigrain tortillas	4
8 oz	cooked chicken, cut into strips	250 g
1	mango, sliced	1
1/4	red onion, cut into thin rings	1/4
4 cups	loosely packed mesclun mix	1 L

1. In a small bowl, combine mayonnaise and chutney.
2. Spread 2 tbsp (25 mL) of the mayonnaise mixture on each tortilla. On the bottom third of each tortilla, place one-quarter of each of the chicken strips, mango slices, red onion rings and mesclun mix. Fold in the 2 sides, then fold the bottom of the wrap up over the filling and roll until tight.

✓ **KID APPROVED**

Diabetes Food Choice Values Per Serving	
3	Carbohydrates
2	Meat & Alternatives
1	Fat

NUTRIENTS Per Serving		
Calories: 417	Carbohydrate: 51.9 g	Calcium: 50 mg
Fat: 13.4 g	Fiber: 6.1 g	Iron: 0.8 mg
Sodium: 791 mg	Protein: 22.6 g	

Very high in: Dietary fiber, vitamin A, niacin, vitamin B$_6$ and folate
High in: Vitamin C and magnesium

Chicken, Hummus and Sautéed Veggie Wraps

• *Preparation time: 10 minutes / Cooking time: 20 minutes*

1 lb	small boneless skinless chicken breasts	500 g
	Salt and freshly ground black pepper	
	Vegetable cooking spray	
1 tbsp	olive oil	15 mL
2	cloves garlic, minced	2
1	green bell pepper, julienned	1
1	red bell pepper, julienned	1
1	yellow bell pepper, julienned	1
1	onion, cut into thin strips	1
2	carrots, julienned	2
½ cup	water	125 mL
2 to 3 tsp	chili powder	10 to 15 mL
½ cup	Spicy Hummus (page 104)	125 mL
4	10-inch (25 cm) whole wheat tortillas	4

1. Season chicken breasts with salt and pepper.

2. Heat a large skillet over medium heat. Spray with vegetable cooking spray. Cook chicken, turning once, for 5 minutes per side or until chicken is no longer pink inside and has reached an internal temperature of 170°F (77°C). Remove to a clean plate and let cool. Cut into strips.

3. In the same skillet, heat olive oil over medium-high heat. Sauté garlic, green, red and yellow peppers, onion and carrots, stirring frequently, until beginning to brown, about 5 minutes. Add water and chili powder; season to taste with salt and pepper. Reduce heat to medium and cook until vegetables are tender-crisp and water has evaporated, about 5 minutes.

4. Spread 2 tbsp (25 mL) Spicy Hummus up the middle of each tortilla. Top with chicken and vegetables. Roll up tortillas.

✓ KID APPROVED

NUTRIENTS Per Serving		
Calories: 366	Carbohydrate: 51 g	Calcium: 62 mg
Fat: 7.2 g	Fiber: 7.3 g	Iron: 2.8 mg
Sodium: 448 mg	Protein: 33.6 g	

Very high in: Dietary fiber, vitamin A, vitamin C, niacin, vitamin B$_6$, folate, magnesium and zinc • **High in:** Iron and thiamine

---

MAKES 4 SERVINGS

Rena Hooey, ON

This recipe is easy to prepare and full of flavor.

TIP
This recipe can be fully prepared and refrigerated overnight for a great lunch, or its components can be stored separately in airtight containers for several days. Pop cold wraps in a toaster oven or microwave to heat through.

Planned Extras
Cook extra chicken breasts and cut into strips to use as salad toppers or in stir-fries.

SERVING IDEA:
Serve with fruit salad for a delicious lunch.

Diabetes Food Choice Values Per Serving	
2½	Carbohydrates
3	Meat & Alternatives

Sweet Potato and Bean Wraps

• *Preparation time: 10 minutes / Cooking time: 6 minutes*

1	sweet potato	1
6	10-inch (25 cm) flour tortillas	6
1	can (14 oz/398 mL) low-fat refried beans	1
2 cups	lightly packed spinach leaves	500 mL
1	avocado, sliced	1

1. Pierce sweet potato with a fork. Microwave on High for 5 minutes or until tender. Slice lengthwise, scoop out flesh and mash in a bowl.

2. On the bottom third of each tortilla, place one-sixth of each of the sweet potato, refried beans, spinach and avocado. Fold in the 2 sides, then fold the bottom of the wrap up over the filling and roll until tight.

3. Microwave wraps on High for 45 seconds or until heated through.

✓ **KID APPROVED**

Diabetes Food Choice Values Per Serving	
3½	Carbohydrates
2	Fats

NUTRIENTS Per Serving		
Calories: 383	Carbohydrate: 60.4 g	Calcium: 81 mg
Fat: 11.0 g	Fiber: 9.6 g	Iron: 4.3 mg
Sodium: 575 mg	Protein: 11.7 g	

Very high in: Dietary fiber, iron, vitamin A, thiamine, niacin, folate and magnesium • **High in:** Riboflavin, vitamin B_6 and zinc

Chunky Peanut Butter Twisters

Lydia Butler, ON

A twist on traditional peanut butter sandwiches, these healthy wraps are portable, easy to make and delicious as an appetizer, breakfast or quick lunch. We served these to a group of little girls having an afternoon tea party in the garden — they didn't last long!

TIPS

To toast pecans, heat a skillet over medium-high heat. Add pecans and toast, shaking occasionally, for about 4 minutes or until lightly browned and fragrant.

Serve the rolls as individual sandwiches or cut in half rather than making the bite-sized pieces suggested in the recipe.

These twisters can be wrapped in plastic wrap and refrigerated for up to 12 hours.

• **Preparation time: 10 to 15 minutes**

½ cup	peanut butter	125 mL
¼ cup	unsweetened shredded coconut	50 mL
¼ cup	pure maple syrup	50 mL
2 tbsp	finely chopped dried figs	25 mL
2 tbsp	finely chopped dried apricots	25 mL
2 tbsp	finely chopped dried cranberries	25 mL
Pinch	ground cinnamon	Pinch
3	10-inch (25 cm) whole wheat tortillas	3
3 tbsp	finely chopped toasted pecans (see tip, at right)	45 mL

1. In a small bowl, combine peanut butter, coconut, maple syrup, figs, apricots, cranberries and cinnamon.

2. Spread ⅓ cup (75 mL) peanut butter mixture on each tortilla. Sprinkle each with 1 tbsp (15 mL) pecans. Roll up tortillas and cut each into 6 pieces.

✓ **KID APPROVED**

Peanut Butter Banana Wrap
Tammy Coles, ON

When you need a quick and easy lunch for your little one (or for yourself), spread 1 tbsp (15 mL) peanut butter on a whole wheat tortilla. Place a banana at one end and roll up. For variety, you could add honey or some raisins or sunflower seeds, or replace the peanut butter with another nut butter or chocolate hazelnut spread.

NUTRIENTS Per Serving		
Calories: 95	Carbohydrate: 12.6 g	Calcium: 12 mg
Fat: 5.0 g	Fiber: 1.5 g	Iron: 0.5 mg
Sodium: 85 mg	Protein: 2.7 g	

Diabetes Food Choice Values Per Serving	
1	Carbohydrate
1	Fat

Judith Swaine, NS

Here's a fast, tasty snack that both kids and adults will love.

Hawaiian Toast

• ***Preparation time: 5 minutes / Cooking time: 5 to 7 minutes***
• *Preheat oven to 375°F (190°C) with rack set in center*
• *Baking sheet*

1	slice multigrain bread	1
1	slice lean ham	1
1	pineapple ring	1
2 tbsp	shredded part-skim mozzarella cheese	25 mL
2 tbsp	shredded Cheddar cheese	25 mL

1. Lightly toast bread. Place on baking sheet and top with ham, pineapple, mozzarella and Cheddar.
2. Bake in preheated oven for 5 to 7 minutes or until cheese is melted and bubbling.

 ✓ KID APPROVED

SERVING IDEA: To get a vegetable serving into the meal, accompany with raw veggie sticks or Fruity Slaw (page 147).

Do It Yourself

Prepackaged lunch items and snack packs are typically high in fat, salt and calories and low in essential nutrients. Create a more nutritious, less expensive version by packing whole-grain crackers, lower-fat cheese, 100% fruit juice and raw vegetables into a divided container.

Diabetes Food Choice Values Per Serving

1½ Carbohydrates
1½ Meat & Alternatives

NUTRIENTS Per Serving		
Calories: 232	Carbohydrate: 28 g	Calcium: 285 mg
Fat: 6.8 g	Fiber: 3.2 g	Iron: 1.9 mg
Sodium: 598 mg	Protein: 15.6 g	

Very high in: Calcium, thiamine and niacin • **High in:** Riboflavin, folate, vitamin B_{12}, magnesium and zinc • **A source of:** Dietary fiber

Pita Surprise

MAKES 1 SERVING

Patricia Wright, Dietitian, ON

• *Preparation time: 5 minutes*

¼	apple, chopped (with or without peel)	¼
	Ground cinnamon	
1	mini whole wheat pita	1
1 tsp	shredded Cheddar cheese	5 mL

1. Sprinkle chopped apple with enough cinnamon to coat evenly.
2. Cut an opening in the top of the pita. Spoon apple pieces into pita. Spoon cheese on top of apples.

✓ **KID APPROVED**

Small children can prepare this fun snack themselves, with parents on hand to help. The mini pitas can be cut or torn in half, allowing little hands to spoon in the ingredients easily.

> **SERVING IDEA:** Baby carrots with light ranch dip would add crunch and a veggie serving. Add a glass of milk for calcium.

TIP
Prepare the filling and have it waiting wrapped in the fridge, so hungry kids can fill their own pitas when they get home from school.

Snacks Adults Will Love

No matter how amazing a meal is, a few hours later, your energy will start to wear off and a snack may be necessary. When selected wisely, snacks boost nutrient intake. Here are some of our favorites:

- raw vegetables served with a delicious dip such as Spicy Hummus (page 104)
- whole-grain crackers or flatbread with your favorite lower-fat cheese or a healthy spread
- a mixture of toasted nuts and dried fruits
- fruit with yogurt, cottage cheese or a yogurt dip
- warm applesauce with a sprinkle of cinnamon and homemade hot chocolate or a cup of your favorite herbal tea (try Masala Chai, page 90, or Mexican Hot Chocolate, page 91)
- half a whole-grain bagel topped with nut butter
- cereal bars or granola bars that are free of hydrogenated vegetable oils (try our Apricot Coconut Bars, page 323)
- homemade hearty muffins with a handful of nuts, yogurt or a piece of cheese
- roasted pumpkin or sunflower seeds or toasted chickpeas sprinkled with your favorite seasoning
- whole-grain cereal with milk and fresh fruit

NUTRIENTS Per Serving		
Calories: 51	Carbohydrate: 9.7 g	Calcium: 21 mg
Fat: 1.1 g	Fiber: 1.2 g	Iron: 0.3 mg
Sodium: 57 mg	Protein: 1.4 g	

Diabetes Food Choice Values Per Serving	
½	Carbohydrates

**Kimberly Green,
Dietitian, ON**

*Grown-ups and kids
can make this healthy
snack together —
a great activity for
a rainy day!*

Raisin-Apple Tortilla Roll-Ups

• *Preparation time: 5 minutes / Cooking time: 4 minutes*

1	apple	1
2 tbsp	low-fat cream cheese, softened	25 mL
2 tsp	liquid honey	10 mL
½ cup	raisins	125 mL
4	6-inch (15 cm) whole wheat tortillas	4
¼ tsp	ground cinnamon	1 mL
½ tsp	granulated sugar	2 mL

1. *Grown-ups:* Finely chop apple, or assist children in using a knife to safely core and finely chop.

2. *Kids:* Measure out cream cheese and honey and combine them in a small bowl. Measure out raisins and stir in. Stir in apples. Divide cream cheese mixture evenly among tortillas and spread using a butter knife or spreader. Sprinkle each with cinnamon and sugar.

3. *Grown-ups:* Roll up tortillas and secure with toothpicks, if necessary. Place seam side down, one at a time, on a microwave-safe plate. Microwave each roll on Medium (50%) for 1 minute or until warmed through. Enjoy together!

✓ **KID APPROVED**

Diabetes Food Choice Values Per Serving	
2½	Carbohydrates
½	Fat

NUTRIENTS Per Serving		
Calories: 186	Carbohydrate: 41.2 g	Calcium: 31 mg
Fat: 1.9 g	Fiber: 3.1 g	Iron: 1.2 mg
Sodium: 179 mg	Protein: 4.1 g	
A source of: Dietary fiber		

Tuna Avocado Salad

MAKES 4 SERVINGS

Cindy McKenna, NS

• *Preparation time: 10 minutes*

1	can (6½ oz/170 g) water-packed tuna, drained	1
1	avocado, peeled, pitted and cut into bite-size pieces	1
1	small tomato, diced	1
½	small red onion, finely chopped	½
¼ cup	frozen corn kernels, thawed	50 mL
2 tbsp	chopped fresh parsley	25 mL
2 tbsp	olive oil	25 mL
1 tsp	lemon juice	5 mL
	Freshly ground black pepper (optional)	
	Hot pepper sauce (optional)	

1. In a small bowl, combine tuna, avocado, tomato, red onion, corn, parsley, olive oil, lemon juice, pepper (if using) and hot pepper sauce (if using).

Preparing Avocados

First cut around the avocado lengthwise, cutting through to the pit. Twist one half to separate the avocado into two halves. To easily pop out the pit, use a sharp knife to pierce the pit; turn the knife and twist. Cut avocado flesh inside the skin in a criss-cross pattern; remove avocado pieces with a large spoon. Avocados brown easily, so once cut, dip the pieces in lemon juice.

A great lunchbox idea, this salad can be served on its own over a green salad or stuffed into a whole wheat pita or flour tortilla for a delicious healthy sandwich.

TIP
This recipe makes enough salad to serve as a side dish for 4 or as lunch for 2. For a stylish presentation for 2, reserve the hollowed-out avocado skins to use as serving dishes and top each serving with a sprig of fresh parsley.

NUTRIENTS Per Serving		
Calories: 201	Carbohydrate: 9.4 g	Calcium: 19 mg
Fat: 14.5 g	Fiber: 4.1 g	Iron: 1.1 mg
Sodium: 121 mg	Protein: 10.3 g	

Very high in: Niacin, folate and vitamin B_{12}
High in: Dietary fiber and vitamin B_6

Diabetes Food Choice Values Per Serving	
1	Meat & Alternatives
2	Fats

Beverages

Sometimes you want a nice cool and refreshing beverage on a hot summer day or a warm and comforting hot drink on a winter morning. These delicious recipes will fit the bill. As a bonus, many of them provide key nutrients such as calcium.

smoothies

Smoothies are a great way to get your nutrition fix in a hurry. Check out the smoothie recipes (pages 86–88) and try your own combinations. Just choose a protein (yogurt, soft tofu or even peanut butter), fruit (berries, peaches and bananas work well) and a liquid (such as milk, soy beverage or fruit juice) and blend. Some great combos for smoothies are:

- plain yogurt + banana + strawberries + orange juice
- plain soft tofu + frozen blueberries + vanilla soy beverage
- peanut butter + frozen banana + milk

Which Vitamins and Minerals Are Especially Important for Women?

Women often struggle to get enough of three important nutrients: calcium, iron and folate.

- Calcium, along with vitamin D, supports healthy bones throughout life. It is of particular concern after menopause, when hormonal changes can reduce the amount of calcium being absorbed by the body. Calcium is abundant in milk products.

- Iron is important for healthy blood and for energy. It is found in lean red meat, whole grains and green leafy vegetables, among other sources. Iron from animal foods is better absorbed than iron from plant sources.

- Folate is a B vitamin that is especially important for women of child-bearing age as it helps to prevent neural tube defects in babies. It can be found in green leafy vegetables, broccoli, asparagus, lentils, chickpeas, oranges and orange juice, papayas and strawberries, to name a few sources.

Tropical Cooler

Eileen Campbell

The idea for this refreshing cooler came from the beaches of southern Thailand. Carts line the beach, offering fruit concoctions to cool you down in the tropical heat. Great for a warm summer day in any country!

• *Preparation time: 2 minutes*

1	ripe banana	1
1 cup	diced seedless watermelon	250 mL
1 cup	pineapple juice	250 mL

1. In blender, on high speed, blend banana, watermelon and pineapple juice until smooth and creamy.

✓ **KID APPROVED**

To Juice or Not to Juice

Freshly squeezed juice is a refreshing way to enjoy nutrients from fruits and vegetables, but be aware that drinking juice rather than eating the whole fruit or veggie reduces your intake of fiber. And be mindful of portions — drinking too much juice can cause you to consume extra calories. Think of how many fruits or vegetables you have put through the juicer to make that one glass.

TIP
Add ice cubes if the fruit is not cold enough.

VARIATIONS
Any of your favorite fruits will work. Always use a banana for creaminess, then add 1 cup (250 mL) diced fruit and 1 cup (250 mL) fruit juice. Some fruit suggestions are: pineapple, mango, cantaloupe, honeydew, papaya, kiwi, frozen or fresh berries. Some juice suggestions are: orange, apple, cranberry, white grape, tropical blend, pomegranate, blueberry.

For a special party treat, add a shot of rum, coconut rum or vodka.

NUTRIENTS Per Serving		
Calories: 145	Carbohydrate: 36.4 g	Calcium: 29 mg
Fat: 0.4 g	Fiber: 1.6 g	Iron: 0.7 mg
Sodium: 3 mg	Protein: 1.5 g	

Very high in: Vitamin C • **High in:** Vitamin B_6, folate and magnesium

Diabetes Food Choice Values Per Serving	
2	Carbohydrates

Donna Bottrell,
Dietitian, ON

This is a great drink for kids when their parents are having the real thing.

Juice Spritzers

It's easy to create your own juice spritzer recipe. Select a juice, such as blueberry, pomegranate or cranberry. Fill a wine glass one-quarter full of juice, top with sparkling water and a wedge of fruit, then sit back and relax.

Grape Juice Sangria

• *Preparation time: 2 minutes*

1 cup	grape juice	250 mL
½ cup	orange juice	125 mL
3 cups	sparkling water	750 mL
1	orange, cut into wedges	1
	Ice cubes	

1. In a jug, combine grape juice, orange juice, sparkling water and orange wedges. Add ice.

✓ KID APPROVED

SERVING IDEA: Serve this party drink with kid-friendly appetizers such as Lightened-Up Guacamole and Chips (page 102).

Diabetes Food Choice Values Per Serving	
1	Carbohydrate

NUTRIENTS Per Serving		
Calories: 68	Carbohydrate: 16.7 g	Calcium: 46 mg
Fat: 0.1 g	Fiber: 0.7 g	Iron: 0.2 mg
Sodium: 4 mg	Protein: 0.9 g	
Very high in: Vitamin C		

Mango Lassi

MAKES 2 SERVINGS

Eileen Campbell

1	ripe mango, peeled and chopped	1
½ cup	low-fat plain or vanilla yogurt	125 mL
½ cup	milk	125 mL
	Liquid honey	
½ cup	ice cubes	125 mL

1. In blender, on high speed, blend mango, yogurt, milk, honey to taste and ice for 2 minutes or until smooth.

 **KID APPROVED**

Mangoes

If you'll be using the mango right away, be sure to buy a ripe one. Mangoes are ripe when they can be easily indented with your thumb. Avoid mangoes that are so ripe they feel mushy.

Mangoes have large, flat stones in the middle. It is a little tricky to remove the fruit, but if you follow these simple instructions, the task should be easier: Make an initial cut about ½ inch (1 cm) from the center and cut off a long slice of mango. Do the same on the other side. For each of these pieces, use a sharp knife to score the flesh in long lines, first lengthwise, then crossways, cutting almost through to the skin to create small cubes. Using a spoon, scoop cubes from skin. Peel the stone section, remove any flesh from the outside edges and cut into cubes.

This refreshing drink is a favorite at Indian restaurants. Now you can make it at home to serve with the spicy recipes in this book.

TIPS

If fresh mangoes are not available, you may be able to find frozen mangoes in the freezer section of your grocery store. Substitute 1 cup (250 mL) frozen mango chunks.

This drink keeps well in the refrigerator overnight.

NUTRIENTS Per Serving		
Calories: 190	Carbohydrate: 38.8 g	Calcium: 203 mg
Fat: 2.7 g	Fiber: 3.3 g	Iron: 0.3 mg
Sodium: 72 mg	Protein: 6.2 g	

Very high in: Vitamin A, vitamin C and vitamin B$_{12}$ • **High in:** Calcium, riboflavin, vitamin B$_6$ and folate • **A source of:** Dietary fiber

Diabetes Food Choice Values Per Serving
2½ Carbohydrates

Jill Miller, Dietitian, ON

Children love bananas, and this is a great way to add another fruit serving to their day.

TIPS

Serve in glasses or in a Thermos for an on-the-go breakfast.

For a delicious frozen dessert, try freezing this smoothie in ice pop molds. It's a wonderful alternative for children who are a little fussy.

Banana Smoothie

• Preparation time: 1 minute

1	ripe banana	1
½ cup	low-fat plain yogurt	125 mL
½ cup	water	125 mL
½ cup	milk	125 mL
3	ice cubes	3

1. In blender, on high speed, blend banana, yogurt, water, milk and ice for 45 seconds or until smooth.

✓ **KID APPROVED**

> **SERVING IDEA:** Serve with a piece of whole-grain toast and peanut butter.

Over-Ripe Bananas

If you can't use bananas that are becoming ripe, pop them into a resealable plastic bag and freeze them. They will turn black, but once they are thawed and the skins are removed, they make a perfect addition to smoothies.

Diabetes Food Choice Values Per Serving	
1	Carbohydrate

NUTRIENTS Per Serving		
Calories: 122	Carbohydrate: 20.6 g	Calcium: 189 mg
Fat: 2.3 g	Fiber: 1.0 g	Iron: 0.2 mg
Sodium: 71 mg	Protein: 5.9 g	

Very high in: Vitamin B_{12} • **High in:** Calcium, riboflavin and vitamin B_6

Decadent Fruit Smoothie

Eileen Campbell

This smoothie, adapted from a recipe on the back of a tofu package, tastes sweet and rich, like dessert!

TIP

For extra frothiness, add 1 cup (250 mL) crushed ice when blending.

• *Preparation time: 5 minutes*

1	ripe banana	1
10 oz	peach-mango-flavored dessert tofu	300 g
1 cup	frozen peach or mango slices	250 mL
1 cup	orange juice	250 mL
	Liquid honey or granulated sugar (optional)	

1. In blender, on high speed, blend banana, tofu, peach slices and orange juice until smooth.
2. Sweeten with honey to taste, if desired. Serve cold.

✓ **KID APPROVED**

NUTRIENTS Per Serving		
Calories: 123	Carbohydrate: 25.4 g	Calcium: 32 mg
Fat: 1.5 g	Fiber: 1.7 g	Iron: 0.9 mg
Sodium: 7 mg	Protein: 3.6 g	

Very high in: Vitamin C • **High in:** Folate

Diabetes Food Choice Values Per Serving

1½ Carbohydrates

Shefali Raja, Dietitian, BC

Shefali's boys came up with the idea of having smoothies and started to experiment. This recipe was a keeper.

Flaxseed Oil

Since flaxseed oil becomes damaged if exposed to heat, it cannot be used to cook with. Instead, use cold oil in a salad dressing. Always store flaxseed oil in the refrigerator.

Strawberry Orange Flaxseed Smoothie

• *Preparation time: 5 minutes*

3	strawberries, hulled	3
½ cup	plain soy beverage	125 mL
½ cup	orange juice	125 mL
2 tbsp	vanilla-flavored soy protein powder	25 mL
1 tsp	flaxseed oil	5 mL
1 to 2	ice cubes	1 to 2

1. In blender, on high speed, blend strawberries, soy beverage, orange juice, protein powder, flaxseed oil and ice for 30 seconds or until smooth.

✓ **KID APPROVED**

SERVING IDEA: This smoothie is a great accompaniment to our Big-Batch Banana Blueberry Muffins (page 285).

Diabetes Food Choice Values Per Serving

1	Carbohydrate
3	Meat & Alternatives

NUTRIENTS Per Serving

Calories: 228	Carbohydrate: 20.1 g	Calcium: 210 mg
Fat: 7.8 g	Fiber: 4.0 g	Iron: 4.4 mg
Sodium: 258 mg	Protein: 23.7 g	

Very high in: Vitamin C, iron, thiamine, niacin and folate
High in: Dietary fiber, calcium, magnesium and zinc

Honeyed Fruity Milk Shake

MAKES 4 SERVINGS

Dairy Farmers of Canada

This drink tastes like a Creamsicle and makes a great pick-me-up.

• *Preparation time: 4 to 5 minutes*

4	oranges, peeled, seeded and coarsely chopped	4
1 cup	milk	250 mL
2 tsp	liquid honey	10 mL
½ tsp	vanilla	2 mL
4	ice cubes	4
	Ground nutmeg (optional)	

1. In blender, on high speed, blend oranges, milk, honey and vanilla until smooth. With blender on low speed, add ice cubes one at a time. Blend for 15 to 20 seconds or until ice is crushed.

2. Pour into 4 tall glasses and sprinkle with nutmeg. Serve immediately.

✓ **KID APPROVED**

SERVING IDEA: Serve for breakfast with a slice of Oat Bran Banana Bread (page 282) for a fiber boost.

NUTRIENTS Per Serving		
Calories: 103	Carbohydrate: 21.2 g	Calcium: 125 mg
Fat: 1.4 g	Fiber: 2.4 g	Iron: 0.2 mg
Sodium: 26 mg	Protein: 3.3 g	

Very high in: Vitamin C • **High in:** Folate
A source of: Dietary fiber

Diabetes Food Choice Values Per Serving

1	Carbohydrate

Masala Chai

Eileen Campbell

Indian chai is a spiced milk tea that has become increasingly popular throughout the world. It is generally made using rich black tea, full-fat milk, a mix of various spices and a sweetener. The spices used vary from region to region and among households in India. The most common mix includes cardamom, cinnamon, ginger, cloves and pepper.

TIPS

If whole spices are hard to find, replace with the following quantities of ground spices: ½ tsp (2 mL) ginger, 1 tsp (5 mL) cardamom, ¼ tsp (1 mL) cinnamon, ¼ tsp (1 mL) cloves and ¼ tsp (1 mL) black pepper (or 2¼ tsp/ 11 mL of your favorite sweet spices).

If you don't have a mortar and pestle, you can use a clean coffee grinder to crush the spices. Just make sure to keep a coffee grinder exclusively for spices rather than using the same one for both spices and coffee.

• *Preparation time: 5 minutes / Cooking time: 15 minutes*

Chai Masala Mix

12	green cardamom pods	12
6	whole cloves	6
5	whole black peppercorns	5
1	cinnamon stick, broken	1
1	1-inch (2.5 cm) piece gingerroot	1
3 cups	water	750 mL
2 cups	milk or vanilla soy beverage	500 mL
2 tsp	loose black tea leaves (or 4 tea bags)	10 mL
	Liquid honey or granulated sugar	

1. *Prepare the Chai Masala Mix:* Using a mortar and pestle, crush cardamom, cloves, peppercorns, cinnamon and ginger.
2. In a large heavy-bottomed saucepan, over medium-high heat, bring crushed spices, water, milk, tea leaves and honey almost to a boil (watch carefully to prevent tea from bubbling over). Reduce heat to low and simmer for 10 minutes.
3. Strain out spices and tea and pour into 4 mugs.

Diabetes Food Choice Values Per Serving	
½	Carbohydrate

NUTRIENTS Per Serving		
Calories: 65	Carbohydrate: 6.9 g	Calcium: 147 mg
Fat: 2.5 g	Fiber: 0.3 g	Iron: 0.2 mg
Sodium: 56 mg	Protein: 4.1 g	
High in: Riboflavin		

Mexican Hot Chocolate

MAKES 6 SERVINGS

Eileen Campbell

This frothy hot chocolate has subtle Mexican spice to warm you up on a chilly day.

TIP
If you have a manual frother, whirl the hot chocolate until very frothy before serving.

• *Preparation time: 2 minutes / Cooking time: 5 minutes*

½ cup	granulated sugar	125 mL
½ cup	water	125 mL
⅓ cup	unsweetened cocoa powder	75 mL
½ tsp	ground cinnamon	2 mL
5 cups	milk	1.25 L
½ tsp	vanilla	2 mL
½ tsp	almond extract	2 mL

1. In a large saucepan, over medium heat, heat sugar, water, cocoa powder and cinnamon until sugar dissolves. Add milk; heat until steaming (do not boil). Remove from heat and stir in vanilla and almond extract.

✓ KID APPROVED

NUTRIENTS Per Serving		
Calories: 178	Carbohydrate: 29.1 g	Calcium: 246 mg
Fat: 4.6 g	Fiber: 1.5 g	Iron: 0.9 mg
Sodium: 85 mg	Protein: 7.6 g	

Very high in: Riboflavin • **High in:** Calcium and magnesium

Diabetes Food Choice Values Per Serving

2	Carbohydrates

Appetizers, Dips and Sauces

Appetizers are a wonderful way to get your taste buds ready for the meal that will follow. While not every meal needs an appetizer, many folks like to munch on something before a meal at a dinner party. The tasty morsels in this chapter fit the bill but won't fill you up. For a unique dinner party, try serving an array of appetizers, dips and sauces, and skip the main meal!

making recipes kid-friendly

Kids are more likely to eat food they take part in preparing — especially if it's something new or different. Get excited about what you're preparing and make the presentation of the food appealing to their young eyes. Excitement can be contagious! Here are some ideas to help you make food more enticing for kids:

- Serve dip. Kids love to dip things, so serve sauce on the side, if appropriate.

- Adjust spices to suit their taste. Most young children prefer their food to be plain and simple.

- Pick vegetables they love and serve them often. When you serve a vegetable they are not so fond of, disguise it by puréeing or mincing it.

- Make foods that are user-friendly for small hands, such as Chicken Parmesan Strips (page 171) with Sweet-and-Sour Sauce (page 110).

- Be creative. Use cookie cutters to serve pizza in interesting shapes, cut radishes into roses, make smiley faces on pancakes (use blueberries to paint eyes, nose and a mouth), arrange veggies on a platter to look like a skeleton at Halloween or a tree during the holiday season.

- Let kids assemble recipes such as tacos at the table.

How Much Alcohol Fits with a Healthy Lifestyle?

One of the problems with enjoying appetizers before dinner is that they are often accompanied by a drink. It's important to watch your consumption of alcohol for a number of reasons. At 7 calories per gram, alcohol contributes almost as many calories per gram as fat. An average drink supplies between 100 and 150 calories, which adds up quickly if you enjoy a couple of drinks every day. This can be a real concern for those who are watching their weight.

Health Canada recommends no more than one drink per day for women and two drinks per day for men. (That doesn't mean you can save up all week for a weekend bash.) If you drink less than this amount, great. One drink is considered equal to 5 ounces (150 mL) of wine, 12 ounces (375 mL) of beer or $1\frac{1}{2}$ ounces (45 mL) of spirits or liquor, such as Scotch.

Don't use alcohol to quench your thirst. Always drink water first. And be aware that alcohol can increase your appetite and speed digestion, making you feel hungry faster. When you go to an event where alcohol will be served, set a moderate limit for the evening and plan to get home safe!

What If My Child Is a Picky Eater?

It's common and natural for kids to be picky eaters as they go through different growth phases, but it can drive parents crazy! Luckily, there are many proven solutions to help you and the kids through this difficult time:

- Keep a wide variety of healthy food choices readily available.
- Set a good example by trying a new food each week.
- Offer new foods for your kids to try, but don't force them to eat anything. You do need to be persistent, however; don't give up when they say no. Try again another day.
- Prepare healthy meals, but let your kids choose how much and whether they will eat. Remember, you probably didn't like steamed spinach when you were eight either!
- Keep portions small so they don't feel overwhelmed.
- Encourage your kids to get involved in the kitchen. To build their interest in food, talk about how various foods are grown, or where they come from. Visit a farm or start your own garden.
- Make sure they are not filling up on less nutritious snacks or drinks that might interfere with a hearty appetite at mealtime.

Finally, try to relax (we know it's tough!). If you force the issue, chances are pretty good that your kids will rebel. With time and patience, most children outgrow the picky phase and start to sample new foods.

Corry Dunphy, Dietitian, SK

In loving memory of Corry's friend and mentor, Lori Sargeant-Radomski, RD, who shared this recipe with her many years ago. She has been taking it to potlucks, where everyone always wants a copy of the recipe. She has lowered the fat content by using light cream cheese and increased the fiber by using whole wheat pitas.

VARIATION

If you like spice, increase the amount of jalapeño or use fresh chopped instead of pickled.

Mini Jalapeño and Cream Cheese Pitas

• *Preparation time: 15 to 20 minutes / Cooking time:5 minutes*

1 tsp	vegetable oil	5 mL
1	onion, chopped	1
8 oz	light or ultra-light cream cheese, softened	250 g
2	tomatoes, finely chopped	2
1/4 cup	real bacon bits or chopped cooked bacon	50 mL
2 tbsp	chopped pickled jalapeño peppers (or to taste)	25 mL
18	whole wheat mini pitas, halved	18

1. In a small skillet, heat oil over medium heat. Sauté onion until softened, about 5 minutes.
2. In a large bowl, combine sautéed onion, cream cheese, tomatoes, bacon bits and jalapeños.
3. Stuff each mini pita half with cream cheese mixture.

✓ **KID APPROVED**

Diabetes Food Choice Values Per Serving

1/2   Fat

NUTRIENTS Per Serving		
Calories: 32	Carbohydrate: 3.3 g	Calcium: 10 mg
Fat: 1.6 g	Fiber: 0.4 g	Iron: 0.3 mg
Sodium: 71 mg	Protein: 1.6 g	

Cheese and Olive Toasts

MAKES 48 PIECES (1 PER SERVING)

Judy Jenkins, Dietitian, NS

Offer this easy and tasty treat to your family while dinner is cooking.

TIPS

Use whole wheat English muffins for added fiber.

If your child does not like olives, they can be omitted.

- *Preparation time: 10 minutes / Cooking time: 10 minutes*
- *Preheat oven to 400°F (200°C)*
- *Baking sheet*

1½ cups	shredded old Cheddar cheese	375 mL
1 cup	chopped pitted black olives	250 mL
½ cup	light mayonnaise	125 mL
1 tbsp	chopped green onion	15 mL
½ tsp	curry powder	2 mL
½ tsp	salt	2 mL
6	English muffins, halved	6

1. In a large bowl, combine cheese, olives, mayonnaise, green onion, curry powder and salt.
2. Place muffin halves on baking sheet and spread with cheese mixture. Cut each into 4 pieces.
3. Bake in preheated oven for 10 minutes or until cheese has melted.

❄ FREEZER FRIENDLY
✓ KID APPROVED

NUTRIENTS Per Serving		
Calories: 43	Carbohydrate: 3.9 g	Calcium: 41 mg
Fat: 2.4 g	Fiber: 0.3 g	Iron: 0.3 mg
Sodium: 119 mg	Protein: 1.5 g	

Diabetes Food Choice Values Per Serving
½ Fat

Sara Duchene-Milne,
Dietitian, ON

This easy snack or appetizer is fast to assemble and is great in the spring and summer months, when fresh tomatoes and herbs are in season. We used cherry or grape tomatoes because they taste great year-round.

TIP
You can use larger tomatoes, if desired. Three medium tomatoes or 5 Roma (plum) tomatoes will make about the same amount of chopped.

SERVING IDEA:
This makes a great starter when you're entertaining guests. For the main course, serve Broiled Cilantro Ginger Salmon (page 207) with Black Bean Salsa (page 106) and Steamed Asian Vegetable Medley (page 263). Finish with Chocolate Fondue (page 311).

Easy Tomato Basil Bruschetta

• **Preparation time: 15 minutes / Cooking time: 8 minutes**
• *Preheat broiler*
• *Baking sheet*

6	slices light rye bread	6
2 tbsp	extra-virgin olive oil, divided	25 mL
18	cherry or grape tomatoes, coarsely chopped	18
5	leaves fresh basil, chopped	5
2	large roasted red bell peppers (from a jar or see recipe, page 98), drained and coarsely chopped	2
1	clove garlic, minced	1
2 tbsp	freshly grated Parmesan cheese	25 mL
2 tsp	hot pepper sauce (optional)	10 mL
1 tsp	freshly ground black pepper	5 mL
½ tsp	salt	2 mL
¼ cup	feta cheese (optional)	50 mL

1. Arrange bread on baking sheet. Brush lightly with 1 tbsp (15 mL) of the olive oil. Toast under preheated broiler for 3 minutes or until light brown.

2. In a medium bowl, toss cherry tomatoes, basil, red peppers, garlic, Parmesan, the remaining olive oil, hot pepper sauce (if using), pepper and salt. Distribute evenly on top of bread. Sprinkle with feta cheese, if using.

3. Broil until heated through, about 5 minutes. Cut each slice of bread in half diagonally.

✔ KID APPROVED

Diabetes Food Choice Values Per Serving	
1	Carbohydrate
1	Fat

NUTRIENTS Per Serving		
Calories: 130	Carbohydrate: 16 g	Calcium: 53 mg
Fat: 6.1 g	Fiber: 2.6 g	Iron: 1.2 mg
Sodium: 443 mg	Protein: 3.7 g	

Very high in: Vitamin C • **High in:** Folate
A source of: Dietary fiber

Mango Lassi (page 85)

Lightened-Up Guacamole and Chips (page 102)

Chicken and Corn Chowder (page 128)

Hungarian Goulash Soup (page 131)

Grilled Cilantro Shrimp Skewers

MAKES 6 SERVINGS

Eileen Campbell

Serve this quick and easy appetizer with Mango Mint Mojo (page 109), Chimichurri (page 108) or Peach Salsa (variation, page 105).

- *Preparation time: 10 minutes / Marinating time: 30 minutes Cooking time: 5 minutes*
- *Six 6-inch (15 cm) wooden skewers*
- *Baking sheet, greased*

2	cloves garlic, minced	2
¼ cup	chopped fresh cilantro	50 mL
2 tbsp	olive oil	25 mL
½ tsp	ground coriander	2 mL
	Grated zest and juice of 2 limes	
	Salt and freshly ground black pepper	
1 lb	extra-large shrimp, peeled and deveined	500 g

1. In a small bowl, combine garlic, cilantro, olive oil, coriander, lime zest, lime juice and salt and pepper to taste.

2. Place shrimp in a shallow dish and pour in marinade. Cover and refrigerate for at least 30 minutes or for up to 2 hours. Meanwhile, soak skewers in hot water for 30 minutes and preheat broiler.

3. Thread shrimp evenly onto skewers and place on prepared baking sheet.

4. Broil, turning once, for 2½ minutes per side or until shrimp are pink and opaque.

✓ **KID APPROVED**

TIP
Barbecue Method: Preheat barbecue to 350°F (180°C) and cook for 2½ minutes per side, or until shrimp are pink and opaque.

Planned Extras
Cook extra shrimp and serve over a green salad for a main course another day.

NUTRIENTS Per Serving		
Calories: 94	Carbohydrate: 1.7 g	Calcium: 34 mg
Fat: 4.4 g	Fiber: 0.2 g	Iron: 1.4 mg
Sodium: 85 mg	Protein: 11.6 g	

Very high in: Vitamin B$_{12}$ • **High in:** Niacin

Diabetes Food Choice Values Per Serving

1½ Meat & Alternatives

Eileen Campbell

Dazzle your dinner guests with this colorful and tasty platter. Don't tell them how easy it was to prepare. Any of the individual components can be served alone, but the platter is a party star. Place the components attractively on a large serving platter, along with 1 cup (250 mL) of purchased spiced olives, and garnish with fresh basil leaves.

TIP

You can also roast peppers in a 400°F (200°C) oven or under the broiler. Place the peppers on a baking sheet and roast, turning often, until blistered and charred. Proceed as above.

Planned Extras

Make lots of roasted peppers when they are in season and freeze 1 to 2 peppers in small freezer bags. Use later in pasta dishes, as a salad topping, in Easy Tomato Basil Bruschetta (page 96) or in Mediterranean Lentil and Rice Salad (page 155).

Antipasto Platter

• **Preparation time: 30 minutes / Cooking time: 20 minutes**
• *Preheat barbecue to 350°F (180°C)*

Roasted Red Peppers

| 2 | red bell peppers | 2 |

1. Place peppers directly on preheated barbecue grill and cook, turning frequently with tongs, until skins are blistered and blackened, about 6 minutes. Remove from barbecue and place in a food-grade plastic bag (or a pot with a lid). Allow some air to remain in the bag and tie loosely (the steam in the bag will help loosen the skin of the peppers). Let cool for about 15 minutes or until you can easily handle the peppers.

2. Remove from bag, peel off skins, and remove stem, core and seeds. Cut into strips and place on platter.

Fire-Grilled Artichoke Hearts

• *6-inch (15 cm) metal skewers, or wooden skewers, soaked*

| 2 | cans (each 14 oz/398 mL) whole artichoke hearts, drained and rinsed | 2 |

1. Thread artichoke hearts onto skewers (3 artichoke hearts will fit comfortably on each skewer) and grill on preheated barbecue until lightly marked with grill marks on all sides, about 5 minutes.

2. Remove artichoke hearts from skewers, cut in half and place on platter.

Marinated Mushrooms

1 cup	water	250 mL
2 tbsp	olive oil	25 mL
1 tbsp	white wine vinegar	15 mL
Pinch	salt	Pinch

(Marinated Mushrooms, continued…)

	Grated zest of 1 lemon, 1 lime and 1 orange	
8 oz	mushrooms	250 g

1. In a medium saucepan, over medium-high heat, bring water, olive oil, vinegar, salt and lemon, lime and orange zest to a boil. Add mushrooms and return to a boil. Reduce heat to medium and simmer for 5 minutes or until mushrooms are tender. Using a slotted spoon, remove mushrooms and place in a serving dish.

2. Increase heat to high and boil liquid until reduced by half. Pour over mushrooms.

3. Place serving dish on platter.

Bocconcini and Grape Tomato Lollipops

1	container (7 oz/200 g) mini bocconcini	1
1 cup	grape tomatoes	250 mL
1 tbsp	basil pesto	15 mL

1. Place bocconcini and tomatoes in a shallow dish and brush with pesto. Cover and refrigerate for at least 15 minutes or for up to 1 hour.

2. Thread 1 piece of cheese and 1 tomato onto a long toothpick. Repeat until all cheese and tomatoes are used. Add to the platter.

✓ KID APPROVED

SERVING IDEA: *Party Menu:* In addition to this platter, lay out Grilled Cilantro Shrimp Skewers (page 97), Lightened-Up Guacamole and Chips (page 102), fresh vegetable sticks and whole wheat pita wedges with Spicy Hummus (page 104).

TIP
If you cannot find mini bocconcini, use small cubes of part-skim mozzarella.

NUTRIENTS Per Serving		
(based on an equal distribution of all appetizers among 12 people)		
Calories: 119	Carbohydrate: 8.6 g	Calcium: 139 mg
Fat: 7.7 g	Fiber: 2.9 g	Iron: 1.3 mg
Sodium: 228 mg	Protein: 6.0 g	
High in: Vitamin C • **A source of:** Dietary fiber		

Diabetes Food Choice Values Per Serving	
½	Meat & Alternatives
1	Fat

Greek Veggie Kabob

Eileen Campbell

Greek salad on a stick — how cool is that?

TIP
Ranch dressing makes a good substitute for tzatziki sauce, and children might prefer it.

6	grape or cherry tomatoes	6
12	½-inch (1 cm) slices English cucumber	12
12	½-inch (1 cm) cubes feta cheese	12
12	½-inch (1 cm) squares red bell pepper	12
6	black olives, pitted	6
⅓ cup	tzatziki sauce (store-bought or see recipe, page 59)	75 mL

1. Thread ingredients onto skewers in the following order: 1 tomato, 1 slice cucumber, 1 cube cheese, 1 square red pepper, 1 slice cucumber, 1 cube cheese, 1 square red pepper, 1 olive.
2. Serve with tzatziki sauce for dipping.

✓ **KID APPROVED**

Diabetes Food Choice Values Per Serving

½	Meat & Alternatives
½	Fat

NUTRIENTS Per Serving

Calories: 56	Carbohydrate: 2.4 g	Calcium: 86 mg
Fat: 4.4 g	Fiber: 0.4 g	Iron: 0.3 mg
Sodium: 216 mg	Protein: 2.5 g	

Sangria Wine Jelly

• **Preparation time: 10 minutes / Cooking time: 10 minutes / Setting time: 24 hours**

MAKES FOUR TO FIVE 1-CUP (250 ML) JARS (1 tbsp/15 ML PER SERVING)

Patti Thomson, Dietitian, MB

Serve this unusual jelly with your favorite cheeses or pâtés when entertaining.

2	oranges	2
1	lemon	1
3½ cups	granulated sugar	875 mL
1⅓ cups	dry red or white wine	325 mL
1	pouch (3 oz/85 mL) liquid fruit pectin	1
3 tbsp	brandy	45 mL

1. Grate zest from 1 orange and the lemon. Squeeze juice from both. Peel, section and chop remaining orange.

2. In a large saucepan, combine orange zest and juice, lemon zest and juice, orange pulp, sugar and wine. Over high heat, stirring constantly, bring to a full rolling boil that cannot be stirred down. Boil hard, stirring constantly, for 1 minute. Remove from heat, immediately stir in pectin and brandy, and quickly skim off any foam.

3. Pour jelly into warm sterilized jars to within ¼ inch (0.5 cm) of rim. (The orange pieces might float to the top.) Seal immediately with sterilized two-piece lids with new centers. Process in a boiling water canner for 10 minutes.

4. Place in a cool spot for at least 24 hours to allow jelly to set. Check lids for seal. Refrigerate any jars that have not sealed properly and use within 3 weeks. Store sealed jars in a cool, dry place for up to 1 year. Refrigerate after opening.

SERVING IDEA: Serve with chicken, pork, Brie or hors d'oeuvres of your choice.

NUTRIENTS Per Serving		
Calories: 45	Carbohydrate: 11.6 g	Calcium: 2 mg
Fat: 0.0 g	Fiber: 0.1 g	Iron: 0.0 mg
Sodium: 0 mg	Protein: 0.0 g	

Diabetes Food Choice Values Per Serving

½	Carbohydrate

This recipe was an instant hit with the tasting panel for its great flavor, and it has less fat than commercial guacamole and chips. Kids love it.

TIPS
The tortilla chips will keep for up to 2 weeks in an airtight plastic bag at room temperature.

Use the baked tortillas as an inexpensive replacement for store-bought crispy flat breads.

Planned Extras
Make extra tortilla chips and use for other dips or with cheese another day.

Lightened-Up Guacamole and Chips

• **Preparation time: 20 minutes / Cooking time: 10 to 15 minutes per batch of tortillas**

• *Preheat oven to 350°F (180°C)*

2	ripe avocados, peeled and mashed	2
1	tomato, chopped (optional)	1
1	clove garlic, minced (or ½ tsp/2 mL garlic powder)	1
½ cup	fat-free plain yogurt	125 mL
⅓ cup	tomato salsa (mild, medium or hot)	75 mL
2 tbsp	chopped green onion (optional)	25 mL
2 tsp	freshly squeezed lemon juice	10 mL
1 tsp	ground cumin (or to taste)	5 mL
1 tsp	chili powder (or to taste)	5 mL
8 to 10	10-inch (25 cm) multigrain or whole wheat tortillas	8 to 10

1. In a large bowl, combine avocados, tomato (if using), garlic, yogurt, salsa, green onion (if using), lemon juice, cumin and chili powder.

2. In batches, place tortillas directly on the middle rack of preheated oven and toast, turning once, for 10 to 15 minutes or until golden brown and starting to crisp (check periodically to make sure they are not getting too brown). Let cool on a wire rack, then break into dipping-size pieces.

3. Serve guacamole in a dish, surrounded by toasted tortilla chips.

✓ **KID APPROVED**

Diabetes Food Choice Values Per Serving	
1½	Carbohydrates
2	Fats

NUTRIENTS Per Serving		
Calories: 227	Carbohydrate: 28.5 g	Calcium: 31 mg
Fat: 10.0 g	Fiber: 6.1 g	Iron: 0.5 mg
Sodium: 411 mg	Protein: 6.4 g	

Very high in: Dietary fiber • **A source of:** Folate

Hot Salmon and Artichoke Dip

MAKES 12 SERVINGS

Cindi Jackson, BC

- *Preparation time: 15 minutes / Cooking time: 10 to 15 minutes per batch of tortillas, plus 30 minutes for dip*
- *Preheat oven to 350°F (180°C)*
- *9-inch (23 cm) glass pie plate*

5	10-inch (25 cm) whole wheat or multigrain tortillas	5
8 oz	light cream cheese, softened	250 g
¼ cup	light sour cream	50 mL
¼ cup	light mayonnaise	50 mL
1	can (7½ oz/213 g) sockeye salmon (no salt added), drained, skin and large bones removed	1
1	can (14 oz/398 mL) artichokes packed in water, drained and chopped	1
1 cup	drained canned white kidney beans, rinsed	250 mL
1 cup	shredded part-skim mozzarella cheese	250 mL
½ cup	chopped green onions	125 mL
¼ tsp	freshly ground black pepper	1 mL

This dish was designed for Cindi's mom-in-law, Joan. She loves salmon, and really enjoys this fragrant, yummy dip.

VARIATIONS

Substitute any cooked seafood, fresh or canned, for the salmon. Leftover cooked salmon, crab and chopped shrimp all work well.

If your family does not favor fish, substitute ¾ cup (175 mL) frozen spinach, thawed and well drained, for the salmon.

1. In batches, place tortillas directly on the middle rack of preheated oven and toast, turning once, for 10 to 15 minutes or until golden brown and starting to crisp (check periodically to make sure they are not getting too brown). Remove from oven and leave oven set to 350°F (180°C). Let tortillas cool on a wire rack, then break into dipping-size pieces.

2. Meanwhile, in a large bowl, combine cream cheese, sour cream and mayonnaise. Stir in salmon, artichokes, beans, mozzarella, green onions and pepper. Spoon into pie plate.

3. Bake for 30 minutes or until heated to an internal temperature of 165°F (74°C).

4. Serve dip in a dish, surrounded by toasted tortilla chips.

NUTRIENTS Per Serving		
Calories: 196	Carbohydrate: 22.3 g	Calcium: 153 mg
Fat: 8.6 g	Fiber: 3.2 g	Iron: 1.7 mg
Sodium: 292 mg	Protein: 12 g	

High in: Niacin, folate and magnesium • **A source of:** Dietary fiber

Diabetes Food Choice Values Per Serving	
1	Carbohydrate
1	Meat & Alternatives
1	Fat

Spicy Hummus

Catha McMaster, ON

Hummus makes a great sandwich spread for a vegetarian lunch, and is a delicious and nutritious between-meal snack with crackers, pitas or celery sticks. Most hummus recipes call for tahini (sesame butter), which is not always easy to find. This one, without tahini, is still excellent.

TIPS

If the hummus is too thick for your taste, blend in a little water.

Hummus will keep for up to 1 week in the refrigerator.

Planned Extras

Make extra to use as a spread on lunchbox sandwiches, with veggie sticks for a quick after-school snack and in Chicken, Hummus and Sautéed Veggie Wraps (page 75).

• Preparation time: 5 minutes

1	can (19 oz/540 mL) chickpeas, drained and rinsed (about 2 cups/500 mL)	1
2	cloves garlic	2
¼ tsp	ground cumin	1 mL
¼ tsp	ground coriander	1 mL
¼ tsp	hot pepper sauce	1 mL
1 tbsp	freshly squeezed lemon juice	15 mL

1. In blender or food processor, on medium speed, blend chickpeas, garlic, cumin, coriander and hot pepper sauce for 30 seconds or until finely chopped. Add lemon juice and blend until smooth.

✓ KID APPROVED

SERVING IDEA: Serve hummus in a hollowed-out red pepper for a nice presentation when entertaining.

Diabetes Food Choice Values Per Serving

1	Carbohydrate

NUTRIENTS Per Serving

Calories: 88	Carbohydrate: 16.9 g	Calcium: 23 mg
Fat: 0.9 g	Fiber: 3.2 g	Iron: 0.9 mg
Sodium: 187 mg	Protein: 3.7 g	

High in: Vitamin B$_6$ and folate • **A source of:** Dietary fiber

Mint Yogurt Dip

• *Preparation time: 5 minutes*

½	clove garlic, minced	½
2 cups	plain yogurt	500 mL
2 tbsp	chopped fresh mint (or 1 tbsp/15 mL dried mint or dill)	25 mL

1. In a medium bowl, combine garlic, yogurt and mint.

Marketa Graham,
Dietitian, ON

Enjoy as a vegetable dip or a dipping sauce for grilled vegetables and meats. It's delicious with Big-Batch Mediterranean Bulgur Meatloaf (page 195).

NUTRIENTS Per Serving

Calories: 40	Carbohydrate: 4.7 g	Calcium: 122 mg
Fat: 1.0 g	Fiber: 0.2 g	Iron: 0.4 mg
Sodium: 44 mg	Protein: 3.3 g	

Very high in: Vitamin B$_{12}$

**Diabetes Food Choice
Values Per Serving**

½	Carbohydrate

Pineapple Salsa

• *Preparation time: 5 minutes*

1 cup	tomato salsa	250 mL
1 cup	diced fresh or drained canned pineapple	250 mL
¼ to ½ cup	chopped fresh cilantro	50 to 125 mL

1. In a medium bowl, combine salsa, pineapple and cilantro. Serve immediately or cover and refrigerate until ready to use.

Eileen Campbell

Store-bought tomato salsa is a great base for more interesting fruit salsa combinations. Serve as a dip with baked tortilla chips.

TIP
Store in an airtight container in the refrigerator for up to 3 days.

VARIATION
Peach Salsa: Substitute fresh or canned peaches for the pineapple and mint for the cilantro.

NUTRIENTS Per Serving

Calories: 24	Carbohydrate: 6.0 g	Calcium: 16 mg
Fat: 0.1 g	Fiber: 1.1 g	Iron: 0.3 mg
Sodium: 264 mg	Protein: 0.8 g	

**Diabetes Food Choice
Values Per Serving**

1	Extra

Eileen Campbell

This salsa is high in fiber and great taste.

TIP
If your family does not like heat, cut back on the amount of jalapeño or omit it.

Black Bean Salsa

● *Preparation time: 5 minutes / Chilling time: 2 hours*

3	tomatoes, diced	3
1	small red onion, finely chopped	1
1	jalapeño pepper, ribs and seeds removed, finely chopped	1
1	can (19 oz/540 mL) black beans, drained and rinsed (about 2 cups/ 500 mL)	1
½ cup	chopped fresh cilantro	125 mL
1 tbsp	olive oil	15 mL
½ tsp	salt	2 mL
	Juice of 2 limes	

1. In a large bowl, combine tomatoes, red onion, jalapeño, beans, cilantro, olive oil, salt and lime juice. Cover and refrigerate for at least 2 hours or overnight to allow flavors to meld.

Black Beans

Popular in Mexican cooking, black beans are served in burritos, enchiladas and as refried beans. Add chilled cooked beans to salads; they are especially good with fresh corn, chopped tomato, and cilantro.

Diabetes Food Choice Values Per Serving	
½	Carbohydrate
½	Fat

NUTRIENTS Per Serving		
Calories: 83	Carbohydrate: 13.5 g	Calcium: 28 mg
Fat: 1.9 g	Fiber: 4.4 g	Iron: 1.1 mg
Sodium: 326 mg	Protein: 3.9 g	

High in: Dietary fiber and folate

Pico de Gallo

MAKES 8 SERVINGS

Eileen Campbell

• *Preparation time: 10 minutes / Chilling time: 1 hour*

1	clove garlic, finely chopped	1
2 cups	chopped seeded tomatoes	500 mL
1 cup	diced Spanish onion	250 mL
½ cup	minced fresh cilantro	125 mL
1 tbsp	minced seeded jalapeño pepper	15 mL
1 tbsp	freshly squeezed lime juice	15 mL
½ tsp	salt	2 mL

1. In a medium bowl, combine garlic, tomatoes, onion, cilantro, jalapeño, lime juice and salt. Cover and refrigerate for at least 1 hour or overnight to allow flavors to meld.

This condiment (literally "rooster's beak" in Spanish) is also known as salsa cruda ("raw sauce") and salsa fresca ("fresh sauce"). It goes well with veggie quesadillas, nacho chips and fajitas.

TIPS

Increase the amount of jalapeño pepper, or leave the seeds in, if you like heat. Omit it if your family prefers a milder flavor.

One medium lime will yield 1 to 2 tbsp (15 to 25 mL) juice.

NUTRIENTS Per Serving		
Calories: 18	Carbohydrate: 4.2 g	Calcium: 11 mg
Fat: 0.0 g	Fiber: 0.7 g	Iron: 0.2 mg
Sodium: 148 mg	Protein: 0.7 g	

Diabetes Food Choice Values Per Serving

1	Extra

Chimichurri

Eileen Campbell

This simple Argentine-style steak sauce makes a perfect accompaniment to barbecued steak, chicken, pork or lamb.

TIPS

If you don't have a mortar and pestle, you can purée all the ingredients in a blender. You will end up with a vibrant green, pasty sauce that can be used to add flavor to homemade burgers. You can either mix it right into the meat (use about 3 tbsp/45 mL per 1 lb/500 g meat) or add a dollop on top of the cooked burgers as a garnish.

For an unusual dip for fresh vegetables, combine chimichurri with an equal quantity of low-fat mayonnaise.

• *Preparation time: 10 minutes*

6	cloves garlic	6
3	bay leaves	3
1 ½	jalapeño peppers, seeded and coarsely chopped	1 ½
1 tsp	salt	5 mL
1 cup	finely minced fresh parsley	250 mL
¼ cup	finely minced fresh oregano	50 mL
¼ cup	white vinegar	50 mL
¼ cup	extra-virgin olive oil	50 mL

1. Using a mortar and pestle, mash garlic, bay leaves, jalapeños and salt until a smooth paste forms.
2. Transfer to a small bowl and add parsley and oregano. Whisk in vinegar and oil until well mixed.

Diabetes Food Choice Values Per Serving	
1	Fat

NUTRIENTS Per Serving		
Calories: 47	Carbohydrate: 1.5 g	Calcium: 19 mg
Fat: 4.6 g	Fiber: 0.5 g	Iron: 0.6 mg
Sodium: 194 mg	Protein: 0.3 g	

Mango Mint Mojo

MAKES 8 SERVINGS

Eileen Campbell

• Preparation time: 10 minutes

12	leaves fresh mint	12
1	ripe mango, peeled, pitted and chopped	1
½ cup	freshly squeezed lime juice	125 mL

1. In blender, on high speed, purée mint, mango and lime juice until smooth.

✓ **KID APPROVED**

> **SERVING IDEA:** Serve as an accompaniment to Simple Grilled Fish (page 203) or Grilled Garlic-Ginger Chicken Breasts (page 166).

Mangoes

If you'll be using the mango right away, be sure to buy a ripe one. Mangoes are ripe when they can be easily indented with your thumb. Avoid mangoes that are so ripe they feel mushy.

Mangoes have large, flat stones in the middle. It is a little tricky to remove the fruit, but if you follow these simple instructions, the task should be easier: Make an initial cut about ½ inch (1 cm) from the center and cut off a long slice of mango. Do the same on the other side. For each of these pieces, use a sharp knife to score the flesh in long lines, first lengthwise, then crossways, cutting almost through to the skin to create small cubes. Using a spoon, scoop cubes from skin. Peel the stone section, remove any flesh from the outside edges and cut into cubes.

The sweetness of mango and the freshness of lime juice and mint make a dynamite combination. This sauce tastes so good that you might want to eat it right out of the bowl!

TIP
If possible, prepare early in the day to allow the flavors to develop. It keeps well in the refrigerator for up to 2 days.

NUTRIENTS Per Serving		
Calories: 21	Carbohydrate: 5.8 g	Calcium: 8 mg
Fat: 0.1 g	Fiber: 0.6 g	Iron: 0.2 mg
Sodium: 1 g	Protein: 0.2 g	

Diabetes Food Choice Values Per Serving

½	Carbohydrate

Sweet-and-Sour Sauce

Patti Thomson,
Dietitian, MB

*Patti uses this simple
sauce as a dip for
meatballs. It is one of
her children's favorites.*

• *Preparation time: 5 minutes / Cooking time: 10 minutes*

1 cup	apricot jam	250 mL
2 tbsp	finely chopped red bell pepper	25 mL
1 tbsp	reduced-sodium soy sauce	15 mL
2 tsp	cider vinegar	10 mL

1. In a small saucepan, combine jam, red pepper, soy sauce
   and vinegar. Bring to a boil over medium heat; reduce heat
   and simmer, stirring occasionally, until sauce is slightly
   thickened, about 10 minutes.

✓ KID APPROVED

SERVING IDEA: Use as a dipping sauce for meatballs or
Chicken Parmesan Strips (page 171).

**Diabetes Food Choice
Values Per Serving**

| 2 | Carbohydrates |

NUTRIENTS Per Serving		
Calories: 132	Carbohydrate: 34.9 g	Calcium: 12 mg
Fat: 0.1 g	Fiber: 0.2 g	Iron: 0.3 mg
Sodium: 121 mg	Protein: 0.6 g	

Zesty Sauce

MAKES 8 SERVINGS

Tracy Hale MacLeod, NS

• *Preparation time: 5 minutes*

3	cloves garlic, minced	3
2/3 cup	ketchup	150 mL
2/3 cup	sweet chili sauce	150 mL
1/2 cup	fancy molasses	125 mL
1/3 cup	freshly squeezed lemon juice	75 mL
1/4 cup	prepared mustard	50 mL
1/2 tsp	freshly ground black pepper	2 mL

1. In a medium bowl, combine garlic, ketchup, chili sauce, molasses, lemon juice, mustard and pepper. Serve immediately or cover and refrigerate until ready to use.

SERVING IDEA: Try this sauce in BBQ Chicken Salad Sandwiches (page 69).

This sauce is tangy but not overwhelming and is excellent with ribs, meatballs and chicken.

TIPS
Store in an airtight container in the refrigerator for up to 1 week.

One medium lemon will yield about 3 tbsp (45 mL) juice, so you'll need a couple of lemons to prepare this recipe.

NUTRIENTS Per Serving

Calories: 114	Carbohydrate: 27.1 g	Calcium: 61 mg
Fat: 0.5 g	Fiber: 2.0 g	Iron: 1.5 mg
Sodium: 623 mg	Protein: 1.3 g	

Very high in: Magnesium • **A source of:** Dietary fiber

Diabetes Food Choice Values Per Serving

1 1/2 Carbohydrates

Soups

A hearty bowl of soup makes a great meal when there is no time to cook a traditional dinner. Just add some fresh multigrain bread or whole wheat rolls, a piece of cheese, a precut packaged salad from the grocery store or some fruit, and a glass of milk or tomato juice. Most of our soups can be made in a slow cooker, so if you have one of these convenient appliances, your soup will be ready and waiting when you come through the door. The "Slow Cooker Friendly" tag in the recipes will tell you which ones are best suited to slow cooking.

a meal in a bowl

Many of our soup recipes make perfect "soup for dinner" meals, as they contain meat or legumes and vegetables. When you're looking for a meal-in-a-bowl, try:

- Chicken and Corn Chowder (page 128)
- Cilantro Bean Soup (page 124)
- Curried Coconut Chicken Soup (page 126)
- Taco Soup (page 130)
- Minestrone with Turkey Sausage (page 129)
- Big-Batch Chicken Vegetable Soup (page 125)
- Hearty Chicken-Peanut Soup (page 127)
- Hungarian Goulash Soup (page 131)

To make a soup meal even easier:

- Make big batches of soup and freeze in meal-size microwave-safe containers, ready to defrost for a fast lunch or dinner. To serve, heat frozen soup in the microwave on High for 8 to 12 minutes, stirring twice, until bubbling, or heat thawed soup on High for 3 minutes.
- Prepare all the ingredients the night before and place them in the slow cooker before you go out in the morning (see box, opposite).

No More Tears!

Onions add great flavor to dishes such as soups and stews. A common complaint about cutting onions is that it makes you cry. Here's a technique to make the process easier, faster and less tearful:

Use a very sharp knife (the compounds in onions that make your eyes water are more likely to be released with a dull knife) and move as quickly as safety permits. Cut the onion in half from top to bottom. Place the cut halves, flat side down, on a clean cutting board. Slice off the stem end, but not the root end, which will hold the onion together as it is cut. Remove the skin and make vertical cuts lengthwise without cutting through the root end. Make a few horizontal cuts from the cut edge toward the root, then chop across the onion to make small dice. Keep in mind that the bottom of the onion should not be sliced through; it should remain intact throughout this procedure.

Lemon Grass

These long stalks resemble dry sticks and are extremely aromatic when sliced or crushed. To use, peel the toughest outside layer and bruise the stalk with the back of a knife, or peel all outer layers to expose the tender inner core and mince. Store fresh lemon grass wrapped in the fridge for up to 2 weeks or in the freezer for up to 3 months.

You may also find finely chopped lemon grass packed in small plastic tubs in the freezer or refrigerated section of some grocery stores. This is the easiest and most economical way to purchase lemon grass.

Making Soup in a Slow Cooker

Get all of your ingredients ready the night before and sauté any vegetables that need precooking. For soups that include ground meat, cook the meat separately from the vegetables, making sure it is completely cooked. Refrigerate the cooked vegetables and meat in separate airtight containers. In the morning, add all of the ingredients to the slow cooker and leave set to Low. In about 8 hours, give or take a bit, you'll arrive home to the tantalizing aroma of freshly made soup.

Aside from the convenience, there are some other advantages to using a slow cooker:

- Because it cooks at a very low temperature, it doesn't heat up the kitchen.
- It allows you to use less expensive meats. Cooked over such a long period, meats become tender and juicier, and they shrink less than they would if cooked on the stovetop or in the oven.

Soup Garnishes

A fun way to let members of your family personalize their soup is to set out an array of garnishes. Garnishes serve a variety of purposes, adding color, texture and contrast as well as flavor. The following garnishes will make a world of difference to the taste and appearance of your soup and will increase your enjoyment of it:

- fresh herbs, either chopped or whole leaves
- puréed vegetables of a contrasting color, splashed or swirled in patterns
- croutons, plain or flavored
- vegetables, such as carrots and zucchini, cut paper-thin
- a dollop of yogurt or sour cream with herbs
- grated cheese
- gratings of colorful vegetables, such as red cabbage and bok choy

Janis Evans, Dietitian,
ON

*A great soup when
asparagus is in season —
the potatoes help to
make it creamy without
much actual cream.*

TIP
This soup is fairly thick.
If you prefer a thinner
version, add more broth.

Creamy Asparagus and Potato Soup

• *Preparation time: 15 minutes / Cooking time: 25 minutes*

1 tbsp	vegetable oil	15 mL
1	small onion, chopped	1
1	clove garlic, minced	1
4	potatoes, diced	4
1 lb	asparagus, cut into 1-inch (2.5 cm) pieces	500 g
3 cups	chicken or vegetable broth	750 mL
3 tbsp	light (5%) cream	45 mL
	Salt and freshly ground black pepper	
	Chopped fresh parsley	

1. In a large saucepan, heat oil over medium heat. Sauté onion and garlic until onion is tender, about 5 minutes. Add potatoes, asparagus and broth; reduce heat, cover and simmer for 20 minutes or until vegetables are tender. Remove from heat.

2. Working in batches, transfer soup to blender and purée on high speed until smooth.

3. Return soup to saucepan, stir in cream and heat over low heat. Season with salt and pepper to taste.

4. Ladle into bowls and garnish with parsley.

❄ **FREEZER FRIENDLY**

SERVING IDEA: Serve with Black Bean Salsa (page 106) and whole wheat pitas for dipping.

Diabetes Food Choice Values Per Serving

1	Carbohydrate
½	Fat

NUTRIENTS Per Serving		
Calories: 107	Carbohydrate: 18.5 g	Calcium: 33 mg
Fat: 2.2 g	Fiber: 2.2 g	Iron: 0.8 mg
Sodium: 349 mg	Protein: 3.4 g	

Very high in: Folate • **A source of:** Dietary fiber

Cream of Broccoli Soup

Lisa Diamond, Dietitian, BC

This is a fast and easy soup for a chilly day. It tastes decadent too!

TIP
You can also use leftover cooked vegetables for this soup. Carrots, cauliflower or a combination work well.

Serve with Sticky Mango Chicken Salad (page 156) and Big-Batch Multigrain Bread (page 280).

• *Preparation time: 10 minutes / Cooking time: 15 minutes*

1	large head broccoli, chopped	1
1	small onion, chopped	1
2 cups	vegetable broth	500 mL
1	can (14 oz/385 mL) evaporated milk	1
½ tsp	dried dillweed	2 mL
	Salt and freshly ground black pepper	
¼ cup	shredded Cheddar, freshly grated Parmesan or shredded Swiss cheese (optional)	50 mL

1. In a large saucepan, over medium heat, combine broccoli, onion and broth. Cover and bring to a boil. Reduce heat and simmer until vegetables are cooked, about 10 minutes. Remove from heat.

2. Working in batches, transfer soup to blender and purée on high speed until smooth.

3. Return soup to saucepan and add evaporated milk and dill. Heat over low heat (do not boil or milk could curdle). Season with salt and pepper to taste. Stir in cheese, if desired.

❄ FREEZER FRIENDLY
✓ KID APPROVED

NUTRIENTS Per Serving		
Calories: 124	Carbohydrate: 17.5 g	Calcium: 311 mg
Fat: 2.3 g	Fiber: 2.5 g	Iron: 1.1 mg
Sodium: 457 mg	Protein: 10 g	

Very high in: Vitamin C, calcium, riboflavin and folate
High in: Vitamin A and magnesium • **A source of:** Dietary fiber

Diabetes Food Choice Values Per Serving	
1	Carbohydrate

Karine Gravel, Dietitian,
QC

*Ginger has a great
affinity for carrots,
and this soup, with its
appetizing color, is a
sweet treat that both
children and adults
will love.*

Gingerroot

Use the side of a spoon
to scrape off the skin
before chopping or
grating. Gingerroot keeps
well in the freezer for up
to 3 months and can be
grated from frozen.

Carrot and Ginger Soup

• *Preparation time: 10 minutes / Cooking time: 45 to
50 minutes*

3 cups	water	750 mL
2	cloves garlic, crushed	2
4 cups	sliced carrots	1 L
½ cup	chopped onion	125 mL
1 tbsp	vegetable bouillon powder	15 mL
2 tsp	pure maple syrup	10 mL
1 tsp	curry powder	5 mL
½ tsp	grated gingerroot	2 mL
1½ cups	milk	375 mL

1. In a large saucepan, bring water to a boil. Add garlic, carrots, onion, bouillon powder, maple syrup, curry powder and ginger; return to a boil. Reduce heat, cover and simmer for 40 to 45 minutes or until carrots are tender. Remove from heat.

2. Working in batches, transfer soup to blender and purée on high speed until smooth.

3. Return soup to saucepan and add milk. Heat over low heat (do not boil or milk will curdle).

❄ FREEZER FRIENDLY
✓ KID APPROVED

SERVING IDEA: Served with Raisin-Apple Tortilla Roll-Ups (page 80), this is a great lunch for small children.

Diabetes Food Choice Values Per Serving	
½	Carbohydrate
½	Fat

NUTRIENTS Per Serving		
Calories: 66	Carbohydrate: 11.2 g	Calcium: 87 mg
Fat: 1.5 g	Fiber: 1.9 g	Iron: 0.3 mg
Sodium: 319 mg	Protein: 2.6 g	
Very high in: Vitamin A		

Leek and Sweet Potato Soup

MAKES 8 1-CUP (250 ML) SERVINGS

Eileen Campbell

When Eileen was growing up, her mother always made leek and potato soup with white potatoes and sometimes shredded cooked chicken. This version offers a new twist, with sweet potatoes instead of white.

• *Preparation time: 10 minutes / Cooking time: 45 minutes*

2 tbsp	vegetable oil	25 mL
4 cups	chopped leeks (white and light green parts only)	1 L
4 cups	diced peeled large sweet potatoes	1 L
4 cups	reduced-sodium chicken or vegetable broth	1 L
1	can (14 oz/398 mL) evaporated milk	1
1 tsp	dried dillweed	5 mL
	Salt and freshly ground black pepper	

1. In a large saucepan, heat oil over medium heat. Sauté leeks for 10 minutes or until lightly browned. Add potatoes and broth; bring to a boil. Reduce heat, cover and simmer for 30 minutes or until potatoes are soft. Remove from heat.

2. Working in batches, transfer soup to blender and purée until smooth.

3. Return soup to saucepan and add evaporated milk and dill. Heat over low heat (do not boil or milk could curdle). Season to taste with salt and pepper.

○ **SLOW COOKER FRIENDLY**
❄ **FREEZER FRIENDLY**
✓ **KID APPROVED**

TIP
If you choose to prepare this recipe in a slow cooker instead of on the stovetop (see page 113), complete Steps 1 and 2, then return soup to the stoneware. Cook on Low for 8 hours, then add the milk, dill, and salt and pepper to taste and heat on High for about 15 minutes, until the mixture is hot but not bubbly.

VARIATION
Replace the sweet potatoes with butternut squash and the leeks with yellow onions.

NUTRIENTS Per Serving		
Calories: 164	Carbohydrate: 22.4 g	Calcium: 231 mg
Fat: 5.1 g	Fiber: 2 g	Iron: 1.0 mg
Sodium: 402 mg	Protein: 7.9 g	

Very high in: Vitamin A • **High in:** Calcium and riboflavin
A source of: Dietary fiber

Diabetes Food Choice Values Per Serving	
1	Carbohydrate
1	Fat

Eileen Campbell

Garlic, ginger, lemon grass, lime and coconut milk bring the flavors of Thailand to your dinner table.

TIPS

This recipe is best when squash is in season. You can often find peeled and chopped butternut squash in the produce section of the supermarket. Buy it, as it will save you time and effort: no blisters that way!

For convenience, buy a jar of minced ginger.

If you can't find kaffir lime leaves locally, substitute grated lime zest (3 leaves = the zest of 1 lime).

If you choose to prepare this recipe in a slow cooker instead of on the stovetop (see page 113), complete Step 2 in the slow cooker, then follow the remainder of the method at right. Heat on High for about 20 minutes after adding the coconut milk and lime leaves.

VARIATION

If you are lucky enough to have any leftovers, this soup is great as a sauce over grilled fish, chicken or pork.

Thai-Style Squash Soup

• **Preparation time: 15 minutes / Cooking time: 45 minutes**
• *Preheat oven to 350°F (180°C)*

1	head garlic	1
1 tbsp	olive oil	15 mL
2 tbsp	vegetable oil	25 mL
1	onion, diced	1
2 tbsp	finely minced gingerroot	25 mL
2 tbsp	finely minced lemon grass	25 mL
1	large butternut squash, peeled, seeded and diced	1
3¼ cups	reduced-sodium chicken broth	800 mL
1	can (14 oz/398 mL) light coconut milk	1
	Salt and freshly ground black pepper	
4	kaffir lime leaves (optional)	4

1. Cut top off head of garlic to expose the cloves. Place on a small piece of foil wrap. Drizzle with olive oil. Cover with foil and bake in preheated oven for 30 minutes or until cloves are soft.

2. Meanwhile, in a large saucepan, heat vegetable oil over medium heat. Sauté onion, ginger and lemon grass until tender, about 5 minutes. Add squash and broth; bring to a boil. Reduce heat, cover and simmer for 30 minutes. Remove from heat. Squeeze roasted garlic into soup, making sure not to get any skin in soup.

3. Working in batches, transfer soup to blender and purée on high speed until smooth.

4. Return soup to saucepan and stir in coconut milk. Season with salt and pepper to taste. Add kaffir lime leaves, if using. Heat over low heat for 10 minutes or until heated through and lime flavor infuses soup.

○ **SLOW COOKER FRIENDLY**
❋ **FREEZER FRIENDLY**
✓ **KID APPROVED**

Diabetes Food Choice Values Per Serving	
1	Carbohydrate
1	Fat

NUTRIENTS Per Serving		
Calories: 118	Carbohydrate: 16.4 g	Calcium: 55 mg
Fat: 5.9 g	Fiber: 2.1 g	Iron: 0.8 mg
Sodium: 184 mg	Protein: 2.3 g	

Very high in: Vitamin A • **High in:** Vitamin C
A source of: Dietary fiber

My Mother's Borscht

MAKES TEN 1-CUP (250 ML) SERVINGS

Madeleine Mitchell, ON

- *Preparation time: 30 to 35 minutes / Cooking time: 1 1/2 to 2 hours*

6	beets, with their green tops	6
2 cups	chopped onions	500 mL
1 1/2 cups	chopped carrots	375 mL
1 cup	chopped celery	250 mL
2	cloves garlic, chopped	2
1	can (19 oz/540 mL) diced tomatoes (about 2 1/3 cups/575 mL)	1
2 cups	chopped peeled potatoes	500 mL
2 cups	chicken broth or water	500 mL
1 tbsp	white vinegar	15 mL
1 tbsp	Worcestershire sauce	15 mL
1 tsp	chopped fresh dill (optional)	5 mL
	Hot pepper sauce	
	Light sour cream and chopped fresh dill	

This dish is a must for anyone who loves beets. Borscht can be served hot or cold.

TIPS

If you prefer your vegetables sautéed in oil, add 1 tbsp (15 mL) vegetable oil to the saucepan and heat over medium heat, then sauté the onions, carrots and celery. But keep in mind that doing this will affect the nutrient analysis, since you are adding fat to the recipe.

Make sure to garnish as suggested — the sour cream and fresh dill add a special touch.

If you choose to prepare this recipe in a slow cooker instead of on the stovetop (see page 113), do not precook the beet roots. Also, wait to add the beet greens and stems until about 20 minutes before cooking is complete and finish cooking on High.

VARIATION

Besides the vegetables listed in the recipe, Madeleine has used fresh tomatoes, cabbage, spinach and peppers, virtually cleaning out the vegetable crisper.

1. Cut beet tops about 1 inch (2.5 cm) from beet roots. Wash thoroughly and drain. Coarsely chop greens and stems; set aside.

2. In a large covered saucepan, over medium-high heat, cook unpeeled beet roots in lots of boiling water. Cook for 20 to 30 minutes or until fork-tender. Cool quickly by running cold water over the beets; slip skins off under running water. Chop beets into 1/2-inch (1 cm) cubes and return to saucepan. Add beet greens and stems, onions, carrots, celery, garlic, tomatoes, potatoes, broth, vinegar, Worcestershire sauce, dill and hot pepper sauce to taste. Cover and cook over medium heat for 1 to 1 1/2 hours or until vegetables are just tender.

3. Ladle into bowls and garnish with sour cream and dill.

○ SLOW COOKER FRIENDLY

NUTRIENTS Per Serving		
Calories: 81	Carbohydrate: 18.0 g	Calcium: 57 mg
Fat: 0.3 g	Fiber: 3.0 g	Iron: 1.4 mg
Sodium: 345 mg	Protein: 2.7 g	

Very high in: Vitamin A • **High in:** Folate
A source of: Dietary fiber

Diabetes Food Choice Values Per Serving
1/2 Carbohydrate

Eileen Campbell

A touch of heat from the jalapeño gives this soup southwest flair.

TIPS

If you prefer your vegetables sautéed in oil, add 1 tbsp (15 mL) vegetable oil to the saucepan and heat over medium heat, then sauté the celery, onion, mushrooms, green pepper and jalapeño with the chili powder. But keep in mind that doing this will affect the nutrient analysis, since you are adding fat to the recipe.

If you choose to prepare this recipe in a slow cooker instead of on the stovetop (see page 113), wait to add the peppers until about 30 minutes before cooking is completed and finish cooking on High. Peppers tend to get bitter with long cooking.

VARIATION

If your family does not like heat, substitute 1 tbsp (15 mL) chopped fresh parsley for the jalapeño.

Chunky Southwest Vegetable Soup

● *Preparation time: 10 minutes / Cooking time: 30 minutes*

1 cup	chopped celery	250 mL
1 cup	chopped onion	250 mL
1 cup	chopped mushrooms	250 mL
1/2 cup	chopped green bell pepper	125 mL
1 tbsp	minced jalapeño pepper	15 mL
1 tsp	chili powder	5 mL
1	can (19 oz/540 mL) diced tomatoes (about 2 1/3 cups/575 mL)	540 mL

1. In a large saucepan, over medium heat, combine celery, onion, mushrooms, green pepper, jalapeño and chili powder. Add tomatoes, then fill can twice with water and add to saucepan; bring to a boil. Reduce heat, cover and simmer for 25 minutes.

○ **SLOW COOKER FRIENDLY**

SERVING IDEA: Serve with Spicy Hummus (page 104) and whole wheat pita bread.

Diabetes Food Choice Values Per Serving
1   Extra

NUTRIENTS Per Serving		
Calories: 49	Carbohydrate: 11.2 g	Calcium: 55 mg
Fat: 0.4 g	Fiber: 2.5 g	Iron: 1.6 mg
Sodium: 167 mg	Protein: 1.9 g	

Very high in: Vitamin C • **A source of:** Dietary fiber

Vegetable Chowder with Cheddar

MAKES SIX 1-CUP (250 ML) SERVINGS

Eileen Campbell

This hearty soup is great on a cold winter day.

TIP
If you choose to prepare this recipe in a slow cooker instead of on the stovetop (see page 113), wait to add the milk, cayenne, salt and pepper until about 30 minutes before cooking is completed and finish cooking on High.

• *Preparation time: 15 minutes / Cooking time: 35 minutes*

1 tbsp	vegetable oil	15 mL
1	small onion, chopped	1
1 cup	diced carrots	250 mL
1/2 cup	diced celery	125 mL
1 cup	diced peeled potato	250 mL
3 cups	chicken or vegetable broth	750 mL
1 cup	hot milk or evaporated milk	250 mL
Pinch	cayenne pepper	Pinch
	Salt and freshly ground black pepper	
1 cup	whole wheat croutons	250 mL
1/2 cup	shredded Cheddar cheese	125 mL

1. In a large saucepan, heat oil over medium heat. Sauté onion, carrots and celery until tender, about 5 minutes. Stir in potato. Add broth and bring to a boil. Reduce heat, cover and simmer for 25 minutes or until vegetables are just soft. Stir in milk, cayenne pepper and salt and pepper to taste.

2. Ladle into warmed bowls and garnish with croutons and cheese.

○ **SLOW COOKER FRIENDLY**
✓ **KID APPROVED**

NUTRIENTS Per Serving		
Calories: 140	Carbohydrate: 13.4 g	Calcium: 139 mg
Fat: 6.7 g	Fiber: 1.9 g	Iron: 0.6 mg
Sodium: 591 mg	Protein: 5.9 g	
Very high in: Vitamin A		

Diabetes Food Choice Values Per Serving	
1/2	Carbohydrate
1/2	Meat & Alternatives
1	Fat

Barley Vegetable Soup

Claude Gamache, Dietitian, QC

When the weather's cold, a big pot of soup simmering on the stove warms the heart as well as the hearth. Whole-grain barley gives this soup its robust flavor.

TIPS

If you prefer your vegetables sautéed in oil, add 1 tbsp (15 mL) vegetable oil to the saucepan and heat over medium heat, then sauté the celery, onion and carrot before adding the tomatoes, broth, barley and pepper. But keep in mind that doing this will affect the nutrient analysis, since you are adding fat to the recipe.

If you choose to prepare this recipe in a slow cooker instead of on the stovetop, see page 113 for instructions.

• Preparation time: 15 minutes / Cooking time: 65 minutes

1	can (19 oz/540 mL) diced tomatoes (about 2⅓ cups/575 mL)	1
6 cups	chicken broth	1.5 L
½ cup	diced celery	125 mL
½ cup	diced onion	125 mL
½ cup	diced carrot	125 mL
½ cup	barley	125 mL
	Freshly ground black pepper	

1. In a large saucepan, over medium heat, combine tomatoes, broth, celery, onion, carrot, barley and pepper to taste; bring to a boil. Reduce heat, cover and simmer for 1 hour or until barley is soft.

○ **SLOW COOKER FRIENDLY**
❄ **FREEZER FRIENDLY**

SERVING IDEA: A piece of cheese and some crusty bread will make this a satisfying lunch.

Diabetes Food Choice Values Per Serving

½	Carbohydrate

NUTRIENTS Per Serving		
Calories: 78	Carbohydrate: 15 g	Calcium: 42 mg
Fat: 0.3 g	Fiber: 1.9 g	Iron: 1.4 mg
Sodium: 789 mg	Protein: 2.8 g	
High in: Vitamin A		

Country Lentil Soup

Eileen Campbell

• Preparation time: 10 minutes / Cooking time: 25 minutes

1 tbsp	vegetable oil	15 mL
1 cup	diced onion	250 mL
½ cup	diced carrot	125 mL
½ cup	diced celery	125 mL
4 cups	vegetable or chicken broth	1 L
1 cup	dried red lentils, well rinsed	250 mL
¼ tsp	dried thyme	1 mL
	Salt and freshly ground black pepper	
½ cup	chopped fresh flat-leaf parsley	125 mL

This hearty soup can be satisfying for lunch or dinner. Soups made with legumes are sources of fiber.

1. In a large saucepan, heat oil over medium heat. Sauté onion, carrot and celery until softened, about 5 minutes. Add broth, lentils and thyme; bring to a boil. Reduce heat, cover and simmer for 20 minutes or until lentils are soft. Remove from heat.

2. Working in batches, transfer soup to blender. Purée on high speed until creamy. Add up to 1 cup (250 mL) water if purée is too thick. Season with salt and pepper to taste. Return to saucepan to reheat, if necessary.

3. Ladle into bowls and garnish with parsley.

○ **SLOW COOKER FRIENDLY**

❄ **FREEZER FRIENDLY**

SERVING IDEA: Accompany with half a tuna or chicken sandwich, a milk pudding and fruit.

TIPS

If you choose to prepare this recipe in a slow cooker instead of on the stovetop (see page 113), transfer soup to the stoneware after bringing it to a boil in Step 1. At this point, you can refrigerate it overnight and drop in the stoneware in the morning. When the soup is cooked, continue with Step 2.

If you prefer, when puréeing soups you can use a stick blender and blend the soup right in the pot. This will save you some cleanup time, but the result will be less smooth.

VARIATIONS

Substitute green lentils, well rinsed and drained, canned chickpeas or white kidney beans for the red lentils. Decrease the simmering time to 15 minutes if using canned legumes.

To make this a heartier soup, add 1 cup (250 mL) of diced cooked lean ham after puréeing.

NUTRIENTS Per Serving		
Calories: 117	Carbohydrate: 18.7 g	Calcium: 29 mg
Fat: 2.0 g	Fiber: 3.7 g	Iron: 2.7 mg
Sodium: 504 mg	Protein: 3.7 g	

Very high in: Folate • **High in:** Vitamin A and iron
A source of: Dietary fiber

Diabetes Food Choice Values Per Serving	
½	Carbohydrate
½	Meat & Alternatives

Cilantro Bean Soup

Eileen Campbell

A great way to use up fresh cilantro, this flavorful purée needs only a multigrain roll with cheese to make it a filling lunch or dinner. A high-fiber soup choice!

TIP

If you choose to prepare this recipe in a slow cooker instead of on the stovetop, see page 113 for instructions.

VARIATIONS

You do not have to blend this soup if you would rather have it chunky.

Vary the beans by substituting black beans, kidney beans or chickpeas.

Substitute sweet potato for the white for a change of taste.

• *Preparation time: 15 minutes / Cooking time: 35 minutes*

1 tbsp	vegetable oil	15 mL
2	onions, chopped	2
1 cup	diced carrots	250 mL
½ cup	diced celery	125 mL
½ tsp	ground cumin	2 mL
½ tsp	ground coriander	2 mL
1	can (19 oz/540 mL) white beans, drained and rinsed (about 2 cups/ 500 mL)	1
1	tomato, seeded and chopped	1
3½ cups	reduced-sodium chicken or vegetable broth	875 mL
1 cup	roughly chopped fresh cilantro	250 mL
1 cup	diced peeled potato	250 mL
	Salt and freshly ground black pepper	
	Additional chopped fresh cilantro (optional)	

1. In a large saucepan, heat oil over medium heat. Sauté onions, carrots and celery until softened, about 5 minutes. Stir in cumin and coriander; cook for 1 minute. Add beans, tomato, broth, cilantro, potato and salt and pepper to taste; bring to a boil. Reduce heat, cover and simmer for 25 minutes or until vegetables are just soft. Remove from heat.

2. Working in batches, transfer soup to blender and purée on high speed until smooth. Return to pot and reheat, if necessary.

3. Ladle into bowls and garnish with cilantro, if desired.

○ **SLOW COOKER FRIENDLY**

SERVING IDEA: Pack this for lunch on a chilly day with half a multigrain bagel, yogurt and fruit.

Diabetes Food Choice Values Per Serving

1	Carbohydrate
½	Meat & Alternatives

NUTRIENTS Per Serving		
Calories: 147	Carbohydrate: 25.5 g	Calcium: 56 mg
Fat: 2.1 g	Fiber: 5.5 g	Iron: 1.7 mg
Sodium: 454 mg	Protein: 7.6 g	

Very high in: Vitamin A • **High in:** Dietary fiber and folate

Big-Batch Chicken Vegetable Soup

MAKES TWENTY 1-CUP (250 ML) SERVINGS

Candice Wilke, BC

• **Preparation time: 40 minutes / Cooking time: 1¼ hours**

8 to 10	skinless chicken drumsticks (about 2 lbs/1 kg total)	8 to 10
12	mushrooms, sliced	12
4	stalks celery, diced	4
4	leeks (white and light green parts only), chopped	4
4	carrots, diced	4
3	large tomatoes, chopped	3
1	large onion, chopped	1
1	can (5½ oz/156 mL) tomato paste	1
10 cups	chicken broth	2.5 L
¼ cup	chopped fresh parsley	50 mL
	Salt and freshly ground black pepper (optional)	

1. In a large pot, combine drumsticks, mushrooms, celery, leeks, carrots, tomatoes, onion, tomato paste, broth, parsley and salt and pepper to taste (if using). Bring to a boil over high heat. Reduce heat, cover and simmer for 30 minutes or until chicken is falling off the bone and vegetables are soft.

2. Remove drumsticks and debone. Discard bones and return chicken to saucepan. Bring back to a boil for a few minutes to reheat chicken.

○ **SLOW COOKER FRIENDLY**
✻ **FREEZER FRIENDLY**
✓ **KID APPROVED**

Freeze this big-batch soup in microwave-safe containers for fast lunches or weeknight meals.

TIPS

When you're going to be freezing meal-sized portions of soup, ladle hot soup into airtight containers, leaving at least 1 inch (2.5 cm) headspace, and let it cool slightly. Refrigerate until completely cold, then freeze for up to 3 months.

This recipe is prepared without sautéing the vegetables in fat. If you prefer, add 1 tbsp (15 mL) vegetable oil to the saucepan and heat over medium heat, then sauté the celery, leeks and carrots before adding all the other ingredients. But keep in mind that doing this will affect the nutrient analysis, since you are adding fat to the recipe.

If you choose to prepare this recipe in a slow cooker instead of on the stovetop, see page 113 for instructions.

NUTRIENTS Per Serving		
Calories: 68	Carbohydrate: 7.5 g	Calcium: 33 mg
Fat: 1.4 g	Fiber: 1.8 g	Iron: 1.2 mg
Sodium: 507 mg	Protein: 6.2 g	
Very high in: Vitamin A		

Diabetes Food Choice Values Per Serving	
½	Meat & Alternatives

Eileen Campbell

This Thai restaurant favorite is easy to make at home and was popular with our taste-testers. You can close your eyes and imagine you are in Thailand. For a less spicy dish for children, reduce the amount of curry paste, or leave it out, and cut back on the amount of ginger.

TIPS
Puréed ginger, available in jars from your grocery store, will save a few minutes in preparation time.

For a more authentic flavor, use kaffir lime leaves, when available, instead of grated zest. Substitute 3 leaves for the zest of 1 lime.

SERVING IDEA:
Make an authentic Thai meal by adding Pineapple Vegetable Rice (page 274) with Grilled Cilantro Shrimp Skewers (page 97).

Curried Coconut Chicken Soup

• *Preparation time: 10 minutes / Cooking time: 25 minutes*

1	can (14 oz/398 mL) light coconut milk	1
1 tsp	red curry paste	5 mL
2 cups	reduced-sodium chicken broth	500 mL
3	stalks lemon grass, split in half lengthwise (or 1 tsp/5 mL finely grated lemon zest)	3
2	boneless skinless chicken breasts (about 8 oz/250 g total), cut into thin strips	2
1/4 cup	finely grated gingerroot	50 mL
1 tbsp	fish sauce (approx.)	15 mL
1	lime	1
2 cups	baby spinach leaves	500 mL
1	green onion, chopped	1
1/2 cup	chopped fresh cilantro	125 mL

1. Take 1/2 cup (125 mL) from the top layer of coconut milk and place in a large saucepan over medium heat. Heat to bubbling, then stir in red curry paste. Reduce heat and simmer for 5 minutes. Add remaining coconut milk and broth; increase heat to medium and bring to a boil. Add lemon grass, chicken, ginger and fish sauce; return to a boil. Reduce heat and simmer, uncovered, until chicken is cooked through, about 8 minutes.

2. Grate zest from the lime, then squeeze the juice. Add lime zest, 1 tbsp (15 mL) lime juice and baby spinach to the soup; simmer for 5 minutes. Remove lemon grass and discard. Taste and add lime juice and fish sauce, if desired.

3. Ladle into bowls and garnish with green onion and cilantro.

❄ FREEZER FRIENDLY
✓ KID APPROVED

Diabetes Food Choice Values Per Serving	
1/2	Carbohydrate
1	Meat & Alternatives

NUTRIENTS Per Serving		
Calories: 130	Carbohydrate: 7.4 g	Calcium: 25 mg
Fat: 5.8 g	Fiber: 0.6 g	Iron: 0.7 mg
Sodium: 498 mg	Protein: 12.2 g	
Very high in: Niacin		

Hearty Chicken-Peanut Soup

MAKES TWELVE 1-CUP (250 ML) SERVINGS

Lydia Butler, ON

This flavorful soup is a meal in itself and is Lydia's family favorite after a hike or winter ski. This soup uses both reduced-sodium broth and canned chicken soup as a base. The delicious vegetables and beans add fiber.

• *Preparation time: 15 minutes / Cooking time: 25 minutes*

2 tsp	vegetable oil	10 mL
3	cloves garlic, minced	3
1	small onion, chopped	1
1	jalapeño pepper, seeded and minced	1
½	red bell pepper, diced	½
2	cans (each 10 oz/284 mL) condensed chicken and wild rice soup, undiluted	2
1	can (19 oz/540 mL) black beans, drained and rinsed (about 2 cups/ 500 mL)	1
5 cups	reduced-sodium chicken broth	1.25 L
2 cups	water	500 mL
2 cups	chopped cooked chicken breast	500 mL
1½ cups	diced peeled sweet potatoes	375 mL
1 cup	salsa	250 mL
1 tsp	ground cumin	5 mL
⅓ cup	creamy peanut butter	75 mL

1. In a large saucepan, heat oil over medium-high heat. Sauté garlic, onion, jalapeño and red pepper until tender, about 5 minutes. Add chicken and wild rice soup, black beans, broth, water, chicken, sweet potatoes, salsa and cumin; bring to a boil. Reduce heat, cover and simmer for 10 minutes. Using a whisk, stir in peanut butter. Simmer for 5 minutes or until potatoes are soft.

❄ **FREEZER FRIENDLY**
✓ **KID APPROVED**

NUTRIENTS Per Serving		
Calories: 171	Carbohydrate: 16.9 g	Calcium: 33 mg
Fat: 6.4 g	Fiber: 4.2 g	Iron: 1.2 mg
Sodium: 872 mg	Protein: 13.3 g	

Very high in: Vitamin A and niacin • **High in:** Dietary fiber, vitamin B_6 and magnesium

Diabetes Food Choice Values Per Serving

½	Carbohydrate
1½	Meat & Alternatives

This delicious, creamy soup was a great hit with our taste-testers, both children and adults. The evaporated milk gives it a richness that suggests it is higher in fat than it actually is. The addition of sweet potato and red pepper helps increase your intake of beta carotene and vitamin C.

TIPS

When using margarine, choose a non-hydrogenated version to limit consumption of trans fats.

If you choose to prepare this recipe in a slow cooker instead of on the stovetop (see page 113), wait to add the milk until about 30 minutes before cooking is completed; cook on High until heated through.

VARIATIONS

This soup works just as well without the chicken. Try replacing it with drained canned clams for variety. With clams, a little hot pepper sauce makes a nice addition.

Ask your family what other ingredients they would like to add to customize the soup.

Chicken and Corn Chowder

• *Preparation time: 10 minutes / Cooking time: 30 minutes*

1 tbsp	margarine	15 mL
1 cup	diced onion	250 mL
1 cup	diced celery	250 mL
½ cup	diced red bell pepper	125 mL
1	boneless skinless chicken breast (about 4 oz/125 g), cubed	1
4 cups	reduced-sodium chicken broth	1 L
1 cup	diced peeled sweet potato	250 mL
1 cup	frozen corn kernels, thawed	250 mL
1	can (14 oz/385 mL) evaporated milk	1
1 tbsp	chopped fresh parsley	15 mL

1. In a large saucepan, melt margarine over medium heat. Sauté onion, celery and red pepper until softened, about 5 minutes. Add chicken, broth, sweet potato and corn; bring to a boil. Reduce heat, cover and simmer for 25 minutes or until chicken and potatoes are cooked through. Add evaporated milk and parsley; heat over low heat (do not boil or milk will curdle).

○ **SLOW COOKER FRIENDLY**
❄ **FREEZER FRIENDLY**
✓ **KID APPROVED**

Diabetes Food Choice Values Per Serving	
½	Carbohydrate
1	Meat & Alternatives

NUTRIENTS Per Serving		
Calories: 118	Carbohydrate: 14.2 g	Calcium: 145 mg
Fat: 2.7 g	Fiber: 1.3 g	Iron: 0.5 mg
Sodium: 362 mg	Protein: 9.8 g	

Very high in: Vitamin A • **High in:** Vitamin C and niacin
A source of: Iron, folate and magnesium

Roasted Beet, Walnut and
Arugula Salad (page 143)

Vegetable Quinoa Salad (page 153)

Jerk Chicken Salad (page 158)

Stir-Fried Chicken with
Mango and Cashews (page 170)

Minestrone with Turkey Sausage

MAKES EIGHT 1²/₃-CUP (400 ML) SERVINGS

Ann Kastner, ON

A dinner soup filled with great chunks of savory sausage and loaded with vegetables.

TIPS
If you choose to prepare this recipe in a slow cooker instead of on the stovetop (see page 113), precook the pasta separately and add it at the end, cooking just until heated through.

There are about 2 cups (500 mL) of beans in a 19-oz (540 mL) can.

VARIATION
Other vegetables you can use include shredded green cabbage or kale, red bell pepper, potatoes, mushrooms and zucchini.

• *Preparation time: 20 minutes / Cooking time: 80 minutes*

1 tbsp	vegetable oil	15 mL
1 lb	turkey sausage, cut into chunks	500 g
1	clove garlic, minced	1
1	large onion, chopped	1
½ cup	diced celery	125 mL
½ cup	diced carrot	125 mL
½ cup	diced green bell pepper	125 mL
1	can (28 oz/796 mL) tomatoes	1
4 cups	reduced-sodium chicken broth	1 L
1	bay leaf	1
2 tbsp	chopped fresh parsley	25 mL
1 tsp	salt	5 mL
½ tsp	dried basil	2 mL
¼ tsp	dried thyme	1 mL
¼ tsp	freshly ground black pepper	1 mL
1	can (19 oz/540 mL) kidney beans, drained and rinsed	1
1 cup	tubetti pasta or other tiny pasta	250 mL
	Freshly grated Parmesan cheese	

1. In a large saucepan, heat oil over medium heat. Sauté sausage, garlic, onion, celery, carrot and green pepper until sausage is browned and vegetables are softened, about 10 minutes; drain fat. Add tomatoes, broth, bay leaf, parsley, salt, basil, thyme and pepper; bring to a boil. Reduce heat, cover and simmer for 1 hour. Add beans and pasta; simmer until pasta is tender, about 10 minutes.

2. Ladle into bowls and sprinkle with Parmesan cheese.

○ **SLOW COOKER FRIENDLY**
❄ **FREEZER FRIENDLY**

NUTRIENTS Per Serving		
Calories: 238	Carbohydrate: 26.5 g	Calcium: 74 mg
Fat: 6.9 g	Fiber: 5.8 g	Iron: 3.0 mg
Sodium: 949 mg	Protein: 17.9 g	

Very high in: Niacin, folate, vitamin B₁₂ and zinc • **High in:** Dietary fiber, vitamin A, vitamin C, iron, thiamine, riboflavin, vitamin B₆ and magnesium

Diabetes Food Choice Values Per Serving	
1	Carbohydrate
2	Meat & Alternatives

**Heather Komar,
Dietitian, AB**

*This is a delicious way
to get picky eaters to
eat more beans and
legumes. It is so thick it
could be called a stew.*

TIPS

The sodium content of
this recipe is reduced
by using tomato paste
instead of tomato sauce
and homemade seasoning
instead of commercial
taco seasoning mix.

The best type of nacho
chips are those that are
oven-baked, as they are
lower in fat.

You can adjust the hot
seasoning up or down,
depending on your
family's taste.

If you choose to prepare
this recipe in a slow
cooker instead of on the
stovetop (see page 113),
wait to add the hot pepper
sauce until the end and
cook just until the flavors
meld.

Taco Soup

• *Preparation time: 10 minutes / Cooking time: 30 minutes*

1 lb	extra-lean ground beef	500 g
1	can (28 oz/796 mL) tomatoes	1
1	can (19 oz/540 mL) kidney beans, drained and rinsed (about 2 cups/ 500 mL)	1
1	can (19 oz/540 mL) black beans, drained and rinsed (about 2 cups/ 500 mL)	1
1	can (5½ oz/156 mL) tomato paste	1
2 cups	water	500 mL
1 cup	frozen corn kernels, thawed	250 mL
2 tbsp	chili powder	25 mL
1 tsp	dried oregano	5 mL
1 tsp	hot pepper sauce	5 mL
½ tsp	ground cumin	2 mL
¼ tsp	hot pepper flakes	1 mL
	Shredded Cheddar cheese and crushed nacho chips	

1. In a large saucepan, over medium-high heat, brown ground
   beef, breaking up with a spoon. Drain off any fat. Add
   tomatoes, kidney beans, black beans, tomato paste, water,
   corn, chili powder, oregano, hot pepper sauce, cumin and
   hot pepper flakes. Cook for 20 minutes, adding water if
   soup is too thick.
2. Ladle into bowls and garnish with cheese and nacho chips.

○ **SLOW COOKER FRIENDLY**
❄ **FREEZER FRIENDLY**
✓ **KID APPROVED**

SERVING IDEA: Serve with brown rice and a green salad on
the side. Cool off your taste buds with a scoop of fruit sorbet
for dessert.

Diabetes Food Choice Values Per Serving

½	Carbohydrate
1½	Meat & Alternatives

NUTRIENTS Per Serving

Calories: 167	Carbohydrate: 21.5 g	Calcium: 55 mg
Fat: 3.6 g	Fiber: 6.9 g	Iron: 3.2 mg
Sodium: 420 mg	Protein: 13.8 g	

Very high in: Dietary fiber, niacin, vitamin B$_{12}$ and zinc

Hungarian Goulash Soup

• **Preparation time: 30 minutes / Cooking time: 2½ to 3½ hours**

2 tsp	vegetable oil	10 mL
8 oz	stew beef, cubed	250 g
1 tbsp	all-purpose flour	15 mL
2	onions, chopped	2
2	stalks celery, chopped	2
1	clove garlic, crushed	1
3 tbsp	paprika	45 mL
4 cups	beef broth	1 L
3	carrots, sliced	3
3	potatoes, diced	3
2	bay leaves	2
¼ cup	white vinegar	50 mL
2 tbsp	tomato paste	25 mL
1 tsp	dried thyme	5 mL
1 tsp	dried parsley	5 mL
½ tsp	freshly ground black pepper	2 mL
½ tsp	Worcestershire sauce	2 mL

MAKES TEN 1-CUP (250 ML) SERVINGS

Phyllis Levesque, Dietitian, ON

This soup, meaty and full of vegetables, is almost a stew. It tastes even better reheated the next day!

TIP
The browning step can be omitted, but the flavor won't be as rich.

1. Heat a large saucepan over medium-high heat. Toss beef with flour. Add oil to pan and swirl to coat. Add beef and brown on all sides. Transfer to a plate and set aside.

2. In the same saucepan, sauté onions, celery, garlic and paprika in the fat remaining in the pan for 1 minute. Add broth, stirring well to scrape up any brown bits stuck to bottom of pan. Add browned beef, carrots, potatoes, bay leaves, vinegar, tomato paste, thyme, parsley, pepper and Worcestershire sauce; bring to a boil. Reduce heat, cover and simmer for 2 to 3 hours, until meat is tender.

SERVING IDEA: Serve with whole wheat rolls and have Pears in Tosca Sauce (page 298) for dessert.

NUTRIENTS Per Serving		
Calories: 121	Carbohydrate: 16.8 g	Calcium: 32 mg
Fat: 3.0 g	Fiber: 2.7 g	Iron: 1.7 mg
Sodium: 408 mg	Protein: 7.9 g	

Very high in: Vitamin A and vitamin B_{12} • **High in:** Niacin, vitamin B_6 and zinc • **A source of:** Dietary fiber

Diabetes Food Choice Values Per Serving	
½	Carbohydrate
1	Meat & Alternatives

Salads

Salad for dinner? Yes, why not? Quick, easy and refreshing, salads are a great way to eat more vegetables and fruit. You can even use leftover meats and meat alternatives as an ingredient. Try some of our great entrée salads such as Jerk Chicken Salad (page 158) Sticky Mango Chicken Salad (page 156) or Deconstructed Sushi (page 161).

Is Olive Oil a Healthy Choice?

Yes, olive oil is a good choice in many recipes, particularly in salad dressings, because it is high in monounsaturated fats and has a unique, delicious taste. Extra-virgin olive oil has a lower smoke point than other oils, so it shouldn't be used for high-temperature cooking, but you can safely use it to sauté vegetables over medium heat.

balsamic vinegar

Balsamic vinegar means "vinegar-like balm." It adds wonderful flavor and, since it doesn't contain any fat, is particularly useful if you're trying to eat healthy. Here are some ideas for how to use it:

- Mix 1 to 2 drops with $\frac{1}{4}$ cup (50 mL) extra-virgin olive oil to make a dip for crusty Italian bread.
- Stir 1 tbsp (15 mL) into gravy for a roast — it will really improve the flavor!
- Stir into roasted vegetables such as onions, tomatoes, fennel, bell peppers and eggplant.
- Sprinkle over white fish after steaming, grilling or broiling.
- Add to fresh tomato sauce and toss with pasta.
- Add a few drops to lemonade.
- Enjoy our Balsamic Strawberry Sauce (page 297)

Nuts Are Healthy, But Aren't They High in Fat?

Nuts are high in both fat and calories. For example, $\frac{1}{4}$ cup (50 mL) of dry-roasted almonds supplies about 18 grams of fat (about the same as in 4 teaspoons/20 mL of butter or margarine) and 210 calories. Although the fat is unsaturated, it is important to moderate the amount of nuts you eat because of the calories they add. Used wisely, nuts can add great taste, texture and variety to your meals. Nuts also provide important nutrients such as vitamin E, potassium, calcium, magnesium, iron, B vitamins, folate and fiber. Here are some ways to add nuts to your menu:

- Add pecans, walnuts or almonds to salads.
- Add peanuts, cashews or almonds to stir-fries.
- Use crushed nuts as a crust for baked fish.
- Make your own trail mix by adding nuts to seeds, raisins, dates or other dried fruits.

Cooking Common Grains

The amount of time and the amount of liquid required to cook grains varies depending on the type and size of the grain, as does the yield of the cooked grain. The table below is a guideline only. When in doubt, check the package directions

Grain (1 cup/250 mL)	Water or broth	Cooking time	Yield
Brown rice	2 cups (500 mL)	45 minutes	3 cups (750 mL)
Wild rice	3 cups (750 mL)	60 minutes	4 cups (1 L)
Millet	3 cups (750 mL)	25 minutes	$3\frac{1}{2}$ cups (875 mL)
Pearl barley	3 cups (750 mL)	35 minutes	$3\frac{1}{2}$ cups (875 mL)
Pot barley	3 cups (750 mL)	60 minutes plus	$3\frac{1}{2}$ cups (875 mL)
Quinoa	2 cups (500 mL)	15 minutes	$2\frac{1}{2}$ cups (625 mL)
Kamut or wheat berries	2 cups (500 mL)	60 minutes	3 cups (750 mL)

To cook, combine grain and liquid in a large pot with a tight-fitting lid; bring to a boil. Reduce heat and simmer, covered, for the suggested cooking time or until liquid is absorbed. Fluff with a fork.

Edie Shaw-Ewald,
Dietitian, NS

*Why bother with
purchased salad
dressing when you can
make a delicious and
fresh version at home?*

TIP
Keeps in the refrigerator
for up to 5 days. If it
solidifies, just bring it out
and let it come to room
temperature. Give bottle
a shake.

VARIATION
This recipe can be
changed up in many
ways, so be creative. Here
are some ideas: add 2 tsp
(10 mL) freshly squeezed
lemon or lime juice, liquid
honey, puréed sun-dried
tomatoes or chopped
herbs.

Homemade Vinaigrette

• Preparation time: 5 minutes

1 to 2	cloves garlic, minced	1 to 2
1/4 cup	vinegar (cider, balsamic, white, etc.)	50 mL
1 tbsp	Dijon mustard	15 mL
1/4 tsp	salt	1 mL
Pinch	freshly ground black pepper	Pinch
Pinch	granulated sugar	Pinch
3/4 cup	extra-virgin olive oil	175 mL

1. In a small bowl, whisk together garlic to taste, vinegar,
   mustard, salt, pepper and sugar. Slowly whisk in olive oil
   (or combine in a jar and shake).

Extra-Virgin Olive Oil
Extra-virgin olive oil comes from the first pressing of the olives and
goes through the least amount of processing. It is the most expensive
of olive oils — but also the most flavorful.

Diabetes Food Choice Values Per Serving	
3	Fats

NUTRIENTS Per Serving		
Calories: 146	Carbohydrate: 0.6 g	Calcium: 3 mg
Fat: 16.3 g	Fiber: 0.0 g	Iron: 0.2 mg
Sodium: 78 mg	Protein: 0.1 g	

Blueberry Vinaigrette

Selina Chan, Dietitian, BC

• *Preparation time:15 minutes*

½ cup	fresh or frozen blueberries, thawed	125 mL
⅓ cup	liquid honey	75 mL
¼ cup	balsamic vinegar	50 mL
2 tbsp	vegetable oil	25 mL
2 tbsp	water	25 mL

1. In a small bowl, mash blueberries with a fork. Whisk in honey, vinegar, oil and water.

 **KID APPROVED**

This stunning dressing was a big hit with our taste-testers. We served it simply over mixed greens, garnished with fresh blueberries.

TIPS

If you prefer, you can prepare the vinaigrette in a blender. Simply add all the ingredients and purée until smooth.

Keeps in the refrigerator for up to 5 days.

NUTRIENTS Per Serving		
Calories: 69	Carbohydrate: 11.9 g	Calcium: 1 mg
Fat: 2.7 g	Fiber: 0.2 g	Iron: 0.1 mg
Sodium: 1 mg	Protein: 0.1 g	

Diabetes Food Choice Values Per Serving	
1	Carbohydrate
½	Fat

Asian Vinaigrette

Donna Bottrell,
Dietitian, ON

This dressing is used in several of the recipes in this book; make a large batch to keep on hand for Edamame Salad (page 160) or some of our other great side salads.

TIP
Keeps in the refrigerator for up to 5 days.

Planned Extras
Always make extra of this dressing to use in our salad recipes.

• **Preparation time: 10 minutes**

2	green onions, finely chopped	2
½ cup	rice wine vinegar	125 mL
¼ cup	unsweetened apple juice	50 mL
2 tbsp	sesame oil	25 mL
2 tbsp	reduced-sodium soy sauce	25 mL
1 tbsp	grated gingerroot	15 mL
1 tsp	granulated sugar	5 mL

1. In blender, on high speed, blend green onions, vinegar, apple juice, sesame oil, soy sauce, ginger and sugar until well combined.

✓ **KID APPROVED**

Diabetes Food Choice Values Per Serving
½ Fat

NUTRIENTS Per Serving		
Calories: 17	Carbohydrate: 1.2 g	Calcium: 2 mg
Fat: 1.4 g	Fiber: 0.1 g	Iron: 0.1 mg
Sodium: 60 mg	Protein: 0.1 g	

Poppy and Sesame Seed Dressing

MAKES 8 SERVINGS

Shauna Lindzon,
Dietitian, ON

• *Preparation time: 5 minutes*

½ cup	vegetable oil	125 mL
¼ cup	cider vinegar	50 mL
3 tbsp	granulated sugar	45 mL
2 tbsp	sesame seeds	25 mL
1 tbsp	poppy seeds	15 mL
2 tsp	chopped green onion	10 mL
¼ tsp	paprika	1 mL
¼ tsp	Worcestershire sauce	1 mL

1. In a small bowl, whisk together oil, vinegar, sugar, sesame seeds, poppy seeds, green onion, paprika and Worcestershire sauce.

This dressing would taste spectacular with Strawberry Spinach Salad (page 142); use it in place of the dressing called for there.

TIP
Keeps in the refrigerator for up to 5 days.

NUTRIENTS Per Serving		
Calories: 160	Carbohydrate: 5.7 g	Calcium: 20 mg
Fat: 15.4 g	Fiber: 0.3 g	Iron: 0.4 mg
Sodium: 3 mg	Protein: 0.8 g	

Diabetes Food Choice Values Per Serving	
½	Carbohydrate
3	Fats

Tomato Basil Buttermilk Dressing

This creamy low-fat dressing will enhance any green salad.

TIPS

Keeps in the refrigerator for up to 5 days.

Sour milk can be used instead of buttermilk. To prepare, combine 2 tsp (10 mL) lemon juice or vinegar with 1 cup (250 mL) milk and let stand for 5 minutes.

• *Preparation time: 10 minutes*

1	Roma (plum) tomato, seeded and finely chopped	1
1	small clove garlic, minced	1
1 cup	buttermilk	250 mL
6 tbsp	chopped fresh basil	90 mL
1/3 cup	light mayonnaise	75 mL
1/2 tsp	granulated sugar	2 mL
1/4 tsp	freshly ground black pepper	1 mL

1. In blender, on high speed, blend tomato, garlic, buttermilk, basil, mayonnaise, sugar and pepper until well combined.

**Diabetes Food Choice
Values Per Serving**

1/2   Fat

NUTRIENTS Per Serving

Calories: 35	Carbohydrate: 2.2 g	Calcium: 33 mg
Fat: 2.6 g	Fiber: 0.1 g	Iron: 0.1 mg
Sodium: 63 mg	Protein: 1.0 g	

Spring Vegetable Salad

MAKES 6 TO 8 SERVINGS

Katie Compton, ON

• *Preparation time: 20 minutes / Cooking time: 3 to 5 minutes*

2 tbsp	green pumpkin seeds	25 mL
1	bag (10 oz/300 g) ready-to-eat spring mix salad	1
1	bag (10 oz/300 g) baby spinach	1
1	small red bell pepper, cut into thin strips	1
1	carrot, grated	1
8	spears asparagus, blanched and cut into 1-inch (2.5 cm) pieces	8
1/4	red onion, thinly sliced	1/4
2 tbsp	balsamic vinegar	25 mL
1 tbsp	freshly squeezed lemon juice	15 mL
2 tsp	pure maple syrup	10 mL
1/2 tsp	Dijon mustard	2 mL
1/4 tsp	minced garlic	1 mL
1/4 tsp	salt	1 mL
Pinch	hot pepper flakes	Pinch
	Freshly ground black pepper	
1/3 cup	flaxseed, grapeseed or other vegetable oil	75 mL
1/4 cup	goat cheese or feta cheese, crumbled	50 mL

Pumpkin seeds add an interesting crunch to this colorful salad, rich in nutrients.

TIPS

If you have leftover cooked asparagus, use it up in this recipe.

Look for chili-and-garlic-infused flaxseed oil in health food stores or the natural food section of larger grocery stores. It can be used in place of the garlic, hot pepper flakes and flaxseed oil.

Leftover dressing can be stored in the refrigerator in an airtight container for up to 1 month.

VARIATION

The pumpkin seeds can be replaced with sunflower seeds or slivered almonds.

1. In a small dry skillet, over medium heat, lightly toast pumpkin seeds for 3 to 5 minutes. Set aside.

2. In a large salad bowl, combine spring mix, spinach, red pepper, carrot, asparagus and red onion.

3. In a small bowl, whisk together vinegar, lemon juice, maple syrup, mustard, garlic, salt, hot pepper flakes and pepper to taste. Slowly whisk in flaxseed oil; continue to whisk until dressing appears thickened.

4. Pour half of the dressing over salad and toss to coat. Sprinkle with toasted pumpkin seeds and goat cheese. Serve the remaining dressing on the side.

NUTRIENTS Per Serving		
Calories: 144	Carbohydrate: 8.8 g	Calcium: 80 mg
Fat: 11.4 g	Fiber: 2.4 g	Iron: 2.0 mg
Sodium: 141 mg	Protein: 3.9 g	

Very high in: Vitamin A, vitamin C and folate
High in: Magnesium • **A source of:** Dietary fiber

Diabetes Food Choice Values Per Serving	
2	Fats

Irene Doyle, Dietitian, PEI

This looks like a rainbow on a plate.

TIPS

Toast sesame seeds in a dry skillet over medium heat, shaking occasionally, until lightly browned, about 5 minutes.

The dressing can be made ahead and stored in the refrigerator for up to 24 hours. Toss with the vegetables just before serving.

Bell Peppers

Red, green and yellow bell peppers provide an array of vitamins and taste great with eggplant, tomatoes, summer squash, onions, garlic or corn. Basil and marjoram provide complementary flavors. Other good flavor partners include vinegar, capers, olives, mozzarella, goat cheese and Parmesan cheese. Kids love to eat peppers raw with some light ranch dressing as a dip.

When you slice a pepper open, be sure your knife is firmly inside the pepper to keep the knife from bouncing off the rubbery surface. Always remove the cap and stem and scoop out the seeds before cutting.

Diabetes Food Choice Values Per Serving	
1½ Fats	

Snow Pea and Bell Pepper Salad

• Preparation time: 10 minutes / Cooking time: 2 minutes

6 oz	snow peas, trimmed	175 g
4 oz	bean sprouts (or other sprouts)	125 g
1	red bell pepper, cut into strips	1
1	yellow bell pepper, cut into strips	1
1	green bell pepper, cut into strips	1
1 tbsp	sesame seeds, toasted (see tip, at left)	15 mL

Dressing

2	cloves garlic, minced	2
½ cup	orange juice	125 mL
¼ cup	olive oil	50 mL
¼ cup	red wine vinegar	50 mL

1. In a small saucepan, bring 1 cup (250 mL) water to a boil. Blanch snow peas for 2 minutes or until just tender; drain and rinse under cold water. Pat dry.
2. In a large salad bowl, combine snow peas, sprouts and red, yellow and green peppers.
3. *Prepare the dressing:* In a small bowl, whisk together garlic, orange juice, oil and vinegar.
4. Pour dressing over salad and toss to coat. Sprinkle with sesame seeds.

✓ KID APPROVED

SERVING IDEA: This colorful salad would complement Tandoori Haddock (page 204). Serve with brown rice or whole wheat noodles for a delicious dinner.

NUTRIENTS Per Serving		
Calories: 99	Carbohydrate: 7.3 g	Calcium: 19 mg
Fat: 7.6 g	Fiber: 1.5 g	Iron: 0.9 mg
Sodium: 4 mg	Protein: 1.9 g	
Very high in: Vitamin C		

Garden Patch Spinach Salad

Eileen Campbell

Full of good things, this colorful salad is scrumptious.

TIP
Any of our dressing recipes will work well with this salad.

Planned Extras
Make extra and serve it the next day, topped with grilled chicken or shrimp.

• *Preparation time: 5 minutes*

1	avocado, peeled, pitted and diced	1
4 cups	baby spinach	1 L
1 cup	grated carrot	250 mL
1 cup	julienned red bell pepper	250 mL
1 cup	grape tomatoes, halved	250 mL
1 cup	canned chickpeas, drained and rinsed	250 mL
1/2 cup	sunflower seeds	125 mL
1/4 to 1/2 cup	lower-fat dressing of your choice	50 to 125 mL

1. In a large salad bowl, combine avocado, spinach, carrot, pepper, tomatoes, chickpeas and sunflower seeds. Serve with dressing on the side.

Change It Up!

This salad is very versatile — vary the ingredients according to what you have on hand. Here are some ideas:

Greens: romaine, spring mix, your favorite bag salad mix

Vegetables: green or yellow bell peppers, zucchini strips, cooked cubed sweet potato, diced celery, tomato wedges, shredded red cabbage, broccoli florets, water chestnuts, fresh chopped herbs

Fruits: dried cranberries, raisins or apricots, pineapple chunks, diced mango, diced apple or pear, blueberries, strawberries, raspberries

Cheese: grated Parmesan, shredded Cheddar, cubed feta

Nuts and seeds: sesame seeds, walnuts, pecans, pumpkin seeds

Legumes: lentils, black beans, white kidney beans

NUTRIENTS Per Serving		
Calories: 140	Carbohydrate: 12.7 g	Calcium: 42 mg
Fat: 9.0 g	Fiber: 4.6 g	Iron: 1.6 mg
Sodium: 188 mg	Protein: 4.6 g	

Very high in: Vitamin A, vitamin C, folate and magnesium
High in: Dietary fiber, thiamine, vitamin B$_6$

Diabetes Food Choice Values Per Serving	
1/2	Carbohydrate
1/2	Meat & Alternatives
1 1/2	Fats

Samantha Thiessen,
Dietitian, ON

This delicious salad is full of crunch and great flavor. Both kids and adults love it, especially the strawberry garnish and the sweet dressing.

TIP
Toast pine nuts or almonds in a dry skillet over medium heat, shaking occasionally, until lightly browned, about 5 minutes.

Strawberry Spinach Salad

● *Preparation time: 10 minutes*

Dressing

1/4 cup	frozen orange juice concentrate, thawed	50 mL
1 tbsp	fat-free or low-fat mayonnaise	15 mL
1 tbsp	low-fat plain yogurt	15 mL
1/4 tsp	granulated sugar	1 mL
4 cups	lightly packed baby spinach	1 L
1 cup	sliced strawberries	250 mL
1/4 cup	pine nuts or slivered almonds, toasted (see tip, at left)	50 mL

1. *Prepare the dressing:* In a small bowl, combine orange juice concentrate, mayonnaise, yogurt and sugar.
2. Wash, trim and tear spinach into a large salad bowl. Add strawberries and pine nuts; toss gently. Immediately before serving, drizzle with dressing.

✓ KID APPROVED

SERVING IDEA: Add some freshly grated Parmesan cheese and serve with a multigrain roll.

Diabetes Food Choice Values Per Serving	
1/2	Carbohydrate
1	Fat

NUTRIENTS Per Serving		
Calories: 112	Carbohydrate: 13.3 g	Calcium: 51 mg
Fat: 6.2 g	Fiber: 2.1 g	Iron: 1.5 mg
Sodium: 59 mg	Protein: 2.9 g	

Very high in: Vitamin A, vitamin C and folate
High in: Magnesium • **A source of:** Dietary fiber

Roasted Beet, Walnut and Arugula Salad

Eileen Campbell

- **Preparation time: 15 minutes / Cooking time: 45 minutes**
- *Preheat oven to 375°F (190°C)*

2½ lbs	fresh beets	1.25 kg
	Salt and freshly ground black pepper	
3	large oranges	3
1	shallot, finely diced	1
¼ cup	red wine vinegar	50 mL
¾ cup	extra-virgin olive oil	175 mL
2	bunches (each about 5 oz/150 g) arugula, washed and trimmed	2
½ cup	toasted walnuts (see tip, at right)	125 mL

1. Wash beets and cut away tops and tails. Wrap in foil and bake in preheated oven for about 45 minutes or until just tender. Unwrap, let cool and peel under running water. Cut into chunks and season to taste with salt and pepper.

2. Meanwhile, grate the zest of 1 orange into a small bowl. Cut orange in half and squeeze juice onto the zest. Add shallot. Whisk in vinegar, then oil.

3. Peel the remaining oranges and cut into wedges.

4. Place arugula in a large salad bowl and place beets on top. Drizzle with a little orange dressing. Top with orange slices and sprinkle with walnuts. Serve the remaining dressing on the side.

> **SERVING IDEA:** Add cubed feta or goat cheese and serve with a slice of Big-Batch Multigrain Bread (page 280) for an enjoyable cold lunch.

Roasting beets brings out their sweetness. Combining them with orange vinaigrette enhances the flavor even more. Enjoy this salad as part of a special dinner when entertaining friends and family.

TIP
Toast walnuts in a dry skillet over medium heat, shaking occasionally, until lightly browned, about 5 minutes.

VARIATION
Substitute 4 cups (1 L) packed baby spinach for the arugula.

Arugula
Arugula is an aromatic salad green popular in Italian cuisine. Aside from its use in salads, it can be cooked with pasta, used to top freshly baked pizza, or used in pesto, either in addition to basil or as a (non-traditional) substitute. If you cannot find it, watercress provides a similar peppery flavor. You can also substitute fresh baby spinach, but the flavor will not be the same.

NUTRIENTS Per Serving		
Calories: 222	Carbohydrate: 19.8 g	Calcium: 116 mg
Fat: 15.4 g	Fiber: 4.5 g	Iron: 2.2 mg
Sodium: 105 mg	Protein: 4.7 g	

Very high in: Vitamin C, folate and magnesium
High in: Dietary fiber, iron and vitamin A

Diabetes Food Choice Values Per Serving	
½	Carbohydrate
3	Fats

Valérie Murray, QC

This is a very tasty and different salad. Valérie sometimes adds diced tomato, grated carrot, slices of zucchini or pieces of cheese.

TIPS

If you are taking this salad to work for lunch, make sure to dip the avocado in lemon or lime juice to prevent it from browning.

If hearts of palm are difficult to find in your area, add extra artichoke hearts.

Hearts of Palm and Artichoke

• *Preparation time:15 minutes*

2 cups	salad greens	500 mL
2	canned hearts of palm, cut into rounds	2
2	canned artichoke hearts, quartered	2
1 tbsp	sesame seeds	15 mL
1 tbsp	olive oil	15 mL
1 tsp	balsamic vinegar	5 mL
	Juice of 1 lemon or lime	
	Salt and freshly ground black pepper	
1	avocado, peeled and diced	1

1. In a large salad bowl, combine greens, hearts of palm and artichokes. Sprinkle with sesame seeds.

2. In a small bowl, combine oil, vinegar, lemon juice, and salt and pepper to taste.

3. Add avocado to the salad, then dressing; toss gently to combine.

> **SERVING IDEA:** This would be great served with Grilled Garlic-Ginger Chicken Breasts (page 166) and a baked sweet potato.

Hearts of Palm

This uncommon ingredient is worth a try! The edible inner portion of the stem of the cabbage palm tree, hearts of palm are native to Florida and other tropical locales. They come in cans, packed in water, and can be found in the specialty canned vegetable section of your grocery store (usually beside canned artichokes). They resemble white asparagus, without the tips. The delicate flavor is a bit like an artichoke. Once opened, they should be transferred to an airtight nonmetal container. Refrigerate in their own liquid and use within 1 week in salads or main dishes.

Diabetes Food Choice Values Per Serving
2½ Fats

NUTRIENTS Per Serving		
Calories: 144	Carbohydrate: 9.1 g	Calcium: 44 mg
Fat: 12.2 g	Fiber: 5.0 g	Iron: 1.4 mg
Sodium: 95 mg	Protein: 2.9 g	

Very high in: Folate • **High in:** Dietary fiber, vitamin C and magnesium

Asian Carrot Cucumber Pickle

MAKES 4 SERVINGS

Eileen Campbell

• *Preparation time: 10 minutes*

¹/₂ cup	rice wine vinegar	125 mL
2 tbsp	granulated sugar	25 mL
1 tsp	olive oil	5 mL
¹/₂ tsp	salt	2 mL
¹/₄ tsp	freshly ground black pepper	1 mL
¹/₂	large English cucumber, halved and thinly sliced	¹/₂
2 cups	thinly sliced carrots	500 mL
2 tbsp	finely chopped red bell pepper	25 mL

1. In a medium bowl, whisk vinegar, sugar, oil, salt and pepper until sugar is dissolved. Add cucumber, carrots and red pepper; toss to coat. Serve right away or cover and refrigerate for up to 30 minutes.

✓ KID APPROVED

This refreshing, light salad counteracts spicy Asian food, but it needs to be made just before you serve it. If kept for longer than a few hours, the vegetables will go limp. If you need to make it ahead, prepare the marinade and keep it separate from the vegetables. Combine just before serving for wonderfully crisp pickles.

TIP
If you prefer, you can seed the cucumbers for a cleaner look.

VARIATIONS
For an authentic Thai touch, garnish the salad with chopped dry-roasted peanuts or cilantro.

A little chopped red chili pepper is a nice addition for adults who like heat.

If you don't have rice wine vinegar, white vinegar will work, but the flavor will be slightly different. Chinese rice vinegars (and most Asian rice vinegars) are milder and less acidic than regular vinegar and are often seasoned with salt and sugar.

NUTRIENTS Per Serving		
Calories: 72	Carbohydrate: 15.6 g	Calcium: 29 mg
Fat: 1.4 g	Fiber: 2.0 g	Iron: 0.4 mg
Sodium: 330 mg	Protein: 1.0 g	
Very high in: Vitamin A • **A source of:** Dietary fiber		

Diabetes Food Choice Values Per Serving	
¹/₂	Carbohydrate
¹/₂	Fat

Ann McConkey,
Dietitian, MB

Here's a new twist on everyone's favorite coleslaw. The peanut butter adds even more crunch to this scrumptious salad.

TIPS

To save time, you can purchase pre-shredded packaged coleslaw vegetables.

Soften the peanut butter in the microwave, if necessary, for easier blending.

This dressing can be made without a blender: just mince the garlic and ginger and whisk together all of the ingredients in a bowl.

If preparing in advance, it's best to keep the vegetables separate from the dressing until about 1 hour before service to maintain the crispness.

VARIATION

Adapt the ingredients to suit your taste. For example, add grated carrot or chopped cilantro, use green onions instead of sweet, or try almond butter instead of peanut butter.

Ginger Lime Peanut Slaw

> • *Preparation time: 10 minutes / Chilling time: 1 hour*

8 cups	shredded green cabbage	2 L
1 to 2	green or red bell peppers, chopped (optional)	1 to 2
½ to 1	sweet onion, chopped (optional)	½ to 1

Dressing

1	clove garlic (or 1 tsp/5 mL garlic powder)	1
¾ cup	crunchy peanut butter	175 mL
¼ cup	rice or cider vinegar	50 mL
3 tbsp	packed brown sugar	45 mL
1 to 2 tbsp	soy sauce	15 to 25 mL
1 to 2 tbsp	freshly squeezed lime juice	15 to 25 mL
1 tbsp	grated gingerroot (or 1 tsp/5 mL ground ginger)	15 mL
1 tsp	sesame oil (optional)	5 mL
1 to 2 tbsp	water (optional)	15 to 25 mL

1. In a large bowl, combine cabbage, green peppers (if using) and onion (if using).
2. *Prepare the dressing:* In blender, on high speed, blend garlic, peanut butter, vinegar, brown sugar, soy sauce, lime juice, ginger and sesame oil (if using) until smooth, adding water if necessary to thin dressing.
3. Pour dressing over salad and toss to coat. Cover and refrigerate for 1 hour to allow flavors to meld.

✓ **KID APPROVED**

> **SERVING IDEA:** For a vegetarian meal, serve with Tofu Patties (page 225) on whole wheat Kaiser rolls.

Diabetes Food Choice Values Per Serving

½	Carbohydrate
½	Meat & Alternatives
1½	Fats

NUTRIENTS Per Serving

Calories: 147	Carbohydrate: 12.1 g	Calcium: 40 mg
Fat: 9.8 g	Fiber: 2.6 g	Iron: 0.8 mg
Sodium: 196 mg	Protein: 5.6 g	

High in: Vitamin C, niacin, folate and magnesium
A source of: Dietary fiber

Fruity Slaw

Eileen Campbell

This fast side dish uses a bag of precut slaw and adds just a few other ingredients. Have your children choose their favorite fruits to add to the mix.

• *Preparation time: 2 minutes / Chilling time: 1 hour*

1	bag (16 oz/500 g) precut coleslaw	1
1 cup	chopped mixed fresh or drained canned fruits (see tip, at right)	250 mL
½ cup	finely chopped red onion	125 mL
¼ cup	sunflower seeds	50 mL
¼ cup	raisins or dried cranberries	50 mL
¼ cup	Asian Vinaigrette (page 136)	50 mL

1. In a large bowl, combine coleslaw, fruit, onion, sunflower seeds and raisins. Pour in vinaigrette and toss to coat. Cover and refrigerate for 1 hour to allow flavors to meld.

✔ KID APPROVED

SERVING IDEA: This is great with Turkey Apple Burgers (variation, page 179) on whole wheat buns.

TIPS

Many of your favorite fruits will work in this recipe, but avoid fruits that discolor easily, such as apples, pears and bananas. Try pineapple, mango, orange, kiwi, watermelon or cantaloupe.

Precut coleslaw is a great ingredient for time-starved cooks. Use it in this recipe or in soups and stir-fries. Precut broccoli slaw works well too!

This is not a salad to make ahead: the fruits will deteriorate, and their juices will make the salad soggy.

NUTRIENTS Per Serving		
Calories: 153	Carbohydrate: 23.6 g	Calcium: 81 mg
Fat: 6.3 g	Fiber: 4.3 g	Iron: 1.6 mg
Sodium: 86 mg	Protein: 4.5 g	

Very high in: Vitamin C and folate
High in: Dietary fiber, thiamine, vitamin B$_6$ and magnesium

Diabetes Food Choice Values Per Serving	
1	Carbohydrate
1	Fat

Eileen Campbell

This new take on potato salad uses a lemony vinaigrette instead of high-fat mayonnaise dressing.

Warm New Potato Salad with Citrus Vinaigrette

• **Preparation time: 10 minutes / Cooking time: 15 to 20 minutes**

2 lbs	tiny new potatoes (unpeeled), scrubbed	1 kg
2 tsp	salt	10 mL

Vinaigrette

1	clove garlic, crushed	1
¼ cup	chopped fresh chives	50 mL
¼ cup	chopped green onions	50 mL
	Grated zest of 1 lemon	
¼ cup	freshly squeezed lemon juice	50 mL
¼ cup	extra-virgin olive oil	50 mL
2 tsp	grainy mustard	10 mL
½ tsp	salt	2 mL
½ tsp	freshly ground black pepper	2 mL

1. In a medium saucepan, over medium-high heat, cook potatoes, salt and enough water to cover for 15 to 20 minutes or until just tender.

2. *Meanwhile, prepare the vinaigrette:* In a large serving bowl, whisk together garlic, chives, green onions, lemon zest, lemon juice, olive oil, mustard, salt and pepper.

3. Drain potatoes and transfer to serving bowl with vinaigrette while still warm; stir well to combine. Serve immediately.

 ✓ KID APPROVED

SERVING IDEA: Delicious alongside grilled salmon, chicken or your favorite meat. Add a green vegetable to complete the meal.

Diabetes Food Choice Values Per Serving	
1½	Carbohydrates
2	Fats

NUTRIENTS Per Serving		
Calories: 195	Carbohydrate: 26.7 g	Calcium: 22 mg
Fat: 9.3 g	Fiber: 2.4 g	Iron: 1.3 mg
Sodium: 516 mg	Protein: 2.8 g	

High in: Vitamin C and vitamin B$_6$ • **A source of:** Dietary fiber

Mediterranean Tuna Risotto Salad

MAKES 10 SERVINGS

Eileen Campbell

Eileen has fond memories of this salad, which was a staple in her university days. Filling and flavorful, it is easy to make.

TIP
You can serve this as a main course, if you wish, instead of as a side salad. As a main course, it serves 6.

VARIATION
Substitute 10 oz (300 g) cooked diced chicken breast or cooked shrimp or crab for the tuna.

Arborio Rice

Arborio is an Italian rice traditionally used for risotto and great for making a creamy rice pudding. The surface starch should not be washed off before cooking, as it gives the finished dish its creamy texture.

• *Preparation time: 10 minutes / Cooking time: 20 minutes*

4 cups	water	1 L
2 cups	Arborio rice	500 mL
2	cans (each 6½ oz/170 g) water-packed albacore tuna, drained and flaked	2
1	red bell pepper, finely chopped	1
½	small red onion, diced	½
½ cup	oil-packed sun-dried tomatoes, drained and finely chopped	125 mL
½ cup	chopped pitted Kalamata olives	125 mL
½ cup	finely chopped celery or fennel	125 mL
½ cup	chopped fresh Italian (flat-leaf) parsley	125 mL
2 tbsp	olive oil	25 mL
2 tbsp	red wine vinegar	25 mL
	Salt and freshly ground black pepper	
	Sliced tomatoes and fresh parsley sprigs	

1. In a large saucepan, bring water to a boil. Add rice and bring back to a boil. Stir well, then reduce heat, cover and simmer for about 15 minutes or until rice is al dente (tender to the bite). Drain and rinse under cold water to cool rice. Set aside to cool completely.

2. In a large salad bowl, combine cooked rice, tuna, red pepper, red onion, sun-dried tomatoes, olives, celery and parsley. Stir in oil and vinegar. Taste and adjust seasoning with salt and pepper. Garnish with fresh tomatoes and parsley.

SERVING IDEA: Serve on top of mixed greens and garnish with sliced tomato and parsley.

NUTRIENTS Per Serving		
Calories: 242	Carbohydrate: 35.4 g	Calcium: 22 mg
Fat: 6.7 g	Fiber: 1.5 g	Iron: 1.0 mg
Sodium: 320 mg	Protein: 9.7 g	

Very high in: Vitamin C • **High in:** Niacin and vitamin B_{12}

Diabetes Food Choice Values Per Serving	
2	Carbohydrates
1	Meat & Alternatives
1	Fat

Couscous Salad

Christine Plante, QC

This colorful and appetizing salad makes a great lunchbox meal. It can be served cold as a salad or hot as a side dish. Either way, it tastes great.

TIPS
Herbs that work well in this salad include flat-leaf (Italian) parsley, cilantro, dill, mint and chives.

VARIATION
To make a main dish out of this salad, simply add cooked chicken.

Planned Extras
Make lots so you can bring some to work with you and send some off with your kids.

• **Preparation time: 30 minutes / Standing time: 15 minutes / Chilling time: 1 hour**

2	shallots, finely chopped	2
1	English cucumber, diced	1
1	tomato, diced	1
1	carrot, grated	1
1	clove garlic, minced	1
½	red or yellow bell pepper, diced	½
1 ½ cups	frozen corn kernels, thawed	375 mL
1 cup	canned chickpeas, drained and rinsed	250 mL
½ cup	chopped spinach	125 mL
½ cup	light Italian vinaigrette	125 mL
1 tbsp	red wine vinegar	15 mL
	Salt, freshly ground black pepper and fresh herbs of your choice	
2 cups	couscous	500 mL
2 cups	boiling water	500 mL

1. In a large bowl, combine shallots, cucumber, tomato, carrot, garlic, red pepper, corn, chickpeas and spinach. Stir in vinaigrette, vinegar, and salt, pepper and herbs to taste until well combined. Set aside.

2. Place couscous in another large bowl and pour in boiling water; stir with a fork, cover and let stand for 15 minutes or until all the water is absorbed. Fluff with a fork.

3. Add couscous to vegetables. Cover and refrigerate for at least 1 hour or for up to 2 days.

4. Serve cold or heat in the microwave for 2 to 3 minutes per 2-cup (500 mL) amount.

✓ **KID APPROVED**

> **SERVING IDEA:** This filling salad would be great served warm with our Moroccan Lamb Tagine (page 198) or Marrakech Chicken (page 165).

Diabetes Food Choice Values Per Serving

2 ½ Carbohydrates
½ Fat

NUTRIENTS Per Serving		
Calories: 233	Carbohydrate: 47.5 g	Calcium: 36 mg
Fat: 1.8 g	Fiber: 3.7 g	Iron: 1.3 mg
Sodium: 285 mg	Protein: 7.9 g	

Very high in: Folate • **High in:** Vitamin A, vitamin C, niacin and vitamin B_6 • **A source of:** Dietary fiber

Roasted Vegetables and Couscous with Goat Cheese

MAKES 8 SERVINGS

Eileen Campbell

This delicious salad uses leftover ratatouille. When entertaining, serve it layered in a pretty glass bowl.

VARIATION
In the winter, take advantage of seasonal vegetables and roast cubed root vegetables such as carrots, parsnips, turnips, sweet potatoes and squash. Use 3 to 4 cups (750 mL to 1 L) instead of the ratatouille mixture.

• Preparation time: 10 minutes / Standing time: 15 minutes

1 1/2 cups	whole wheat couscous	375 mL
2 cups	hot vegetable broth	500 mL
1/2 cup	cubed goat cheese or feta cheese	125 mL
1/2	batch Big-Batch Oven-Roasted Ratatouille (page 266), cooled	1/2
1	package (8 oz/250 g) mixed salad greens	1
1 cup	reduced-fat sun-dried tomato dressing	250 mL

1. Place couscous in a large bowl and pour in boiling stock; stir with a fork, cover and let stand for 15 minutes or until all the stock is absorbed. Fluff with a fork. Set aside and let cool.

2. In a large salad bowl, combine cooled couscous, goat cheese and cooled ratatouille. Top with greens.

3. Just before serving, pour dressing evenly over greens and drizzle down the sides of the couscous and ratatouille.

NUTRIENTS Per Serving		
Calories: 395	Carbohydrate: 41.5 g	Calcium: 115 mg
Fat: 12.5 g	Fiber: 7.1 g	Iron: 2.2 mg
Sodium: 714 mg	Protein: 10.1 g	

Very high in: Dietary fiber and vitamin C
High in: Iron, vitamin A and folate

Diabetes Food Choice Values Per Serving	
2	Carbohydrates
2 1/2	Fats

Bulgur Parsley Salad

Eileen Campbell

This Middle Eastern salad is a version of the famous tabbouleh. It is typically served cold as part of a mezza (appetizer) selection, but if you prefer, it can be served with a meal.

TIP

If you're making lots of this salad and planning to store some, omit the tomatoes. Cover and store in the refrigerator for up to 1 week. Add the tomatoes just before serving.

VARIATIONS

The salad is very versatile — adapt it by adding your favorite vegetables or legumes, such as shredded carrots or chickpeas.

This version contains lots more parsley than bulgur, but you can adjust the amounts if you prefer one over the other. Just make sure to use the same amount of boiling water as you do bulgur (e.g., if you increase the bulgur to 1 cup/250 mL, use 1 cup/ 250 mL boiling water).

Planned Extras

Make lots and pack into lunchboxes. Try stuffing it in a pita and topping with cooked chicken.

• *Preparation time: 10 minutes / Standing time: 20 minutes*

½ cup	bulgur, rinsed and drained	125 mL
½ cup	boiling water	125 mL
6 tbsp	freshly squeezed lemon juice	90 mL
2	tomatoes, chopped	2
1	bunch (6 oz/175 g) fresh parsley, washed and roughly chopped	1
½ cup	diced green onions	125 mL
½ cup	finely chopped fresh mint	125 mL
6 tbsp	extra-virgin olive oil	90 mL
1 tsp	salt	5 mL

1. Place bulgur in a large bowl and pour in boiling water. Cover and let stand for 15 minutes. Squeeze out excess water. Stir in lemon juice and let stand for 5 minutes. Stir in tomatoes, parsley, green onions, mint, olive oil and salt until well combined.

SERVING IDEA: Serve with Grilled Cilantro Shrimp Skewers (page 97) for a unique appetizer course.

Diabetes Food Choice Values Per Serving	
½	Carbohydrate
2	Fats

NUTRIENTS Per Serving		
Calories: 140	Carbohydrate: 10.9 g	Calcium: 54 mg
Fat: 10.5 g	Fiber: 2.5 g	Iron: 2.5 mg
Sodium: 309 mg	Protein: 2.4 g	

Very high in: Vitamin A and vitamin C
High in: Iron and folate • **A source of:** Dietary fiber

Vegetable Quinoa Salad

**MAKES
10 SERVINGS**

Deloris Del Rio, QC

• *Preparation time: 15 minutes / Cooking time: 15 to 20 minutes*

1 cup	quinoa, well rinsed and drained	250 mL
2 cups	cold water	500 mL
2	tomatoes, chopped	2
2	large sprigs Italian (flat-leaf) parsley (leaves only), chopped	2
1/4	English cucumber, chopped	1/4
1/3 cup	chopped red, green, yellow or mixed bell peppers	75 mL

Vinaigrette

3 tbsp	extra-virgin olive oil	45 mL
2 tbsp	freshly squeezed lemon juice	25 mL
1 1/2 tsp	hot pepper flakes (optional)	7 mL
1/2 tsp	salt	2 mL
1/2 tsp	freshly ground black pepper	2 mL
1/2 tsp	dried lavender flowers (optional)	2 mL

Quinoa (pronounced keen-wa) is an ancient grain from South America that is considered a complete protein. It can be used in any recipe in which you would use rice, and can be served hot or cold. It is easy to cook.

TIPS

If you are not a fan of the strong flavors of chili and/or lavender, leave them out. You could also substitute your favorite homemade or store-bought dressing; 1/4 cup (50 mL) is required to coat the salad. Remember, you do not want it soaked in dressing, just enough to enhance the natural flavors.

Only lavender that has been grown specifically for food use should be used in cooking. Avoid lavender sold for decoration or potpourri, as it may have been treated to preserve the color.

This salad is best served fresh, but it will keep for up to 2 days in the refrigerator.

1. In a medium saucepan, over medium heat, bring quinoa and water to a boil. Reduce heat and boil gently for 10 to 15 minutes or until the white germ separates from the seed. Cover, remove from heat and let stand for 5 minutes. Remove lid, let cool and fluff with a fork.

2. Meanwhile, in a large bowl, combine tomatoes, parsley, cucumber and bell peppers. Stir in cooled quinoa.

3. *Prepare the vinaigrette:* In a small bowl, whisk together olive oil, lemon juice, hot pepper flakes (if using), salt, pepper and lavender (if using).

4. Pour vinaigrette over salad and toss to coat.

Quinoa

Here are a couple more recipe ideas for quinoa:
- Combine chilled cooked quinoa with pinto beans, pumpkin seeds, green onions and cilantro. Season to taste and enjoy this south-of-the-border-inspired salad.
- Add nuts and fruits to cooked quinoa and serve as a breakfast porridge, topped with milk or yogurt.

NUTRIENTS Per Serving		
Calories: 108	Carbohydrate: 13.6 g	Calcium: 17 mg
Fat: 5.1 g	Fiber: 1.6 g	Iron: 1.8 mg
Sodium: 123 mg	Protein: 2.6 g	
High in: Magnesium		

Diabetes Food Choice Values Per Serving	
1/2	Carbohydrate
1	Fat

Eileen Campbell

Kamut is a chewy whole grain that holds up well in salad mixtures. This salad would be great packed in a lunchbox or rolled into a tortilla.

TIPS

If you cannot find kamut, replace it with wheat berries or brown rice (see cooking info on page 133).

This salad keeps very well for up to 1 week in the refrigerator.

Planned Extras

Cook extra kamut and use as a base for a stir-fry.

Greek Kamut Salad

• *Preparation time: 10 minutes / Soaking time: 6 hours / Cooking time: 1 hour*

1 cup	kamut	250 mL
2	green onions, chopped	2
1	small carrot, grated	1
½	red bell pepper, finely diced	½
½ cup	finely diced English cucumber	125 mL
¼ cup	finely chopped fresh parsley	50 mL
¼ cup	finely chopped black olives	50 mL
¼ cup	freshly squeezed lemon juice	50 mL
2 tbsp	olive oil	25 mL
½ tsp	dried oregano	2 mL
	Salt and freshly ground black pepper	
½ cup	crumbled feta cheese	125 mL

1. Rinse kamut well in cold water. Place in a small saucepan and cover with water. Let soak for at least 6 hours or overnight.

2. Rinse and replace the water in the pan, making sure there is twice as much water as kamut. Bring to a boil over high heat, then reduce heat to medium and cook until kamut is soft, about 1 hour. Drain and rinse under cold water to cool kamut. Drain well. Set aside to cool completely.

3. In a large bowl, combine cooled kamut, green onions, carrot, red pepper, cucumber, parsley, olives, lemon juice, olive oil, oregano, and salt and pepper to taste. Sprinkle with crumbled feta.

> **SERVING IDEA:** Serve with grilled chicken, mixed greens and a glass of milk for a satisfying lunch or dinner.

Diabetes Food Choice Values Per Serving	
1	Carbohydrate
1½	Fats

NUTRIENTS Per Serving		
Calories: 152	Carbohydrate: 19.9 g	Calcium: 64 mg
Fat: 6.3 g	Fiber: 5.0 g	Iron: 1.2 mg
Sodium: 146 mg	Protein: 4.6 g	
High in: Dietary fiber and vitamin C		

Mediterranean Lentil and Rice Salad

**MAKES
10 SERVINGS**

Eileen Campbell

This salad travels well, making it a great lunchbox choice. It can work on its own or be served with veggie sticks.

TIPS
For 3 cups (750 mL) cooked brown rice, cook 1 cup (250 mL) rice with 2 cups (500 mL) water.

If you serve this as a main course instead of as a side salad, it serves 6.

This salad keeps well for up to 1 week in the refrigerator.

Planned Extras
Use to stuff pitas or whole wheat wraps for lunchboxes or another dinner.

• Preparation time: 10 minutes

2	roasted red bell peppers, patted dry and julienned	2
1	can (19 oz/540 mL) lentils, drained and rinsed	1
3 cups	cooked brown rice	750 mL
1 cup	chopped fresh Italian (flat-leaf) parsley	250 mL
½ cup	thinly sliced green onions	125 mL
¼ cup	slivered dried apricots	50 mL

Dressing

¼ cup	olive oil	50 mL
2 tbsp	freshly squeezed lemon juice	25 mL
2 tbsp	balsamic vinegar	25 mL
1 tsp	liquid honey	5 mL
1 tsp	ground cumin	5 mL
½ tsp	ground coriander	2 mL
	Salt and freshly ground black pepper	

1. In a large bowl, combine red peppers, lentils, rice, parsley, green onions and apricots.
2. *Prepare the dressing:* In a small bowl, whisk together olive oil, lemon juice, vinegar, honey, cumin, coriander, and salt and pepper to taste.
3. Pour dressing over salad and toss to coat.

✓ **KID APPROVED**

SERVING IDEA: Add a glass of milk and an apple to create a healthy lunch.

NUTRIENTS Per Serving		
Calories: 182	Carbohydrate: 27.0 g	Calcium: 31 mg
Fat: 6.2 g	Fiber: 3.4 g	Iron: 2.4 mg
Sodium: 138 mg	Protein: 5.7 g	

Very high in: Vitamin C and folate • **High in:** Iron and magnesium • **A source of:** Dietary fiber

Diabetes Food Choice Values Per Serving	
1½	Carbohydrates
1	Fat

Rory Hornstein,
Dietitian, AB

The sweet flavor of mango in this main-course salad is a favorite of Rory's son and was well liked by all of our taste-testers, young and old.

TIPS

The longer the chicken marinates, the better it tastes! Marinate overnight, and it will be ready the next day for a fast lunch or dinner.

One medium lime will yield 1 to 2 tbsp (15 to 25 mL) juice.

Toast pine nuts or almonds in a dry skillet over medium heat, shaking occasionally, until lightly browned, about 5 minutes.

Sticky Mango Chicken Salad

- **Preparation time: 15 minutes / Marinating time: 1 hour / Cooking time: 9 minutes**
- *Baking sheet, greased*

Marinade

2 tbsp	mango chutney	25 mL
1 tbsp	packed dark brown sugar	15 mL
2 tsp	freshly squeezed lime juice	10 mL
1 tsp	reduced-sodium soy sauce	5 mL
	Freshly ground black pepper	
2	boneless skinless chicken breasts (about 8 oz/250 g), cut into strips	2

Dressing

3 tbsp	vegetable oil	45 mL
1 tbsp	balsamic vinegar	15 mL
1 tsp	granulated sugar	5 mL
	Salt and freshly ground black pepper	

Salad

1/2	large mango, peeled, pitted and chopped (or 3/4 cup/175 mL frozen mango pieces, thawed)	1/2
6 cups	packed baby spinach	1.5 L
1/3 cup	dried cranberries (or your favorite dried fruit)	75 mL
1 1/2 tbsp	toasted pine nuts or slivered almonds (optional)	22 mL

1. *Prepare the marinade:* In a medium bowl, combine chutney, brown sugar, lime juice, soy sauce and pepper to taste.
2. Add chicken strips to marinade and toss to coat. Cover and refrigerate for at least 1 hour or overnight, tossing occasionally. Preheat broiler.
3. Remove chicken from marinade and discard marinade. Place chicken on prepared baking sheet.

4. Broil chicken for 6 minutes. Turn and broil for about 3 minutes or until chicken is turning golden and is no longer pink inside.

5. *Meanwhile, prepare the dressing:* In a small bowl, whisk together oil, vinegar, sugar, and salt and pepper to taste.

6. *Assemble the salad:* In a large bowl, combine mango, spinach, cranberries and half of the pine nuts (if using). Pour in dressing and toss to coat.

7. Make a bed of salad on each of 4 plates and top with chicken. Sprinkle with the remaining pine nuts (if using).

 **KID APPROVED**

> **SERVING IDEA:** Serve for lunch with a whole-grain roll and a glass of milk.

Mangoes

If you'll be using the mango right away, be sure to buy a ripe one. Mangoes are ripe when they can be easily indented with your thumb. Avoid mangoes that are so ripe they feel mushy.

Mangoes have large, flat stones in the middle. It is a little tricky to remove the fruit, but if you follow these simple instructions, the task should be easier: Make an initial cut about ½ inch (1 cm) from the center and cut off a long slice of mango. Do the same on the other side. For each of these pieces, use a sharp knife to score the flesh in long lines, first lengthwise, then crossways, cutting almost through to the skin to create small cubes. Using a spoon, scoop cubes from skin. Peel the stone section, remove any flesh from the outside edges and cut into cubes.

NUTRIENTS Per Serving		
Calories: 266	Carbohydrate: 25.7 g	Calcium: 56 mg
Fat: 11.6 g	Fiber: 2.2 g	Iron: 1.7 mg
Sodium: 220 mg	Protein: 16.7 g	
Very high in: Vitamin A, niacin and folate • **High in:** Vitamin C, vitamin B$_6$ and magnesium • **A source of:** Dietary fiber		

Diabetes Food Choice Values Per Serving	
1½	Carbohydrates
2	Meat & Alternatives
1	Fat

Jerk Chicken Salad

Chriss Polson, BC

This meal-sized salad adjusts easily to make more or less. Add more cayenne pepper if you like a spicy kick! The chicken, beans and corn can all be prepared the evening before, which makes this quick and easy.

TIP

If you prefer, you can grill the chicken rather than stir-frying.

• *Preparation time: 30 minutes / Marinating time: 1 hour / Cooking time: 25 minutes*

Marinade/Dressing

¾ cup	lightly packed brown sugar	175 mL
½ cup	raspberry vinegar	125 mL
½ cup	water	125 mL
3 tbsp	ground allspice	45 mL
½ tsp	cayenne pepper (or to taste)	2 mL
	Salt and freshly ground black pepper	
4	boneless skinless chicken breasts (about 1 lb/500 g), cut into strips	4
½ cup	frozen corn kernels, thawed	125 mL
½ cup	canned black beans or kidney beans, drained and rinsed	125 mL
1	head romaine lettuce (small to medium), washed and torn (or 8 cups/2 L lettuce mix of your choice)	1
1	carrot, sliced	1
½ cup	sliced cucumber	125 mL
½ cup	sliced bell pepper (any color)	125 mL

1. *Prepare the marinade/dressing:* In a large bowl, combine brown sugar, vinegar, water, allspice, cayenne, and salt and pepper to taste.

2. Place chicken in a shallow dish and pour in half of the marinade/dressing. Cover and refrigerate for at least 1 hour or overnight.

3. Add corn and beans to the remaining marinade/dressing. Cover and refrigerate for at least 1 hour or overnight.

4. Remove chicken from marinade and discard marinade. Working in small batches, stir-fry chicken for 5 to 6 minutes or until no longer pink inside. Don't crowd the pan, or the chicken will steam instead of browning.

5. To the corn-bean mixture, add romaine, carrot, cucumber and bell pepper; toss to coat vegetables with dressing.

6. Make a bed of salad on each of 4 plates and top with chicken.

✓ KID APPROVED

Black Beans

Popular in Mexican cooking, black beans are served in burritos, enchiladas and as refried beans. Add chilled cooked beans to salads; they are especially good with fresh corn, chopped tomato, and cilantro.

SERVING IDEA:
Serve with brown and wild rice or a multigrain roll. Add a glass of milk to cover all the food groups.

NUTRIENTS Per Serving		
Calories: 353	Carbohydrate: 50.1 g	Calcium: 116 mg
Fat: 2.9 g	Fiber: 6.1 g	Iron: 3.3 mg
Sodium: 187 mg	Protein: 34.6 g	

Very high in: Dietary fiber, vitamin A, vitamin C, niacin, vitamin B_6, folate and magnesium • **High in:** Iron, thiamine, riboflavin, vitamin B_{12} and zinc

Diabetes Food Choice Values Per Serving	
2½	Carbohydrates
3	Meat & Alternatives

Edamame Salad

MAKES 6 SERVINGS

Eileen Campbell

Edamame, or fresh soybeans, have become very popular recently. This simple but tasty dish is great on its own or as part of a composed salad plate for lunch or dinner.

TIPS

To cook edamame, add 2 cups (500 mL) to ½ cup (125 mL) boiling water. Reduce heat, cover and simmer for 4 minutes. Drain well.

If you buy the beans still in the pod, have your children help shell them. It's even okay if they eat a few along the way — they are full of dietary fiber and taste delicious!

This salad will keep for up to 3 days in the refrigerator.

• Preparation time: 5 minutes / Chilling time: 1 hour

1	red bell pepper, diced	1
2 cups	cooked edamame beans (removed from pods)	500 mL
2 cups	cooked corn kernels	500 mL
⅓ cup	Asian Vinaigrette (page 136)	75 mL

1. In a large bowl, combine red pepper, edamame, corn and vinaigrette. Cover and refrigerate for at least 1 hour to allow flavors to meld.

✓ **KID APPROVED**

SERVING IDEA: Make a composed salad plate by adding Vegetable Quinoa Salad (page 153). Garnish with toasted sesame seeds.

Edamame

Edamame is the Japanese word for fresh green soybeans. To retain their freshness and natural flavor, they are parboiled and quick-frozen. In East Asia, the soybean has been used for over 2,000 years as a major source of protein. Edamame is consumed as a snack and a vegetable dish, used in soups and processed into sweets. As a snack, the pods are lightly boiled in salted water, then the seeds are squeezed directly from the pods into the mouth, using the fingers. Be careful not to eat the pods!

Diabetes Food Choice Values Per Serving	
1	Carbohydrate
1	Meat & Alternatives

NUTRIENTS Per Serving		
Calories: 147	Carbohydrate: 19.0 g	Calcium: 92 mg
Fat: 5.4 g	Fiber: 3.9 g	Iron: 1.0 mg
Sodium: 60 mg	Protein: 9.1 g	

Very high in: Vitamin C and folate • **High in:** Thiamine, niacin and magnesium • **A source of:** Dietary fiber

Chicken in Butter Sauce (page 172)

Thai Turkey Stir-Fry (page 178)

Vegetable Stir-Fry with Beef (page 185)

African Beef Stew (page 187)

Deconstructed Sushi

• Preparation time: 10 minutes

2	cans (each 7 ½ oz/240 g) crabmeat, drained (or imitation crab)	2
1	large carrot, peeled and grated	1
1	English cucumber (unpeeled), cut in 4 lengthwise and chopped	1
1	avocado, peeled and cubed	1
4 cups	cooked short-grain white rice	1 L
¼ cup	chopped drained pink pickled ginger	50 mL
2	sheets nori (dried seaweed)	2
⅓ cup	bottled Thai red curry sauce or Szechwan sauce	75 mL
	Finely chopped green onion, wasabi, sesame seeds and soy sauce (optional)	

1. In a large bowl, combine crabmeat, carrot, cucumber, avocado, rice and ginger.
2. Using kitchen scissors, cut nori into small strips or squares. Add to crabmeat mixture. Pour in Thai curry sauce and toss to coat. If desired, garnish with green onion and sesame seeds. Serve with soy sauce and wasabi (if using) on the side.

✓ **KID APPROVED**

SERVING IDEA: This pairs well with a cup of iced, milky Chai or green tea.

Patricia Chuey, Dietitian, BC

This meal offers all the flavor of sushi, with far less work. Leftovers, if any, make a quick lunch the next day.

TIPS
Look for pickled ginger, nori and wasabi in Asian markets. If you can't find them, you can omit them; the salad will still be good.

For the Thai red curry sauce, we used Sharwood's, a coconut milk–based sauce. Make sure not to buy curry paste.

NUTRIENTS Per Serving		
Calories: 232	Carbohydrate: 38 g	Calcium: 31 mg
Fat: 5.9 g	Fiber: 3.2 g	Iron: 1.4 mg
Sodium: 173 mg	Protein: 7.2 g	

Very high in: Vitamin A • **High in:** Folate
A source of: Dietary fiber

Diabetes Food Choice Values Per Serving	
2	Carbohydrates
½	Meat & Alternatives
½	Fat

Chicken and Turkey

Poultry is one of the best sources of complete protein because, once the skin is removed, it is a very lean meat. Chicken and turkey are also extremely versatile, and can be used in everything from appetizers and soups to sandwiches, casseroles and entrées.

Garam Masala

This traditional spice blend from Northern India usually combines ground cumin, coriander, cardamom, black peppercorns, cloves, bay leaf and cinnamon. The mixture is often added near the end of the cooking time or as a garnish. If you cannot find it locally, create your own with this simple recipe:

1	2-inch (5 cm) cinnamon stick, broken	1
¼	whole nutmeg	¼
1 tbsp	cardamom seeds	15 mL
1 tsp	cumin seeds	5 mL
1 tsp	whole cloves	5 mL
1 tsp	black peppercorns	5 mL

Place all spices in a clean coffee grinder and grind for about 40 seconds or until spices are fully ground. Store at room temperature in an airtight jar for up to 3 months. Try garam masala in our Chicken in Butter Sauce (page 172).

stir-frying

This cooking method is a good one for healthy meal preparation, as only a little bit of oil (1 tbsp/15 mL) is required. You can include lots of vegetables, with your choice of protein, and serve over brown rice or whole wheat pasta. Here are some ideas for the ingredients and amounts needed to make four hearty stir-fry servings:

- **Protein:** 1 lb (500 g) thin strips of chicken breast, turkey, lean beef or pork; 1 lb (500 g) shrimp or scallops; 2 cups (500 mL) tofu or legumes
- **Vegetables:** 6 cups (1.5 L) thinly cut veggies — always include onions, then choose from mushrooms, carrots, cauliflower, broccoli, bell peppers, spinach, zucchini, yellow squash, snow peas, sugar snap peas, green peas, corn, cabbage, parsnips
- **Sauce:** ¾ to 1 cup (175 to 250 mL) homemade or commercial stir-fry sauce (look for those with lower sodium content), or combine ¼ cup (50 mL) sauce with ½ to ¾ cups (125 to 175 mL) broth or water
- **Seasonings:** minced garlic, grated gingerroot, chopped fresh herbs, chopped chili peppers (seeded for less heat), hot pepper sauce (for more seasoning ideas, check out "Add Taste, not Fat or Salt" on page 39)
- **Garnish:** Sesame seeds, chopped fresh herbs, crispy noodles

Recipes such as Stir-Fried Chicken with Mango and Cashews (page 170) or Thai Turkey Stir-Fry (page 178) will give you a good idea of the techniques involved in putting a stir-fry together.

Don't Contaminate, Use Another Plate

When you're barbecuing meat or poultry, pay extra attention to food safety. To avoid cross-contamination, don't place cooked meat on the plate you used to carry it to the barbecue when it was raw. Always take a clean platter out to the barbecue. Be sure, as well, to clean all the utensils, such as forks, spatulas and tongs you used to handle the raw meat if you intend to use them on the cooked product. If your meat has been marinated, discard any leftover marinade (because it was exposed to raw meat, it may contain contaminants).

Skewer Savvy

If you're using wooden skewers when barbecuing, soak them in water first for 10 to 30 minutes. This ensures they won't burn on the grill.

Eileen Campbell

A roast chicken that is crispy on the outside and juicy on the inside is hard to beat.

TIP

Using a V-shaped rack is an excellent and healthy way to roast chicken. The open cavity of the chicken is placed over the rack, allowing the chicken to roast upright. If you don't have a V-shaped rack, you can just place the chicken in the roasting pan. However, the overall result is better with the rack — the chicken skin crisps all around, and any excess fat drips off into the pan.

VARIATIONS

Try other seasoning combinations for this roast chicken. Make it international by using Marrakech Rub (page 181), tandoori paste or a mixture of hoisin and chili sauces.

For a one-dish meal, add cubed root vegetables, such as sweet potatoes, carrots, potatoes and turnips, around the chicken for the last hour of cooking. For the last 10 minutes of cooking, add apple or pear slices.

Lemon-Thyme Roast Chicken

• **Preparation time: 10 minutes / Cooking time: 1³/₄ to 2¹/₄ hours**

• *Roasting pan with V-shaped rack*

1	whole roasting chicken (5 to 6 lbs/2.5 to 3 kg)	1
4	cloves garlic, minced	4
¼ cup	olive oil	50 mL
2 tbsp	chopped fresh thyme	25 mL
1 tsp	freshly ground black pepper	5 mL
	Grated zest and juice of 1 lemon	
	Salt	

1. Prepare chicken by trimming excess fat from body or cavity. Rinse inside and out under cold running water and pat dry.

2. In a bowl large enough to hold the chicken, whisk together garlic, olive oil, thyme, pepper, lemon zest, lemon juice and salt to taste. Place chicken in bowl and turn to coat completely, inside and out. Cover and refrigerate for at least 1 hour or overnight. Preheat oven to 450°F (230°C) and remove top rack.

3. Place chicken on rack in roasting pan and baste with marinade. Roast for 15 to 20 minutes. Reduce heat to 375°F (190°C) and roast for 1¹/₂ to 2 hours (depending on the size of the chicken) or until skin is dark golden and crispy, drumsticks wiggle when touched, and a meat thermometer inserted into the thickest part of a thigh registers 185°F (85°C). Remove from oven and let rest, tented with foil, for 10 to 15 minutes before carving. (This allows the juices to redistribute and provides a much moister chicken.)

✓ **KID APPROVED**

SERVING IDEA: For a great Sunday dinner, add Oven-Roasted Lemon Potatoes (page 269) and steamed broccoli.

Diabetes Food Choice Values Per Serving	
3	Meat & Alternatives

NUTRIENTS Per Serving		
Calories: 231	Carbohydrate: 1.1 g	Calcium: 14 mg
Fat: 14.5 g	Fiber: 0.2 g	Iron: 1.0 mg
Sodium: 74 mg	Protein: 23.5 g	

Very high in: Niacin and vitamin B₆ • **High in:** Zinc

Marrakech Chicken

MAKES 4 SERVINGS

Eileen Campbell

- *Preparation time: 15 to 20 minutes / Marinating time: 1 hour / Cooking time: 1¼ hours*
- *13- by 9-inch (3 L) baking dish, lightly greased / Baking sheet*

2	bone-in chicken leg quarters	2
2	bone-in chicken breasts	2
2 tbsp	Marrakech Rub (page 181)	25 mL
2	onions, chopped	2
2	large tomatoes, chopped	2
1	green bell pepper, diced	1
½ cup	dried fruit (raisins, apricots, cranberries, prunes)	125 mL
½ cup	pitted olives (green or black)	125 mL
3 cups	Tomato Master Sauce (page 232) or commercial pasta sauce	750 mL

1. Remove skin from chicken pieces and trim fat. Cut leg quarters at joint into thigh and drumsticks. Place all chicken pieces in prepared baking dish and rub with Marrakech Rub, coating evenly. Cover and refrigerate for 1 hour or overnight. Preheat oven to 375°F (190°C).

2. Place onions, tomatoes, green pepper, dried fruit and olives over and around chicken pieces in baking dish. Pour tomato sauce over chicken and vegetables. Cover dish with foil and place on baking sheet.

3. Bake for 45 minutes. Remove from oven, remove foil and make sure chicken is well covered with sauce. Return to oven, uncovered, and bake for about 30 minutes or until juices run clear when chicken is pierced and chicken reaches an internal temperature of 170°F (77°C).

 FREEZER FRIENDLY

> **SERVING IDEA:** For a Moroccan-themed dinner, serve with Couscous with Currants and Carrots (page 273).

This saucy dish has flavors reminiscent of North Africa.

TIPS
If you prefer, you can use all legs or all breasts instead of 2 of each. But keep in mind that the nutritional analysis will change, and the fat will increase if you use legs only.

If your family does not like olives, just leave them out.

Choose a dried fruit that everyone likes.

This recipe makes 4 generous servings. For smaller appetites, you could get 6 servings out of it. This will lower the calories and nutrients in each serving.

Planned Extras
This recipe makes more sauce than you really need. Freeze the leftover sauce for up to 3 months and use to top pasta another day.

NUTRIENTS Per Serving		
Calories: 348	Carbohydrate: 34.9 g	Calcium: 90 mg
Fat: 9.9 g	Fiber: 5.4 g	Iron: 3.4 mg
Sodium: 752 mg	Protein: 32.5 g	

Very high in: Vitamin C, niacin, vitamin B$_6$, magnesium and zinc • **High in:** Dietary fiber, vitamin A, iron, thiamine, riboflavin, folate and vitamin B$_{12}$

Diabetes Food Choice Values Per Serving	
1½	Carbohydrates
3	Meat & Alternatives

Judy Jenkins, Dietitian, NS

This simple grilled chicken can be enhanced with any of the great salsas or dips in this book.

TIP
Broiler Method: After removing chicken from marinade, place in a lightly greased 9-inch (2.5 L) square baking pan and pour in marinade. Broil, turning once, for 5 to 6 minutes per side or until chicken is no longer pink inside and has reached an internal temperature of 170°F (77°C).

Planned Extras
Extra cooked chicken is always useful to add a quick protein boost to salads, stir-fries and soups.

Grilled Garlic-Ginger Chicken Breasts

• *Preparation time: 5 minutes / Marinating time: 10 minutes / Cooking time: 6 to 10 minutes*

2 tbsp	freshly squeezed lemon juice	25 mL
2 tsp	minced garlic	10 mL
2 tsp	minced gingerroot	10 mL
2 tsp	olive oil	10 mL
1 tsp	ground cumin	5 mL
4	boneless skinless chicken breasts (1 lb/500 g total)	4
	Freshly ground black pepper	

1. In a shallow dish, whisk together lemon juice, garlic, ginger, olive oil and cumin. Add chicken and turn to coat. Let stand at room temperature for 10 minutes, or cover and refrigerate for up to 4 hours. Preheat barbecue to medium.

2. Remove chicken from marinade and discard marinade. Place chicken on barbecue and cook, turning once, for 3 to 5 minutes per side or until chicken is no longer pink inside and has reached an internal temperature of 170°F (77°C). Season to taste with pepper.

 ❄ **FREEZER FRIENDLY**

SERVING IDEA: Serve with Stir-Fried Chinese Greens (page 259) and Basmati Rice Pulau (page 275) for a yummy and healthy dinner.

Diabetes Food Choice Values Per Serving	
3	Meat & Alternatives

NUTRIENTS Per Serving		
Calories: 145	Carbohydrate: 1.2 g	Calcium: 11 mg
Fat: 3.4 g	Fiber: 0.1 g	Iron: 0.8 mg
Sodium: 61 mg	Protein: 26.0 g	
Very high in: Niacin and vitamin B_6		

Easy Salsa Chicken

• *Preparation time: 2 minutes / Cooking time: 25 minutes*

Vicky Guitar, NB

1 tbsp	vegetable oil	15 mL
4	boneless skinless chicken breasts (1 lb/500 g total)	4
Pinch	salt	Pinch
Pinch	freshly ground black pepper	Pinch
1½ cups	salsa	375 mL
1 cup	shredded nacho cheese blend	250 mL

When you're short on time and need a quick dinner the whole family will enjoy, serve this easy Mexican dish with green peas and leftover brown rice.

TIP
This dish can also be cooked in a 350°F (180°C) oven for 20 to 30 minutes; you can broil it for 5 minutes at the end to melt the cheese.

1. In a large skillet, heat oil over medium-high heat. Brown chicken breasts on both sides until lightly browned on the outside but still pink inside. Season chicken with salt and pepper and add salsa. Reduce heat and simmer for about 15 minutes or until chicken is no longer pink inside and has reached an internal temperature of 170°F (77°C). Sprinkle each chicken breast with cheese and cook for 5 minutes or until cheese is melted.

✓ KID APPROVED

SERVING IDEA: For a Mexican-themed dinner, serve with brown rice (cooked with vegetable juice instead of just water) and corn kernels. Finish the meal with Dessert Nachos (page 300).

NUTRIENTS Per Serving		
Calories: 309	Carbohydrate: 7.2 g	Calcium: 222 mg
Fat: 14.3 g	Fiber: 1.6 g	Iron: 1.1 mg
Sodium: 864 mg	Protein: 38.5 g	

Very high in: Niacin and vitamin B_6 • **High in:** Calcium, vitamin B_{12}, magnesium and zinc

Diabetes Food Choice Values Per Serving	
4	Meat & Alternatives

Eileen Campbell

The traditional version of Chicken Maryland combines fried chicken with corn fritters, batter-fried bananas and grilled pineapple rings. This lightened-up version combines the same ingredients, but in a much healthier way. It's always a crowd pleaser, and small children love it.

TIPS

If children don't like the herbs, they can easily be left out.

This recipe makes 4 generous servings. For smaller appetites, serve half a chicken breast per person. This will lower the calories and nutrients in each serving.

SERVING IDEA:
Serve with a large tossed green salad or crisp steamed broccoli and Sweet Corn Fritters (page 267).

Oven-Baked Chicken Maryland

• **Preparation time: 10 minutes / Cooking time: 20 to 30 minutes**
• *Preheat oven to 350°F (180°C)*
• *Baking sheet, greased*

4	boneless skinless chicken breasts (1 lb/500 g total)	4
2	large bananas, halved crosswise	2
1	egg, beaten	1
½ cup	milk	125 mL
1 cup	cornmeal	250 mL
1 tsp	salt	5 mL
1 tsp	freshly ground black pepper	5 mL
1 tbsp	dried Italian herb seasoning	15 mL
	Vegetable cooking spray	
2	pineapple rings (fresh or canned), halved	2

1. Place chicken breasts on a large cutting board and cover with plastic wrap. Flatten breasts with a kitchen mallet to create very thin cutlets. Roll one banana half tightly inside each chicken cutlet. Secure with toothpicks.

2. In a shallow dish, combine egg and milk. In another shallow dish, combine cornmeal, salt, pepper and herbs.

3. Dip each rolled-up cutlet in egg mixture, then into cornmeal mixture, coating well. Place on baking sheet with pineapple ring halves. Spray chicken lightly with vegetable cooking spray. Discard any excess egg and cornmeal mixtures.

4. Bake in preheated oven for 20 to 30 minutes or until chicken is golden brown, no longer pink inside and has reached an internal temperature of 170°F (77°C).

5. Remove toothpicks, cut each cutlet in half diagonally and serve with pineapple on top or on the side.

✓ **KID APPROVED**

Diabetes Food Choice Values Per Serving	
2	Carbohydrates
3	Meat & Alternatives

NUTRIENTS Per Serving		
Calories: 311	Carbohydrate: 32.3 g	Calcium: 51 mg
Fat: 4.5 g	Fiber: 2.8 g	Iron: 1.4 mg
Sodium: 382 mg	Protein: 34.6 g	

Very high in: Niacin, vitamin B$_6$ and magnesium • **High in:** Riboflavin, folate, vitamin B$_{12}$ and zinc • **A source of:** Dietary fiber

Chicken Stuffed with Mushrooms and Cheese

MAKES 6 TO 12 SERVINGS

Nadine Day, Dietitian, ON

- **Preparation time: 10 minutes / Cooking time: 1 hour**
- Preheat oven to 350°F (180°C)
- Baking sheet
- 11- by 7-inch (2 L) glass baking dish

5	portobello mushrooms, stems and gills removed	5
6 tbsp	olive oil, divided	90 mL
	Salt and freshly ground black pepper	
2	cloves garlic, minced	2
8 oz	soft goat cheese, crumbled	250 g
1 tbsp	chopped fresh thyme	15 mL
6	boneless skinless chicken breasts (1½ lbs/750 g total)	6

1. Place mushrooms on baking sheet and drizzle with 3 tbsp (45 mL) of the olive oil. Season to taste with salt and pepper. Bake in preheated oven for 15 minutes or until soft. Let cool and finely chop.

2. In a small bowl, combine roasted mushrooms, garlic, goat cheese and thyme.

3. Cut chicken breasts horizontally from the side, cutting about 80% through. Open them like you are opening a book. Divide mushroom filling evenly among chicken breasts. Close breasts over filling and secure with toothpicks.

4. In a large skillet, heat the remaining olive oil over medium heat. Cook filled chicken on both sides until outside is lightly crisped. Transfer to baking dish.

5. Bake in preheated oven for 40 minutes or until chicken is no longer pink inside and has reached an internal temperature of 170°F (77°C).

6. Remove toothpicks and slice each breast into 2 pieces on the bias.

This dish is perfect for a special dinner, but easy enough that you can make it on a weeknight.

TIP
This recipe makes 6 to 12 servings. For smaller appetites, serve half a chicken breast per person. The nutrient analysis below is based on the smaller portion. If serving a full chicken breast, the nutrients will be double.

VARIATIONS
If your family doesn't like mushrooms or goat cheese, replace the filling with roasted red bell pepper strips and ricotta cheese mixed with some dried basil.

Another delicious filling is sliced mango and roasted red bell pepper with cream cheese.

NUTRIENTS Per Serving		
Calories: 202	Carbohydrate: 3.7 g	Calcium: 36 mg
Fat: 11.8 g	Fiber: 1.0 g	Iron: 1.1 mg
Sodium: 108 mg	Protein: 20.3 g	

Very high in: Riboflavin and niacin • **A source of:** Vitamin B_6

Diabetes Food Choice Values Per Serving	
2½	Meat & Alternatives
1	Fat

Stir-Fried Chicken with Mango and Cashews

Eileen Campbell

If you love the sweet taste of mangoes with chicken, you will love this dish. It's easy to make on a weeknight if you do all the prep work the day before.

TIP
Adults will love the spicy taste from the red chili pepper. If the rest of the family doesn't like heat, take their portions out first, then add the chili at the end.

VARIATIONS
This recipe is not very saucy. If you want to add sauce, combine 1 cup (250 mL) chicken stock with 1 tbsp (15 mL) cornstarch. Add to the finished dish and heat to thicken. Taste and adjust seasoning with salt and pepper.

Fresh or canned pineapple chunks can replace the mango.

• *Preparation time: 15 minutes / Cooking time: 35 minutes*

2 tbsp	vegetable oil, divided	25 mL
1½ lbs	boneless skinless chicken breasts, cut into thin strips	750 g
2	red bell peppers, julienned	2
1	onion, peeled and sliced lengthwise into thick wedges	1
1	small fresh red chili pepper, seeded and finely chopped (optional)	1
2 tbsp	fish sauce	25 mL
2 tsp	reduced-sodium soy sauce	10 mL
1 tsp	granulated sugar	5 mL
2 cups	diced fresh or frozen mango, thawed	500 mL
½ cup	unsalted dry-roasted cashew pieces	125 mL
	Salt and freshly ground black pepper	

1. Heat a wok or large skillet over medium heat. Add 1 tbsp (15 mL) of the oil and swirl to coat the surface. When oil is hot but not smoking, add chicken in batches and stir-fry until it turns white and is almost cooked through, about 3 minutes. Remove each batch to a plate until all the chicken is cooked. Set aside.

2. Add the remaining oil, then the red peppers, onion and chili pepper to the wok; stir-fry for 1 minute. Stir in fish sauce, soy sauce and sugar. Add chicken, mango and cashews; stir-fry for 10 to 15 minutes or until chicken is no longer pink inside. Season to taste with salt and pepper.

✓ **KID APPROVED**

SERVING IDEA: Serve over basmati or jasmine rice or whole wheat rotini. If desired, start the meal with snow peas and carrot sticks with ranch dip.

Diabetes Food Choice Values Per Serving
½ Carbohydrate
2½ Meat & Alternatives

NUTRIENTS Per Serving		
Calories: 219	Carbohydrate: 13.9 g	Calcium: 20 mg
Fat: 8.9 g	Fiber: 1.6 g	Iron: 1.1 mg
Sodium: 443 mg	Protein: 21.5 g	

Very high in: Vitamin C, niacin, vitamin B_6 and magnesium

Chicken Parmesan Strips

- **Preparation time: 15 minutes / Marinating time: 15 minutes to 4 hours / Cooking time: 20 minutes**
- *Baking sheet, greased*

1 lb	boneless skinless chicken breasts, cut into strips	500 g
½ cup	skim milk	125 mL
⅓ cup	dry bread crumbs or corn flakes cereal, finely crushed	75 mL
3 tbsp	freshly grated Parmesan cheese	45 mL
2 tsp	dried parsley	10 mL
¼ tsp	freshly ground black pepper	1 mL
	Salt	

1. Place chicken in a shallow dish and pour in milk. Cover and refrigerate for at least 15 minutes or for up to 4 hours. Preheat oven to 375°F (190°C).

2. In another shallow dish, combine bread crumbs, Parmesan, parsley and pepper. Remove chicken strips from milk and dip in crumb mixture, coating well. Place on prepared baking sheet. Discard any excess milk and crumb mixture.

3. Bake for 20 minutes or until chicken is no longer pink inside.

❄ **FREEZER FRIENDLY**

✓ **KID APPROVED**

> **SERVING IDEA:** For a completely kid-friendly meal, serve with Oven-Baked Potato Wedges (page 271) and Fruity Slaw (page 147). They'll go nuts over Pink Strawberry Wiggles (page 325) for dessert.

Patsy Turple, NB

Kids will love this simple chicken dish. Offer Sweet-and-Sour Sauce (page 110) on the side for a special treat.

VARIATIONS
Add other dried herbs, such as thyme, basil or oregano.

Replace some of the bread crumbs with ground flaxseed.

NUTRIENTS Per Serving		
Calories: 191	Carbohydrate: 8.0 g	Calcium: 106 mg
Fat: 3.7 g	Fiber: 0.5 g	Iron: 1.2 mg
Sodium: 211 mg	Protein: 29.6 g	

Very high in: Niacin and vitamin B_6 • **High in:** Vitamin B_{12} and magnesium

Diabetes Food Choice Values Per Serving	
½	Carbohydrate
3	Meat & Alternatives

Chicken in Butter Sauce

Eileen Campbell

Indian Butter Chicken is a favorite the world over. The traditional recipe is very high in fat, with lots of butter and whipping cream. We have reduced the fat content without losing any of the flavor. The ingredient list looks long, but the recipe is really quite simple and is worth the effort.

TIPS

Tandoori paste is available in the ethnic food aisle of most supermarkets, usually on the shelf with Indian sauces.

One medium lemon will yield about 3 tbsp (45 mL) juice.

• **Preparation time: 15 minutes / Marinating time: 1 hour / Cooking time: 35 to 40 minutes**
• *11- by 7-inch (2 L) baking pan*

3 tbsp	tandoori paste (see tip, at left)	45 mL
2 tbsp	freshly squeezed lemon juice	25 mL
2 tbsp	low-fat plain yogurt	25 mL
1 1/2 lbs	boneless skinless chicken breasts, cut into 1-inch (2.5 cm) chunks	750 g

Sauce

1/4 cup	tomato paste	50 mL
1/2 cup	water	125 mL
1	1-inch (2.5 cm) cube gingerroot, very finely grated	1
1	fresh green chili pepper, seeded and finely chopped	1
4 tsp	freshly squeezed lemon juice	20 mL
1 tbsp	chopped fresh cilantro	15 mL
1 tsp	ground cumin	5 mL
1 tsp	garam masala (store-bought or see recipe, page 162)	5 mL
3/4 tsp	salt	4 mL
1/4 tsp	granulated sugar	1 mL
1/4 tsp	chili powder	1 mL
1 tbsp	unsalted butter	15 mL
1 cup	half-and-half (10%) cream	250 mL

1. In a large bowl, combine tandoori paste, lemon juice and yogurt. Add chicken and stir well to coat. Cover and refrigerate for at least 1 hour or overnight. Preheat oven to 350°F (180°C).

2. Arrange chicken in a single layer in baking pan and pour in marinade. Bake for 20 to 25 minutes or until no longer pink inside.

3. *Meanwhile, prepare the sauce:* In a small bowl, combine tomato paste and water. Stir in ginger, chili pepper, lemon juice, cilantro, cumin, garam masala, salt, sugar and chili powder.

4. In a large saucepan, melt butter over medium heat. Stir in sauce and bring to a simmer. Add cooked chicken and any juice from the baking pan; simmer for about 10 minutes to combine flavors. Add cream and cook for 3 minutes to heat through (do not boil).

❄️ **FREEZER FRIENDLY**

> **SERVING IDEAS:** Serve over steamed basmati rice, garnished with chopped fresh cilantro. Accompany with steamed green beans or asparagus.
>
> For an Indian-themed dinner party, serve with Basmati Rice Pulau (page 275), green beans and Mango Lassi (page 85).

Gingerroot

Use the side of a spoon to scrape off the skin before chopping or grating. Gingerroot keeps well in the freezer for up to 3 months and can be grated from frozen.

TIP
Themed dinners are a great way to explore new cultural foods. Consider an Indian-themed party (see menu, at left) and have everyone come dressed in cultural attire!

NUTRIENTS Per Serving		
Calories: 175	Carbohydrate: 4.6 g	Calcium: 53 mg
Fat: 6.2 g	Fiber: 0.5 g	Iron: 0.9 mg
Sodium: 460 mg	Protein: 24.3 g	
Very high in: Niacin and vitamin B$_6$		

Diabetes Food Choice Values Per Serving	
3	Meat & Alternatives

Fusion Chicken

Tina Profiri, ON

Tina's family wanted a dish that incorporated the tastes of many different cultures, and this is what they created. The use of mild curry powder makes it delicate and delicious. It tastes even better the second day!

TIP

If desired, once you've ladled Fusion Chicken onto plates, top each portion with a dollop of non-fat plain yogurt and sprinkle with chopped fresh cilantro.

VARIATIONS

For a vegetarian version, replace the chicken breast with chickpeas and the chicken broth with vegetable broth.

If you prefer, replace half of the chicken breasts with boneless skinless chicken thighs.

SERVING IDEA:
Serve over basmati rice with steamed cauliflower and Greek Kamut Salad (page 154).

• Preparation time: 20 minutes / Cooking time: 25 to 30 minutes

3 tbsp	all-purpose flour	45 mL
1 tsp	salt	5 mL
1/2 tsp	ancho or regular chili powder	2 mL
1 lb	boneless skinless chicken breasts, cut into small cubes	500 g
2 tbsp	vegetable oil (approx.)	25 mL
1 tbsp	mild curry powder	15 mL
4	shallots, sliced	4
2	cloves garlic, minced	2
1	red bell pepper, finely chopped	1
1 1/4 cups	reduced-sodium chicken broth	300 mL
1/3 cup	golden raisins	75 mL
2 tbsp	tomato paste	25 mL
1 tbsp	freshly squeezed lime juice	15 mL

1. In a large plastic bag, combine flour, salt and chili powder; add chicken and shake to coat.
2. In a large skillet, heat oil over medium-high heat. Add chicken, discarding excess flour. Brown chicken on all sides. Add curry powder and toss to coat chicken; cook for 1 minute or until chicken is no longer pink inside. Remove chicken to a plate and set aside.
3. In the same skillet, sauté shallots and garlic, adding oil if necessary, for 2 minutes. Stir in red pepper, broth, raisins, tomato paste and lime juice. Return chicken to skillet; reduce heat and simmer for 15 to 20 minutes or until chicken is heated through and sauce has thickened.

❄ FREEZER FRIENDLY
✓ KID APPROVED

Diabetes Food Choice Values Per Serving	
1/2	Carbohydrate
3	Meat & Alternatives

NUTRIENTS Per Serving		
Calories: 202	Carbohydrate: 14.1 g	Calcium: 24 mg
Fat: 6.3 g	Fiber: 1.5 g	Iron: 1.4 mg
Sodium: 568 mg	Protein: 22.3 g	

Very high in: Vitamin C, niacin and vitamin B$_6$
High in: Magnesium

Spicy Orange Chicken

• *Preparation time: 15 minutes / Cooking time: 1 hour*

4 lbs	skinless bone-in chicken breasts and thighs	2 kg
¼ cup	all-purpose flour	50 mL
1 tbsp	olive oil	15 mL
3	cloves garlic, crushed	3
1 cup	orange juice	250 mL
2 tbsp	packed brown sugar	25 mL
2 tbsp	white vinegar	25 mL
1 tsp	dried basil	5 mL
1 tsp	salt	5 mL
¾ tsp	ground nutmeg	4 mL
	Freshly ground black pepper	

Jessie Kear, Dietitian, ON

This 1970s recipe, originally called "Irene's Spicy Chicken," was part of a recipe exchange between students in Montreal. Jessie has spiced it up and reduced the fat to satisfy the more adventurous palate and the healthy lifestyle of the 21st century. It smells wonderful while it's cooking, and the taste is fantastic!

TIP
For a thicker sauce, remove the cover for the last 10 minutes of cooking.

1. Cut chicken breasts in half. Place all chicken pieces in a large plastic bowl with a cover and sprinkle with flour. Cover and shake chicken until well coated. Discard extra flour.

2. In a large saucepan, heat olive oil over medium heat. Brown chicken on all sides. (Do not overheat, as this will cause the flour to blacken.)

3. In a small bowl, whisk together garlic, orange juice, brown sugar, vinegar, basil, salt, nutmeg and pepper until sugar is dissolved.

4. Pour sauce over chicken in saucepan; reduce heat, cover tightly and simmer, stirring occasionally, for about 50 minutes or until chicken is no longer pink inside and sauce has thickened slightly.

❄️ **FREEZER FRIENDLY**
✓ **KID APPROVED**

SERVING IDEA: Serve with quinoa and a bright green vegetable, such as broccoli or spinach.

NUTRIENTS Per Serving		
Calories: 260	Carbohydrate: 9.7 g	Calcium: 25 mg
Fat: 7.5 g	Fiber: 0.3 g	Iron: 1.6 mg
Sodium: 409 mg	Protein: 36.4 g	

Very high in: Niacin, vitamin B_6 and zinc
High in: Riboflavin, vitamin B_{12} and magnesium

Diabetes Food Choice Values Per Serving	
½	Carbohydrate
4	Meat & Alternatives

Maureen Falkiner,
Dietitian, BC

*This unusual dish is
like Thanksgiving
dinner in a casserole.
Our taste panel
absolutely loved it.*

Cranberry Chicken Bake

• *Preparation time: 10 minutes / Cooking time: 50 minutes*
• *Preheat oven to 350°F (180°C)*
• *8-inch (2 L) square baking pan, lightly greased*

1	package (4 oz /125 g) stuffing mix	1
	Vegetable cooking spray	
1	onion, chopped	1
3	eggs	3
1½ cups	diced cooked chicken or turkey	375 mL
1½ cups	ricotta cheese	375 mL
	Salt and freshly ground black pepper	
1 cup	whole-berry cranberry sauce	250 mL

1. Prepare stuffing mix according to package directions and spread on bottom of prepared pan.

2. Heat a small skillet over medium heat. Spray with vegetable cooking spray. Sauté onion until softened, about 5 minutes.

3. In a large bowl, combine sautéed onion, eggs, chicken, ricotta, and salt and pepper to taste. Pour over stuffing.

4. Bake in preheated oven for 45 minutes or until egg mixture is firm and a tester inserted in the center comes out clean.

5. While still hot, stir cranberry sauce and spread over top. Serve hot or cold.

✓ KID APPROVED

SERVING IDEA: In keeping with the Thanksgiving theme, add steamed green beans and a slice of Pumpkin Spice Nut Bread (page 283) for dessert.

Diabetes Food Choice Values Per Serving	
2	Carbohydrates
3	Meat & Alternatives

NUTRIENTS Per Serving		
Calories: 367	Carbohydrate: 32.3 g	Calcium: 160 mg
Fat: 15.9 g	Fiber: 0.7 g	Iron: 1.6 mg
Sodium: 433 mg	Protein: 23.7 g	

Very high in: Niacin • **High in:** Vitamin A, calcium, riboflavin, vitamin B$_6$, folate, vitamin B$_{12}$ and zinc

Cranberry Chicken Chili

• *Preparation time: 15 minutes / Cooking time: 50 minutes*

1 tbsp	vegetable oil	15 mL
3	stalks celery, chopped	3
2	cloves garlic, chopped	2
1	large onion, chopped	1
8 oz	mushrooms, sliced	250 g
1	large green bell pepper, chopped	1
1½ lbs	lean ground chicken or turkey	750 g
2	bay leaves	2
2 tbsp	chili powder	25 mL
1 tbsp	chopped fresh parsley	15 mL
1 tsp	hot pepper flakes	5 mL
1	can (19 oz/540 mL) stewed tomatoes, chopped or mashed	1
1	can (19 oz/540 mL) dark red kidney beans, drained and rinsed	1
½ cup	vegetable juice (optional)	125 mL
1 cup	fresh or frozen cranberries	250 mL

Judy Jenkins, Dietitian, NS

This is a great recipe for a crowd, and a nice change from beef chili. The cranberries and green peppers float, making a colorful presentation that's perfect for the festive season.

TIPS

If you cannot find fresh or frozen cranberries, use dried ones for a sweeter taste. We did this for the recipe test, and the results were outstanding.

Instead of dirtying a cutting board or food processor, use kitchen scissors or a knife to chop canned tomatoes right in the can.

The longer you cook this dish, the more the flavor develops. However, be careful not to cook it so long that the beans disintegrate.

1. Heat a large saucepan over medium heat. Add oil and swirl to coat pan. Sauté celery, garlic, onion, mushrooms and half the green pepper until tender. Remove vegetables to a plate.

2. Add chicken to saucepan and brown, breaking up with a spoon, until no longer pink. Drain off any fat and return to saucepan. Stir in sautéed vegetables, bay leaves, chili powder, parsley and hot pepper flakes; cook for 5 minutes. Add tomatoes; cook for 5 minutes. Stir in beans, being careful not to break them. Dilute mixture with vegetable juice if too thick. Reduce heat and simmer for 30 minutes (or longer — see tip, at right), adding vegetable juice if necessary.

3. Add cranberries and remaining green pepper just before serving.

SERVING IDEA:
Serve with a multigrain roll and fruit salad for a satisfying meal.

❄ FREEZER FRIENDLY
✓ KID APPROVED

NUTRIENTS Per Serving

Calories: 175	Carbohydrate: 4.6 g	Calcium: 53 mg
Fat: 6.2 g	Fiber: 0.5 g	Iron: 0.9 mg
Sodium: 460 mg	Protein: 24.3 g	

Very high in: Niacin and vitamin B_6

Diabetes Food Choice Values Per Serving

½	Carbohydrate
2	Meat & Alternatives
1	Fat

Amélie Roy-Fleming and Marie-Eve Richard, Nutrition Students, QC

This recipe is a great introduction to Thai cuisine. It's not too spicy, so it appeals to all ages, making it a great way for parents to introduce new foods and cultures to their family.

Thai Turkey Stir-Fry

• *Preparation time: 15 minutes / Cooking time: 25 minutes*

1 tbsp	vegetable oil	15 mL
2	cloves garlic, finely chopped	2
1	2-inch (5 cm) piece gingerroot, grated	1
1 lb	boneless skinless turkey breast, cut into strips	500 g
1	head bok choy (about 1 lb/500 g), chopped	1
1	red bell pepper, julienned	1
½ cup	light coconut milk	125 mL
1 tsp	grated lime zest	5 mL
2 tbsp	freshly squeezed lime juice	25 mL
1 tbsp	reduced-sodium soy sauce	15 mL
1 tsp	red curry paste	5 mL
	Salt and freshly ground black pepper	
2 tsp	chopped fresh cilantro	10 mL

1. Heat a wok or large skillet over medium-high heat. Add oil and swirl to coat wok. Sauté garlic, ginger and turkey for about 10 minutes or until turkey is lightly browned on the outside and no longer pink inside. Add bok choy and red pepper; sauté for 4 minutes. Stir in coconut milk, lime zest, lime juice, soy sauce and curry paste; bring to a boil. Reduce heat and simmer for 10 minutes or until sauce has thickened slightly. Season to taste with salt and pepper.

2. Ladle onto plates and garnish with cilantro.

✓ **KID APPROVED**

> **SERVING IDEA:** Serve over jasmine rice or whole wheat pasta. Finish the meal with tropical fruits, such as mango, pineapple and papaya.

Diabetes Food Choice Values Per Serving

3	Meat & Alternatives

NUTRIENTS Per Serving		
Calories: 227	Carbohydrate: 10.0 g	Calcium: 234 mg
Fat: 8.0 g	Fiber: 3.0 g	Iron: 3.8 mg
Sodium: 315 mg	Protein: 29.7 g	

Very high in: Vitamin A, vitamin C, iron, niacin, vitamin B$_6$, folate, magnesium and zinc • **High in:** Calcium, riboflavin and vitamin B$_{12}$ • **A source of:** Dietary fiber

Turkey Apple Meatloaf

- *Preparation time: 15 minutes / Cooking time: 45 to 60 minutes*
- *Preheat oven to 350°F (180°C)*
- *9- by 5-inch (2 L) loaf pan, lightly greased*

2	cloves garlic, minced	2
1	egg	1
1	tart apple, such as Mutsu or Granny Smith, finely chopped	1
1 lb	lean ground turkey	500 g
½ cup	chopped onion	125 mL
⅓ cup	oat bran	75 mL
⅓ cup	ground flaxseed	75 mL
3 tbsp	prepared yellow mustard	45 mL
1 tbsp	ketchup	15 mL
1 tsp	salt	5 mL

1. In a large bowl, combine garlic, egg, apple, turkey, onion, oat bran, flaxseed, mustard, ketchup and salt. Pack into prepared loaf pan.
2. Bake in preheated oven for 45 to 60 minutes or until a meat thermometer inserted in the center registers an internal temperature of 175°F (80°C).

❄️ FREEZER FRIENDLY
✓ KID APPROVED

> **SERVING IDEA:** Serve with Lightened-Up Scalloped Potatoes (page 270) and Simple Stir-Fried Kale (page 260).

Gillian Proctor, Dietitian, AB

This recipe is a good one for kids to help make. They will enjoy adding ingredients to the bowl and patting down the loaf in the pan. (Just make sure they wash their hands before and after!)

Ground turkey is lean and pairs well with the tartness of apple.

VARIATION
Turkey Apple Burgers: This mixture can also be used to make burgers, which can be cooked on a barbecue or grill or in the oven. They're excellent served on a whole wheat bun with sliced tomato and a spoonful of low-fat cucumber dressing.

Planned Extras
Make extra turkey mixture and form into burger patties. After cooking, freeze in freezer bags for quick healthy lunches. Reheat burgers in the microwave on High for about 1 minute.

An extra meatloaf can be sliced to use in sandwiches or frozen for another day.

NUTRIENTS Per Serving		
Calories: 197	Carbohydrate: 11.4 g	Calcium: 51 mg
Fat: 10.3 g	Fiber: 3.2 g	Iron: 1.9 mg
Sodium: 583 mg	Protein: 16.9 g	

Very high in: Niacin • **High in:** Vitamin B6, magnesium and zinc • **A source of:** Dietary fiber

Diabetes Food Choice Values Per Serving	
½	Carbohydrate
2	Meat & Alternatives

Beef, Pork and Lamb

Beef, pork and lamb are among the best sources of vitamin B$_{12}$, high-quality protein, iron and zinc. Because these are animal sources, they also contain cholesterol and saturated fat. The best way to get great nutrition from these meats is to choose lean cuts and watch your portion sizes.

Iron Boosters

Iron in food comes in two forms: **heme iron** from animal sources, which is well absorbed by the body; and **non-heme iron**, mainly from plant sources, which is not as well absorbed. The best sources of heme iron include clams, oysters, beef, poultry, pork, veal, lamb and fish. Non-heme iron is found in eggs, legumes such as white beans, soybeans, lentils, chickpeas, sesame seeds, dried apricots, nuts, bread, oatmeal, wheat germ, canned beets, canned pumpkin, dried raisins, baked potato, prune juice and blackstrap molasses. Some products, such as breakfast cereals, tofu, egg noodles and pasta, are enriched with iron.

You can improve your absorption of non-heme iron by eating heme-iron foods such as meat and fish in combination with plant-based non-heme-iron foods such as pasta (for example, add chicken to pasta salad). Vitamin C also increases iron absorption, so eat non-heme iron foods along with those rich in vitamin C. For example, add tomatoes to your bean salad or top breakfast cereal with strawberries and accompany with a glass of orange juice.

rubs and marinades

Rubs and marinades are a great way to add flavor to meat, fish and poultry, with little or no fat and salt.

Dry rubs

A rub is usually a mixture of fresh or dried herbs and spices, sometimes with a little oil, crushed garlic or mustard added. It is rubbed onto the surface of meat, fish and poultry. Rubs are recommended for meats that require only a short cooking time. After applying a dry rub, refrigerate the food for at least 1 hour or for up to 8 hours to let it absorb the flavors.

Marinades

Marinades enhance flavor and keep meat tender. They often contain acid ingredients, such as citrus juice or vinegar, which have a slight tenderizing effect on small cuts of meat that are moderately tender, such as chicken pieces, chops and steaks. When making marinades, don't add salt, as it draws moisture out, causing meat to be dry.

To use a marinade, place meat in a baking dish or a resealable plastic bag, add the marinade and turn to coat evenly. Cover or seal and refrigerate for the length of time indicated in your chosen recipe. Brush or scrape off excess marinade before cooking, particularly if it contains herbs or other aromatics that burn easily, and pat dry. Discard leftover marinade.

Big-Batch Marrakech Rub for Chicken, Pork or Lamb

Mix up a batch of this zesty rub and keep it for days when you want to make Marrakech Chicken (page 165) or Roast Lamb with Marrakech Rub (page 197). It's also great for seasoning vegetables for roasting or meats for grilling.

Makes ³⁄₄ cup (175 mL)

¼ cup	paprika	50 mL
2 tbsp	ground coriander	25 mL
2 tbsp	ground cumin	25 mL
2 tbsp	ground cinnamon	25 mL
1 tbsp	cayenne pepper	15 mL
1 tbsp	ground allspice	15 mL
1 tsp	ground ginger	5 mL
1 tsp	ground cloves	5 mL

Combine all ingredients and store in a covered container for up to 6 months.

Eileen Campbell

This is an ideal meal for entertaining because it can be prepared ahead of time and placed in the slow cooker earlier in the day to be ready for your company at night. The steak is so tender that even small children, who do not usually like to chew meat, will enjoy it.

Planned Extras

Use leftover meat to make delicious sandwiches for another meal.

Slow-Cooked Chili Flank Steak or Brisket

- **Preparation time: 20 minutes / Cooking time: 20 minutes / Slow cooker time: 6 to 8 hours**

- *Slow cooker*

2 lbs	flank steak or beef brisket	1 kg
½ tsp	freshly ground black pepper	2 mL
1 tbsp	vegetable oil	15 mL
3	stalks celery, with leaves, cut into chunks and leaves chopped	3
2	cloves garlic, minced	2
1	onion, cut into chunks	1
1 cup	reduced-sodium beef broth	250 mL
1	can (19 oz/540 mL) chili-flavored or regular stewed tomatoes, with juice (about 2⅓ cups/575 mL)	1
1	large carrot, cut into chunks	1
1	bay leaf	1
½ tsp	dried thyme	2 mL
2 tsp	chili powder	10 mL

1. Cut beef into large pieces that will comfortably fit in your slow cooker. Season with pepper.
2. In a large skillet, heat oil over medium-high heat. Cook beef for 3 to 4 minutes per side or until browned on all sides. Transfer beef to slow cooker.
3. In the fat remaining in the skillet, sauté celery (including leaves), garlic and onion until lightly browned, about 5 minutes. Add to slow cooker.

4. Add stock to skillet and scrape up any brown bits from the bottom. Pour liquid into slow cooker.

5. To the slow cooker, add tomatoes and juice, carrot, bay leaf, thyme and chili powder; stir to combine. Cover and cook on Low for 6 to 8 hours or until beef is fork-tender. Discard bay leaf.

6. Slice beef across the grain and arrange on a platter. Skim fat from sauce, pour over meat and serve.

❄ FREEZER FRIENDLY
✓ KID APPROVED

SERVING IDEA: Serve with Spinach Spaghettini (page 272) and steamed green beans for a tasty and easy dinner.

Timing Is Everything

Every meal needs planning to ensure that everything is ready at the same time. Try to balance your recipe choices to combine dishes that can cook unattended on the stove, in the oven or in the microwave with those that require last-minute attention. A good menu balance could include a slow-cooked meat dish and rice, along with a salad and quick-cooking vegetables.

Break the menu into steps and make a preparation plan. For example, if you need diced onions or chopped garlic for several recipes, do all the chopping at once and measure out the amount for each.

You can also prepare in advance any items that will hold well overnight. Some ingredients — such as grains, legumes, pasta and sauces, salsas and dips — can be cooked in quantity and used throughout the week for quick meal additions. These healthy additions will be lifesavers on days when you're pressed for time.

Planned Extras
Use leftover sauce to create a tasty beef and vegetable soup. Add the trimmings from the meat, some chopped fresh (or leftover) vegetables, such as carrot, celery, potato, sweet potato, cabbage or peppers, and enough extra liquid or beef stock to create a soupy mixture. Heat on high, then reduce heat and simmer for 30 minutes or until vegetables are just tender.

NUTRIENTS Per Serving		
Calories: 256	Carbohydrate: 8.2 g	Calcium: 71 mg
Fat: 12.1 g	Fiber: 2.2 g	Iron: 3.1 mg
Sodium: 619 mg	Protein: 26.4 g	

Very high in: Vitamin A, niacin, vitamin B_{12} and zinc
High in: Iron and vitamin B_6 • **A source of:** Dietary fiber

Diabetes Food Choice Values Per Serving	
3	Meat & Alternatives

This easy beef dish needs to be marinated ahead of time, but it cooks quickly and tastes delicious.

TIP

Kimchee (pickled spiced cabbage), a traditional Korean accompaniment, is usually served on the side. If you have an Asian market in your area, look for jars of kimchee where condiments are displayed.

Planned Extras

Marinate and cook extra meat. Let cool, slice and store in the fridge for a fast topper for an entrée salad.

Bulgogi – Korean Barbecued Beef

• *Preparation time: 10 minutes / Marinating time: 30 minutes / Cooking time: 4 to 6 minutes*

1 lb	thin-cut sirloin steak	500 g
4	green onions, finely chopped	4
2	cloves garlic, crushed	2
1 tbsp	finely grated gingerroot	15 mL
1/4 cup	reduced-sodium soy sauce	50 mL
1/4 cup	liquid honey	50 mL
1 tbsp	sesame seeds	15 mL
1 tbsp	sesame oil	15 mL

1. Pierce steaks with a fork to allow marinade to penetrate.

2. In a large sealable plastic bag, combine green onions, garlic, ginger, soy sauce, honey, sesame seeds and sesame oil. Add steak, seal bag and toss to coat. Refrigerate for at least 30 minutes or for up to 4 hours. Preheat barbecue or grill to medium-high.

3. Remove steak from marinade and discard marinade. Place steak on barbecue or grill and cook for 2 to 3 minutes per side or until desired doneness. Remove steak to a plate and tent with foil. Let rest for 5 minutes, then slice across the grain into strips.

SERVING IDEA: Serve over rice with stir-fried vegetables or in a flour tortilla with stir-fried vegetables. To keep with the Asian theme, serve wedges of fresh Asian pear or lychees for dessert.

Diabetes Food Choice Values Per Serving	
1	Carbohydrate
3	Meat & Alternatives

NUTRIENTS Per Serving		
Calories: 262	Carbohydrate: 22.0 g	Calcium: 34 mg
Fat: 9.5 g	Fiber: 1.0 g	Iron: 3.1 mg
Sodium: 577 mg	Protein: 22.8 g	

Very high in: Niacin, vitamin B_{12} and zinc
High in: Iron, riboflavin, vitamin B_6 and magnesium

Vegetable Stir-Fry with Beef

MAKES 4 SERVINGS

General Mills

You don't need to spend time chopping vegetables for this recipe, so it's great when you need a quick meal. If you buy the beef precut, the prep time will be even less.

• *Preparation time: 10 minutes / Cooking time: 15 minutes*

Sauce

1/2 cup	water	125 mL
2 tbsp	soy sauce	25 mL
1 tbsp	liquid honey	15 mL
1 tsp	cornstarch	5 mL
3/4 tsp	ground ginger	4 mL
1/2 tsp	garlic powder	2 mL
1/4 tsp	freshly ground black pepper	1 mL
1 tbsp	vegetable oil	15 mL
1 lb	top sirloin beef, cut into thin strips	500 g
1	package (1 lb/500 g) frozen vegetables (Japanese or California mix)	1
2 tbsp	water	25 mL
1	can (14 oz/398 mL) baby corn, drained and rinsed (optional)	1

1. *Prepare the sauce:* In a small bowl, combine water, soy sauce, honey, cornstarch, ginger, garlic powder and pepper.

2. Heat a wok or large skillet over medium-high heat. Add oil and swirl to coat wok. Stir-fry beef for 3 to 4 minutes or until browned on all sides. Remove to a plate.

3. Add frozen vegetables and water to wok. Cover and cook, stirring frequently, for about 8 minutes or until hot and tender-crisp. Add beef, sauce and baby corn (if using). Cook, stirring constantly, until sauce is thickened and bubbling and beef is fork-tender, about 3 minutes.

SERVING IDEA: Serve over hot cooked rice, couscous or pasta.

NUTRIENTS Per Serving		
Calories: 249	Carbohydrate: 17.2 g	Calcium: 68 mg
Fat: 7.8 g	Fiber: 4.2 g	Iron: 3.3 mg
Sodium: 588 mg	Protein: 26.9 g	

Very high in: Niacin, vitamin B_{12} and zinc • **High in:** Dietary fiber, vitamin A, vitamin C, iron, riboflavin and vitamin B_6

Diabetes Food Choice Values Per Serving	
1/2	Carbohydrate
3	Meat & Alternatives

Beef Stroganoff

The Campbell Company of Canada

On a busy weeknight, it's always great to have a simple recipe, like this one, that requires little prep and only one pan to clean.

VARIATIONS
Use different types of mushrooms to vary the look and flavor.

If you like a spicier dish, add hot pepper sauce or more pepper.

• *Preparation time: 10 minutes / Cooking time: 35 minutes*

	Vegetable cooking spray	
12 oz	boneless sirloin grilling steak, cut into strips	375 g
1	large onion, sliced	1
¾ cup	sliced mushrooms	175 mL
3 cups	reduced-sodium beef broth	750 mL
1	can (10 oz/284 mL) condensed low-fat cream of mushroom soup, undiluted	1
2½ cups	fusilli pasta or spiral egg noodles	625 mL
1 cup	frozen peas	250 mL
1 tbsp	Worcestershire sauce	15 mL
¼ tsp	freshly ground black pepper	1 mL
¾ cup	light sour cream or plain yogurt	175 mL

1. Heat a large saucepan over medium-high heat. Spray with vegetable cooking spray. Working in batches, stir-fry beef for 3 to 4 minutes or until browned on all sides. Remove beef to a large bowl as each batch is completed.

2. Reduce heat to medium and add onion and mushrooms to saucepan; cook for 3 minutes or until lightly colored. Stir into beef.

3. In the same saucepan, combine broth and soup; bring to a boil. Add fusilli; bring back to a gentle boil and cook, stirring often, until fusilli is al dente (tender to the bite), about 12 minutes. Stir in peas, Worcestershire sauce and pepper; reduce heat and simmer for 3 minutes. Stir in beef mixture and sour cream; cook for about 5 minutes or until heated through.

Diabetes Food Choice Values Per Serving	
3	Carbohydrates
3	Meat & Alternatives

NUTRIENTS Per Serving		
Calories: 447	Carbohydrate: 59.7 g	Calcium: 150 mg
Fat: 8.1 g	Fiber: 4.8 g	Iron: 5.0 mg
Sodium: 1002 mg	Protein: 32.6 g	

Very high in: Iron, thiamine, riboflavin, niacin, folate, vitamin B_{12} and zinc • **High in:** Dietary fiber, vitamin B_6 and magnesium

African Beef Stew

MAKES 6 SERVINGS

Claude Gamache,
Dietitian, QC

- *Preparation time: 10 minutes / Cooking time: 3 hours*
- *Preheat oven to 350°F (180°C)*
- *12-cup (3 L) Dutch oven or casserole dish with cover*

2 lbs	lean stew beef, cubed	1 kg
5	stalks celery, diced	5
2	onions, diced	2
1	green bell pepper, diced	1
1	red bell pepper, diced	1
1 cup	diced zucchini	250 mL
¼ cup	lightly packed brown sugar	50 mL
¼ cup	white vinegar or cider vinegar	50 mL
½ tsp	Worcestershire sauce	2 mL
	Hot pepper sauce	
	Salt and freshly ground black pepper	

This easy stew has a touch of sweetness and a splash of heat.

TIPS

Slow Cooker Method: Combine all ingredients in slow cooker. Cover and cook on Low for 6 to 8 hours or until beef is fork-tender.

If you prefer your vegetables sautéed in oil, add 1 tbsp (15 mL) vegetable oil to the saucepan and heat over medium heat before adding the vegetables. But keep in mind that doing this will affect the nutrient analysis, since you are adding fat to the recipe.

1. In Dutch oven, combine beef, celery, onions, green pepper, red pepper, zucchini, brown sugar, vinegar, Worcestershire sauce, hot pepper sauce to taste, and salt and pepper to taste.
2. Cook in preheated oven for 3 hours or until beef is fork-tender. Season to taste with hot pepper sauce, salt and pepper.

Planned Extras

Make extra stew and save it for another day. Top with biscuit dough for a simple pot pie.

○ **SLOW COOKER FRIENDLY**
❋ **FREEZER FRIENDLY**
✓ **KID APPROVED**

SERVING IDEA: Serve with mashed potatoes and a whole-grain roll. Complete the meal with frozen yogurt for dessert.

NUTRIENTS Per Serving		
Calories: 310	Carbohydrate: 17.6 g	Calcium: 45 mg
Fat: 10.9 g	Fiber: 1.7 g	Iron: 3.7 mg
Sodium: 130 mg	Protein: 34.6 g	

Very high in: Vitamin C, iron, niacin, vitamin B_6, vitamin B_{12} and zinc • **High in:** Riboflavin and magnesium

Diabetes Food Choice Values Per Serving	
½	Carbohydrate
4	Meat & Alternatives

Slow-Cooked Beef Stew

Eileen Campbell

Do all the preparation the night before and place this stew in the slow cooker before you go to work in the morning. When you come home on a cold winter evening, a delicious meal will be ready for you.

TIP

If you prefer, you could cook this on High for 4 to 5 hours instead.

SERVING IDEA:
Serve with egg noodles or Bannock (page 284) and a green salad for a complete and satisfying meal.

• **Preparation time: 15 minutes / Chilling time: 4 hours / Cooking time: 10 minutes / Slow cooker time: 8 to 10 hours**

• *Slow cooker*

1½ cups	dry red wine	375 mL
3 tbsp	vegetable oil, divided	45 mL
1	bay leaf	1
2 tsp	dried parsley	10 mL
1 tsp	dried thyme	5 mL
¼ tsp	freshly ground black pepper	1 mL
2 lbs	lean stew beef, cut into cubes	1 kg
⅓ cup	all-purpose flour	75 mL
1	large onion, chopped	1
2	cloves garlic, minced	2
2 cups	sliced mushrooms	500 mL
18	small white onions, thawed if frozen	18
1 cup	beef broth	250 mL
1 tbsp	tomato paste	15 mL

1. In a large bowl, whisk together wine, 1 tbsp (15 mL) of the oil, bay leaf, parsley, thyme and pepper. Stir in beef, coating evenly. Cover and refrigerate for at least 4 hours or overnight.

2. Drain beef, reserving 1 cup (250 mL) marinade. Place beef in slow cooker, sprinkle with flour and toss to coat.

3. In a small skillet, heat 1 tbsp (15 mL) of the oil over medium heat. Sauté chopped onion until lightly browned, about 5 minutes. Add garlic and sauté for a few seconds. Using a slotted spoon, transfer onions and garlic to slow cooker.

4. Add the remaining oil to skillet. Sauté mushrooms for 5 minutes or until they release their liquid. Using a slotted spoon, transfer mushrooms to slow cooker.

5. Add reserved marinade, small onions, beef broth and tomato paste to slow cooker; stir well. Cover and cook on Low for 8 to 10 hours or until beef is fork-tender.

❄ FREEZER FRIENDLY

Diabetes Food Choice Values Per Serving	
3	Meat & Alternatives
1	Fat

NUTRIENTS Per Serving		
Calories: 260	Carbohydrate: 8.7 g	Calcium: 23 mg
Fat: 12.6 g	Fiber: 1.0 g	Iron: 3.2 mg
Sodium: 188 mg	Protein: 26.8 g	

Very high in: Niacin, vitamin B_{12} and zinc
High in: Iron, riboflavin and vitamin B_6

Tasty Meatballs in Tomato Sauce

MAKES 6 SERVINGS

Eileen Campbell

Eileen's family has a tradition of making hedgehog meatballs using ground beef and white rice with canned tomato soup. This version adds carrots and uses brown rice and homemade tomato sauce for greater nutrition. Meatballs are always kid-approved.

• Preparation time: 10 minutes / Cooking time: 45 minutes

1	egg (or 2 egg whites), slightly beaten	1
1 lb	lean ground beef	500 g
2 cups	Tomato Master Sauce (page 232), divided	500 mL
½ cup	grated carrot	125 mL
¼ cup	finely chopped onion	50 mL
¼ cup	cooked brown rice	50 mL
½ tsp	salt	2 mL
¼ tsp	freshly ground black pepper	1 mL
	Vegetable cooking spray	
1 tbsp	chopped fresh parsley	15 mL

1. In a large bowl, combine egg, ground beef, ¼ cup (50 mL) of the tomato sauce, carrot, onion, rice, salt and pepper. With clean hands, shape into 18 meatballs.

2. Heat a large skillet over medium heat. Spray with vegetable cooking spray. Cook meatballs until browned on all sides, about 10 minutes. Spoon off any fat. Pour the remaining tomato sauce over meatballs and bring to a boil. Reduce heat, cover and simmer, stirring frequently, for 35 minutes or until meatballs are no longer pink inside.

3. Serve 3 meatballs per person and ladle sauce on top. Sprinkle with parsley.

❄ **FREEZER FRIENDLY**
✓ **KID APPROVED**

SERVING IDEA: Serve with mashed sweet potatoes and a green vegetable.

TIP
If you don't have time to make Tomato Master Sauce, and you don't have any stored in the freezer, you can use store-bought tomato sauce.

VARIATION
Substitute an equal amount of ground chicken or turkey for the beef.

Planned Extras
Extra meatballs, without sauce, always come in handy. Serve them another day with dipping sauce, over pasta or inside a whole wheat submarine bun for a completely different meal.

NUTRIENTS Per Serving		
Calories: 249	Carbohydrate: 10.9 g	Calcium: 44 mg
Fat: 12.7 g	Fiber: 1.4 g	Iron: 2.4 mg
Sodium: 390 mg	Protein: 17.3	

Very high in: Niacin, vitamin B_{12} and zinc
High in: Vitamin A, iron, riboflavin and magnesium

Diabetes Food Choice Values Per Serving	
½	Carbohydrate
2	Meat & Alternatives
1	Fat

Paul Carvalho and
Monica Braz, Dietitian,
ON

*Monica and her
husband love to create
recipes together. This
is one of their tasty
dishes.*

VARIATIONS

Substitute an equal
amount of ground pork
or turkey for the beef.

If you prefer not to add
wine, apple juice can be
substituted.

South African Curried Minced Meat

• *Preparation time: 10 minutes / Cooking time: 45 minutes*

1 tbsp	vegetable oil	15 mL
2	onions, chopped	2
1 lb	lean ground beef	500 g
2 tsp	minced garlic	10 mL
3 tbsp	curry powder	45 mL
1 1/2 cups	diced canned tomatoes, with juice	375 mL
1 cup	water	250 mL
1/2 cup	white wine (optional)	125 mL
1 tsp	Worcestershire sauce	5 mL
1	bay leaf	1
	Salt and freshly ground black pepper	

1. Heat a large saucepan over medium heat. Add oil and swirl to coat pan. Sauté onions, ground beef and garlic, breaking up beef, until beef is browned, about 10 minutes. Add curry powder and cook for 2 minutes. Add tomatoes and juice, water, wine (if using), Worcestershire sauce and bay leaf; bring to a boil. Reduce heat and simmer, uncovered, adding water if mixture becomes too dry, for 30 minutes or until meat is saucy but not too wet. Taste and adjust seasoning with salt and pepper. Discard bay leaf.

❄ **FREEZER FRIENDLY**

SERVING IDEA: Serve over brown rice, with steamed broccoli on the side.

Diabetes Food Choice Values Per Serving
1 1/2 Meat & Alternatives
1 Fat

NUTRIENTS Per Serving		
Calories: 176	Carbohydrate: 6.2 g	Calcium: 39 mg
Fat: 9.8 g	Fiber: 1.5 g	Iron: 2.2 mg
Sodium: 103 mg	Protein: 12.0 g	

Very high in: Niacin, vitamin B_{12} and zinc • **High in:** Iron

Orange Hoisin Pork

MAKES 4 SERVINGS

Eileen Campbell

Asian ingredients provide delicious flavor to a simple pork roast.

- **Preparation time: 10 minutes / Marinating time: 30 minutes / Cooking time: 25 to 30 minutes**
- *Shallow baking pan, lined with foil*

⅓ cup	plum sauce	75 mL
⅓ cup	hoisin sauce	75 mL
1 tbsp	grated gingerroot	15 mL
1 tbsp	grated orange zest	15 mL
1 tsp	hot pepper sauce (optional)	5 mL
1 lb	pork tenderloin	500 g
	Salt and freshly ground black pepper	

1. In a small bowl, combine plum sauce, hoisin sauce, ginger, orange zest and hot pepper sauce (if using).

2. Place tenderloin in prepared baking pan and season to taste with salt and pepper. Baste generously with sauce mixture, cover and refrigerate for 30 minutes to allow pork to absorb flavors. Meanwhile, place rack in top third of oven and preheat oven to 450°F (230°C).

3. Roast, uncovered, in preheated oven for 25 to 30 minutes or until just a hint of pink remains in pork and it has reached an internal temperature of 160°F (71°C). Remove from oven and let rest for 5 minutes before slicing.

✓ **KID APPROVED**

SERVING IDEA: This quick entrée is great with Stir-Fried Chinese Greens (page 259) and brown rice.

NUTRIENTS Per Serving		
Calories: 218	Carbohydrate: 15.9 g	Calcium: 15 mg
Fat: 4.0 g	Fiber: 0.7 g	Iron: 1.8 mg
Sodium: 411 mg	Protein: 28.0 g	

Very high in: Thiamine, riboflavin, niacin, vitamin B₁₂ and zinc • **High in:** Vitamin B₆

Diabetes Food Choice Values Per Serving	
1	Carbohydrate
3	Meat & Alternatives

Patti Thomson,
Dietitian, MB

*This savory one-dish
meal can be prepared
in advance and popped
in the oven when you
get home at night.*

SERVING IDEA:
Serve with a green salad,
your favorite raw veggies
or sliced fruit.

Baked Pork Chops with Vegetable Rice

• **Preparation time: 5 minutes / Cooking time: 55 to 60 minutes**
• *Preheat oven to 350°F (180°C)*
• *13- by 9-inch (3 L) baking dish with cover*

2 tsp	vegetable oil	10 mL
6	boneless pork loin chops, trimmed	6
1	onion, chopped	1
1	clove garlic, minced	1
1 cup	long-grain white rice	250 mL
1 tsp	curry powder	5 mL
1 tsp	ground cumin	5 mL
1 tsp	dried oregano	5 mL
2 cups	diced or sliced zucchini	500 mL
2 cups	chicken broth	500 mL
1 1/2 cups	chopped Roma (plum) tomatoes	375 mL
1 cup	diced bell pepper (red or yellow)	250 mL
1/2 tsp	salt	2 mL
1/4 tsp	freshly ground black pepper	1 mL
1	bay leaf	1

1. In a large skillet, heat oil over medium-high heat. Brown chops on both sides, about 4 minutes per side. Remove to a plate.

2. Add onion and garlic to skillet and sauté for about 5 minutes or until softened. Add rice, curry powder, cumin and oregano; stir to coat rice. Add zucchini, stock, tomatoes, bell pepper, salt, pepper and bay leaf; bring to a boil. Reduce heat, cover and simmer for 10 minutes. Transfer to baking dish.

3. Nestle pork chops into rice mixture in baking dish and pour any juices from meat over top.

4. Cover and bake in preheated oven for 30 to 35 minutes or until rice is tender, liquid is absorbed and just a hint of pink remains in pork and it has reached an internal temperature of 160°F (71°C). Discard bay leaf.

**Diabetes Food Choice
Values Per Serving**

1 1/2	Carbohydrates
3	Meat & Alternatives

NUTRIENTS Per Serving		
Calories: 337	Carbohydrate: 31.7 g	Calcium: 59 mg
Fat: 11.4 g	Fiber: 2.3 g	Iron: 1.9 mg
Sodium: 554 mg	Protein: 24.9 g	

Very high in: Vitamin C, thiamine, niacin, vitamin B$_6$ and zinc
High in: Vitamin A, riboflavin, vitamin B$_{12}$ and magnesium
A source of: Dietary fiber

Stuffed Roast Pork (page 194)

Moroccan Lamb Tagine (page 198)

Tandoori Haddock (page 204)

Italian Seafood Stew (page 209)

Big-Batch Mediterranean Bulgur Meatloaf

- **Preparation time: 15 minutes / Cooking time: 45 minutes**
- Preheat oven to 350°F (180°C)
- Two 9- by 5-inch (2 L) loaf pans, lightly greased

¾ cup	bulgur, washed and drained	175 mL
1½ cups	hot water	375 mL
2	eggs	2
1	onion, finely chopped	1
1 lb	lean ground pork	500 g
1 lb	ground chicken	500 g
¼ cup	finely chopped fresh parsley	50 mL
2 tbsp	freshly squeezed lemon juice	25 mL
2 tsp	ground cinnamon	10 mL
1 tsp	ground allspice	5 mL
1 tsp	paprika	5 mL
½ tsp	salt	2 mL
½ tsp	freshly ground black pepper	2 mL
	Olive oil	

1. Place bulgur in a large bowl and pour in hot water. Cover and let stand for 10 minutes or until most of the water is absorbed. Squeeze out excess water. Add eggs, onion, ground pork, ground chicken, parsley, lemon juice, cinnamon, allspice, paprika, salt and pepper; mix ingredients together, using very clean hands, and divide in half. Pack each half into a prepared loaf pan. Brush lightly with olive oil.

2. Bake in preheated oven for about 45 minutes or until a meat thermometer inserted in the center of a loaf registers an internal temperature of 175°F (80°C).

❄ FREEZER FRIENDLY
✓ KID APPROVED

Sidebar

MAKES 2 LOAVES OR 16 SERVINGS

Marketa Graham, Dietitian, ON

Cinnamon and bulgur give this meatloaf Mediterranean flair. It's great with Mint Yogurt Dip (page 105).

VARIATION
Substitute an equal amount of lean or extra-lean ground beef for the pork.

Planned Extras
Slice and freeze one meatloaf in a freezer bag. Save for busy evenings when there is no time to cook. Or, for a great lunch, defrost a slice, heat in the microwave and stuff into a pita with Mint Yogurt Dip (page 105), cucumber slices, tomato slices and lettuce or spinach.

SERVING IDEA:
Serve with Mint Yogurt Dip (page 105). Add Yummy Asparagus (page 256), or simply cook some frozen mixed vegetables. Finish with Toffee Bars (page 322) for dessert.

NUTRIENTS Per Serving		
Calories: 202	Carbohydrate: 8.4 g	Calcium: 19 mg
Fat: 11.2 g	Fiber: 1.4 g	Iron: 1.3 mg
Sodium: 152 mg	Protein: 16.5 g	

Very high in: Niacin • **High in:** Vitamin B$_{12}$ and zinc

Diabetes Food Choice Values Per Serving	
½	Carbohydrate
2	Meat & Alternatives

Stuffed Roast Pork

Judy Jenkins, Dietitian, NS

This was one of our taste panel's favorite recipes. It may look time-consuming, but it is easier than you think and is certainly worth the effort.

TIPS

If you would like to make a smaller amount, the recipe can be cut in half.

To save you time and effort, your butcher can butterfly the pork loin roast for you.

Toast almonds in a dry skillet over medium heat until lightly browned and fragrant, about 3 minutes.

> • *Preparation time: 20 minutes / Cooking time: 110 minutes / Resting time: 10 to 15 minutes*
> • *Preheat oven to 400°F (200°C)*
> • *Roasting pan with rack*

Stuffing

3	eggs, beaten	3
1	clove garlic, finely chopped	1
1 lb	spinach, cooked and chopped	500 g
12 oz	mild Italian sausage, casings removed	375 g
1 cup	slivered almonds, toasted (see tip, at left)	250 mL
½ cup	dry bread crumbs	125 mL
1 tbsp	chopped fresh parsley	15 mL
1 tbsp	dried French onion soup mix	15 mL
½ tsp	dried thyme	2 mL
Pinch	freshly ground black pepper	Pinch
3½ to 4 lb	boneless pork loin roast	1.75 to 2 kg
½	clove garlic, chopped	½
1 tsp	vegetable oil	5 mL
½ tsp	dried thyme	2 mL
1 cup	red currant jelly, melted	250 mL
	Additional red currant jelly	

1. *Prepare the stuffing:* In a large bowl, combine eggs, garlic, spinach, sausage, almonds, bread crumbs, parsley, onion soup mix, thyme and pepper. Set aside.

2. Place pork loin roast fat side down and, starting at the thickest edge, slice horizontally through the meat, stopping 1 inch (2.5 cm) from the other side of the roast, so that it will open like a book. Lightly pound the butterflied roast. Remove any fat thicker than ¼ inch (0.5 cm) from outside of roast.

3. Spread stuffing mixture evenly on cut side of roast. Starting at the long side, roll up jelly-roll style and tie securely with string. Place seam side down on rack in roasting pan. Combine garlic, oil and thyme and rub on roast.

4. Roast in preheated oven for 20 minutes. Reduce heat to 350°F (180°C) and roast for 70 minutes. Baste pork with red currant jelly and roast for about 20 minutes or until juices run clear when pork is pierced and it has reached an internal temperature of 160°F (71°C). Remove from oven and let rest, tented with foil, for 10 to 15 minutes before carving. (This allows the juices to redistribute and provides a much moister roast.)

5. Slice roast and serve with additional red currant jelly.

> **SERVING IDEA:** On the weekend, when you have time to go all out, serve with Ginger Carrots (page 257) and Lightened-up Scalloped Potatoes (page 270) or Oven-Roasted Lemon Potatoes (page 269). Finish with Lemon Blueberry Panna Cotta (page 299) for dessert.

Dry Bread Crumbs

You can purchase dry bread crumbs or make your own. To make ½ cup (125 mL) dry bread crumbs, crumble one slice of bread into a food processor or blender and pulse until crumbs are desired consistency. Spread crumbs in a single layer on a baking sheet and bake at 350°F (180°C), shaking pan frequently, for 6 to 8 minutes or until lightly browned, crisp and dry. (Or microwave, uncovered, on High for 1 to 2 minutes, stirring every 30 seconds.)

Planned Extras
Make the big batch and serve the remainder with Roasted Beet, Walnut and Arugula Salad (page 143) for another dinner or lunch.

NUTRIENTS Per Serving		
Calories: 319	Carbohydrate: 20.8 g	Calcium: 87 mg
Fat: 14.6 g	Fiber: 1.8 g	Iron: 2.6 mg
Sodium: 387 mg	Protein: 26.2 g	

Very high in: Vitamin A, thiamine, niacin, vitamin B_{12}, magnesium and zinc • **High in:** Iron, riboflavin, vitamin B_6 and folate

Diabetes Food Choice Values Per Serving	
1	Carbohydrate
3½	Meat & Alternatives

Murphy's Casserole

Eileen Campbell

This comfort food favorite never seems to go out of fashion. Our tasting panel ate it up quickly.

VARIATIONS

For a spicy twist, add ½ tsp (2 mL) curry powder to the flour and omit the chives and paprika.

Other soup and meat combinations also work: try cream of chicken with cooked diced chicken; cream of mushroom with sautéed mushrooms and the cooked protein of your choice; or cream of tomato with cooked ground beef. Create your own family favorite!

• **Preparation time: 10 minutes / Cooking time: 65 minutes**
• *Preheat oven to 375°F (190°C)*
• *11- by 7-inch (2 L) casserole dish with cover, greased*

2 tbsp	all-purpose flour	25 mL
1 tsp	chopped fresh parsley	5 mL
1 tsp	chopped fresh chives	5 mL
Pinch	freshly ground pepper	Pinch
4	large potatoes, peeled and sliced lengthwise into thin slices	4
2 cups	diced lean ham	500 mL
1	leek (white and light green parts only), thinly sliced	1
1 cup	thinly sliced onion	250 mL
1 cup	shredded Cheddar cheese	250 mL
1	can (10 oz/284 mL) condensed cream of celery soup, undiluted	1
	Paprika and fresh parsley	

1. In a small bowl, combine flour, parsley, chives and pepper.

2. In prepared casserole dish, layer half of the potatoes, all of the ham, leek and onion, and half of the flour mixture and cheese. Top with the other half of the potatoes and the remaining flour mixture. (Reserve the remaining cheese.) Combine soup with enough water to make 2 cups (500 mL) and pour evenly over casserole. Sprinkle to taste with paprika and parsley.

3. Cover and bake in preheated oven for 50 minutes. Uncover and add reserved cheese. Bake, uncovered, for 15 minutes or until cheese is lightly browned and center is hot. Let cool for 5 minutes.

 **✓ KID APPROVED**

SERVING IDEA: Serve with snow peas and your favorite dip or steamed green peas.

Diabetes Food Choice Values Per Serving

2	Carbohydrates
2	Meat & Alternatives

NUTRIENTS Per Serving

Calories: 273	Carbohydrate: 34.2 g	Calcium: 135 mg
Fat: 8.5 g	Fiber: 2.5 g	Iron: 1.3 mg
Sodium: 847 mg	Protein: 15.6 g	

Very high in: Thiamine, niacin and vitamin B$_6$ • **High in:** Vitamin B$_{12}$, magnesium and zinc • **A source of:** Dietary fiber

Roast Lamb with Marrakech Rub

MAKES 8 SERVINGS

Eileen Campbell

This simple roast with the flavors of Morocco is easy to prepare if you have a batch of Marrakech Rub (page 181) on hand. It's great served hot, but would also be good cold, with salad.

• *Preparation time: 5 minutes / Marinating time: 1 hour / Cooking time: 45 to 60 minutes*

• *Roasting pan with rack, lightly sprayed with vegetable cooking spray*

3 lb	boneless leg of lamb, trimmed	1.5 kg
2 tbsp	Marrakech Rub (page 181)	25 mL
2 cups	reduced-sodium chicken broth	500 mL
1 cup	sliced dried apricots	250 mL

1. Place lamb in a large container and rub with Marrakech Rub. Cover and refrigerate for at least 1 hour or overnight. Preheat oven to 375°F (190°C).

2. Place lamb on rack in roasting pan and roast for 25 minutes. Add 1 cup (250 mL) of the stock and the apricots to the drippings in the pan. Roast, adding more stock as the liquid evaporates, for 20 to 35 minutes or until lamb has reached an internal temperature of 150°F (65°C) for medium-rare, or until desired doneness. Remove to a plate and cover with foil. Let rest for 15 minutes before carving.

> **SERVING IDEA:** Serve with Bulgur Parsley Salad (page 152) and mashed sweet potatoes.

NUTRIENTS Per Serving		
Calories: 241	Carbohydrate: 11.8 g	Calcium: 28 mg
Fat: 7.7 g	Fiber: 1.8 g	Iron: 3.3 mg
Sodium: 201 mg	Protein: 30.7 g	

Very high in: Riboflavin, niacin, vitamin B$_{12}$ and zinc • **High in:** Iron

Diabetes Food Choice Values Per Serving	
½	Carbohydrate
4	Meat & Alternatives

Moroccan Lamb Tagine

Eileen Campbell

Tender lamb seasoned with Moroccan spices joins apricots, orange peel and tomatoes in this classic North African dish. Tagine *refers to gently simmered meat, fish or vegetable dishes that have a sweet and savory flavor. It is also the name of the earthenware dish with a conical lid that this type of stew is typically prepared in. The adults on our taste panel loved this one.*

VARIATIONS

Midway through the cooking process, you could add cooked chickpeas or diced sweet potato or butternut squash. Just before serving, orange segments, slivered almonds and chopped fresh cilantro would be authentic additions.

The recipe also works well with bone-in chicken, diced pork or stew beef. If using chicken, reduce the simmering time to 30 to 45 minutes or until chicken is fork-tender.

- **Preparation time: 20 minutes / Cooking time: 2 hours, 25 minutes**
- *Dutch oven*

2 tbsp	olive oil, divided	25 mL
2 lbs	boneless leg of lamb, trimmed and cut into cubes	1 kg
4	cloves garlic, chopped	4
1	large onion, chopped	1
1 tbsp	ground cumin	15 mL
1 tbsp	ground coriander	15 mL
1 tbsp	paprika	15 mL
1 tbsp	ground ginger	15 mL
1/2 tsp	freshly ground black pepper	2 mL
3	large strips orange peel	3
1	cinnamon stick	1
1	can (28 oz/796 mL) diced tomatoes, with juice	1
1 cup	reduced-sodium chicken broth	250 mL
1 cup	dried apricots	250 mL

1. In Dutch oven, heat 1 tbsp (15 mL) of the olive oil over medium heat. Add half of the lamb and cook until browned on all sides, about 8 minutes. Remove to a plate. Add the remaining oil to the pan and cook the remaining lamb. Add to plate.

2. Add garlic and onion to Dutch oven; sauté, stirring to scrape up any brown bits from the bottom of the pan, for 5 minutes or until golden. Stir in cumin, coriander, paprika, ginger and pepper; sauté for 1 minute. Add lamb, orange peel, cinnamon stick, tomatoes, broth and apricots; bring to a boil. Reduce heat, cover and simmer very gently for about 2 hours or until meat is fork-tender. Discard orange peel and cinnamon stick.

❄ **FREEZER FRIENDLY**

Diabetes Food Choice Values Per Serving	
1/2	Carbohydrate
3	Meat & Alternatives

NUTRIENTS Per Serving		
Calories: 242	Carbohydrate: 19.7 g	Calcium: 76 mg
Fat: 8.1 g	Fiber: 3.7 g	Iron: 4.3 mg
Sodium: 256 mg	Protein: 24.3 g	

Very high in: Iron, riboflavin, niacin, vitamin B$_{12}$ and zinc • **High in:** Vitamin C, vitamin B$_6$ and magnesium • **A source of:** Dietary fiber

Mediterranean Lamb Curry Couscous

MAKES 6 SERVINGS

Elisabeth McDonald, USA

• Preparation time: 10 minutes / Cooking time: 30 minutes

	Vegetable cooking spray	
1 lb	ground lamb	500 g
1 cup	finely diced onion	250 mL
1 cup	finely diced celery	250 mL
1 cup	finely diced carrot	250 mL
1 cup	finely diced broccoli (fresh or frozen)	250 mL
1 tsp	curry powder	5 mL
1 tsp	garlic powder	5 mL
1 tsp	dried parsley	5 mL
1 tsp	ground turmeric (optional)	5 mL
1 tsp	fancy molasses or liquid honey	5 mL
1 1/4 cups	water	300 mL
2/3 cup	whole wheat couscous	150 mL

1. Heat a large skillet over medium heat. Spray with vegetable cooking spray. Cook ground lamb, breaking up clumps, until evenly browned, about 15 minutes. Transfer to a colander and rinse under hot running water to remove excess fat. Drain well. Rinse out skillet.

2. Reheat skillet over medium heat. Spray with vegetable cooking spray. Sauté onion, celery, carrot and broccoli for 5 minutes. Add curry powder, garlic powder, parsley, turmeric (if using) and molasses. Stir in water, cover and bring to a boil. Return lamb to skillet and cook for 5 minutes. Stir in couscous. Cover, remove from heat and let stand for 5 minutes. Fluff with a fork.

❄ FREEZER FRIENDLY
✓ KID APPROVED

This complete one-pot meal is a lifesaver that Elisabeth created for nights when her family only has about 45 minutes to make and eat dinner before heading out to evening activities. She often dices the vegetables ahead of time to save an extra 10 minutes on those nights.

VARIATIONS

If your family does not like curry seasoning, omit the curry powder and turmeric and add salt and pepper to taste.

Substitute ground chicken, turkey or beef for the lamb.

SERVING IDEA:
While this meal is delicious on its own, if you're serving a hungry crowd, you could add a simple green salad topped with tomatoes and cucumbers. Or double the vegetables in the recipe.

NUTRIENTS Per Serving		
Calories: 254	Carbohydrate: 24.2 g	Calcium: 50 mg
Fat: 10.5 g	Fiber: 4.3 g	Iron: 2.1 mg
Sodium: 78 mg	Protein: 16.5 g	

Very high in: Vitamin A, niacin, vitamin B$_{12}$ and zinc
High in: Dietary fiber, iron and folate

Diabetes Food Choice Values Per Serving	
1	Carbohydrate
2	Meat & Alternatives

Fish and Seafood

Fish and seafood are high-quality proteins that are low in fat. Some oily fish, such as salmon and sardines, are also high in omega-3 fatty acids. Adding more of these foods to your meal plan is a healthy eating strategy.

buying and storing fish

Look for fish that has a clean, fresh smell. If it smells like ammonia, it's likely old or has been mishandled. If little particles of flesh come off when you run your hand across the fillet, the flesh is breaking down and the fish is old.

If you'll be eating fish within 48 hours of purchasing, keep it in the coldest part of the fridge. Otherwise, freeze it.

Fish Is Fast

Microwaving, poaching, baking, grilling and broiling are all fast, low-fat ways to cook fish. Pan-frying in a small amount of vegetable oil also works. Most fish cooks in about 10 minutes per inch (2.5 cm) of thickness.

Fennel

Fennel is composed of a white or pale green bulb from which closely overlapping stalks topped with feathery green leaves grow. The three components — bulb, stalks and leaves — can all be used in cooking. Fennel bulbs taste great roasted with olive oil, onions and grated Parmesan cheese, or raw, thinly sliced with oranges in a salad. The stalks can be used for soups, stocks and stews, and the leaves can be used as an herb. Fennel's gentle flavor works well with seafood.

To prepare a fennel bulb, cut the stalks away where they meet the bulb. If you are not using the intact bulb, cut it in half, remove the base, then rinse it with water before cutting it further. The best way to slice a bulb is to do so vertically. If your recipe requires diced or julienned fennel, it is best to first remove the harder core from the center. Try fennel in our Italian Seafood Stew (page 209).

Is Fish Safe for Pregnant or Nursing Women?

Some fish, specifically shark, swordfish, king mackerel, tilefish and fresh or frozen tuna, should be consumed with caution because they contain high levels of mercury. Pregnant or nursing women, or those who might become pregnant, should limit their consumption of these fish to 6 ounces (170 g) a week. However, they can safely eat two average meals a week (6 oz/170 g per meal) of low-mercury seafood such as shrimp, salmon, catfish or canned tuna specifically labelled as skipjack.

Buying, Storing and Using Herbs

Fresh Herbs

When you buy fresh herbs, snip off the bottom of the stems, then pluck off any damaged leaves. (Soft stems can be eaten along with the rest of the herb.) Put the stems in a glass of water, leaving the leaves exposed above the glass. Cover with a plastic bag and place in the refrigerator for up to 1 week. Change the water every other day. When you are ready to use the herbs, rinse them, pat dry, then chop or use cooking scissors to cut them until very fine.

If you have extra fresh herbs, you can store them for up to 3 months in the freezer. First, wash and dry them, then place them in freezer bags, being sure to mark the date on the bag. Herbs that freeze well include tarragon, basil, dill, chives and parsley.

Dried Herbs

Dried herbs, while convenient, don't have the same pure flavor as fresh herbs. Because of their more intense flavor, substitute dried herbs for fresh at a ratio of 1:3 (e.g., 1 tsp/5 mL dried for 1 tbsp/15 mL fresh). To release the flavor of dried herbs, crumble them between your fingers or use a grinder. If you cannot detect any aroma when you do this, it is time to replace the herb.

Most dried herbs have about a year's shelf life. If you don't use a lot of a particular herb, buy it in small quantities from the bulk food store. Though people often store dried herbs above the stove, this is not recommended, as the heat and exposure to light can cause herbs to lose flavor. A dark, cool, dry place is best.

Oven-Fried Fish

Eileen Campbell

You won't be tempted by deep-fried battered fish once you taste this simple, healthy version.

TIPS

For the fish fillets, try tilapia, sole, haddock or orange roughy.

If you cannot find seasoned bread crumbs for fish in your supermarket, create your own by combining regular dry bread crumbs with a little salt, lemon pepper and dried parsley.

• *Preparation time: 10 minutes / Cooking time: 10 minutes*
• *Preheat oven to 350°F (180°C)*
• *Baking sheet, greased*

1	egg	1
½ cup	milk	125 mL
½ cup	all-purpose flour	125 mL
1	pouch (2 oz/57 g) seasoned bread crumbs for fish (see tip, at left)	1
4	thin white fish fillets (about 1½ lbs/ 750 g total)	4
	Vegetable cooking spray	

1. In a shallow bowl, whisk egg and milk. Place flour on one plate and bread crumbs on another.

2. Dip both sides of fish in flour, then in egg mixture. Coat well with crumbs. Place on prepared baking sheet and spray top lightly with vegetable cooking spray. Discard any excess flour, egg and crumb mixtures.

3. Bake in preheated oven for 10 minutes or until fish is opaque and flakes easily with a fork.

✓ **KID APPROVED**

SERVING IDEA: Serve with a slice of lemon, Oven-Baked Potato Wedges (page 271) and Fruity Slaw (page 147). Lemon Blueberry Panna Cotta (page 299) would be a nice light finish to this meal.

Diabetes Food Choice Values Per Serving	
1	Carbohydrate
4	Meat & Alternatives

NUTRIENTS Per Serving		
Calories: 262	Carbohydrate: 18.6 g	Calcium: 78 mg
Fat: 4.4 g	Fiber: 1.0 g	Iron: 1.9 mg
Sodium: 368 mg	Protein: 34.3 g	

Very high in: Niacin, folate, vitamin B_{12} and magnesium
High in: Thiamine, riboflavin and vitamin B_6

Simple Grilled Fish

MAKES 4 SERVINGS

Eileen Campbell

- *Preparation time: 5 minutes / Cooking time: 5 to 10 minutes*
- *Preheat broiler*
- *Rimmed baking sheet, lightly greased*

1 tbsp	chopped fresh parsley	15 mL
1 tbsp	butter, melted	15 mL
	Juice of 1 lemon	
4	orange roughy fillets (about 1¾ lbs/ 875 g total)	4

1. In a small bowl, combine parsley, butter and lemon juice.
2. Place fish fillets on prepared baking sheet and baste both sides with butter mixture.
3. Broil for 5 to 10 minutes or until fish is opaque and flakes easily with a fork.

 **KID APPROVED**

> **SERVING IDEA:** Enjoy this fish with Pineapple Salsa (page 105), Black Bean Salsa (page 106) or Mango Mint Mojo (page 109), Vegetable Quinoa Salad (page 153) and Yummy Asparagus (page 256).

Sometimes the best-tasting food comes from simple ingredients with the right accompaniments. Serve this dish with steamed broccoli and whole wheat rolls — you'll have a complete meal ready within minutes so you can get on with your busy schedule.

VARIATION
You could substitute tilapia, sole, haddock or halibut for the orange roughy.

Planned Extras
Use leftover cooked fish to make an excellent variation on our Tasty Fish Cakes (page 205).

NUTRIENTS Per Serving		
Calories: 170	Carbohydrate: 1.1 g	Calcium: 63 mg
Fat: 4.3 g	Fiber: 0.1 g	Iron: 0.4 mg
Sodium: 150 mg	Protein: 30.1 g	

Very high in: Niacin, vitamin B$_6$, vitamin B$_{12}$ and magnesium
High in: Thiamine, riboflavin and zinc

Diabetes Food Choice Values Per Serving	
3	Meat & Alternatives

Tandoori Haddock

Eileen Campbell

Purchased tandoori paste makes an easy marinade for white fish. This Indian-inspired dish can be made quickly for a great weeknight meal.

TIP

Most supermarkets now carry tandoori paste. You can usually find it in the ethnic food aisle where Indian and Asian sauces are displayed.

VARIATION

This works well with most firm white fish fillets or steaks, such as halibut or orange roughy. We have even tested it with salmon, and it works great! Adjust the broiling time depending on the thickness of the fish.

- *Preparation time: 5 minutes / Marinating time: 20 to 30 minutes / Cooking time: 10 minutes*
- *Rimmed baking sheet, lightly greased*

¼ cup	tandoori paste (see tip, at left)	50 mL
¼ cup	low-fat yogurt	50 mL
1 tbsp	freshly squeezed lemon juice	15 mL
4	haddock fillets (about 14 oz/420 g total)	4

1. In a shallow dish, combine tandoori paste, yogurt and lemon juice. Add fish, turning to coat evenly. Cover and refrigerate for 20 to 30 minutes. Meanwhile, preheat broiler, with rack set 4 inches (10 cm) from the top.

2. Place fish on baking sheet and broil for 10 minutes or until fish is opaque and flakes easily with a fork and the top is lightly browned.

> **SERVING IDEA:** For a balanced meal, serve with Basmati Rice Pulau (page 275) and steamed sugar snap peas.

Diabetes Food Choice Values Per Serving

3	Meat & Alternatives

NUTRIENTS Per Serving

Calories: 113	Carbohydrate: 4.3 g	Calcium: 65 mg
Fat: 1.2 g	Fiber: 0.3 g	Iron: 1.2 mg
Sodium: 538 mg	Protein: 20.2 g	

Very high in: Niacin and vitamin B_{12} • **High in:** Vitamin B_6 and magnesium

Tasty Fish Cakes

Eileen Campbell

A great way to use up leftover cooked salmon and mashed potatoes, but just as good made with canned salmon.

• *Preparation time: 10 minutes / Chilling time: 30 minutes / Cooking time: 4 minutes*

1	can (7½ oz/213 g) salmon, drained, skin and large bones removed (or 6 oz/ 175 g leftover cooked salmon)	1
1 cup	puréed or mashed potatoes	250 mL
¼ cup	finely chopped green onion	50 mL
¼ cup	finely diced red bell pepper	50 mL
3 tbsp	chopped fresh dill	45 mL
3 tbsp	milk	45 mL
	Salt and freshly ground black pepper	
1	egg, beaten	1
	Vegetable cooking spray	

1. In a medium bowl, combine salmon, potatoes, green onion, red pepper, dill and milk. Season to taste with salt and pepper. Gently stir in egg. Form mixture into four ¾-inch (1.5 cm) thick cakes. Cover and refrigerate for at least 30 minutes or overnight to let flavor develop.

2. Heat a large nonstick skillet over medium heat. Spray with vegetable cooking spray. Add fish cakes and cook for about 2 minutes per side, or until browned on both sides and hot in the center.

TIPS

Use plain puréed or mashed potato, without milk or butter added.

These cakes can be made the night before so they are ready to cook when you get home.

VARIATION

Vary the flavor by using 6 oz (175 g) cooked haddock, crab or diced shrimp instead of salmon. Change the herbs and veggies depending on the fish or seafood you choose.

✓ **KID APPROVED**

SERVING IDEA: Serve with Snow Pea and Bell Pepper Salad (page 140) or a green vegetable or salad with lemon wedges on the side. To add a grain to the meal, enjoy our Rhubarb Bread Pudding (page 303) for dessert.

NUTRIENTS Per Serving		
Calories: 149	Carbohydrate: 12.2 g	Calcium: 125 mg
Fat: 5.1 g	Fiber: 1.0 g	Iron: 0.8 mg
Sodium: 179 mg	Protein: 13.1 g	

Very high in: Niacin and vitamin B$_{12}$ • **High in:** Vitamin C

Diabetes Food Choice Values Per Serving	
½	Carbohydrate
2	Meat & Alternatives

Eileen Campbell

Do you avoid cooking fish because you are worried about the smell it sometimes leaves in the kitchen? In this recipe, the fish is enclosed in foil, and no smell escapes at all.

TIP

The rule of thumb for cooking fish is 10 minutes per inch (2.5 cm) of thickness. The thicker the fish, the longer you need to cook it.

Planned Extras

Always cook extra to make Tasty Fish Cakes (page 205) for another meal.

Salmon in a Parcel

• ***Preparation time: 5 minutes / Cooking time: 20 minutes***
• *Preheat oven to 450°F (230°C)*
• *Rimmed baking sheet*

4	salmon fillets (about 1 lb/500 g total)	1
1	lemon, thinly sliced	1
½ cup	chopped fresh dill	125 mL
1 tbsp	olive oil	15 mL

1. Cut 4 pieces of foil big enough to completely wrap each piece of fish. Place 1 salmon fillet in the center of each piece of foil. Top each with lemon slices, sprinkle with dill and drizzle with olive oil. Fold foil over fish and crimp in the center. Tuck excess foil under, pinching to seal edges. Place foil packets on baking sheet.

2. Bake in preheated oven for about 20 minutes or until salmon is opaque and flakes easily with a fork.

> **SERVING IDEA:** Serve with steamed broccoli and Baked Springtime Risotto (page 277).

Diabetes Food Choice Values Per Serving

3	Meat & Alternatives

NUTRIENTS Per Serving

Calories: 218	Carbohydrate: 3.0 g	Calcium: 32 mg
Fat: 14.4 g	Fiber: 1.3 g	Iron: 0.6 mg
Sodium: 56 g	Protein: 19.9 g	

Very high in: Niacin, vitamin B_6 and vitamin B_{12}
High in: Vitamin C, thiamine and folate

Broiled Cilantro Ginger Salmon

MAKES 6 SERVINGS

Eileen Campbell

This was a major hit with our taste panel. Broiling the fish on one side only keeps it moist, delicious and full of flavor.

- **Preparation time: 10 minutes / Marinating time: 30 minutes / Cooking time: 7 to 10 minutes**
- Rimmed baking sheet, greased

3	cloves garlic, roughly chopped	3
2 tbsp	grated gingerroot	25 mL
½ tsp	salt	2 mL
½ cup	chopped fresh cilantro	125 mL
2 tbsp	olive oil	25 mL
½ tsp	freshly ground black pepper	2 mL
	Grated zest of 2 limes	
6	salmon fillets (about 2¼ lbs/ 1.125 kg total)	6

1. Using a mortar and pestle (or a food processor), crush garlic, ginger and salt to form a paste. Stir in cilantro, olive oil, pepper and lime zest.
2. Place salmon on a plate and coat top evenly with paste. Cover and refrigerate for at least 30 minutes or for up to 2 hours. Preheat broiler, with rack set 4 inches (10 cm) from the top.
3. Transfer salmon to prepared baking sheet and broil for 7 to 10 minutes or until salmon is opaque and flakes easily with a fork.

✓ KID APPROVED

SERVING IDEA: Serve with our Black Bean Salsa (page 106), Steamed Asian Vegetable Medley (page 263) and quinoa.

TIP
This can also be cooked on a barbecue with two or more burners. Preheat one side to medium, place salmon on the other side and close the lid. This indirect cooking method is great for delicate proteins like fish. There will be enough heat to cook the salmon without burning it or drying it out.

Planned Extras
Extra salmon is great served cold with a salad.

NUTRIENTS Per Serving		
Calories: 327	Carbohydrate: 1.3 g	Calcium: 26 mg
Fat: 21.4 g	Fiber: 0.2 g	Iron: 0.6 mg
Sodium: 276 mg	Protein: 30.4 g	

Very high in: Thiamine, niacin, vitamin B_6 and vitamin B_{12}
High in: Folate and magnesium

Diabetes Food Choice Values Per Serving

4½ Meat & Alternatives

**Donna Bottrell,
Dietitian, ON**

*A quick and easy fish
dish with Asian flair.*

TIP
Leftover orange juice
concentrate can be used
to make orange juice or
to prepare Fruit Frenzy
Pops (page 327) or the
dressing for Strawberry
Spinach Salad (page 142).

Orange Hoisin Salmon

• *Preparation time: 5 minutes / Cooking time: 7 to 10 minutes*
• *Preheat broiler, with rack set 4 inches (10 cm) from the top*
• *Rimmed baking sheet, lightly greased*

2 tbsp	hoisin sauce	25 mL
1 tbsp	frozen orange juice concentrate	15 mL
2 tsp	grated orange zest	10 mL
2 tsp	liquid honey	10 mL
Pinch	salt	Pinch
Pinch	freshly ground black pepper	Pinch
4	salmon fillets (about 1½ lbs/750 g total)	4
	Vegetable cooking spray	

1. In a small bowl, combine hoisin sauce, orange juice
   concentrate, orange zest and honey.
2. Place salmon on baking sheet and baste both sides with
   hoisin mixture. Season with salt and pepper.
3. Broil for 7 to 10 minutes or until fish is opaque and flakes
   easily with a fork.

 **KID APPROVED**

> **SERVING IDEA:** Serve over Pineapple Vegetable Rice
> (page 274) with a green salad.

Diabetes Food Choice Values Per Serving	
½	Carbohydrate
4	Meat & Alternatives

NUTRIENTS Per Serving		
Calories: 314	Carbohydrate: 8.4 g	Calcium: 26 mg
Fat: 17.1 g	Fiber: 0.4 g	Iron: 0.6 mg
Sodium: 210 mg	Protein: 29.7 g	

Very high in: Thiamine, niacin, vitamin B_6 and vitamin B_{12}
High in: Folate and magnesium

Italian Seafood Stew

MAKES 8 SERVINGS

Eileen Campbell

• *Preparation time: 15 minutes / Cooking time: 15 to 20 minutes*

½	head fennel	½
2 tbsp	olive oil	25 mL
2	cloves garlic, crushed	2
1	large onion, diced	1
1	red bell pepper, diced	1
4 cups	Tomato Master Sauce (page 232) or good-quality commercial marinara sauce	1 L
	Juice of 1 lemon	
1½ lbs	large shrimp, peeled and deveined	750 g
8 oz	mussels, in shell	250 g
1 lb	halibut fillets, skin removed and cut into chunks	500 g
1 tbsp	hot pepper sauce (optional)	15 mL
2 tbsp	chopped fresh parsley	25 mL

This is a great dinner party dish that is easy to put together yet tastes like you've been slaving all day over the stove.

VARIATION
If you cannot find or do not like fennel, substitute 3 stalks celery, thinly sliced, and garnish with the leaves.

1. Remove stalks, base and hard core of fennel, reserving the fronds (feathery leaves). Chop the remainder into 1-inch (2.5 cm) chunks. Chop 2 tbsp (25 mL) of the fronds and set aside.

2. In a large saucepan, heat oil over medium heat. Sauté fennel chunks, garlic, onion and red pepper until onion is lightly browned, about 5 minutes. Add tomato sauce and bring to a boil. Reduce heat, cover and simmer for 5 minutes. Stir in lemon juice. Add shrimp, mussels and halibut; cover and simmer for 5 to 10 minutes or until shrimp are pink and opaque, mussels have opened and halibut is opaque. Discard any mussels that do not open. Add hot pepper sauce, if using.

3. Ladle into bowls and sprinkle with parsley and fennel fronds.

SERVING IDEA: Serve with crusty Italian bread for dunking and have biscotti and a latte for dessert.

NUTRIENTS Per Serving		
Calories: 214	Carbohydrate: 10.7 g	Calcium: 110 mg
Fat: 7.4 g	Fiber: 2.1 g	Iron: 3.6 mg
Sodium: 360 mg	Protein: 26.4 g	

Very high in: Iron, vitamin C, riboflavin, niacin, vitamin B$_{12}$ and magnesium • **High in:** Vitamin B$_6$ • **A source of:** Dietary fiber

Diabetes Food Choice Values Per Serving

3½ Meat & Alternatives

Heather Barnes,
Dietitian, ON

*We have deliberately
kept this dish mild so
that children can enjoy
it. If you like heat,
increase the amount
of curry paste.*

TIPS

Up to 1 tbsp (15 mL)
curry paste can be used,
depending on your taste.

When the shrimp is cooked,
immediately remove the
skillet from the heat to
avoid overcooking it.

Fish Sauce

Fish sauce is a clear
brown extraction of
salted small fish, such as
anchovies, sold in bottles.
It is the quintessential
ingredient of several Asian
cuisines (particularly
Thailand's), used to season
savory dishes, just as soy
sauce is used in Chinese
cooking. Don't worry; the
final taste is not fishy and
the powerful scent fades
on cooking. There is no
substitute, but if you
cannot find it, replace it
with soy sauce.

Easy Shrimp Curry

• *Preparation time: 15 minutes / Cooking time: 15 minutes*

Sauce

1 cup	light coconut milk	250 mL
1 tbsp	packed brown sugar	15 mL
1 tbsp	reduced-sodium soy sauce or fish sauce	15 mL
2 tsp	cornstarch	10 mL
	Vegetable cooking spray	
1/4	red onion, chopped	1/4
2	bell peppers (any color), chopped	2
1 tsp	red curry paste (or to taste)	5 mL
8 oz	shrimp, peeled and deveined	250 g

1. *Prepare the sauce:* In a small bowl, whisk together coconut milk, brown sugar, soy sauce and cornstarch.

2. Heat a large skillet over medium heat. Spray with vegetable cooking spray. Sauté red onion until just soft, about 5 minutes. Add bell peppers and curry paste; cook until peppers are slightly soft, about 5 minutes. Add sauce and shrimp; bring to a boil. Reduce heat, cover and simmer for 5 minutes or until shrimp are pink and opaque.

✓ **KID APPROVED**

SERVING IDEA: Serve with brown rice. For dessert, enjoy Baked Granola Apples (page 296) with a glass of cold milk.

Diabetes Food Choice Values Per Serving	
1 1/2	Carbohydrates
2	Meat & Alternatives

NUTRIENTS Per Serving		
Calories: 275	Carbohydrate: 28.0 g	Calcium: 71 g
Fat: 9.9 g	Fiber: 2.4 g	Iron: 3.1 mg
Sodium: 474 mg	Protein: 19.9 g	

Very high in: Vitamin A, vitamin C, niacin and vitamin B_{12} • **High in:** Iron, vitamin B_6 and magnesium • **A source of:** Dietary fiber

Stir-Fried Scallops with Curried Sweet Peppers

MAKES 4 SERVINGS

Edie Shaw-Ewald, Dietitian, NS

• *Preparation time: 10 minutes / Cooking time: 10 minutes*

2 tbsp	curry powder (or 2 tsp/10 mL mild curry paste)	25 mL
1 tbsp	olive oil, divided	15 mL
Pinch	salt	Pinch
1	red bell pepper, julienned	1
1	green bell pepper, julienned	1
1	yellow bell pepper, julienned	1
1 lb	sea scallops, halved horizontally	500 g
½ cup	white wine, apple juice or water	125 mL
1 tsp	dark sesame oil	5 mL
1 tbsp	chopped fresh cilantro	15 mL

This is an easy, elegant dish with just a few ingredients. Edie loves to serve it to guests, and her two sons love it too. She sometimes adjusts the amount of curry powder for those who do not like the dish too spicy. Be careful not to overcook the scallops, as they are delicate.

1. In a large bowl, combine curry powder, 1 tsp (5 mL) of the oil and salt. Add scallops and toss to coat.

2. In a wok or a large skillet, heat the remaining oil over medium-high heat. Add scallops and stir-fry for 1 minute. Add red, green and yellow peppers; stir-fry for 1 minute. Add wine and cook, stirring, for 3 to 4 minutes or until scallops are firm and opaque. Stir in sesame oil.

3. Using a slotted spoon, remove scallops and vegetables to a serving bowl. Boil sauce, uncovered, for 3 to 5 minutes, or until thickened. Taste and add salt, if needed.

4. Pour sauce over scallops and vegetables and sprinkle with cilantro. Serve immediately.

> **SERVING IDEA:** This is great served over fine pasta, such as angel hair. Fruit salad and a glass of milk will finish the meal nicely.

NUTRIENTS Per Serving		
Calories: 201	Carbohydrate: 10.8 g	Calcium: 74 mg
Fat: 7.3 g	Fiber: 2.3 g	Iron: 2.4 mg
Sodium: 601 mg	Protein: 20.4 g	

Very high in: Vitamin C, vitamin B_{12} and magnesium • **High in:** Iron, niacin, vitamin B_6 and zinc • **A source of:** Dietary fiber

Diabetes Food Choice Values Per Serving

3	Meat & Alternatives

Vegetarian Main Courses

Even meat eaters enjoy a vegetarian main course from time to time. It's a great way to add variety to your meal plan, and many vegetarian entrées offer more dietary fiber than meat-based entrées. Vegetarian meals can also be economical and are a great way to introduce the family to some new tastes.

eating more legumes

Legumes (sometimes called pulses) include dried peas, beans and lentils. They are a great fit with healthy eating, providing carbohydrate and quality protein, as well as several essential nutrients. They are also low in fat.

Here are some suggestions for adding legumes to your meals:

- Purée cooked beans or lentils and add to tomato-based sauces for pasta or tacos.
- Add lentils and split peas to soups and casseroles.
- Use cooked brown lentils instead of ground beef in dishes such as lasagna, pasta sauces and shepherd's pie.
- Sprinkle cooked chickpeas or lentils on a pizza, along with other toppings.

- Purée cooked legumes and add to meat or veggie burger mixtures.
- Make Easy Pasta with Beans (page 235), a classic Italian one-pot dinner.
- Add cooked lentils to rice pilaf (try our Mediterranean Lentil and Rice Salad, page 155).
- Enjoy a mixed bean salad with vinaigrette dressing for a quick, nutritious lunch or snack.
- Add cooked beans or lentils to salads for extra fiber.
- Use chickpeas, black beans or other beans to make dips such as Spicy Hummus (page 104).
- Add black beans to salsa and use to top a baked potato or fish (try Black Bean Salsa, page 106).

The Gas Problem

Some people avoid legumes because of the uncomfortable and potentially embarrassing gas that results from eating them. There are several steps you can take to reduce this problem. Be sure to rinse canned beans well under cold running water before using. If using dried beans, discard the soaking water and cook them well in fresh water. Adding beans to your diet gradually can also help.

What About Soy?

Soybeans are a source of high-quality protein and supply vitamins, minerals and fiber. They also contain phytochemicals called isoflavones, natural estrogen-like substances that that are being investigated for their health benefits. Because of their isoflavone content, soy foods may not be advisable for breast cancer survivors, although more research is needed in this area. However, for most people, soybean products offer the opportunity to add variety to their menu. Try our Edamame Salad (page 160) or Tofu Veggie Kabobs (page 229).

Cooking Dried Beans

Cooked legumes, such as kidney beans and chickpeas, can be purchased in cans for convenience. However, if you have the time, cooking dried beans and peas yourself can be more economical. Here's how to do it properly. (These are guidelines only; when in doubt, check the package directions.)

Soaking

All dried beans need to be soaked before they are cooked to replace the water lost in drying. A general rule is to use 3 cups (750 mL) water for every 1 cup (250 mL) beans. After soaking, discard soaking water, rinse and replace with fresh water before cooking (this helps cut down on the substance that causes gas). Note that while dried lentils are classified as a legume, they don't need to be presoaked.

- **Overnight Soak:** Let beans and water stand overnight in refrigerator. Drain. (Beans soaked using this method cook more quickly and keep their shape better.)
- **Quick Soak:** In a large saucepan, bring water and beans to a boil; cover and boil for 2 minutes. Remove from heat and let stand for 1 hour. Drain.
- **Microwave Soak:** In a microwave-safe casserole dish, combine hot water and beans. Cover and microwave on High for 15 minutes or until boiling. Let stand for 1 hour. Drain.

Cooking

To cook soaked beans, use 3 cups (750 mL) water for every 1 cup (250 mL) soaked beans and follow one of the methods below. The longer you store beans, the more they dry out and the longer you need to cook them. Never add salt or seasoning until the beans are tender; otherwise, the skin will toughen and they will never soften.

- **Stovetop Cooking:** In a large saucepan, combine water and soaked beans. Cover and bring to a full rolling boil. Reduce heat and simmer for 45 to 60 minutes or until fork-tender.
- **Microwave Cooking:** In a microwave-safe casserole dish, combine water and soaked beans. Cover and microwave on High for 10 to 15 minutes or until boiling. Stir and microwave on Medium (50%) for 15 minutes. Stir again and microwave on Medium (50%) for 10 to 20 minutes or until fork-tender.

Greens and Grains Gratin

Nicole Fetterly, BC

Get glowing reviews for greens! This hearty dish makes a delicious meal when served with a baked potato, or stands out as a superb side dish.

TIP

The gratin can be made ahead through Step 4; cover and refrigerate for up to 8 hours. You may need to increase the baking time by 10 minutes, but check it after 30 minutes.

- *Preparation time: 20 minutes / Standing time: 15 minutes / Cooking time: 40 minutes*
- *Preheat oven to 350°F (180°C)*
- *Ovenproof skillet*

$\frac{1}{3}$ cup	bulgur	75 mL
$\frac{1}{3}$ cup	millet (or more bulgur)	75 mL
1 $\frac{1}{3}$ cup	boiling water	325 mL
1	bunch greens (such as spinach, collard greens, Swiss chard)	1
4 tsp	olive oil, divided	20 mL
6	cloves garlic, minced	6
	Salt and freshly ground black pepper	
2 cups	shredded old Cheddar cheese, divided	500 mL
$\frac{1}{4}$ cup	dry bread crumbs	50 mL
$\frac{1}{4}$ cup	finely chopped nuts (such as almonds)	50 mL
2 tbsp	minced fresh flat-leaf parsley	25 mL

1. In a heatproof bowl, combine bulgur and millet. Pour in boiling water, cover and let stand for 15 minutes. Drain off any excess water.

2. Meanwhile, clean greens and tear into small pieces.

3. In ovenproof skillet, heat 1 tbsp (15 mL) of the olive oil over medium-low heat. Sauté garlic until golden, about 2 minutes. Add grains and greens; sauté until grains are slightly browned and greens are wilted, about 5 minutes. Season to taste with salt and pepper. Remove from heat. Transfer half of the mixture to a bowl and set aside.

4. Spread the remaining mixture in the bottom of the skillet. Top with 1 cup (250 mL) of the cheese. Spread reserved half of mixture over cheese.

5. In a small bowl, combine the remaining 1 tsp (5 mL) oil, the remaining 1 cup (250 mL) cheese, bread crumbs, nuts and parsley. Spread evenly over grains mixture.

6. Bake in preheated oven for 30 minutes or until cheese is bubbly and top is golden brown.

Diabetes Food Choice Values Per Serving	
1	Carbohydrate
1 $\frac{1}{2}$	Meat & Alternatives
2	Fats

NUTRIENTS Per Serving		
Calories: 308	Carbohydrate: 21.9 g	Calcium: 377 mg
Fat: 15.0 g	Fiber: 4.0 g	Iron: 3.2 mg
Sodium: 309 mg	Protein: 15.0 g	

Very high in: Vitamin A, calcium, folate, magnesium and zinc
High in: Dietary fiber, iron, riboflavin, niacin, vitamin B_6 and vitamin B_{12}

Teriyaki Rice Noodles with Veggies and Beans

MAKES 8 SERVINGS

Krystal Taylor, Dietitian, ON

• *Preparation time: 8 minutes / Cooking time: 25 minutes*

2 cups	rice noodles	500 mL
1 tbsp	olive oil	15 mL
1	small onion, diced	1
1 cup	chopped carrots	250 mL
1 cup	chopped celery	250 mL
2	cloves garlic, chopped	2
2 cups	broccoli florets	500 mL
½ cup	reduced-sodium teriyaki sauce	125 mL
Dash	hot pepper sauce	Dash
1	can (19 oz/540 mL) mixed beans, drained and rinsed (about 2 cups/ 500 mL)	1

1. Prepare rice noodles according to package directions. Drain and set aside.
2. In a large skillet, heat oil over medium heat. Sauté onion, carrots and celery until onions are softened, about 5 minutes. Add garlic and broccoli; cover and cook for 5 minutes. Stir in teriyaki sauce, hot pepper sauce, beans and rice noodles; cover and cook for 5 minutes.

✓ KID APPROVED

This is a variation on the noodle dish Pad Thai, but it uses beans as the protein instead of shrimp and chicken, which is the more usual combination. Teriyaki sauce is a favorite of children because of its sweet taste.

TIP
Krystal likes her noodles with zip! For a milder flavor, omit the hot pepper sauce.

VARIATION
To change the texture of this recipe, substitute couscous for the rice noodles.

Planned Extras
This recipe reheats well, so it makes for a great packed lunch the next day.

NUTRIENTS Per Serving		
Calories: 264	Carbohydrate: 51.7 g	Calcium: 32 mg
Fat: 2.6 g	Fiber: 5.1 g	Iron: 0.8 mg
Sodium: 616 mg	Protein: 7.7 g	

Very high in: Vitamin A • **High in:** Dietary fiber

Diabetes Food Choice Values Per Serving	
3	Carbohydrates
½	Fat

Vegetarian Chili

**Lindsay Mandryk,
Dietitian, BC**

*When Lindsay was in
university, she used to
make a batch of this
chili and freeze it in
meal-sized portions so
she could have a hot,
healthy meal during
exam time.*

TIPS

If you cannot find
Mexican-flavored
vegetarian ground round,
use regular vegetarian
ground round and add
2 tbsp (25 mL) chili
powder.

Chili makes a great base
for a Mexican meat pie.
Ladle it into a casserole
dish and top with Cheddar
Corn Muffin batter (page
292). Bake in a 350°F
(180°C) oven for about
35 to 45 minutes or until
a tester inserted into the
topping comes out clean.

VARIATION

Substitute a 12-oz
(341 mL) can of peaches-
and-cream corn, drained,
for the carrots.

• **Preparation time: 10 minutes / Cooking time: 20 minutes**

1 tbsp	vegetable oil	15 mL
2	cloves garlic, diced	2
1/2 cup	diced red onion	125 mL
1	package (12 oz/340 g) Mexican-flavored vegetarian ground round	1
1 cup	diced green bell pepper	250 mL
2	cans (each 19 oz/540 mL) diced tomatoes (about 4 3/4 cups/1.175 L)	2
1	can (19 oz/540 mL) red kidney beans, drained and rinsed (about 2 cups/ 500 mL)	1
1 cup	grated carrots	250 mL
1 tbsp	dried parsley	15 mL
1 tsp	hot pepper sauce	5 mL
	Freshly ground black pepper	
1/2 cup	shredded Cheddar cheese	125 mL

1. In a large skillet, heat oil over medium heat. Sauté garlic
   and red onion until softened, about 5 minutes. Add ground
   round, breaking it apart with a wooden spoon to prevent
   clumps; sauté for 2 to 3 minutes or until evenly heated.
   Add green pepper and sauté for 2 to 3 minutes. Add
   tomatoes, beans, carrots, parsley, hot pepper sauce and
   pepper to taste; cook, stirring occasionally, for 10 minutes
   or until beans are heated through.

2. Ladle into serving bowls and sprinkle with cheese.

❄️ FREEZER FRIENDLY
✓ KID APPROVED

SERVING IDEA: Serve with half a bagel and a glass of milk.

**Diabetes Food Choice
Values Per Serving**

1/2	Carbohydrate
2	Meat & Alternatives

NUTRIENTS Per Serving		
Calories: 194	Carbohydrate: 20.3 g	Calcium: 156 mg
Fat: 6.4 g	Fiber: 6.8 g	Iron: 4.1 mg
Sodium: 587 mg	Protein: 14.6 g	

Very high in: Dietary fiber, Vitamin A, thiamine, riboflavin, niacin, vitamin B_{12} and iron • **High in:** Vitamin C, folate and vitamin B_6

Lentils Bolognese

• Preparation time: 10 minutes / Cooking time: 70 minutes

1 cup	brown or red lentils	250 mL
2 cups	water	500 mL
1	bay leaf	1
2 tbsp	olive oil	25 mL
2	cloves garlic, crushed	2
1	onion, diced	1
1 cup	sliced mushrooms	250 mL
1 cup	chopped canned tomatoes	250 mL
1	can (5½ oz/156 mL) tomato paste	1
1	apple, diced	1
½ cup	cider vinegar	125 mL
1 tsp	dried oregano	5 mL
	Juice of 1 lemon	

Elaine Bass, ON

This great recipe is very easy to make and is a great vegetarian take on a traditional Italian dish.

1. In a medium saucepan, bring lentils, water and bay leaf to a boil over high heat. Reduce heat to medium and cook for about 20 minutes or until lentils are soft. Drain and rinse and discard bay leaf. Set aside.

2. In a large saucepan, heat oil over medium heat. Sauté garlic, onion and mushrooms until softened, about 5 minutes. Add cooked lentils, tomatoes, tomato paste, apple, vinegar, oregano and lemon juice; bring to a boil. Reduce heat, cover and simmer for 45 minutes.

❄ FREEZER FRIENDLY

SERVING IDEA: Serve on top of whole wheat spaghetti and sprinkle with freshly grated Parmesan cheese.

NUTRIENTS Per Serving		
Calories: 153	Carbohydrate: 24.7 g	Calcium: 37 mg
Fat: 3.9 g	Fiber: 4.9 g	Iron: 3.5 mg
Sodium: 48 mg	Protein: 7.8 g	

Very high in: Iron and folate • **High in:** Dietary fiber and magnesium

Diabetes Food Choice Values Per Serving	
1	Carbohydrate
½	Meat & Alternative

Donna Bottrell, Dietitian, ON

This colorful and healthy blend of vegetables scented with saffron, lemon and parsley works beautifully served with steamed whole wheat couscous or brown rice.

TIPS

Nothing can really substitute for the flavor of saffron, but the pretty yellow-orange color it creates can be mimicked with ¹/₂ tsp (2 mL) ground turmeric.

There are about 2¹/₃ cups (575 mL) of diced tomatoes in a 19-oz (540 mL) can and about 2 cups (500 mL) of drained chickpeas in a 19-oz can.

SERVING IDEA:
Add whole wheat couscous and serve fresh fruit and yogurt or cheese for dessert.

Moroccan Vegetable Tagine

• **Preparation time: 20 minutes / Cooking time: 45 minutes**

1 tbsp	olive oil	15 mL
2	onions, chopped	2
2	cloves garlic, finely chopped	2
2	Yukon gold potatoes, peeled and cubed	2
2	large carrots, cut into short sticks	2
¹/₂	large sweet potato, peeled and cut into short sticks	¹/₂
1 tbsp	grated gingerroot	15 mL
1 tsp	ground cumin	5 mL
1 tsp	ground cinnamon	5 mL
1	can (19 oz/540 mL) diced tomatoes	1
1	can (19 oz/540 mL) chickpeas, drained and rinsed	1
4 cups	vegetable broth	1 L
Pinch	saffron strands (optional)	Pinch
¹/₄ cup	chopped fresh parsley	50 mL
	Juice of 1 lemon	
	Salt and freshly ground black pepper	
2 tbsp	hot pepper sauce (optional)	25 mL

1. In a large saucepan, heat oil over medium-high heat. Add onions, garlic, potatoes, carrots, sweet potato, ginger, cumin and cinnamon; cook, stirring often, for 10 minutes. Stir in tomatoes; cook for 2 minutes. Stir in chickpeas, broth and saffron (if using); bring to a boil. Reduce heat, cover and simmer for 30 minutes, until vegetables are just tender. Stir in parsley and lemon juice. Season to taste with salt and pepper. Stir in hot sauce (if using).

❄ **FREEZER FRIENDLY**
✓ **KID APPROVED**

Diabetes Food Choice Values Per Serving

1¹/₂ Carbohydrates
¹/₂ Fat

NUTRIENTS Per Serving		
Calories: 175	Carbohydrate: 34.3 g	Calcium: 63 mg
Fat: 2.6 g	Fiber: 5.3 g	Iron: 2.2 mg
Sodium: 712 mg	Protein: 4.8 g	

Very high in: Vitamin A and vitamin B₆ • **High in:** Dietary fiber, vitamin C, iron, folate and magnesium

Chickpea Curry

Lindsay Mandryk, Dietitian, BC

Lindsay created this mild curry, filled with colorful vegetables and rich in fiber, when she was completing the food service portion of her internship in Australia. Her students loved it served with pappadams!

• *Preparation time: 10 minutes / Cooking time: 30 minutes*

2 tbsp	vegetable oil	25 mL
¾ cup	diced onion	175 mL
1 tbsp	curry powder	15 mL
1 to 2 tbsp	all-purpose flour (or 1 tbsp/15 mL cornstarch)	15 to 25 mL
1 cup	water (approx.)	250 mL
⅔ cup	diced red bell pepper	150 mL
⅔ cup	diced yellow bell pepper	150 mL
1 cup	diced zucchini	250 mL
¾ cup	diced butternut squash	175 mL
1	can (19 oz/540 mL) chickpeas, drained and rinsed (about 2 cups/ 500 mL)	1
½ cup	vegetable broth	125 mL
½ cup	snow peas (optional)	125 mL
¼ cup	finely chopped fresh parsley (or 1 tbsp/15 mL dried)	50 mL

1. In a large skillet, heat oil over medium heat. Sauté onions until softened, about 5 minutes. Stir in curry powder. Sprinkle with 1 tbsp (15 mL) flour. Add water, stirring constantly to prevent lumping. Add red and yellow peppers, zucchini and squash; bring to a boil. Cook, stirring often, for 10 minutes, adding more water if sauce is too thick. (If it's too thin, add the remaining flour, mixed with a little water.) Add chickpeas and broth; reduce heat and simmer for 10 minutes, until chickpeas are heated through. Add snow peas (if using) and parsley just before serving.

❄ FREEZER FRIENDLY
✓ KID APPROVED

SERVING IDEA: This curry is delicious inside a whole wheat pita.

NUTRIENTS Per Serving		
Calories: 169	Carbohydrate: 26.3 g	Calcium: 47 mg
Fat: 5.6 g	Fiber: 4.9 g	Iron: 1.7 mg
Sodium: 273 mg	Protein: 4.7 g	

Very high in: Vitamin A, vitamin C and folate
High in: Dietary fiber, vitamin B$_6$ and magnesium

Diabetes Food Choice Values Per Serving	
1	Carbohydrate
1	Fat

Easy Black Beans

Chantal Saad Haddad,
Dietitian, QC

*This spicy recipe is
great for those rushed
days when you're not
very organized and
are wondering what
to make for supper
as you drive home.
When you are more
organized, plan ahead
and soak some beans
instead of using canned.*

TIP
If your family doesn't
like heat, leave out the
chipotle pepper.

Planned Extras
Use with cooked brown
rice to fill tortillas and pitas
for an easy lunchbox meal.

• *Preparation time: 10 minutes / Cooking time: 25 minutes*

1 tsp	vegetable oil	5 mL
1	small onion, chopped	1
1	can (19 oz/540 mL) black beans, drained and rinsed (about 2 cups/ 500 mL)	1
1½ cups	water	375 mL
½ cup	tomato paste	125 mL
1	chipotle pepper in adobo sauce	1
1	bay leaf	1
1 tsp	ground cumin	5 mL
2 tbsp	chopped fresh cilantro (optional)	25 mL

1. In a large skillet, heat oil over medium heat. Sauté onion until softened, about 5 minutes. Stir in beans, water, tomato paste, chipotle pepper, bay leaf and cumin; bring to a boil. Reduce heat and simmer for 15 minutes or until slightly thickened. Discard the chipotle and bay leaf. (If you leave the chipotle in, the dish will be too spicy)!

2. Ladle into bowls and garnish with cilantro, if desired.

❄ **FREEZER FRIENDLY**

SERVING IDEA: Serve with Simple Stir-Fried Kale (page 260) and Basmati Rice Pulau (page 275).

Diabetes Food Choice Values Per Serving	
1	Carbohydrate
1	Meat & Alternative

NUTRIENTS Per Serving		
Calories: 145	Carbohydrate: 26.0 g	Calcium: 56 mg
Fat: 1.8 g	Fiber: 9.2 g	Iron: 3.2 mg
Sodium: 412 mg	Protein: 8.2 g	

Very high in: Dietary fiber and folate
High in: Iron and magnesium

Veggie Quesadillas

• *Preparation time: 10 minutes / Cooking time: 25 minutes*

Eileen Campbell

8	6-inch (15 cm) whole wheat tortillas	8
1 1/2 cups	shredded nacho cheese blend	375 mL
1 cup	finely chopped broccoli	250 mL
1 cup	julienned red bell pepper	250 mL
1 cup	grated carrot	250 mL
1/3 cup	chopped green onions	75 mL

Raw veggies add a crunchy twist to the familiar quesadilla. This one is loaded with nutrient-rich ingredients.

1. Heat a small skillet over medium heat. Heat tortillas, one at a time, for 30 seconds per side, then remove.

2. Sprinkle half the cheese evenly over 4 tortillas. Place broccoli, red pepper, carrot and green onions evenly on top of the cheese. Sprinkle with the other half of the cheese. Top with the remaining 4 tortillas.

3. In the same skillet, over medium heat, cook quesadillas, one at a time, for 2 minutes per side or until surface is crisp and cheese has melted. Transfer to a plate and keep warm in a low oven while making the remaining quesadillas.

4. Cut each quesadilla into 4 wedges and serve.

✓ KID APPROVED

NUTRIENTS Per Serving		
Calories: 316	Carbohydrate: 44.1 g	Calcium: 328 mg
Fat: 13.9 g	Fiber: 5.4 g	Iron: 2.0 mg
Sodium: 632 mg	Protein: 16.4 g	

Very high in: Vitamin A, vitamin C, calcium and folate • **High in:** Dietary fiber, thiamine, riboflavin, niacin, vitamin B_6 and magnesium

Diabetes Food Choice Values Per Serving	
2	Carbohydrates
1	Meat & Alternatives
2	Fats

Bean Burritos

Lorraine Van Heteren, ON

A kid favorite that combines salsa, beans and cheese.

TIP
You can improve the nutritional value of this dish by using whole wheat or multigrain tortillas.

- *Preparation time: 10 minutes / Cooking time: 20 minutes*
- *Preheat oven to 350°F (180°C)*
- *13- by 9-inch (3 L) baking dish, lightly greased*

8	10-inch (25 cm) flour tortillas	8
1 1/2 cups	salsa, divided	375 mL
2	cans (each 14 oz/398 mL) black beans, drained and rinsed (about 3 cups/750 mL)	2
1	can (4 oz/113 g) chopped green chili peppers, drained	1
1/2	Spanish onion, chopped	1/2
	Salt and freshly ground black pepper	
1 1/2 cups	shredded Cheddar or nacho cheese blend, divided	375 mL

1. Microwave tortillas on High for 1 to 2 minutes to soften them and make rolling easier.

2. Spread 1/2 cup (125 mL) of salsa on the bottom of prepared baking dish.

3. In a large bowl, combine beans, chilies, onion and 1/2 cup (125 mL) of the salsa. Season to taste with salt and pepper.

4. Divide bean mixture among the tortillas and spread to within 1/2 inch (1 cm) of edge. Top with 1 cup (250 mL) of the cheese, divided evenly among the tortillas. Roll up tortillas and place seam side down on the salsa in the baking dish. Spread the remaining salsa on top of the tortillas and sprinkle with the remaining cheese.

5. Bake in preheated oven for 20 minutes or until heated through.

❄ **FREEZER FRIENDLY**
✓ **KID APPROVED**

SERVING IDEA: Serve with Spring Vegetable Salad (page 139).

Diabetes Food Choice Values Per Serving

3	Carbohydrates
1	Meat & Alternatives
1 1/2	Fats

NUTRIENTS Per Serving

Calories: 415	Carbohydrate: 59.0 g	Calcium: 226mg
Fat: 12.5 g	Fiber: 9.1 g	Iron: 4.2 mg
Sodium: 1,068 mg	Protein: 9.4 g	

Very high in: Dietary fiber, iron, thiamine, riboflavin, niacin and folate • **High in:** Calcium, magnesium and zinc

Open-Faced Grilled Bean and Cheese Tortillas

- *Preparation time: 5 minutes / Cooking time: 5 to 10 minutes*
- *Preheat oven to 425°F (220°C), with rack set in center of oven*
- *Baking sheet*

4	10-inch (25 cm) flour tortillas	4
1	can (14 oz/398 mL) refried beans	1
½ cup	salsa	125 mL
1 cup	shredded Cheddar cheese	250 mL
¼ cup	finely chopped pickled jalapeño (or to taste)	50 mL
	Sour cream and additional salsa (optional)	

1. Place tortillas on baking sheet and spread evenly with refried beans, then with salsa. Sprinkle evenly with cheese and jalapeños.
2. Bake in preheated oven for 5 to 10 minutes or until cheese is browned.
3. Cut into wedges and serve with sour cream and salsa, if desired, for dipping.

 **✓ KID APPROVED**

SERVING IDEA: Serve with a fresh garden salad tossed with our Homemade Vinaigrette (page 134) spiked with a little lime juice.

MAKES 4 SERVINGS

Chantal Sigouin, Dietitian, ON

Here's another great Tex-Mex meal that the whole family can enjoy — and it's ready in no time!

TIP
Use whole wheat tortillas, low-fat refried beans and reduced-fat cheese to improve the overall nutrition of this dish.

VARIATION
You can reduce the amount of refried beans and add diced cooked chicken or browned ground beef. Add chopped green onion or diced red or green bell pepper for crunch.

NUTRIENTS Per Serving		
Calories: 386	Carbohydrate: 47.1 g	Calcium: 270 mg
Fat: 14.2 g	Fiber: 7.9 g	Iron: 3.8 mg
Sodium: 996 mg	Protein: 17.8 g	

Very high in: Dietary fiber, calcium, iron, niacin, folate, magnesium and zinc • **High in:** Vitamin C, thiamine, riboflavin and vitamin B_6

Diabetes Food Choice Values Per Serving
2½ Carbohydrates
1½ Meat & Alternatives
1½ Fats

Tofu 101

MAKES 4 SERVINGS

Nicole Fetterly, BC

This is the recipe for anyone who wants an easy way to eat tofu! It's fast and impossible to ruin. These delicious cubes taste great in any dish. Serve hot or cold in a salad, pop into a tomato pasta sauce, add to a stir-fry or just eat as is!

TIPS

For the fresh herbs, try cilantro, rosemary and/or flat-leaf (Italian) parsley.

Feel free to experiment with the dressing ingredients — try adding minced jalapeño to spice it up!

• **Preparation time: 5 minutes / Cooking time: 30 minutes**
• *Preheat oven to 400°F (200°C)*
• *8-inch (2 L) square baking pan, lightly greased*

2 tbsp	chopped fresh herbs (see tip, at left)	25 mL
½ cup	water	125 mL
2 tbsp	vegetable oil	25 mL
2 tbsp	soy sauce	25 mL
	Juice of 1 lemon or lime	
½ tsp	freshly ground black pepper	2 mL
1	package (12 oz/375 g) firm or extra-firm tofu	1

1. In prepared baking pan, whisk herbs, water, oil, soy sauce, lemon juice and pepper until well combined.

2. Cut tofu horizontally in half, then make 4 long slices, and finally cut 6 times across, to make forty-eight ½-inch (1 cm) cubes. Place in baking pan in a single layer, making sure all pieces are just covered by dressing.

3. Bake in preheated oven for 15 minutes. Turn tofu over and bake for 15 minutes or until most of the dressing is absorbed.

> **SERVING IDEA:** Add to Stir-Fried Chinese Greens (page 259) and serve over whole wheat spaghetti.

Diabetes Food Choice Values Per Serving

1	Meat & Alternatives
1	Fat

NUTRIENTS Per Serving		
Calories: 130	Carbohydrate: 3.4 g	Calcium: 182 mg
Fat: 10.5 g	Fiber: 1.1 g	Iron: 1.7 mg
Sodium: 463 mg	Protein: 7.8 g	

High in: Calcium and magnesium

Teriyaki Rice Noodles with
Veggies and Beans (page 215)

Vegetarian Chili (page 216)

Sweet Chili Tofu Stir-Fry (page 226)

Whole Wheat Pasta with Rapini,
Grape Tomatoes and Mushrooms (page 236)

Tofu Patties

Sue Minicucci, Dietitian, ON

- **Preparation time: 5 minutes / Cooking time: 20 to 25 minutes**
- *Preheat oven to 325°F (160°C)*
- *9-inch (2.5 L) square baking pan, lightly greased*

10 oz	firm tofu, mashed	300 g
¾ cup	quick-cooking rolled oats	175 mL
2 tbsp	soy sauce	25 mL
½ tsp	dried basil	2 mL
½ tsp	dried oregano	2 mL
½ tsp	garlic powder	2 mL
½ tsp	onion powder	2 mL
	Salt and freshly ground black pepper	

1. In a medium bowl, combine tofu, oats, soy sauce, basil, oregano, garlic powder, onion powder, and salt and pepper to taste. Knead for a few minutes. Shape into 1-inch (2.5 cm) thick patties and place in prepared pan.

2. Bake in preheated oven for 20 to 25 minutes or until lightly browned.

> **SERVING IDEA:** Place on a multigrain bun and top with sliced tomato, leaf lettuce and a dab of your favorite mustard or salsa.

This is a great way to prepare tofu. For children, make mini patties and place on whole-grain dinner rolls with their choice of condiments.

TIP
Look for tofu made with calcium. Look for "calcium sulfate" or "calcium chloride" in the ingredients list to make sure the tofu you are buying is a source of calcium.

NUTRIENTS Per Serving		
Calories: 83	Carbohydrate: 9.5 g	Calcium: 105 mg
Fat: 2.7 g	Fiber: 1.6 g	Iron: 1.5 mg
Sodium: 308 mg	Protein: 6.1 g	
High in: Magnesium		

Diabetes Food Choice Values Per Serving	
½	Carbohydrate
½	Meat & Alternatives

Sweet Chili Tofu Stir-Fry

MAKES 4 SERVINGS

Eileen Campbell

Stir-frying is a fast and easy way to prepare a meal without a lot of added fat. Vegetables and lean protein form the basis for this dish, with a little added sauce and seasoning for flavor. It's a flavorful way to introduce your family to tofu.

• **Preparation time: 15 minutes / Cooking time: 12 minutes**

	Vegetable cooking spray	
5 oz	firm tofu, cut into thin strips	150 g
¾ cup	sliced Spanish onion	175 mL
1 cup	broccoli florets	250 mL
1 cup	baby carrots, cut into bite-size pieces	250 mL
¾ cup	sugar snap peas, trimmed	175 mL
½ cup	julienned red bell pepper	125 mL
½ cup	vegetable broth or water	125 mL
¼ cup	sweet chili sauce	50 mL
1 tsp	grated orange zest	5 mL
1 tbsp	chopped fresh cilantro (optional)	15 mL

1. Heat a wok or large skillet over medium-high heat. Spray with vegetable cooking spray. Brown tofu on both sides, then remove from pan and set aside.

2. Add onion to wok and sauté for 1 minute. Add broccoli, carrots, peas and red pepper; stir-fry until tender-crisp, about 5 minutes. Return tofu to wok and stir in broth, chili sauce and orange zest. Heat until bubbling.

3. Transfer stir-fry to serving platter and sprinkle with cilantro, if using.

✓ **KID APPROVED**

SERVING IDEA: Serve with brown rice and pour a glass of Mango Lassi (page 85).

Diabetes Food Choice Values Per Serving

½	Carbohydrate
½	Meat & Alternatives

NUTRIENTS Per Serving

Calories: 115	Carbohydrate: 17.1 g	Calcium: 118 mg
Fat: 2.6 g	Fiber: 3.0 g	Iron: 1.7 mg
Sodium: 265 mg	Protein: 6.0 g	

Very high in: Vitamin A and vitamin C • **High in:** Folate and magnesium • **A source of:** Dietary fiber

Nutty Tofu and Green Vegetable Stir-Fry

MAKES 4 SERVINGS

Colleen Joice, Dietitian, NS

This spicy, nutty tofu recipe has the flavor of an Asian satay dish and is guaranteed to please both vegetarians and non-vegetarians!

TIP
Freeze the tofu cubes prior to preparation; this enhances the texture of the tofu so it's more poultry-like.

• *Preparation time: 20 minutes / Cooking time: 30 minutes*

1 tbsp	vegetable oil	15 mL
8 oz	firm tofu, cubed	250 g
1	green bell pepper, thinly sliced	1
1 1/2 cups	green beans, trimmed	375 mL
1/2 tsp	salt	2 mL
4	cloves garlic, minced	4
1	onion, chopped	1
1	tomato, chopped	1
1/4 cup	coarsely ground almonds	50 mL
1/2 cup	water (approx.), divided	125 mL
1/2 tsp	granulated sugar	2 mL
1/2 tsp	ground turmeric	2 mL
1/2 tsp	ground cumin	2 mL
1/2 tsp	ground coriander	2 mL

1. In a large skillet, heat oil over medium heat. Lightly brown tofu on all sides, then remove from pan and set aside.

2. Add green pepper, green beans and salt to skillet; stir-fry until tender-crisp, about 5 minutes. Add garlic, onion and tomato; stir-fry for 5 minutes. Stir in tofu pieces. Stir in almonds, 1/4 cup (50 mL) of the water and sugar. Reduce heat to low and cook for 5 minutes. Stir in turmeric, cumin and coriander, then the remaining 1/4 cup (50 mL) water (add more if the mixture becomes too dry and sticks to the pan).

✓ **KID APPROVED**

SERVING IDEA: This dish goes well with jasmine rice or noodles.

NUTRIENTS Per Serving		
Calories: 149	Carbohydrate: 13.6 g	Calcium: 117 mg
Fat: 8.9 g	Fiber: 3.8 g	Iron: 1.8 mg
Sodium: 297 mg	Protein: 6.8 g	

Very high in: Vitamin C • **High in:** Folate and magnesium
A source of: Dietary fiber

Diabetes Food Choice Values Per Serving	
1	Meat & Alternatives
1	Fat

Shefali Raja, Dietitian, BC

Serve this pilaf with plain yogurt for a low-cost, well-balanced comfort meal!

Tofu Vegetable Pilaf

• *Preparation time: 15 minutes / Cooking time: 20 to 25 minutes*

2 tbsp	butter or vegetable oil	25 mL
3 to 4	cinnamon sticks	3 to 4
3 to 4	cardamom pods	3 to 4
1/2 tsp	ground turmeric	2 mL
2	large peeled potatoes, cut into small cubes	2
1	carrot, diced	1
5 oz	firm tofu, diced	150 g
1 cup	frozen peas, thawed	250 mL
2 tbsp	grated gingerroot	25 mL
	Salt	
3 cups	water (approx.)	750 mL
1 1/2 cups	basmati rice, well rinsed	375 mL

1. In a large saucepan, melt butter over medium heat. Stir in cinnamon sticks to taste, cardamom pods to taste and turmeric. Add potatoes, carrot, tofu, peas, ginger and salt to taste; cook, stirring, for 3 to 4 minutes or until well mixed together and starting to brown. Add water and rice; bring to a boil. Reduce heat, cover and simmer for 10 minutes. Check to ensure pilaf is not sticking and stir well to combine. (If more water is needed to ensure that rice is not too dry, add small amounts at a time.) Cover and continue cooking for 5 to 10 minutes or until water is absorbed and rice is just tender. Discard cardamom pods and cinnamon sticks. Fluff with a fork.

✓ **KID APPROVED**

Diabetes Food Choice Values Per Serving	
3 1/2	Carbohydrates
1	Fat

NUTRIENTS Per Serving		
Calories: 325	Carbohydrate: 59.8 g	Calcium: 92 mg
Fat: 5.6 g	Fiber: 3.5 g	Iron: 1.5 mg
Sodium: 62 mg	Protein: 8.7 g	

Very high in: Vitamin A • **High in:** Thiamine, niacin, vitamin B$_6$, folate and magnesium • **A source of:** Dietary fiber

Tofu Veggie Kabobs

- *Preparation time: 15 minutes / Cooking time: 10 minutes*
- *Preheat barbecue to medium*
- *Eight 8-inch (20 cm) wooden skewers, soaked*

Sara Duchene-Milne,
Dietitian, ON

Unusual flavor and a kick of heat make a star out of tofu in this dish. Although the list of ingredients seems long, most of them are spices you are likely to have on hand.

Spice Mixture

2 tbsp	granulated sugar	25 mL
1 tbsp	ground cinnamon	15 mL
1 tbsp	ground nutmeg	15 mL
2 tsp	salt	10 mL
2 tsp	cayenne pepper (or to taste)	10 mL
2 tsp	onion powder	10 mL
2 tsp	dried thyme	10 mL
1 tsp	freshly ground black pepper	5 mL
1/4 cup	olive oil, divided	50 mL
3 tbsp	balsamic vinegar	45 mL
1 tbsp	soy sauce	15 mL
10 oz	firm tofu, cut into large cubes	300 g
1	large zucchini	1
1	large orange bell pepper	1
1	large yellow bell pepper	1
16	cherry tomatoes	16

TIPS
Leftover kabob vegetables make perfect pizza toppings.

The tofu can marinate overnight, covered, in the refrigerator.

VARIATION
This recipe is very versatile. You can use herbed tofu or, for a non-vegetarian meal, cubes of cooked chicken or beef. You could also substitute different vegetables, such as sweet potatoes and onions, and even fresh pineapple.

1. *Prepare the spice mixture:* In a small bowl, combine sugar, cinnamon, nutmeg, salt, cayenne, onion powder, thyme and black pepper. Set aside.

2. In a large bowl, combine 2 tbsp (25 mL) of the olive oil, balsamic vinegar and soy sauce. Add tofu and set aside to marinate while you chop the vegetables.

3. Cut zucchini, orange pepper and yellow pepper into large pieces. In a bowl, combine zucchini, peppers and cherry tomatoes. Add spice mixture and the remaining 2 tbsp (25 mL) olive oil; toss until vegetables are evenly coated.

4. Thread zucchini, peppers, tomatoes and tofu cubes onto skewers. Place on preheated barbecue and cook, turning at least once, for about 10 minutes or until browned.

SERVING IDEA:
Serve these kabobs with rice or pasta or on top of fresh greens.

NUTRIENTS Per Serving		
Calories: 144	Carbohydrate: 13.0 g	Calcium: 124 mg
Fat: 9.2 g	Fiber: 2.7 g	Iron: 2.1 mg
Sodium: 696 mg	Protein: 4.9 g	
Very high in: Vitamin C • **High in:** Iron and magnesium		
A source of: Dietary fiber		

Diabetes Food Choice Values Per Serving

1/2	Carbohydrate
1/2	Meat & Alternatives
1 1/2	Fats

Pasta and Pizza

Pasta and pizza are two family favorites. There's no need to go out to a restaurant or order pizza in when you can easily make delicious and healthy recipes at home.

storing cooked pasta

When cooking pasta, cook more than you need for one recipe. You can store the leftover pasta and use it in other recipes. To store cooked pasta:

- Toss with 1 to 3 tsp (5 to 15 mL) vegetable oil while pasta is still warm. (This ensures the pieces won't stick together when they cool.)
- Place the pasta in a resealable food storage bag and set it, unsealed, in the refrigerator. Once it is cool, seal the bag and lightly turn the contents around to make sure the pasta is not sticking together.
- Use the pasta cold if the recipe calls for it. You can also reheat it by dropping the pasta into a pot of rapidly boiling water for 30 to 60 seconds, just until hot. Don't leave it in the water for longer than 1 minute, or it will become mushy.

Converting to Whole Wheat Pasta

For extra nutrients and fiber, try to eat whole wheat pasta more often than white. If your family is just starting to eat whole wheat pasta, mix it half and half with regular pasta until they get used to it. Gradually increase the percentage of whole wheat until the whole dish is whole-grain! Try a few brands of whole wheat pasta until you find one your family really likes. Whole wheat pasta can be used in any of the pasta recipes in this book.

Perfect Pasta Every Time

To serve four people, use 2 cups (500 mL) of short-cut pasta, such as macaroni or penne, or a 1-inch (2.5 cm) diameter bunch of long-cut pasta, such as spaghetti or fettuccine. One pound (500 g) of short-cut pasta is approximately 5¼ cups (1.3 L).

- Use an 8- to 10-quart pot with a lid and a minimum of 4 quarts (4 L) of fresh boiling water for each pound (500 g) of pasta. The abundance of water prevents the pasta from clumping and allows for even cooking. Do not add salt or oil to the water. Oil prevents sauce from sticking to pasta and adds extra calories. Salt is not necessary; the seasoning will be in the sauce.
- Make sure the water is boiling rapidly before adding the pasta. It should return to a rolling boil within 30 seconds. Stir with a spoon to gently submerge and separate pasta.
- Depending on the shape of the pasta, allow 5 to 12 minutes for dry pasta and 1 to 4 minutes for fresh. Pasta should be cooked until it is "al dente": tender but with a hint of firmness. When in doubt, use the package directions as a guideline
- As soon as the pasta is cooked, drain it into a colander placed in the sink. If left in the cooking water, it will lose its firmness. Shake the colander to remove water, especially for pasta shapes that trap liquid, such as penne. Do not rinse or wash with water or add oil. Rinsing removes the surface starch, and oil creates a barrier. Both actions will prevent sauce from properly clinging to the pasta. (An exception is if you're making a pasta salad, in which case rinsing is fine to cool the pasta.) As soon as the pasta is drained, toss it with sauce. This provides a thorough coating of sauce. Tossing is especially important with cream sauces to make sure the sauce is evenly distributed.

making pizza

When making pizza, the only limit is your imagination — just about anything can be a pizza topping, so be creative! Let your kids help prepare and top the pizza. Start with ½ cup (125 mL) sauce and add 2 to 3 cups (500 to 750 mL) vegetables and/or 2 to 4 oz (60 to 125 g) meat or another protein choice. Sprinkle with 1 to 2 tbsp (15 to 25 mL) fresh herbs (or 1 to 2 tsp/5 to 10 mL dried herbs), if desired, and finish with 1 to 2 cups (250 to 500 mL) of your favorite cheeses.

Here are some suggestions to get you going:

- **Sauce:** Pizza sauce, herbed tomato sauce, tomato salsa or your favorite canned soup (cream of mushroom works great for a mushroom and cheese pizza; cream of chicken works well with cooked chicken, peppers and cheese)
- **Vegetables:** Tomatoes, olives, zucchini, eggplant, onions, mushrooms, roasted bell peppers, hot peppers, broccoli, garlic
- **Meat and Alternatives:** Bacon, browned ground beef, sausage, cooked chicken strips, ham, shrimp, salmon, tofu, beans, lentils
- **Herbs and Seasonings:** Basil, oregano, thyme, parsley, rosemary, dill, garlic powder, onion powder
- **Cheese:** Mozzarella, Cheddar, Swiss, Asiago, Parmesan, feta, goat cheese, blue cheese

Enhancing Store-Bought Sauce

If you use bottled tomato sauce for convenience, enhance it by adding vegetables such as bell peppers, broccoli, mushrooms or onions. Grate them finely into the sauce to slip them past your kids if they're on an "I hate vegetables" kick.

Eileen Campbell

Big-Batch Italian Tomato Master Sauce

This Italian master sauce makes a great base for many pasta dishes. There are several recipes in this book that call for tomato sauce. You could buy a commercial product, but think how much more satisfying it is to have your own special sauce, right there in the freezer.

TIPS

Stovetop Method: If you don't have a slow cooker, you can still make the sauce by adjusting the method slightly. Sauté the onions and garlic in a large pot, then add all of the other ingredients and bring to a boil. Reduce heat, cover and simmer, stirring occasionally, for 4 hours until flavor is developed.

If you prefer a thicker sauce, purée it slightly.

Planned Extras
Make a batch on the weekend. Keep some in the fridge for use during the week and freeze the rest in 2-cup (500 mL) or 3-cup (750 mL) portions for later use. Use on pasta alone, or with beans, vegetables and protein added; as a base for minestrone soup; or to replace any commercial sauce in your recipes.

- **Preparation time: 15 minutes / Cooking time: 5 minutes / Slow cooker time: 8 hours**
- *Large (minimum 6-quart) slow cooker*

3 tbsp	olive oil	45 mL
6	cloves garlic, minced	6
1	large Spanish onion, finely diced	1
1 tsp	salt, divided	5 mL
4	cans (each 28 oz/796 mL) whole plum tomatoes, with juice, chopped	4
4	sprigs fresh basil, divided	4
1 tsp	dried oregano	5 mL
1/2 tsp	freshly ground black pepper	2 mL
	Granulated sugar (optional)	

1. In a large skillet, heat olive oil over medium-high heat. Add garlic and onion; season lightly with some of the salt. Sauté until lightly browned, about 5 minutes.

2. Transfer sautéed vegetables to slow cooker. Stir in tomatoes, 3 of the basil sprigs, oregano, the remaining salt and pepper. Cover and cook on Low for 8 hours, until flavor is developed. If sauce is thin, near the end of the cooking time increase to High and keep lid slightly open until sauce thickens. Discard basil sprigs.

3. Chop the remaining basil sprig and add to sauce. Taste and season with salt and pepper, if desired. Add sugar if sauce is too tart.

○ **SLOW COOKER FRIENDLY**
❄ **FREEZER FRIENDLY**
✓ **KID APPROVED**

Diabetes Food Choice Values Per Serving

1/2	Fat

NUTRIENTS Per Serving		
Calories: 34	Carbohydrate: 5.3 g	Calcium: 36 mg
Fat: 1.4 g	Fiber: 1.0 g	Iron: 1.1 mg
Sodium: 201 mg	Protein: 1.0 g	

Spaghetti Sauce

Judy Jenkins, Dietitian, NS

Don't have a favorite spaghetti sauce? This one is sure to become your favorite.

• *Preparation time: 10 minutes / Cooking time: 35 to 45 minutes*

12 oz	lean ground beef	375 g
1	small onion, chopped	1
1	clove garlic, minced	1
1	can (19 oz/540 mL) stewed tomatoes, with juice, chopped	1
1	can (5½ oz/156 mL) tomato paste	1
¼ cup	chopped green bell pepper	50 mL
1 tbsp	dried basil	15 mL
½ tsp	crushed fennel seeds	2 mL
Pinch	freshly ground black pepper	Pinch

1. In a large skillet, over medium heat, brown ground beef, breaking up chunks. Add onion, garlic, tomatoes, tomato paste, green pepper, basil, fennel seeds and pepper; bring to a boil. Reduce heat and simmer, stirring occasionally, for 20 to 30 minutes or until vegetables are tender and flavor is well developed.

❄ **FREEZER FRIENDLY**
✓ **KID APPROVED**

NUTRIENTS Per Serving		
Calories: 114	Carbohydrate: 8.0 g	Calcium: 37.0 mg
Fat: 4.9 g	Fiber: 1.7 g	Iron: 2.1 mg
Sodium: 168 mg	Protein: 8.1 g	

Very high in: Vitamin B$_{12}$ • **High in:** Iron, niacin and zinc

Diabetes Food Choice Values Per Serving	
1	Meat & Alternatives

Vegetable Pasta Sauce

MAKES 5 CUPS
(1.25 L) OR
8 SERVINGS

Tina Coutts, ON

This chunky sauce is a great way to get your family to eat more vegetables.

VARIATION
Add chopped fresh tomatoes when the sauce is almost done cooking.

Planned Extras
Extra sauce can be the base for a chunky vegetable soup for lunch on a chilly day.

• *Preparation time: 10 minutes / Cooking time: 45 minutes*

	Vegetable cooking spray	
2	carrots, chopped	2
2	small zucchini, chopped	2
1	small onion, chopped	1
1	green bell pepper, chopped	1
8 oz	mushrooms, chopped	250 g
1 to 2	cloves fresh garlic, minced	1 to 2
1	can (19 oz/540 mL) reduced-sodium tomato sauce	1
	Italian herb seasoning	
	Dried oregano	

1. Heat a large nonstick skillet over medium heat. Spray with vegetable cooking spray. Sauté carrots, zucchini, onion, green pepper, mushrooms and garlic until lightly browned, about 5 minutes. Stir in tomato sauce and Italian seasoning and oregano to taste; bring to a boil. Reduce heat and simmer, stirring often, for about 30 minutes or until vegetables are tender and flavor is well developed.

✓ **KID APPROVED**

SERVING IDEA: Serve over whole wheat pasta and stir in cooked extra-lean ground beef, ground soy or crumbled tofu. Sprinkle with a little grated Parmesan or shredded mozzarella cheese to add another food group! Enjoy a glass of milk to round out the meal. Have dried apricots and walnuts for dessert.

Diabetes Food Choice Values Per Serving

½	Carbohydrate
1	Fat

NUTRIENTS Per Serving

Calories: 101	Carbohydrate: 16.2 g	Calcium: 32 mg
Fat: 3.8 g	Fiber: 3.6 g	Iron: 1.0 mg
Sodium: 33 mg	Protein: 2.2 g	

Very high in: Vitamin A • **High in:** Vitamin C and vitamin B_6
A source of: Dietary fiber

Easy Pasta with Beans

**MAKES
10 SERVINGS**

Eileen Campbell

• Preparation time: 3 minutes / Cooking time: 20 minutes

3 cups	Big-Batch Italian Tomato Master Sauce (page 232)	750 mL
1	can (19 oz/540 mL) white kidney beans, drained and rinsed (about 2 cups/500 mL)	1
1 lb	short-cut pasta (penne, rigatoni, rotini or shells)	500 g
2 tbsp	chopped fresh parsley, basil or chives	25 mL
	Freshly grated Parmesan cheese (optional)	

1. In a large saucepan, heat tomato sauce over medium heat until bubbling. Stir in beans. Reduce heat and simmer for 20 minutes, until hot and thickened.

2. Meanwhile, cook pasta in a large pot of boiling water until al dente (tender to the bite). Drain.

3. Transfer pasta to a serving bowl, top with sauce and sprinkle with parsley. Offer Parmesan as a topper, if desired.

✓ KID APPROVED

SERVING IDEAS: Serve this light, healthy meal with a glass of milk or enjoy a container of yogurt with fruit for dessert.

On Friday nights, or whenever you're short on time and energy, serve with a store-bought Caesar salad. Defrost slices of Carrot Cake (page 305) for dessert.

This is a great way to use the Tomato Master Sauce recipe (page 232) — just combine it with canned beans for a fast pasta sauce. This dish can be made even more quickly if you have leftover cooked pasta on hand.

TIP
If you don't have time to prepare the Tomato Master Sauce — and you don't have any stored in the freezer — you can substitute a 28-oz (796 mL) can or jar of tomato pasta sauce.

NUTRIENTS Per Serving		
Calories: 290	Carbohydrate: 53.7 g	Calcium: 63 mg
Fat: 3.8 g	Fiber: 6.0 g	Iron: 3.6 mg
Sodium: 661 mg	Protein: 10.4 g	

Very high in: Dietary fiber, iron, niacin and folate
High in: Thiamine, magnesium and zinc

Diabetes Food Choice Values Per Serving	
3	Carbohydrates
1	Fat

Eileen Campbell

This recipe is a weeknight blessing, as it takes only 15 minutes from start to finish.

TIP

There is no sauce for this pasta. If you prefer a saucy dish, add the tomatoes earlier, with the mushrooms, and cook to release their juices.

Rapini

Rapini, also known as broccoli raab, is a bitter green prized for its assertive flavor. Its pungency and bite adds inspiration to less potent partners such as pasta, rice, polenta and mushrooms. Popular in Italian cuisine, it is steamed, braised, used in stir-fries and added to pizza, pasta and soup. It is low in calories and sodium, has no fat or cholesterol, and is high in vitamins A and C. Rapini also provides iron and calcium and, like other cruciferous vegetables, contains compounds and phytochemicals with cancer-fighting benefits. The potassium, folate, fiber and bioflavonoids found in cruciferous vegetables may help prevent the risk of stroke. Try to eat deep green leafy vegetables daily.

Whole Wheat Pasta with Rapini, Grape Tomatoes and Mushrooms

• *Preparation time: 5 minutes / Cooking time: 10 minutes*

2 cups	short-cut whole wheat pasta (such as rotini or penne)	500 mL
1	head rapini (broccoli raab, or rape), trimmed and chopped into 3-inch (7.5 cm) lengths	1
2 tbsp	extra-virgin olive oil	25 mL
2	green onions, finely chopped	2
2 cups	sliced mushrooms	500 mL
1 cup	grape tomatoes, halved	250 mL
¼ cup	freshly grated Parmesan cheese	50 mL
2 tbsp	chopped fresh basil, chives or parsley (optional)	25 mL

1. Cook pasta according to package directions. When pasta is 3 minutes from being cooked, add rapini. Cook until pasta is al dente (tender to the bite). Drain.

2. Meanwhile, in a large skillet, heat olive oil over medium-high heat. Sauté green onions and mushrooms for 4 minutes. Stir in pasta and rapini; cook, stirring constantly, to reheat pasta. Stir in tomatoes.

3. Serve sprinkled with Parmesan and basil, if using.

SERVING IDEA: Add more protein by topping with strips of grilled pork, steak or chicken. For a vegetarian alternative, top with red kidney beans.

Diabetes Food Choice Values Per Serving	
1½	Carbohydrates
1	Meat & Alternatives
1	Fat

NUTRIENTS Per Serving		
Calories: 287	Carbohydrate: 39.3 g	Calcium: 386 mg
Fat: 9.8 g	Fiber: 7.3 g	Iron: 3.8 mg
Sodium: 259 mg	Protein: 13.9 g	

Very high in: Dietary fiber, vitamin A, vitamin C, calcium, iron, niacin and magnesium • **High in:** Thiamin and zinc

Tomato Basil Fettuccine with Prosciutto

MAKES 6 SERVINGS

Mary Lee McCormick, ON

• **Preparation time: 15 minutes / Cooking time: 25 minutes**

10 oz	whole wheat fettuccini or cracked pepper fettuccini pasta	300 g
2 tbsp	olive oil	25 mL
5 oz	Italian prosciutto, thinly sliced and chopped	150 g
1 cup	sliced mushrooms	250 mL
8 oz	light cream cheese, cut into chunks	250 g
¾ cup	milk	175 mL
	Salt and freshly ground black pepper	
5	Roma (plum) tomatoes, chopped	5
2 tbsp	chopped fresh basil	25 mL

1. Cook fettuccini according to package directions until al dente (tender to the bite). Drain.

2. Meanwhile, in a large skillet, heat oil over medium heat. Sauté prosciutto and mushrooms until mushrooms are tender, about 5 minutes. Reduce heat and add cream cheese and milk, stirring until consistency is creamy. Season to taste with salt and pepper. Simmer, stirring occasionally, for 15 minutes. Do not let boil. Stir in tomatoes and basil. Remove from heat, stir in fettuccini and serve immediately.

✓ **KID APPROVED**

SERVING IDEA: Serve cooked rapini on the side to add a green vegetable to your meal. Finish with a bowl of fresh berries.

This rich, creamy recipe reminded our taste panel of pasta dishes their mothers used to make when they were kids. All of the prep work can be done in advance, so you'll have more time to visit with friends and family. No salt is added, as the prosciutto provides plenty.

TIP
If you have any leftovers, you may need to add milk to thin the sauce when reheating.

NUTRIENTS Per Serving		
Calories: 317	Carbohydrate: 32.1 g	Calcium: 105.0 mg
Fat: 15.1 g	Fiber: 3.8 g	Iron: 2.2 mg
Sodium: 537 mg	Protein: 15.3 g	

Very high in: Thiamine and niacin • **High in:** Iron, riboflavin, vitamin B$_{12}$, magnesium and zinc • **A source of:** Dietary fiber

Diabetes Food Choice Values Per Serving	
2	Carbohydrates
1	Meat & Alternatives
2	Fats

This updated version of a family favorite is so tasty that no one will suspect it's made with whole wheat macaroni.

TIPS

When using margarine, choose a non-hydrogenated version to limit consumption of trans fats.

This dish can be prepared through Step 2 up to 1 day in advance. Cover and refrigerate until ready to bake, and increase baking time to 30 to 40 minutes or until dish is hot all the way through.

SERVING IDEA:
Serve with a large green salad with lots of raw vegetables and, if desired, leftover chunks of ham to add some meat to the meal.

Whole Wheat Macaroni and Cheese

- **Preparation time: 20 minutes / Cooking time: 30 minutes**
- *Preheat oven to 350°F (180°C)*
- *11- by 7-inch (2 L) baking dish, greased*

1½ cups	whole wheat macaroni	375 mL
3 tbsp	margarine	45 mL
3 tbsp	all-purpose flour	45 mL
¾ tsp	salt	4 mL
2 cups	skim milk (approx.)	500 mL
1 tbsp	dehydrated minced onion	15 mL
	Freshly ground black pepper	
2 cups	shredded Cheddar cheese (medium or sharp)	500 mL
¼ cup	dry whole wheat bread crumbs	50 mL
2 tsp	dried parsley	10 mL

1. Cook macaroni according to package directions until al dente (tender to the bite). Drain.

2. Meanwhile, in a large heavy saucepan, melt margarine over medium heat. Whisk in flour and salt to make a smooth paste. Whisk in milk, ½ cup (125 mL) at a time. Cook, stirring frequently, until sauce thickens, about 5 minutes. (Add milk if sauce is too thick). Remove from heat and stir in onion and pepper. Stir in cheese until melted. Stir in macaroni until well coated.

3. Transfer macaroni and cheese to prepared baking dish. Sprinkle with bread crumbs and parsley.

4. Bake in preheated oven for about 15 minutes or until topping is golden.

❄ FREEZER FRIENDLY
✓ KID APPROVED

Diabetes Food Choice Values Per Serving	
2	Carbohydrates
1	Meat & Alternatives
3	Fats

NUTRIENTS Per Serving		
Calories: 357	Carbohydrate: 31.2 g	Calcium: 397 mg
Fat: 19.0 g	Fiber: 3.1 g	Iron: 1.6 mg
Sodium: 746 mg	Protein: 17.3 g	

Very high in: Calcium, vitamin B$_{12}$ and zinc • **High in:** Vitamin A, riboflavin, niacin and magnesium • **A source of:** Dietary fiber

Green Macaroni and Cheese

• Preparation time: 5 minutes / Cooking time: 10 minutes

1	bag (10 oz/300 g) baby spinach	1
2 tbsp	freshly squeezed lemon juice	25 mL
1 tbsp	extra-virgin olive oil	15 mL
12 oz	whole wheat macaroni	375 g
1 cup	shredded white Cheddar cheese	250 mL
1/2 cup	slivered almonds, toasted	125 mL
	Freshly ground black pepper	

1. In food processor, pulse spinach, lemon juice and olive oil for 15 seconds, until roughly puréed (don't overdo it).
2. Cook macaroni according to package directions until al dente (tender to the bite). Drain and return to the pot. Add spinach mixture, tossing to coat evenly. Stir in cheese and almonds. Season to taste with pepper.

✓ KID APPROVED

> **SERVING IDEA:** For kids, serve carrot sticks on the side; for adults, Roasted Beet, Walnut and Arugula Salad (page 143). Toss in slices of leftover steak, chicken or crumbled tofu.

Jody MacLean, NS

Joy makes this for her two small children. Whole spinach leaves tend to be hard for them to chew and swallow, so this is a great way to get some greens into them.

VARIATIONS
Substitute 1/2 cup (125 mL) freshly grated Parmesan cheese for the Cheddar. Because of its stronger flavor, you don't need as much.

Substitute a 1-lb (500 g) container of fat-free cottage cheese for the Cheddar.

For a more grown-up palate, add chopped fresh dill and extra black pepper, and use penne, rotini or fusilli.

Planned Extras
Store any extras in the fridge and reheat for lunch the next day.

NUTRIENTS Per Serving		
Calories: 429	Carbohydrate: 55.6 g	Calcium: 290 mg
Fat: 16.9 g	Fiber: 8.6 g	Iron: 4.6 mg
Sodium: 378 mg	Protein: 19.8 g	

Very high in: Dietary fiber, vitamin A, calcium, iron, niacin, folate, magnesium and zinc • **High in:** Thiamine, riboflavin and vitamin B$_6$

Diabetes Food Choice Values Per Serving	
3	Carbohydrates
1	Meat & Alternatives
2 1/2	Fats

239

Linda Smith, AB

Linda invented this recipe when she was a single mom on social assistance with three small kids to feed. At that time, she used only ground beef, onions, regular macaroni and tomato soup. Nowadays, she uses whole wheat pasta, which her family enjoys immensely, and she has added vegetables and seasonings for flavor. Her children help chop, stir and test for doneness.

TIP
If desired, top with shredded part-skim mozzarella cheese to add some dairy.

Hamburger Noodle Casserole

• *Preparation time: 15 minutes / Cooking time: 25 minutes*

12 oz	whole wheat macaroni	375 g
3	stalks celery, chopped into 1/4-inch (0.5 cm) pieces	3
2	cloves garlic, finely chopped	2
1/2	large onion, chopped into 1/4-inch (0.5 cm) pieces	1/2
1/2	red bell pepper, chopped into 1/4-inch (0.5 cm) pieces	1/2
1/4	jalapeño pepper, seeded and finely chopped	1/4
1 lb	lean ground beef	500 g
1/2 tsp	freshly ground black pepper	2 mL
1/2 tsp	dried basil	2 mL
1/2 tsp	dried oregano	2 mL
2	cans (each 10 oz/284 mL) condensed tomato soup, undiluted	2

1. Cook macaroni according to package directions until al dente (tender to the bite). Drain.

2. Meanwhile, in a large saucepan, over medium heat, sauté celery, garlic, onion, red pepper, jalapeño, ground beef, pepper, basil and oregano, breaking up chunks of beef, until beef is no longer pink, about 10 minutes. Drain off any fat. Stir in tomato soup and heat to boiling. Add pasta and stir well.

❄ FREEZER FRIENDLY
✓ KID APPROVED

SERVING IDEA: Fresh vegetable sticks add crunch to the menu. Serve with ice cold milk. Soft Apple Cinnamon Cookies (page 316) will help complete a low-cost meal.

Diabetes Food Choice Values Per Serving

2 1/2 Carbohydrates
1 1/2 Meat & Alternatives

NUTRIENTS Per Serving		
Calories: 338	Carbohydrate: 44.6 g	Calcium: 47 mg
Fat: 8.9 g	Fiber: 5.2 g	Iron: 3.4 mg
Sodium: 603 mg	Protein: 19.1 g	

Very high in: Niacin, vitamin B_{12}, magnesium and zinc
High in: Dietary fiber, iron, thiamine, riboflavin and vitamin B_6

Linguine with Chili Shrimp

• **Preparation time: 10 minutes / Cooking time: 15 minutes**

8 oz	linguine	250 g
1 tbsp	olive oil	15 mL
2	cloves garlic, minced	2
½	red bell pepper, chopped	½
14 to 16	shrimp, peeled and deveined	14 to 16
½	small red chili pepper, seeded and finely chopped (or a pinch of hot pepper flakes)	½
2 tbsp	butter	25 mL
1 tbsp	freshly squeezed lemon juice	15 mL
	Handful arugula	

1. Cook linguine according to package directions until al dente (tender to the bite). Drain.
2. Meanwhile, in a large skillet, heat olive oil over medium heat. Sauté garlic for a few seconds, being careful not to burn it. Add red pepper; sauté for about 2 minutes or until it begins to soften. Add shrimp and chili pepper; cook for 1 to 2 minutes, or until shrimp are pink and opaque. Remove from heat and add butter and linguine; toss to coat.
3. Serve immediately, drizzled with lemon juice and topped with arugula.

✓ KID APPROVED

SERVING IDEA: Serve with Steamed Asian Vegetable Medley (page 263) for another vegetable serving and finish off the meal with a glass of Mango Lassi (page 85).

MAKES 4 SERVINGS

Samantha Thiessen, Dietitian, ON

This was a huge hit with our tasting panel, even the children. It was gone in just a few minutes.

TIP
The longer you cook the chili pepper, the less heat it has. Removing the seeds also helps to reduce the spiciness.

VARIATION
If you cannot find arugula, substitute baby spinach.

NUTRIENTS Per Serving		
Calories: 335	Carbohydrate: 44.5 g	Calcium: 35 mg
Fat: 10.8 g	Fiber: 2.8 g	Iron: 3.0 mg
Sodium: 243 mg	Protein: 14.4 g	

Very high in: Vitamin C, thiamine, niacin and folate • **High in:** Iron, vitamin B$_{12}$ and magnesium • **A source of:** Dietary fiber

Diabetes Food Choice Values Per Serving	
2½	Carbohydrates
1	Meat & Alternatives
1½	Fats

Karen Boyd, Dietitian, AB

Everyone on our taste panel loved this authentic Thai dish.

TIP
Some of the ingredients may be hard to find, so here are some substitution suggestions: linguine or fettuccini for the rice noodles; soy sauce for the fish sauce; a combination of minced garlic, soy sauce and plum sauce for the hoisin sauce; hot pepper sauce for the chili-garlic sauce; mint or parsley for the cilantro.

SERVING IDEA:
Enjoy a simple dessert of custard and fruit.

Asian Stir-Fried Noodles with Shrimp

• Preparation time: 30 minutes / Soaking time: 30 minutes / Cooking time: 4 to 8 minutes

3 oz	dried wide rice noodles	90 g
2 tbsp	granulated sugar	25 mL
2 tbsp	fish sauce	25 mL
1 tbsp	soy sauce	15 mL
1 tsp	hoisin sauce	5 mL
1 tsp	chili-garlic sauce	5 mL
1 tbsp	vegetable oil	15 mL
2	cloves garlic, minced	2
6 oz	shrimp, peeled and deveined	175 g
1½ cups	bean sprouts	375 mL
10	fresh mint leaves, chopped	10
¼ cup	coarsely chopped fresh cilantro	50 mL
3 tbsp	crushed unsalted dry-roasted peanuts	45 mL
1	lime, cut into wedges	1

1. Soak rice noodles in a bowl of very warm water until pliable but still firm, about 30 minutes. Drain.

2. In a small bowl, combine sugar, fish sauce, soy sauce, hoisin sauce and chili-garlic sauce.

3. Heat a wok or large skillet over medium-high heat. Add oil and swirl to coat wok. Stir-fry garlic and shrimp for 2 to 3 minutes, or until shrimp are pink and opaque. Stir in fish sauce mixture, then noodles. Stir-fry for 1 to 2 minutes or until noodles are tender and liquid is absorbed. (If noodles are too firm at this point, add 1 tbsp/15 mL of water and cook for 1 minute.) Add bean sprouts; stir-fry for 1 to 2 minutes or until slightly limp.

4. Serve immediately, garnished with mint, cilantro and peanuts, with lime wedges on the side.

Diabetes Food Choice Values Per Serving	
2	Carbohydrates
1	Meat & Alternatives
1	Fat

NUTRIENTS Per Serving		
Calories: 227	Carbohydrate: 30.5 g	Calcium: 43 mg
Fat: 7.3 g	Fiber: 1.8 g	Iron: 1.7 mg
Sodium: 1,014 mg	Protein: 10.9 g	

High in: Niacin, vitamin B_6, vitamin B_{12}, folate and magnesium

Shrimp, Vegetables and Whole Wheat Pasta

• **Preparation time: 15 minutes / Cooking time: 10 to 12 minutes**

4 cups	whole wheat pasta (such as fusilli or penne)	1 L
1 tbsp	olive oil	15 mL
3	cloves garlic, minced	3
1	bunch broccoli, chopped	1
1	red bell pepper, sliced	1
2 cups	grape tomatoes, halved	500 mL
12 oz	shrimp, peeled, deveined and halved	375 g
1 tsp	dried Italian herb seasoning	5 mL
½ tsp	salt	2 mL
½ tsp	freshly ground black pepper	2 mL

1. Cook pasta according to package directions until al dente (tender to the bite). Drain.
2. Meanwhile, heat a large skillet over medium-high heat. Add oil and swirl to coat pan. Sauté garlic for 1 minute, being careful not to burn it. Add broccoli, red pepper and tomatoes; sauté for 5 to 7 minutes or until vegetables are tender-crisp. Add shrimp and cook, turning once, until opaque and slightly browned, about 4 minutes. Stir in pasta, Italian seasoning, salt and pepper.

✓ **KID APPROVED**

> **SERVING IDEA:** For a dessert treat, serve Chocolate Fondue (page 311) with fruits for dipping. Or serve lower-fat cheese and grapes or melon slices.

This is a very attractive one-dish meal with lots of color, and it's simple to make and tastes great. It looks like a lot of food on the plate, so it satisfies you visually, but it is loaded with vegetables and there's not too much pasta.

VARIATIONS

Change some of the vegetables for variety. You could try sugar snap peas, snow peas or spinach instead of the broccoli, or yellow pepper or carrot instead of the red pepper. Or use a frozen vegetable blend.

The dish does not have a lot of sauce. If you prefer a saucier dish, add a little pesto or a creamy tomato sauce. If using pesto, omit the Italian seasoning.

NUTRIENTS Per Serving		
Calories: 223	Carbohydrate: 34.2 g	Calcium: 78 mg
Fat: 3.9 g	Fiber: 5.8 g	Iron: 2.9 mg
Sodium: 382 mg	Protein: 16.1 g	

Very high in: Vitamin C, niacin, folate and magnesium • **High in:** Dietary fiber, vitamin A, iron, thiamine, vitamin B_6, vitamin B_{12} and zinc

Diabetes Food Choice Values Per Serving	
1½	Carbohydrates
1	Meat & Alternatives

Judy Jenkins, Dietitian, NS

"This dish is to die for," said Chef Eileen's doggy daycare lady, Vicky. She and her husband taste-tested it and could not get enough. It does take a while to make, so save it for a night when you have time to cook without rushing.

TIP

For the cheese, try part-skim mozzarella, Swiss, white Cheddar, Gouda or Gruyère.

Planned Extras

Make lasagna on the weekend and reheat during the week for a fast meal.

Chicken Lasagna

• **Preparation time: 20 minutes / Cooking time: 75 to 80 minutes**
• *Preheat oven to 350°F (180°C)*
• *13- by 9-inch (3 L) baking pan, lightly greased*

9	lasagna noodles	9
2 tbsp	vegetable oil	25 mL
3	stalks celery, chopped	3
2	large white onions, chopped	2
2	large mushrooms, sliced	2
2	cloves garlic, minced	2
1 1/2	green bell peppers, chopped	1 1/2
1 cup	white wine	250 mL
2 lbs	boneless skinless chicken breasts, chopped into 1-inch (2.5 cm) cubes	1 kg
2	chicken bouillon cubes	2
1 cup	sour cream	250 mL
2 tbsp	all-purpose flour	25 mL
1 tbsp	chopped fresh parsley	15 mL
	Salt and freshly ground black pepper	
3 cups	shredded white cheese (see tip, at left)	750 mL

1. Cook lasagna noodles according to package directions until al dente (tender to the bite). Drain and set aside in cold water.

2. In a large saucepan, heat oil over medium heat. Sauté celery, onions, mushrooms, garlic and green peppers until tender, about 5 minutes. Add wine, chicken and chicken bouillon cubes (do not dilute). Cook until chicken just barely turns white and bouillon cubes are dissolved, about 8 minutes. Using a slotted spoon, remove chicken and vegetables to a plate.

3. To the liquid remaining in the pan, add sour cream, flour, parsley, and salt and pepper to taste. Cook, stirring constantly, for 5 to 8 minutes or until sauce is thickened. Return the chicken-vegetable mixture to the pan and stir to combine.

4. Line bottom of prepared baking pan with 3 noodles. Spread one-third of the chicken-vegetable mixture on top of the noodles, then sprinkle with 1 cup (250 mL) of cheese. Make two more layers of noodles, chicken-vegetable mixture and cheese, ending with cheese.

5. Cover with foil and bake in preheated oven for 35 minutes. Remove foil and bake for 10 minutes or until bubbly on the sides and cheese is lightly browned.

❄ FREEZER FRIENDLY
✓ KID APPROVED

> **SERVING IDEA:** Serve with Strawberry Spinach Salad (page 142) for a very yummy dinner!

Cleaning and Storing Mushrooms

Clean mushrooms with a damp cloth. Do not immerse them in water — they soak it up like a sponge. Store fresh mushrooms in the refrigerator for up to 1 week in a paper bag, rather than in plastic, where they are too moist and become slimy.

NUTRIENTS Per Serving		
Calories: 405	Carbohydrate: 29.3 g	Calcium: 344 mg
Fat: 15.6 g	Fiber: 2.9 g	Iron: 1.9 mg
Sodium: 571 mg	Protein: 35.1 g	

Very high in: Calcium, niacin, vitamin B_6, vitamin B_{12}, folate, magnesium and zinc • **High in:** Vitamin C, thiamine and riboflavin • **A source of:** Dietary fiber

Diabetes Food Choice Values Per Serving

1½	Carbohydrates
3½	Meat & Alternatives

Judy Jenkins, Dietitian, NS

This is a great "planned extra" recipe, using leftover spaghetti and sauce, but it is equally good when made from scratch. It also freezes well for future use. All you need is a microwave and the ingredients, and dinner is served in less than 30 minutes.

TIPS

When using margarine, choose a non-hydrogenated version to limit consumption of trans fats.

If you don't have time to prepare the Spaghetti Sauce — and you don't have any stored in the freezer — you can substitute store-bought meat pasta sauce.

VARIATION

If you can't find provolone, substitute another mild or smoked white cheese.

Microwave Spaghetti Pie

• *Preparation time: 10 minutes / Cooking time: 10 to 14 minutes*

• *10-inch (25 cm) microwave-safe pie plate, lightly greased*

1	egg, beaten	1
1/3 cup	freshly grated Parmesan cheese	75 mL
2 tbsp	melted margarine or butter	25 mL
6 oz	spaghetti, cooked (about 1 1/2 cups/ 375 mL)	175 g
2 cups	shredded mozzarella cheese	500 mL
3 cups	Spaghetti Sauce (page 233)	750 mL
3 oz	sliced provolone cheese (about 5 slices), cut into wedges	90 g

1. In a medium bowl, combine egg, Parmesan and margarine. Add spaghetti and toss to coat.

2. Press noodle mixture into bottom and sides of prepared pie plate to form a crust. Cover with vented waxed or parchment paper and microwave on Medium (50%) for 5 to 7 minutes or until noodles are slightly crisp. Let cool for 3 minutes.

3. Sprinkle crust with mozzarella and pour in spaghetti sauce. Cover with waxed or parchment paper and microwave on Medium (50%) for 5 to 7 minutes or until heated through.

4. Decorate top evenly with provolone. Let stand for 5 minutes to allow provolone to soften. Cut into 6 wedges and serve.

❄ FREEZER FRIENDLY
✓ KID APPROVED

> **SERVING IDEA:** Add a mixed green salad with Homemade Vinaigrette (page 134) and serve fresh strawberries for dessert.

Diabetes Food Choice Values Per Serving	
1 1/2	Carbohydrates
2	Meat & Alternatives
3	Fats

NUTRIENTS Per Serving		
Calories: 427	Carbohydrate: 29.4 g	Calcium: 357 mg
Fat: 24.1 g	Fiber: 1.3 g	Iron: 1.3 mg
Sodium: 1,320 mg	Protein: 22.4 g	

Very high in: Calcium, folate and vitamin B_{12}
High in: Riboflavin, niacin and zinc

Big-Batch Whole Wheat Pizza Dough

MAKES ENOUGH DOUGH FOR TWO 12- TO 15-INCH (30 TO 38 CM) PIZZA CRUSTS

Eileen Campbell

• *Preparation time: 10 minutes / Rising time: 2 hours*
• *Electric mixer with dough hook*

2	packages (each ¼ oz/7 g) instant yeast	2
2 cups	whole wheat flour	500 mL
1 cup	all-purpose flour	250 mL
1 tsp	salt	5 mL
½ tsp	granulated sugar	2 mL
1½ cups	lukewarm water	375 mL
½ tsp	olive oil	2 mL

A homemade crust, when you have time to prepare it, will make a huge difference to the taste of your pizza and provides added nutrition. It seems like a long process, but it is relatively easy — and it's worth the trouble. Try this dough with one of our great pizza recipes, or create your own pizza parlor special!

1. In the mixer bowl, combine yeast, whole wheat flour, all-purpose flour, salt and sugar. Attach dough hook and mixer bowl to mixer. With mixer running on low speed, gradually add water; knead until dough is smooth and elastic, about 10 minutes. Turn mixer off and pour oil down side of bowl. Set to low speed for 15 seconds to coat inside of bowl and cover dough lightly with oil. Remove mixer bowl and cover loosely with plastic wrap.

2. Let rise in a warm, draft-free place until doubled in bulk, about 2 hours.

3. Punch down dough and cut in half to make two balls. Place each ball in an airtight freezer bag and store for up to 3 months, or roll out for immediate usage.

4. To roll out, place dough ball on a floured work surface and form into a circle. Roll out until dough reaches a 12- to 15-inch (30 to 38 cm) diameter. Pierce dough with a fork before adding toppings.

❄ **FREEZER FRIENDLY**

TIP
If you do not have an electric mixer with a dough hook, you can use a food processor or knead the dough by hand. To knead by hand, combine dry ingredients in a large bowl. Make a well in the center and gradually mix in water until a stiff dough forms. Knead in the bowl (adding a little extra flour if the dough is too sticky) until dough holds together, then turn dough out onto a floured work surface and knead until smooth and elastic, about 10 minutes. Coat dough with olive oil. Place in a clean oiled bowl and cover loosely with plastic wrap. Continue with Step 2.

NUTRIENTS Per Serving (⅙ pizza crust)		
Calories: 129	Carbohydrate: 27.0 g	Calcium: 12 mg
Fat: 0.8 g	Fiber: 3.6 g	Iron: 1.6 mg
Sodium: 194 mg	Protein: 5.0 g	
A source of: Dietary fiber		

Diabetes Food Choice Values Per Serving
1½ Carbohydrates

MAKES 6 SERVINGS

Eileen Campbell

You won't be tempted to send out for pizza when you can create this gourmet version in less than 20 minutes.

TIP
If you don't have time to make the dough, you can use a purchased pizza crust.

Artichoke and Veggie Pizza

- • **Preparation time: 10 minutes / Cooking time: 10 to 12 minutes**
- • *Preheat oven to 375°F (190°C)*
- • *12-inch (30 cm) pizza pan, lightly greased*

½	recipe Big-Batch Whole Wheat Pizza Dough (page 247)	½
½	can (7½ oz/213 mL) pizza sauce	½
3	Roma (plum) tomatoes, thinly sliced	3
1	can (14 oz/398 mL) artichoke hearts, drained and halved	1
1 cup	shredded Asiago cheese	250 mL

1. Roll out dough to a 12-inch (30 cm) diameter and fit into prepared pan. Spread pizza sauce evenly over crust to within ½ inch (1 cm) of edge. Place tomato slices evenly around the edge and in the center. Place halved artichoke hearts over tomato slices. Sprinkle pizza evenly with cheese.

2. Bake in preheated oven for 10 to 12 minutes or until cheese is melted and starting to brown and crust is golden and crisp.

❄ **FREEZER FRIENDLY**

Using a Pizza Stone

A pizza stone helps distribute the heat of the oven evenly to your pizza, and the porous nature of the stone absorbs excess moisture, creating a crisper crust. To use one, place pizza stone on bottom rack of preheated oven for at least 1 hour. Spray lightly with vegetable oil before placing pizza directly on top.

Diabetes Food Choice Values Per Serving	
1½	Carbohydrates
½	Meat & Alternatives
1	Fat

NUTRIENTS Per Serving		
Calories: 239	Carbohydrate: 35.6 g	Calcium: 177 mg
Fat: 7.0 g	Fiber: 5.7 g	Iron: 2.4 mg
Sodium: 502 mg	Protein: 10.9 g	

Very high in: Folate and magnesium • **High in:** Dietary fiber, calcium, iron, thiamine, riboflavin, niacin and zinc

Grilled Veggie Pizza

**MAKES
12 SERVINGS**

Janis Evans, Dietitian,
ON

- **Preparation time: 12 to 15 minutes / Cooking time: 18 to 20 minutes**
- *Preheat barbecue to medium*
- *Two 14-inch (35 cm) pizza pans, lightly greased*

2	small eggplants	2
1	zucchini	1
	Olive oil	
1 tbsp	balsamic vinegar	15 mL
1	recipe Big-Batch Whole Wheat Pizza Dough (page 247)	1
½ cup	pizza sauce	125 mL
2 tsp	dried Italian herb seasoning	10 mL
12	stuffed green olives, halved	12
1½ cups	shredded mozzarella cheese	375 mL
1½ cups	shredded Cheddar cheese	375 mL

1. Slice eggplant and zucchini on the diagonal into ¼-inch (0.5 cm) slices. Brush lightly with olive oil. Place on preheated barbecue and grill, turning once, until browned on both sides, about 4 minutes per side.

2. Place grilled vegetables in layers on a platter, sprinkling each layer with balsamic vinegar. Cover and refrigerate for up to 4 hours, or until ready to assemble pizza.

3. Preheat oven to 375°F (190°C). Roll out each dough ball to a 14-inch (35 cm) diameter and fit into prepared pans. Spread ¼ cup (50 mL) tomato sauce over each crust to within ½ inch (1 cm) of edge. Sprinkle each pizza with 1 tsp (5 mL) Italian seasoning. Place zucchini and eggplant slices in a single layer on each pizza. Place olives between slices of zucchini and eggplant. Sprinkle each pizza evenly with half of the mozzarella and half of the Cheddar.

4. Bake in preheated oven for 10 to 12 minutes or until cheeses are melted and starting to brown and crust is golden and crisp.

❄ FREEZER FRIENDLY

TIPS
Grill the vegetables the day before, especially if you have the grill or barbecue on for something else; cover and refrigerate until ready to assemble.

If you don't have time to make the dough, you can use a purchased pizza crust.

For a very special grilled pizza flavor, try browning the pizza dough on the grill (on the pan) for a few minutes before topping with the other ingredients.

If you don't have Italian seasoning, substitute dried basil, oregano, rosemary or thyme, or a combination of all or any two.

SERVING IDEA:
Serve with Snow Pea and Bell Pepper Salad (page 140) for an extra serving of vegetables.

NUTRIENTS Per Serving		
Calories: 281	Carbohydrate: 33.9 g	Calcium: 222 mg
Fat: 12.0 g	Fiber: 6.1 g	Iron: 2.2 mg
Sodium: 579 mg	Protein: 12.5 g	

Very high in: Dietary fiber and folate • **High in:** Calcium, iron, thiamine, niacin and magnesium

Diabetes Food Choice Values Per Serving

1½	Carbohydrates
1	Meat & Alternatives
1½	Fats

Veggie Pizza with Three Cheeses

Jocelyne Jones,
Dietitian, QC

Pizza is a fun meal for the whole family to prepare, as it is quick and easy. What a great way to include more vegetables in your menu!

TIPS

If you don't have time to make the dough, you can use a purchased pizza crust.

If you choose part-skim mozzarella and light feta cheese, you'll decrease the fat in each serving by about 4 g.

- **Preparation time: 30 minutes / Cooking time: 25 to 30 minutes**
- *Preheat oven to 400°F (200°C)*
- *12-inch (30 cm) pizza pan, lightly greased*

½	recipe Big-Batch Whole Wheat Pizza Dough (page 247)	½
¾ cup	mild salsa	175 mL
2 tbsp	olive oil	25 mL
3	green onions, chopped	3
1	red onion, diced	1
1	small green bell pepper, sliced	1
1	small red bell pepper, sliced	1
1 cup	broccoli florets	250 mL
1	can (10 oz/284 mL) sliced mushrooms, drained and rinsed	1
1	can (10 oz/284 mL) water chestnuts, sliced	1
½ cup	sliced black olives	125 mL
1 tsp	dried oregano	5 mL
1 tsp	dried basil	5 mL
1 tsp	freshly ground black pepper	5 mL
2 cups	shredded mozzarella cheese	500 mL
½ cup	freshly grated Parmesan cheese	125 mL
½ cup	crumbled feta cheese	125 mL

1. Roll out dough to a 12-inch (30 cm) diameter and fit into prepared pan. Spread salsa evenly over crust to within ½ inch (1 cm) of edge. Set aside.

2. Heat a medium skillet over medium heat. Add oil and swirl to coat pan. Sauté green onions, red onion, green pepper, red pepper and broccoli for 10 minutes or until tender-crisp. Add mushrooms, water chestnuts and olives and cook for 5 minutes or until tender-crisp. Remove from heat and stir in oregano, basil and pepper.

3. Spread vegetables evenly over pizza crust. Sprinkle evenly with mozzarella, Parmesan and feta.

4. Bake in center of preheated oven for 12 to 15 minutes or until cheeses are melted and starting to brown and crust is golden and crisp.

✓ KID APPROVED

> **SERVING IDEA:** To add an extra serving of vegetables, serve with a green salad or a glass of vegetable juice.

Bell Peppers

Red, green and yellow bell peppers provide an array of vitamins and taste great with eggplant, tomatoes, summer squash, onions, garlic or corn. Basil and marjoram provide complementary flavors. Other good flavor partners include vinegar, capers, olives, mozzarella, goat cheese and Parmesan cheese. Kids love to eat peppers raw with some light ranch dressing as a dip.

When you slice a pepper open, be sure your knife is firmly inside the pepper to keep the knife from bouncing off the rubbery surface. Always remove the cap and stem and scoop out the seeds before cutting.

Other vegetables can be substituted; use whatever you have on hand that your whole family loves.

NUTRIENTS Per Serving		
Calories: 288	Carbohydrate: 25.0 g	Calcium: 338 mg
Fat: 15.8 g	Fiber: 4.5 g	Iron: 2.2 mg
Sodium: 728 mg	Protein: 14.4 g	

Very high in: Vitamin C, calcium and folate • **High in:** Dietary fiber, vitamin A, iron, riboflavin, niacin, vitamin B_6, vitamin B_{12}, magnesium and zinc

Diabetes Food Choice Values Per Serving	
1	Carbohydrate
1 ½	Meat & Alternatives
1 ½	Fats

Compass Group Canada

Jerk sauce lends Caribbean flair and a touch of spice to this pizza.

TIP
If you don't have time to make the dough, you can use a purchased pizza crust.

SERVING IDEA:
Serve with veggie sticks and Spicy Hummus (page 104) for dipping, with Tropical Coolers (page 83) as thirst-quenchers in keeping with the Caribbean theme.

Caribbean Chicken and Pineapple Pizza

- **Preparation time: 15 minutes / Cooking time: 15 to 17 minutes**
- *Preheat oven to 400°F (200°C)*
- *12-inch (30 cm) pizza pan, lightly greased*

4 oz	boneless skinless chicken breasts, cooked and cut into strips	125 g
2 tbsp	Caribbean jerk sauce, divided	25 mL
¼ cup	thinly sliced red onion	50 mL
	Vegetable cooking spray	
½ cup	pizza sauce	125 mL
½	recipe Big-Batch Whole Wheat Pizza Dough (page 247)	½
2 cups	shredded pizza cheese blend, divided	500 mL
1 cup	fresh pineapple chunks	250 mL
1 tbsp	hot banana pepper rings, drained (optional)	15 mL

1. Lightly coat chicken strips with 1½ tbsp (22 mL) of the jerk sauce.

2. Heat a small skillet over medium heat. Spray with vegetable cooking spray. Sauté onions for 5 minutes or until softened. Set aside.

3. In a small bowl, combine pizza sauce and the remaining jerk sauce.

4. Roll out dough to a 12-inch (30 cm) diameter and fit into prepared pan. Spread jerk pizza sauce evenly over crust to within ½ inch (1 cm) of edge. Sprinkle evenly with onions, half of the cheese, chicken strips, pineapple and banana pepper rings (if using). Top with the remaining cheese.

5. Bake in preheated oven for 10 to 12 minutes or until cheese is melted and starting to brown and crust is golden and crisp.

❄ **FREEZER FRIENDLY**
✓ **KID APPROVED**

Diabetes Food Choice Values Per Serving	
1	Carbohydrate
2	Meat & Alternatives

NUTRIENTS Per Serving		
Calories: 253	Carbohydrate: 23.4 g	Calcium: 275 mg
Fat: 10.5 g	Fiber: 2.8 g	Iron: 1.5 mg
Sodium: 617 mg	Protein: 17.7 g	

Very high in: Calcium • **High in:** Niacin and folate
A source of: Dietary fiber

Ham and Pineapple Pizza

MAKES 6 SERVINGS

Donna Bottrell, Dietitian, ON

- **Preparation time: 10 minutes / Cooking time: 10 to 12 minutes**
- *Preheat oven to 375°F (190°C)*
- *12-inch (30 cm) pizza pan, lightly greased*

½	recipe Big-Batch Whole Wheat Pizza Dough (page 247)	½
½	can (7½ oz/213 mL) pizza sauce	½
½ cup	diced lean ham	125 mL
½ cup	diced fresh pineapple	125 mL
1 cup	shredded part-skim mozzarella	250 mL

1. Roll out dough to a 12-inch (30 cm) diameter and fit into prepared pan. Spread pizza sauce evenly over crust to within ½ inch (1 cm) of edge. Sprinkle evenly with ham and pineapple. Top with cheese.

2. Bake in preheated oven for 10 to 12 minutes or until cheese is melted and starting to brown and crust is golden and crisp.

❄️ FREEZER FRIENDLY
✓ KID APPROVED

This Hawaiian-style pizza is a favorite in Donna's house. The sweetness of the pineapple is appealing to kids and adults alike.

TIP
If you don't have time to make the dough, you can use a purchased pizza crust.

VARIATION
For a special treat, substitute diced mango for the pineapple and diced cooked chicken for the ham.

NUTRIENTS Per Serving		
Calories: 154	Carbohydrate: 23.0 g	Calcium: 202 mg
Fat: 1.5 g	Fiber: 3.5 g	Iron: 1.6 mg
Sodium: 467 mg	Protein: 12.9 g	

Very high in: Calcium, thiamine, niacin, folate, magnesium and zinc • **A source of:** Dietary fiber

Diabetes Food Choice Values Per Serving	
1	Carbohydrate
1½	Meat & Alternatives

Vegetables and Sides

When you add interest and flavor to vegetables and grain products, you can enhance the taste of your entrées. Side dishes are also a great way to introduce your family members to new tastes and textures and give them delicious nutrition.

great ways to eat more vegetables

- Make vegetable kabobs by grilling cherry tomatoes, zucchini, red onion, baby potatoes and/or red pepper chunks.
- Make "fries": toss strips of potato or sweet potato in a light coating of oil and bake.
- Keep frozen peas, beans, corn or mixed vegetables in the freezer for a quick meal addition.
- Make your own fresh salsa by combining finely chopped fresh tomatoes, bell peppers, onions and cilantro. Add diced jalapeño or other chili peppers if you like heat.
- Try one of our delicious vegetable soups, such as Chunky Southwest Vegetable Soup (page 120) or My Mother's Borscht (page 119).

Help Kids Enjoy Vegetables

- Purée soft-cooked vegetables and stir them into pasta sauces.
- Serve raw vegetables when kids are hungriest (which may not always be at mealtime).
- Ask your kids what their favorite vegetables are. Provide two vegetables at dinner and give them a choice. They can eat one or both.
- Hide vegetables in unusual places. For instance, add shredded carrots, zucchini or beets to cakes or loaves.
- Make vegetable meals more fun by adding vegetables to wraps, pitas, soups, chili or pizza.
- Kids are always watching, so set a good example by enjoying vegetables yourself.

How Can I Get My Teen to Eat Better?

Teens need plenty of calories and nutrients to support their rapid physical growth. As a result, they have huge appetites and snack constantly. Helping your teens make healthy choices can be challenging, but the investment will pay off for a lifetime. Remember, teens are still watching what you do, so model healthy eating behavior!

Here are some tips that will help you make it easy for your teens to eat well. Be sure to use Canada's Food Guide (www.healthcanada.gc.ca/foodguide) to help you shop:

- Keep your fridge well stocked with vegetables and fruits. Look for those that are dark green or orange, as they're packed with great nutrition.
- Look for yogurt and pudding in convenient, single-serving packages.
- Buy baked munchies instead of deep-fried varieties.
- Pick up roasted soy beans (commonly called soynuts) or a variety of nuts.
- Offer whole-grain cereal and granola bars. Check the label for the best nutrition.
- Prepare Spicy Hummus (page 104) or Greek Veggie Kabob (page 100).
- Organize your kitchen so the healthiest choices are the easiest to grab. Keep less healthy choices out of reach.
- Keep a bowl of fresh fruits on your kitchen table.
- Make sure raw vegetables are always washed, cut and ready to go.
- Have whole-grain crackers and cheese available.
- Always keep milk and 100% juice on hand.
- Make your own popcorn, using your teen's favorite spice as flavoring.
- Have your teens learn to make a few quick and easy recipes for after-school snacks. Try Fruit Wrap (page 72), Hawaiian Toast (page 78) or Pink Strawberry Wiggles (page 325).

When trying to instill good eating habits in teens, it's important to set limits:

- Serve regular meals at regular times, and encourage your teen to be there. If that's not possible, keep portions handy to warm up after scheduled activities.
- If your teens love snacks that are high in fat, salt or sugar, sit down together and talk about healthy alternatives you can have on hand. Talk about their habits when eating out. Discuss what foods you will serve when their friends visit.
- Start a new family tradition — for example, begin each meal with raw vegetables pieces or salad.

Barbecued Vegetables: Healthy Never Tasted So Good

Many vegetables, including eggplant, zucchini, squash, tomatoes, asparagus and potatoes, can be prepared on the backyard grill, and barbecued vegetables are delicious. Use one type of vegetable or a mixture. When creating a mixture, choose vegetables that have the same cooking time (for example, eggplant, zucchini, peppers and mushrooms or potatoes, squash and carrots). Cook tender vegetables such as asparagus on their own, as they need very little time on the grill.

To grill vegetables, cut them as desired, then lightly coat with olive oil and sprinkle with your favorite herbs and spices. If your vegetables are in small pieces, use a vegetable basket designed for grilling to prevent them from dropping through the grates. After cooking, add a splash of balsamic vinegar for a delicious finish.

Roberta Lowcay,
Dietitian, BC

*The title says it all —
both kids and adults
will be back for more.*

Yummy Asparagus

• *Preparation time: 2 minutes / Cooking time: 5 minutes*

1 tbsp	butter	15 mL
1	bunch asparagus, ends trimmed	1
1	clove garlic, minced	1
1 tbsp	freshly grated Parmesan cheese	15 mL

1. In a medium saucepan, melt butter over medium heat.
   Sauté asparagus and garlic, shaking pan constantly, until
   just tender, about 5 minutes. Sprinkle with cheese and
   allow it to melt before serving.

✓ **KID APPROVED**

SERVING IDEA: This dish is delicious served with brown rice
and any of our salmon recipes (pages 206, 207 and 208).

Asparagus

For the best taste and freshness, choose asparagus with a bright green
stalk and tightly closed, purple-tinged stalks. To prepare asparagus,
break off the tough root end.

Diabetes Food Choice Values Per Serving	
½	Fat

NUTRIENTS Per Serving		
Calories: 51	Carbohydrate: 3.6 g	Calcium: 42 mg
Fat: 3.5 g	Fiber: 1.6 g	Iron: 0.7 mg
Sodium: 61 mg	Protein: 2.6 g	
Very high in: Folate		

Shrimp, Vegetables and
Whole Wheat Pasta (page 243)

Veggie Pizza with Three Cheeses (page 250)

Stir-Fried Chinese Greens (page 259)

Baked Springtime Risotto (page 277)

Ginger Carrots

MAKES 4 TO 6 SERVINGS

Roberta Lowcay,
Dietitian, BC

MMMmmmm good — a delicious way to enjoy carrots. Kids love them.

• *Preparation time: 10 minutes / Cooking time: 20 minutes*

4 cups	chopped carrots	1 L
1/2 cup	vegetable or chicken broth	125 mL
2 tsp	minced gingerroot	10 mL
1 tsp	minced garlic	5 mL
1 tsp	packed brown sugar	5 mL
1/4 tsp	freshly squeezed lemon juice	1 mL

1. In a large saucepan, combine carrots, broth, ginger, garlic, brown sugar and lemon juice. Bring to a boil, then reduce heat, cover and simmer for about 20 minutes or until carrots are tender-crisp and liquid is absorbed.

✓ **KID APPROVED**

Gingerroot

Use the side of a spoon to scrape off the skin before chopping or grating. Gingerroot keeps well in the freezer for up to 3 months and can be grated from frozen.

NUTRIENTS Per Serving		
Calories: 34	Carbohydrate: 7.9 g	Calcium: 25 mg
Fat: 0.2 g	Fiber: 2.2 g	Iron: 0.3 mg
Sodium: 128 mg	Protein: 0.7 g	

Very high in: Vitamin A • **A source of:** Dietary fiber

Diabetes Food Choice Values Per Serving	
1	Extra

Julie Bourdua, QC

A simple way of preparing cauliflower that can be put together in a flash.

TIP
If there is not enough soup for the amount of vegetables, add a little water.

VARIATION
Broccoli also works well in this recipe.

Cauliflower au Gratin

- *Preparation time: 10 minutes / Cooking time: 30 minutes*
- *Preheat oven to 350°F (180°C)*
- *9-inch (2.5 L) casserole dish with cover, lightly greased*

1	large cauliflower, cut into florets	1
1	green onion, finely chopped	1
1	can (10 oz/284 mL) condensed reduced-fat cream of broccoli soup, undiluted	1
1 cup	shredded skim-milk mozzarella cheese	250 mL

1. Bring 6 cups (1.5 L) water to a boil. Drop cauliflower into boiling water and cook for 2 minutes; drain well.

2. Place cauliflower in prepared casserole dish and sprinkle with green onion. Stir in soup. Sprinkle with cheese.

3. Cover and bake in preheated oven for 20 minutes or until cauliflower is tender and cheese is melted. Uncover and broil until cheese is browned.

✓ **KID APPROVED**

Diabetes Food Choice Values Per Serving

½   Meat & Alternatives

NUTRIENTS Per Serving		
Calories: 70	Carbohydrate: 8.4 g	Calcium: 165 mg
Fat: 1.2 g	Fiber: 3.4 g	Iron: 0.6 mg
Sodium: 389 mg	Protein: 7.2 g	

Very high in: Vitamin C • **High in:** Calcium and folate
A source of: Dietary fiber

Stir-Fried Chinese Greens

MAKES 6 SERVINGS

Eileen Campbell

This wonderful side dish for grilled fish or chicken is easy to prepare — and even easier if you wash and cut the vegetables the night before.

• *Preparation time: 10 minutes / Cooking time: 10 minutes*

1 tbsp	vegetable oil	15 mL
1	Spanish onion, sliced lengthwise into thick slices	1
1	green bell pepper, julienned	1
1	head bok choy, cut into chunks (about 4 cups/1 L), white stalks and green leaves separated	1
1 cup	broccoli florets	250 mL
1/2 cup	water	125 mL
1 tbsp	hoisin sauce or your favorite stir-fry sauce	15 mL
2 tsp	reduced-sodium soy sauce	10 mL
1/2 tsp	sesame oil	2 mL
1 tbsp	sesame seeds	15 mL

1. Heat a wok or large skillet over medium heat. Add oil and swirl to coat. When oil is hot but not smoking, add onion and stir-fry for 3 minutes. Add green pepper and stir-fry for 2 minutes. Add white ends of the bok choy and the broccoli and stir-fry for 2 minutes. Stir in green bok choy leaves, water, hoisin sauce and soy sauce. Cover and cook for 3 minutes or until broccoli is tender-crisp.

2. Transfer to a serving dish, drizzle with sesame oil and sprinkle with sesame seeds.

✓ **KID APPROVED**

SERVING IDEA: Add Tofu 101 (page 224) and serve over brown rice.

NUTRIENTS Per Serving		
Calories: 75	Carbohydrate: 9.2 g	Calcium: 68 mg
Fat: 3.8 g	Fiber: 1.9 g	Iron: 1.0 mg
Sodium: 125 mg	Protein: 2.5 g	

Very high in: Vitamin A and vitamin C • **High in:** Folate

Diabetes Food Choice Values Per Serving

1	Fat

Simple Stir-Fried Kale

Gerry Kasten, Dietitian, BC

An interesting way to add greens to your menu, this recipe is a very easy way to prepare kale. When Gerry demonstrated this dish during a cooking course for dietetics students, it was gobbled up quickly.

TIPS

Tahini is often used in Middle Eastern cooking and is an ingredient in hummus. It is made from ground sesame seeds and adds a nutty flavor to dishes.

Leave out the hot pepper sauce if your family does not like spice.

• Preparation time: 10 minutes / Cooking time: 3 to 5 minutes

1 tbsp	vegetable oil	15 mL
1 tsp	sesame oil	5 mL
4 cups	julienned kale (tough center rib removed first)	1 L
2	leeks (white and light green parts only), julienned	2
1 tbsp	tahini	15 mL
2 tsp	hot pepper sauce	10 mL
2 tsp	soy sauce	10 mL
	Freshly ground white or black pepper	

1. In a wok or large skillet, heat vegetable oil and sesame oil over high heat. Add kale and leeks; stir-fry for 3 to 5 minutes or until limp.
2. Combine tahini, hot pepper sauce and soy sauce; pour over vegetables. Season to taste with pepper. Serve warm.

Diabetes Food Choice Values Per Serving

1½ Fats

NUTRIENTS Per Serving		
Calories: 116	Carbohydrate: 12.2 g	Calcium: 125 mg
Fat: 7.2 g	Fiber: 2.6 g	Iron: 2.2 mg
Sodium: 204 mg	Protein: 3.5 g	

Very high in: Vitamin A and vitamin C • **High in:** Iron and folate
A source of: Dietary fiber

Stuffed Zucchini

- *Preparation time: 10 minutes / Cooking time: 15 minutes*
- *Preheat oven to 350°F (180°C)*
- *Baking sheet*

Laurie Evans, Dietitian, MB

Here's a unique presentation for a versatile vegetable.

¾ cup	reduced-sodium vegetable broth	175 mL
2	small zucchini, halved lengthwise	2
2	green onions, chopped	2
2	cloves garlic, minced	2
1	tomato, diced	1
½ tsp	dried basil	2 mL
½ tsp	dried thyme	2 mL
¼ tsp	hot pepper sauce	1 mL
¾ cup	shredded Cheddar cheese	175 mL

1. In a large skillet, over medium-high heat, bring broth to a boil. Reduce heat to medium and add zucchini halves, skin side up. Cook for 2 to 3 minutes or until tender. Remove zucchini and let cool. Discard excess liquid.

2. Using a spoon, scoop out zucchini flesh, leaving a shell. Chop zucchini flesh. In a large bowl, combine zucchini flesh, green onions, garlic, tomato, basil, thyme and hot pepper sauce. Fill zucchini shells with mixture and top with cheese. Place filled shells on baking sheet.

3. Bake in preheated oven for 10 minutes or until heated through and cheese is melted.

NUTRIENTS Per Serving		
Calories: 107	Carbohydrate: 5.2 g	Calcium: 175 mg
Fat: 7.1 g	Fiber: 1.4 g	Iron: 0.7 mg
Sodium: 275 mg	Protein: 6.1 g	
High in: Vitamin A and calcium		

Diabetes Food Choice Values Per Serving	
1	Meat & Alternatives
1	Fat

Texan Zucchini

Jo-Anne Palmer, ON

This recipe is quick, easy and tasty with chicken or fish. It is very versatile in that it can be cooked in a skillet, in the oven or on the barbecue (see tips, below).

TIPS

Oven Method: Preheat oven to 375°F (190°C). In a small casserole dish, combine zucchini, corn and salsa. Sprinkle with Parmesan (if using) and garlic powder (if using). Bake in preheated oven for 30 minutes or until zucchini is soft.

Barbecue Method: Preheat barbecue to medium-low. In a medium bowl, combine zucchini, corn, salsa, Parmesan (if using) and garlic powder (if using). Transfer to a double thickness of foil and wrap into a packet. Place packet on preheated barbecue and cook for about 20 minutes, turning after 10 minutes, until zucchini is soft.

• Preparation time: 5 minutes / Cooking time: 20 to 30 minutes

2	small zucchini, cubed	2
1 cup	frozen corn kernels	250 mL
1 cup	chunky salsa	250 mL
2 tbsp	freshly grated Parmesan cheese (optional)	25 mL
1/2 tsp	garlic powder (optional)	2 mL

1. In a small saucepan, over medium-high heat, bring 1/2 cup (125 mL) water to a boil. Add zucchini and corn; cook for 5 to 7 minutes or until zucchini is tender-crisp. Drain and add salsa, Parmesan (if using) and garlic powder (if using). Reduce heat and simmer for 15 to 20 minutes or until zucchini is soft.

✓ **KID APPROVED**

Diabetes Food Choice Values Per Serving	
1/2	Carbohydrate

NUTRIENTS Per Serving		
Calories: 58	Carbohydrate: 13.7 g	Calcium: 26 mg
Fat: 0.4 g	Fiber: 2.5 g	Iron: 0.7 mg
Sodium: 398 mg	Protein: 2.3 g	
A source of: Dietary fiber		

Steamed Asian Vegetable Medley

Eileen Campbell

This versatile, delicately flavored dish encourages families to enjoy a variety of vegetables, which are steamed over soy sauce and sesame oil–flavored water. Choose a selection from each of the color groups, ensuring good color and flavor contrast. Allow 3/4 cup (175 mL) assorted vegetables per person and let each family member make a choice for the dish.

• **Preparation time: 10 minutes / Cooking time: 5 to 10 minutes, depending on quantity**

Green: Sugar snap peas, snow peas, finely chopped bok choy, chopped spinach

Yellow/orange: Baby corn, julienned yellow or orange bell peppers, yellow squash slices, carrot slices

Red: Julienned red bell peppers, cherry tomatoes, radishes

White: Bean sprouts, water chestnuts, turnip strips

Sesame oil

Soy sauce

Toasted sesame seeds (optional)

1. In a medium saucepan, bring 1 cup (250 mL) water to a boil. Place steamer basket over boiling water and fill with vegetables. Drizzle with a small amount of sesame oil and soy sauce. Cover and steam until vegetables are tender-crisp.

2. Transfer to a serving dish and sprinkle with toasted sesame seeds, if desired.

✓ **KID APPROVED**

NUTRIENTS Per Serving		
(based on a 3/4 cup (175 mL) assortment of snow peas, carrots, red bell peppers and water chestnuts without any flavoring)		
Calories: 41	Carbohydrate: 9.2 g	Calcium: 16 mg
Fat: 0.1 g	Fiber: 2.7 g	Iron: 0.7 mg
Sodium: 15 mg	Protein: 1.5 g	
Very high in: Vitamin A and vitamin C • **A source of:** Dietary fiber		

Diabetes Food Choice Values Per Serving
1   Extra

Dianna Bihun, Dietitian, BC

With this recipe, all the chopping can be done in advance, then you can pop the dish in the oven when company arrives. Once the vegetables are roasted, arrange them on a serving platter or around a roasted chicken, beef roast or fillet of salmon.

TIPS

For the herbs, try any combination of thyme, oregano, basil, dill, parsley, chives and rosemary — whatever suits your taste!

To save time, you can buy most veggies already cleaned and ready cut. The oil mixture can also be made a day in advance, covered and stored in the fridge.

Barbecue Method:
These vegetables can also be grilled in a vegetable basket on a lightly greased barbecue preheated to medium. Cook, turning once, until tender, about 10 minutes.

Roasted Vegetables

- **Preparation time: 30 minutes / Cooking time: 30 to 40 minutes**
- *Preheat oven to 325°F (160°C)*
- *13- by 9-inch (3 L) roasting pan or shallow casserole dish, lightly greased*

2	bell peppers (any color)	2
2	parsnips, peeled	2
2	carrots	2
2	potatoes (unpeeled)	2
1	onion	1
1	zucchini	1
1	bulb fennel	1
3	cloves garlic	3
2 tbsp	vegetable oil	25 mL
2 tbsp	pure maple syrup or liquid honey	25 mL
1 tbsp	Dijon mustard	15 mL
2 tbsp	chopped fresh herbs (or 2 tsp/ 10 mL dried) (see tip, at left)	25 mL
	Freshly ground black pepper	

1. Chop peppers, parsnips, carrots, potatoes, onion, zucchini and fennel into bite-size chunks. Spread vegetables and garlic in prepared pan.
2. In a medium bowl, combine oil, maple syrup, mustard and herbs. Pour over vegetables and toss to coat. Sprinkle with pepper to taste.
3. Roast in preheated oven, tossing vegetables once, for 30 to 40 minutes or until fork-tender and golden.

SERVING IDEA: This makes an attractive meal served with Lemon-Thyme Roast Chicken (page 164).

Diabetes Food Choice Values Per Serving	
1	Carbohydrate
1	Fat

NUTRIENTS Per Serving		
Calories: 150	Carbohydrate: 27.9 g	Calcium: 64 mg
Fat: 4.0 g	Fiber: 4.8 g	Iron: 1.6 mg
Sodium: 62 mg	Protein: 2.9 g	

Very high in: Vitamin A, vitamin C and folate
High in: Dietary fiber, vitamin B$_6$ and magnesium

Hot-Bag Vegetables

MAKES 8 SERVINGS

Susanna Herczeg, ON

- *Preparation time: 15 minutes / Cooking time: 17 to 20 minutes*
- *Preheat barbecue to medium*
- *Roasting bag, lightly greased*
- *Vegetable basket for barbecue*

1 cup	chopped carrots	250 mL
1 cup	chopped peeled parsnips	250 mL
1 cup	chopped peeled potato	250 mL
1 cup	chopped red bell pepper	250 mL
1 cup	cauliflower florets	250 mL
1 cup	chopped onion	250 mL
1 tbsp	vegetable oil	15 mL
2 tbsp	seasonings (see tip, at right)	25 mL

1. In a large bowl, toss carrots, parsnips, potato, red pepper, cauliflower, onion, oil and seasonings. Pour into prepared roasting bag. Fold opening of bag twice to ensure it stays closed.

2. Place roasting bag in a vegetable basket on preheated barbecue and cook, turning occasionally, for 17 to 20 minutes or until vegetables are tender.

This is a great recipe for a summer barbecue, but you can also cook it in the oven (see tip, below) and save on cleanup.

TIPS

Roasting bags are heat-resistant clear plastic bags with plastic closures. Look for them in the meat department of your grocery store. They keep your oven splatter-free during the roasting process, saving you time on cleanup. Try using them for roast chicken or pork too!

This recipe will work with any of your favorite fresh vegetables — just chop them into bite-size pieces.

For the seasonings, try any combination of dried basil, dried rosemary, dried thyme, dried parsley, salt, pepper and garlic powder.

For a lower-fat version, replace the oil with chicken broth.

Oven Method: Place roasting bag in preheated 350°F (180°C) oven and roast for 30 to 40 minutes or until vegetables are tender.

NUTRIENTS Per Serving		
Calories: 64	Carbohydrate: 11.4 g	Calcium: 28 mg
Fat: 2.0 g	Fiber: 2.3 g	Iron: 0.7 mg
Sodium: 158 mg	Protein: 1.3 g	
Very high in: Vitamin A and vitamin C • **A source of:** Dietary fiber		

Diabetes Food Choice Values Per Serving
½   Fat

**MAKES
12 SERVINGS**

Eileen Campbell

*Ratatouille, a popular
Mediterranean dish,
combines eggplant,
tomatoes, onions,
peppers, zucchini,
garlic and herbs, all
usually simmered in
olive oil. This version
cooks in the oven with
a little oil and takes
on a toasty flavor. It's
perfect in the summer
months, when fresh
produce is abundant,
but it's delicious all
year round.*

VARIATION

If you make this recipe
in the winter, when
tomatoes are lacking in
flavor, substitute whole
drained canned tomatoes.

Planned Extras

This recipe allows for extra
servings that you can use
in Roasted Vegetables
and Couscous with Goat
Cheese (page 151) or as
filler for vegetable lasagna.

Big-Batch Oven-Roasted Ratatouille

* *Preparation time: 20 minutes / Cooking time: 30 minutes*
* *Preheat oven to 450°F (230°C)*
* *16- by 12-inch (40 by 30 cm) shallow roasting pan*

4	tomatoes, chopped	4
4	cloves garlic, chopped	4
3	small Italian eggplants, cut into ½-inch (1 cm) rounds	3
2	large zucchini, cut into ½-inch (1 cm) rounds	2
1	red bell pepper, cut into chunks	1
1	yellow bell pepper, cut into chunks	1
1	large red onion, cut into chunks	1
3 tbsp	olive oil	45 mL
	Salt and freshly ground black pepper	
1	small bunch fresh basil, roughly torn	1
½ cup	freshly grated Parmesan cheese	125 mL

1. In a large bowl, combine tomatoes, garlic, eggplants, zucchini, red pepper, yellow pepper and red onion. Add olive oil and toss to coat. Transfer to roasting pan and season to taste with salt and pepper.
2. Roast on the top rack of preheated oven for 15 minutes. Stir and roast for 15 minutes or until vegetables are just soft and tinged brown on the edges.
3. Transfer to a serving bowl and stir in basil. Sprinkle with cheese.

> **SERVING IDEA:** Serve warm over whole wheat spaghetti with grated Parmesan cheese.

Diabetes Food Choice Values Per Serving	
1	Fat

NUTRIENTS Per Serving		
Calories: 97	Carbohydrate: 11.7 g	Calcium: 81 mg
Fat: 4.9 g	Fiber: 2.9 g	Iron: 0.6 mg
Sodium: 83 mg	Protein: 3.4 g	
Very high in: Vitamin C • **A source of:** Dietary fiber		

Sweet Corn Fritters

MAKES 16 FRITTERS (2 PER SERVING)

Eileen Campbell

• *Preparation time: 5 minutes / Cooking time: 10 minutes*

1 cup	all-purpose flour	250 mL
2 tsp	granulated sugar	10 mL
½ tsp	baking soda	2 mL
1 tsp	salt	5 mL
2	eggs	2
1 cup	buttermilk	250 mL
2 tbsp	vegetable oil	25 mL
1 cup	frozen corn kernels, thawed	250 mL

These fritters make a great side dish for chicken or pork. Kids love them on their own, with applesauce for dipping.

1. In a large bowl, combine flour, sugar, baking soda and salt.
2. In a small bowl, whisk eggs, buttermilk and oil. Stir into flour mixture until just combined. Stir in corn.
3. Heat a nonstick griddle or skillet over medium heat. For each fritter, pour ¼ cup (50 mL) batter onto the griddle. When bubbles break the surface and the bottom is golden, flip and cook the other side until golden (about 2 minutes per side). Cook remaining batter in batches, keeping fritters warm in a low oven until they are all cooked.

✓ **KID APPROVED**

> **SERVING IDEA:** Serve with Oven-Baked Chicken Maryland (page 168), or your favorite chicken dish, and a green salad with one of our great dressings.

NUTRIENTS Per Serving		
Calories: 137	Carbohydrate: 18.3 g	Calcium: 45 mg
Fat: 5.2 g	Fiber: 0.9 g	Iron: 1.0 mg
Sodium: 413 mg	Protein: 4.7 g	
High in: Folate		

Diabetes Food Choice Values Per Serving	
1	Carbohydrate
1	Fat

MAKES 6 SERVINGS

Charissa McKay,
Dietitian, AB

This side dish makes plain old potatoes fun! The sweet potato gives it a nice orange color.

TIPS

Use plain mashed potato and sweet potato, without milk or butter added.

Every time you cook potatoes, make extra. Use them for this recipe, for breakfast home fries or to add to soups.

VARIATION

Use different combinations of cheeses and add chives, green or red bell pepper or mushrooms for a bit of extra color and flavor.

Potato Cakes with a Twist

• *Preparation time: 10 minutes / Cooking time: 30 minutes*

1	egg, beaten	1
1 cup	mashed potato	250 mL
1 cup	mashed sweet potato	250 mL
½ cup	crumbled feta cheese	125 mL
	Vegetable cooking spray	

1. In a medium bowl, combine egg, mashed potatoes and mashed sweet potatoes until smooth. Stir in feta cheese.
2. Heat a skillet over medium heat and spray with cooking spray. Spoon ½ cup (125 mL) potato mixture into the pan and cook until bottom is golden. Flip and cook until bottom is golden and cake is heated through. Remove to a plate and repeat until all potato mixture is used, spraying pan as needed between batches.

✓ **KID APPROVED**

Diabetes Food Choice Values Per Serving	
1	Carbohydrate
1	Fat

NUTRIENTS Per Serving		
Calories: 119	Carbohydrate: 17.2 g	Calcium: 83 mg
Fat: 4.0 g	Fiber: 1.9 g	Iron: 0.7 mg
Sodium: 166 mg	Protein: 4.2 g	

Very high in: Vitamin A • **High in:** Vitamin B$_{12}$

Oven-Roasted Lemon Potatoes

MAKES 6 SERVINGS

Patti Thomson,
Dietitian, MB

This tasty potato recipe is similar to a dish served in Greek restaurants.

• *Preparation time: 10 minutes / Cooking time: 1 hour*
• *Preheat oven to 400°F (200°C)*
• *Large shallow roasting pan*

1½ lbs	potatoes, peeled and cut in chunks	750 g
3 tbsp	olive oil	45 mL
	Juice of 1 lemon	
½ tsp	dried oregano	2 mL
¼ tsp	freshly ground black pepper	1 mL
	Salt	
1½ cups	chicken broth (approx.)	375 mL

1. Place potatoes in a single layer in roasting pan. Add olive oil, lemon juice, oregano, pepper and salt to taste; toss to coat. Pour in just enough broth to half-cover potatoes.

2. Bake in preheated oven for about 1 hour or until potatoes are tender, golden-brown and crispy on the outside.

✓ **KID APPROVED**

SERVING IDEA: Great served with Roast Lamb with Marrakech Rub (page 197) or Stuffed Roast Pork (page 194) with steamed green beans.

NUTRIENTS Per Serving		
Calories: 131	Carbohydrate: 17.5 g	Calcium: 13 mg
Fat: 6.1 g	Fiber: 1.3 g	Iron: 0.5 mg
Sodium: 230 mg	Protein: 1.9 g	

Diabetes Food Choice Values Per Serving	
1	Carbohydrate
1	Fat

**Helen Haresign,
Dietitian, ON**

*Scalloped potatoes go
well with baked ham
or roast pork. This is a
lower-fat version that
still tastes wonderful.*

Lightened-Up Scalloped Potatoes

• *Preheat oven to 450°F (230°C)*
• *11- by 7-inch (2 L) casserole dish, lightly greased*

2 lbs	potatoes, peeled and sliced	1 kg
1	clove garlic, chopped	1
1	onion, thinly sliced	1
1 tbsp	chopped fresh rosemary	15 mL
1½ cups	beef broth	375 mL

1. In prepared casserole dish, layer potatoes, garlic and onion. Sprinkle with rosemary. Pour in beef broth.
2. Cover and bake in preheated oven for 25 minutes. Uncover and bake for 5 minutes or until potatoes are soft and tops are browned.

 **KID APPROVED**

SERVING IDEA: These potatoes are perfect served with baked ham, Peach Salsa (variation, page 105) and Stuffed Zucchini (page 261).

**Diabetes Food Choice
Values Per Serving**

1½ Carbohydrates

NUTRIENTS Per Serving		
Calories: 107	Carbohydrate: 24.2 g	Calcium: 17 mg
Fat: 0.2 g	Fiber: 1.9 g	Iron: 0.5 mg
Sodium: 234 mg	Protein: 2.8 g	

High in: Vitamin B_6

Oven-Baked Potato Wedges

MAKES 6 SERVINGS

Wendy Benson,
Dietitian, AB

This dish tastes like restaurant potato wedges but has less fat and salt. It's a great way to add more vegetables to a meal.

- *Preparation time: 10 minutes / Cooking time: 15 to 20 minutes*
- *Preheat oven to 450°F (230°C)*
- *Baking sheet, lightly greased*

2 tbsp	vegetable oil	25 mL
½ tsp	salt	2 mL
1 tsp	dried rosemary	5 mL
½ tsp	dried thyme	2 mL
2	russet potatoes (unpeeled), cut into ½-inch (1 cm) wedges	2
1	sweet potato (unpeeled), cut into ½-inch (1 cm) wedges	1

1. In a large bowl, combine oil, salt, rosemary and thyme. Add potatoes and toss to coat. Transfer to prepared baking sheet.
2. Bake in preheated oven, turning wedges occasionally, for 15 to 20 minutes or until browned and tender.

✓ **KID APPROVED**

TIP
Leaving the peel on shortens the preparation time and adds fiber to your meal; just be sure to scrub well with a brush under running water first. Russet potatoes are the best baking potatoes.

VARIATIONS
Different seasonings can dramatically change this potato dish. For spicy flavor, use salt and 2 tbsp (25 mL) chili powder.

If available, add a third potato color with blue (or purple) potatoes.

NUTRIENTS Per Serving		
Calories: 124	Carbohydrate: 18.7 g	Calcium: 26 mg
Fat: 4.7 g	Fiber: 2.4 g	Iron: 1.7 mg
Sodium: 207 mg	Protein: 2.1 g	

Very high in: Vitamin A • **High in:** Vitamin B$_6$
A source of: Dietary fiber

Diabetes Food Choice Values Per Serving	
1	Carbohydrate
1	Fat

Carla Reid, Dietitian, NS

Carla and her husband came up with this recipe when they were looking for a healthy, quick and tasty side dish.

TIPS

To save time, cook the pasta while you are preparing the other ingredients or, better yet, use pasta you have precooked for planned extras.

If you love spinach, add extra — the recipe will still turn out great.

If serving this dish to children, you may want to leave out the hot pepper flakes.

Spinach Spaghettini

• *Preparation time: 10 minutes / Cooking time: 10 minutes*

2 tbsp	olive oil	25 mL
1/2 cup	sliced mushrooms	125 mL
2	cloves garlic, chopped	2
Pinch	salt	pinch
Pinch	hot pepper flakes (optional)	Pinch
1 cup	chopped spinach	250 mL
2 cups	cooked whole wheat spaghettini	500 mL
2 tbsp	freshly grated Parmesan cheese	25 mL

1. In a medium saucepan, heat olive oil over medium-low heat. Sauté mushrooms, garlic, salt and pepper flakes until mushrooms are tender, about 5 minutes. Add spinach and sauté until tender and wilted, about 5 minutes. Add spaghettini and toss until heated.
2. Transfer to a serving bowl and sprinkle with Parmesan.

✓ **KID APPROVED**

Diabetes Food Choice Values Per Serving	
1	Carbohydrate
1 1/2	Fats

NUTRIENTS Per Serving		
Calories: 166	Carbohydrate: 19.8 g	Calcium: 66 mg
Fat: 8.1 g	Fiber: 2.6 g	Iron: 1.2 mg
Sodium: 136 mg	Protein: 5.5 g	
A source of: Dietary fiber		

Couscous with Currants and Carrots

Corilee Watters, Dietitian, BC

This dish goes wonderfully with Moroccan Vegetable Tagine (page 218) or Moroccan Lamb Tagine (page 198).

• *Preparation time: 5 minutes / Cooking time: 20 minutes*

2 cups	chicken broth	500 mL
1	carrot, diced	1
¼ cup	olive oil	50 mL
1 tbsp	grated gingerroot	15 mL
¼ tsp	ground turmeric	1 mL
¼ tsp	ground cinnamon	1 mL
¼ tsp	ground cumin	1 mL
1 cup	couscous	250 mL
½ cup	currants	125 mL

1. In a medium saucepan, over medium-high heat, bring broth to a boil. Add carrot, oil, ginger, turmeric, cinnamon and cumin. Boil until carrot is tender-crisp, about 4 minutes. Remove from heat and stir in couscous and currants. Cover and let stand for 10 minutes, until couscous is softened and has absorbed most of the water. Fluff with a fork.

❄ **FREEZER FRIENDLY**
✓ **KID APPROVED**

TIPS
Store unpeeled gingerroot in the freezer for up to 3 months. You can grate it from frozen for dishes that will be cooked.

Use whole wheat couscous to boost the whole grains in your menu.

NUTRIENTS Per Serving		
Calories: 225	Carbohydrate: 31.0 g	Calcium: 28 mg
Fat: 9.3 g	Fiber: 2.1 g	Iron: 1.1 mg
Sodium: 320 mg	Protein: 4.6 g	

Very high in: Vitamin A • **A source of:** Dietary fiber

Diabetes Food Choice Values Per Serving	
2	Carbohydrates
2	Fats

Eileen Campbell

This is an adaptation of a delicious Thai rice dish. The Thai version includes chicken pieces and shrimp and is served in a hollowed-out pineapple for a stunning presentation. Kids love the sweet taste of the pineapple.

TIPS

To make 3 cups (750 mL) cooked brown rice, use 1 cup (250 mL) rice and 2 cups (500 mL) water.

Every time you cook brown rice, make extra. Use it for this recipe or as a side dish for a stir-fry.

VARIATION

For a more substantial main dish, add leftover cooked chicken, Tofu 101 (page 224) or cooked shrimp.

Pineapple Vegetable Rice

• **Preparation time: 15 minutes / Cooking time: 50 minutes**
• *Preheat oven to 350°F (180°C)*
• *Ovenproof skillet*

2 tbsp	vegetable oil	25 mL
1	clove garlic, finely chopped	1
½ cup	chopped yellow onion	125 mL
½ cup	diced carrot	125 mL
½ cup	diced red bell pepper	125 mL
3 cups	cooked brown rice (see tip, at left)	750 mL
1 cup	fresh or canned pineapple chunks	250 mL
½ cup	unsalted dry-roasted cashew pieces	125 mL
¼ cup	dried cranberries	50 mL
3 tbsp	reduced-sodium soy sauce	45 mL
1 tbsp	granulated sugar	15 mL
½ cup	frozen green peas, thawed	125 mL
1	green onion, chopped	1
2 tbsp	chopped fresh cilantro	25 mL

1. In ovenproof skillet, heat oil over medium heat. Sauté garlic and onion until softened, about 5 minutes. Add carrot and red pepper; sauté until slightly softened, about 5 minutes. Stir in rice, pineapple, cashews, cranberries, soy sauce and sugar.

2. Place skillet in preheated oven and bake for 30 minutes. Remove from oven and stir in green peas. Bake for 10 minutes, until peas are hot.

3. Transfer to a serving bowl and sprinkle with green onion and cilantro.

✓ **KID APPROVED**

Diabetes Food Choice Values Per Serving	
1	Carbohydrate
1	Fat

NUTRIENTS Per Serving		
Calories: 138	Carbohydrate: 20.6 g	Calcium: 16 mg
Fat: 5.5 g	Fiber: 1.8 g	Iron: 0.9 mg
Sodium: 161 mg	Protein: 2.9 g	
High in: Magnesium		

Basmati Rice Pulau

MAKES 6 SERVINGS

Eileen Campbell

• *Preparation time: 10 minutes / Soaking time: 15 minutes / Cooking time: 17 minutes*

• *8-cup (2 L) microwave-safe glass or ceramic baking dish*

1 cup	basmati rice	250 mL
½ cup	chopped almonds, lightly toasted (see tip, at right)	125 mL
½ cup	golden raisins	125 mL
2 tsp	margarine or butter	10 mL
¼ tsp	cumin seeds	1 mL
6	cardamom pods	6
2	whole cloves	2
1	cinnamon stick	1
½ cup	grated carrot	125 mL
½ cup	frozen green peas, thawed	125 mL
½ cup	chopped fresh cilantro (optional)	125 mL

1. Wash rice in 4 to 5 changes of cold water, then soak for 15 minutes in enough water to cover. Wash again in a few changes of water until water is fairly clear. Drain.

2. In baking dish, combine soaked rice, 1½ cups (375 mL) water, almonds, raisins, margarine, cumin, cardamom, cloves and cinnamon stick. Cover and microwave on High for 10 minutes. Check doneness. If needed, return to microwave and cook on High for up to 5 minutes, or until rice is tender and water is almost absorbed. Stir in carrot and peas. Microwave on High for 2 minutes. Discard cardamom, cloves and cinnamon stick.

3. Fluff rice with a fork and sprinkle with cilantro, if desired.

Although you can cook this on the stovetop, the results in a microwave are amazing. The recipe is prepared in the same dish it is served in, cutting down on cleanup!

TIPS
Toast almonds in a dry skillet over medium heat until lightly browned and fragrant, about 3 minutes.

When using margarine, choose a non-hydrogenated version to limit consumption of trans fats.

VARIATION
If your family doesn't like curry spices, omit them and add salt and pepper to taste.

NUTRIENTS Per Serving		
Calories: 224	Carbohydrate: 38.0 g	Calcium: 41 mg
Fat: 6.2 g	Fiber: 2.5 g	Iron: 1.0 mg
Sodium: 27 mg	Protein: 5.4 g	

High in: Vitamin A and magnesium • **A source of:** Dietary fiber

Diabetes Food Choice Values Per Serving	
2	Carbohydrates
1	Fat

Eileen Campbell

Traditional risotto takes 30 minutes on top of the stove and needs constant attention. This simpler method starts on the stovetop and finishes in the oven. The results are still tasty.

VARIATION

Substitute other vegetables or protein for the mushrooms.

Planned Extras

Leftover risotto makes great rice cakes for another meal. Form cooled risotto into rounds and flatten. Heat a skillet over medium-high heat and spray with vegetable cooking spray. Cook risotto cakes for 3 minutes per side or until golden. Serve with tomato sauce, Grilled Garlic-Ginger Chicken Breasts (page 166) and a green salad.

SERVING IDEA:
Serve with Lemon-Thyme Roast Chicken (page 164) and Garden Patch Spinach Salad (page 141).

Oven-Baked Mushroom Risotto

• *Preparation time: 5 minutes / Soaking time: 30 minutes / Cooking time: 40 minutes*

• *Preheat oven to 350°F (180°C)*
• *12-cup (3 L) casserole dish with cover*
• *Baking sheet*

1 cup	assorted dried mushrooms	250 mL
2 cups	boiling water	500 mL
2 tbsp	olive oil	25 mL
8 oz	mushrooms, chopped	250 g
1	onion, chopped	1
1 cup	Arborio rice	250 mL
½ cup	dry white wine (optional)	125 mL
	Salt and freshly ground black pepper	
2 tbsp	freshly grated Parmesan cheese	25 mL
1 tbsp	butter	15 mL

1. Soak dried mushrooms in boiling water for 30 minutes. Drain and reserve liquid. Chop mushrooms.

2. In a medium skillet, heat oil over medium heat. Sauté fresh mushrooms, onion and chopped soaked mushrooms until lightly browned, about 10 minutes. Stir in rice. Transfer to casserole dish.

3. To the reserved mushroom liquid, add wine (if using) and enough water to make 3 cups (750 mL). Stir into mushroom mixture. Season to taste with salt and pepper. Cover casserole and place on baking sheet.

4. Bake in preheated oven for 20 minutes. Remove from oven and stir in cheese and butter. Cover and bake for 10 minutes or until rice is al dente (tender to the bite) and most of the liquid is absorbed.

✓ **KID APPROVED**

Diabetes Food Choice Values Per Serving	
2	Carbohydrates
1	Fat

NUTRIENTS Per Serving		
Calories: 204	Carbohydrate: 36.2 g	Calcium: 31 mg
Fat: 5.7 g	Fiber: 3.0 g	Iron: 1.0 mg
Sodium: 45 mg	Protein: 4.4 g	

High in: Riboflavin, niacin and zinc • **A source of:** Dietary fiber

Baked Springtime Risotto

- *Preparation time: 15 minutes / Cooking time: 40 minutes*
- *Preheat oven to 350°F (180°C)*
- *12-cup (3 L) casserole dish with cover*
- *Baking sheet*

1 tbsp	olive oil	15 mL
1	small onion, diced	1
1	clove garlic, minced	1
1 cup	Arborio rice	250 mL
3 cups	hot chicken broth, divided	750 mL
1/2 tsp	salt (or to taste)	2 mL
10	thin spears asparagus, cut into short pieces	10
1	red bell pepper, cut into thin strips	1
1/4 cup	freshly grated Parmesan cheese	50 mL
1/4 cup	minced fresh parsley	50 mL
	Freshly ground black pepper	

1. In a medium saucepan, heat oil over medium heat. Sauté onion and garlic for 5 minutes or until softened. Add rice and cook, stirring, for about 1 minute or until evenly coated. Add 2 cups (500 mL) of the broth and salt; bring to a simmer. Transfer to casserole dish, cover and place on baking sheet.

2. Bake in preheated oven for 15 minutes. Remove from oven and stir in the remaining broth, asparagus and red pepper. Cover and bake for 15 minutes or until rice is al dente (tender to the bite) and most of the liquid is absorbed.

3. Ladle into serving bowls and sprinkle each serving with cheese, parsley and pepper to taste.

✓ **KID APPROVED**

SERVING IDEA: Mix torn romaine with mandarin oranges and toasted almonds for a delicious side salad. Enjoy with Simple Grilled Fish (page 203).

Andrea Holmes, Dietitian, BC

Here's another great oven-baked rice dish that cooks unsupervised while you spend time with your family preparing the rest of the meal.

VARIATIONS

The first time you add broth, replace 1/2 cup (125 mL) of the chicken broth with an equal amount of dry white wine.

This dish works well with other vegetable combinations — try portobello mushrooms or butternut squash in the fall.

NUTRIENTS Per Serving		
Calories: 138	Carbohydrate: 22.8 g	Calcium: 59 mg
Fat: 2.9 g	Fiber: 1.1 g	Iron: 0.7 mg
Sodium: 551 mg	Protein: 4.3 g	
High in: Vitamin C and folate		

Diabetes Food Choice Values Per Serving	
1	Carbohydrate
1/2	Fat

Breads and Muffins

Breads and muffins are a great way to eat your grains. Try some with interesting tastes, such as Pumpkin Spice Nut Bread (page 283) or Big-Batch Banana Blueberry Muffins (page 285), to add variety as well as nutrients to your healthy menu.

How to Make Quick Breads Healthier

- Replace half of the all-purpose flour with quick-cooking rolled oats or whole wheat flour.
- Substitute wheat germ or bran for $1/4$ cup (50 mL) of the flour in a recipe.
- Replace a portion of the fat with an equal amount of puréed fruit. Puréed peaches work well in muffins and spice cakes; puréed prunes are great in chocolate-based recipes; puréed pears or bananas work well in quick breads and coffee cakes; and unsweetened applesauce is delicious in almost any baked good.
- Add grated carrot, sweet potato or zucchini to increase the nutrient content.
- Substitute dried fruits for chocolate chips or nuts.
- Add seeds (sunflower, pumpkin, sesame, flax) for extra nutrition and crunch.

Storing Whole Wheat Flour

Whole wheat flour contains all three nutrient-rich parts of the wheat berry — the bran, the germ and the endosperm — and has more fiber than all-purpose flour. However, its many healthful oils tend to go rancid quickly. Store unopened whole wheat flour for up to 1 month at room temperature. Once opened, it will last for up to 8 months in the refrigerator. If you're not using it up quickly, your best bet is to store it, tightly sealed, in the refrigerator.

Flaxseed

Flaxseed is a great source of fiber and other nutrients, and it's easy to add flax to your diet. Sprinkle ground flaxseed on cereal, yogurt or casseroles. Whole flaxseed adds flavor and crunch to baked goods such as breads and muffins.

Ground flaxseed became a favorite ingredient during the testing process. It adds a nutty taste and a boost of fiber, without changing the overall taste or quality of the recipe. To cut back on fat and improve the nutrition of your baking recipes, try some of these substitutions:

- **For fat:** Use a 3:1 ratio. For example, for 1 tbsp (15 mL) butter, margarine, shortening or vegetable oil, use 3 tbsp (45 mL) ground flaxseed.

- **For eggs:** For every egg being replaced, mix 1 tbsp (15 mL) ground flaxseed with 3 tbsp (45 mL) water in a small bowl; let stand for 1 to 2 minutes or until mixture becomes gel-like. Add to your recipe as you would an egg.

Whole flaxseed can be stored at room temperature for up to 1 year. Keep ground flaxseed in an airtight container in the fridge for up to 3 months. Since whole flaxseed is difficult to grind at home, buy preground flaxseed if you need it for a recipe. You can usually find it in the natural food section of the grocery store or in a health food store.

Try Ancient for Taste and Whole Grain Goodness

Ancient grains — kamut, spelt, amaranth, quinoa and millet — are trendy these days. Many are sold in bulk, and all are an inexpensive source of excellent nutrition. Another great thing about these grains is that they are relatively easy to cook — for the most part, just add water and simmer. Some, such as spelt, need to be soaked overnight and take a relatively long time to cook, about 45 minutes. Others, such as quinoa, just require a thorough rinsing and cook in about 15 minutes. Most ancient grains have a chewy texture and a mild, nutty flavor.

portioning muffins

To bake muffins evenly, you want to scoop out consistent amounts of batter. A good solution is to use a measuring scoop rather than a spoon. You can find scoops in specialty kitchen stores. They are usually marked with numbers that indicate the different portion sizes: #30 for mini muffins (1-oz/30 g serving), # 16 for medium-sized muffins (2-oz/60 g serving) or #12 for large muffins (3-oz/90 g serving). We used a #16 scoop for all the muffin recipes in the book. If you want to make mini muffins, halve the baking time, then do the usual checks for doneness.

Diane May, Dietitian, SK

One of the taste-testers offered to pay us to make her this bread on a regular basis — it is just that good. It takes a while for the dough to rise; however, the total preparation time is not that long, considering that the recipe makes 5 loaves.

TIPS

If you want to make just 1 loaf, divide the ingredient measures roughly by 5.

Look for 9-grain cereal in the bulk food store or the bulk food section of your grocery store.

Make sure to use self-rising yeast, which you can add directly to the flour.

If you do not have a bowl large enough to contain the dough when it has doubled, divide the dough in half and let each half rise in a separate bowl. Combine the two portions when punching dough down for step 4.

Diane combines the ingredients in a very clean dishpan.

Big-Batch Multigrain Bread

• **Preparation time: 20 minutes / Rising time: 105 to 110 minutes / Cooking time: 40 minutes**

• *Five 9- by 5-inch (2 L) loaf pans, greased on the bottom only*

1 cup	natural bran	250 mL
1 cup	9-grain cereal (such as Red River)	250 mL
1 cup	granulated sugar	250 mL
3 tbsp	self-rising yeast	45 mL
1 tbsp	salt	15 mL
3	eggs, beaten	3
5 cups	lukewarm water	1.25 L
1 cup	vegetable oil	250 mL
¼ cup	fancy molasses	50 mL
8 to 10 cups	all-purpose flour (approx.)	2 to 2.5 L
4 to 5 cups	whole wheat flour (approx.)	1 to 1.25 L

1. In a very large bowl, combine bran, 9-grain cereal, sugar, yeast and salt.

2. In a large bowl, combine eggs, water, oil and molasses. Stir into bran mixture until well combined. Stir in all-purpose flour and whole wheat flour 1 cup (250 mL) at a time until a stiff dough is formed. (Depending on the weather and humidity, you may not need all the flour).

3. On a floured work surface, knead dough until smooth and elastic. Place in clean, lightly oiled large bowl (see tip, at left), cover with a tea towel and let rise until doubled in bulk, about 1 hour.

4. Punch down dough several times to work out air bubbles. Divide into 5 equal pieces and shape into loaves. Place in prepared loaf pans. Cover with towels and let rise for 45 to 50 minutes, or until the top of the dough is nearly level with the top of the loaf pan. Meanwhile, preheat oven to 350°F (180°C).

5. Bake for 40 minutes, rotating pans halfway through, or until tops are golden and firm to the touch. Let cool in pans for 10 minutes, then remove to a wire rack to cool completely.

❄ FREEZER FRIENDLY
✓ KID APPROVED

TIP
You should be able to bake all 5 pans at the same time if you place them carefully on one rack in the oven. If you don't have 5 loaf pans, though, you can bake the loaves in batches. While each batch is baking, cover the remaining loaves with lightly oiled plastic wrap and place in the refrigerator to retard rising. Bring to room temperature for about 15 minutes before baking.

Liquid Sweeteners

- **Honey** is a liquid sugar made by bees. It is sweeter than sugar and has a distinctive flavor. Baked goods made with honey are moist and dense and tend to brown faster than those made with granulated sugar. Use $\frac{1}{2}$ cup (125 mL) honey to replace 1 cup (250 mL) granulated sugar. Unless the recipe includes sour cream or buttermilk, add a pinch of baking soda to neutralize the acidity.

- **Molasses** is a byproduct of refined sugar production. It contains small amounts of B vitamins, calcium and iron. Molasses imparts a dark color and strong flavor to baked foods but is not as sweet as sugar. When substituting molasses for granulated sugar, use $1\frac{1}{3}$ cups (325 mL) unsulfured molasses per 1 cup (250 mL) sugar and reduce the amount of liquid in the recipe by 5 tablespoons (75 mL). Molasses is more acidic than sugar, so add $\frac{1}{2}$ teaspoon (2 mL) baking soda for each cup (250 mL) of molasses used to replace sugar. Replace no more than half the sugar called for in a recipe with molasses.

- **Maple syrup** is made from the sap of sugar maple trees. It is used as syrup on pancakes and waffles and is very good in cookies, pies and cakes. Like honey, it is quite sweet; use $\frac{3}{4}$ cup (175 mL) for every cup (250 mL) of granulated sugar and reduce the amount of liquid in the recipe by 3 tablespoons (45 mL).

- **Brown rice syrup** is an amber-hued syrup that resembles honey but is not as sweet. It can be substituted cup per cup (mL per mL) for granulated sugar, but the amount of liquid in the recipe should be reduced by $\frac{1}{4}$ cup (50 mL) for every cup (250 mL) of rice syrup.

NUTRIENTS Per Serving		
Calories: 193	Carbohydrate: 30.8 g	Calcium: 59 mg
Fat: 6.9 g	Fiber: 3.6 g	Iron: 1.1 mg
Sodium: 157 mg	Protein: 5.5 g	

High in: Magnesium • **A source of:** Dietary fiber

Diabetes Food Choice Values Per Serving	
2	Carbohydrates
$1\frac{1}{2}$	Fats

Oat Bran Banana Bread

- *Preparation time: 15 minutes / Cooking time: 50 to 60 minutes*
- *Preheat oven to 325°F (160°C)*
- *9- by 5-inch (2 L) loaf pan, lightly greased*

1 1/2 cups	whole wheat flour	375 mL
1/2 cup	oat bran	125 mL
1/3 cup	ground flaxseed	75 mL
1 tsp	baking powder	5 mL
1 tsp	baking soda	5 mL
2	egg whites	2
1	whole egg	1
1/2 cup	granulated sugar	125 mL
1/4 cup	vegetable oil or margarine	50 mL
1 tsp	vanilla	5 mL
3/4 cup	low-fat plain yogurt	175 mL
3	ripe bananas, mashed (about 1 1/3 cups/325 mL)	3
2 tbsp	whole flaxseed (optional)	25 mL

1. In a medium bowl, combine flour, oat bran, ground flaxseed, baking powder and baking soda.

2. In a large bowl, beat egg whites, whole egg, sugar, oil and vanilla for 3 to 4 minutes or until creamy. Stir in yogurt until well combined. Stir in bananas. Gradually fold in flour mixture.

3. Spoon batter into prepared loaf pan and smooth top. Sprinkle with whole flaxseed (if using).

4. Bake in preheated oven for 50 to 60 minutes or until top is firm to the touch and a tester inserted in the center comes out clean. Let cool in pan for 10 minutes, then remove to a wire rack to cool completely.

❄ FREEZER FRIENDLY
✓ KID APPROVED

Diabetes Food Choice Values Per Serving	
2	Carbohydrates
1 1/2	Fats

NUTRIENTS Per Serving		
Calories: 193	Carbohydrate: 30.8 g	Calcium: 59 mg
Fat: 6.9 g	Fiber: 3.6 g	Iron: 1.1 mg
Sodium: 157 mg	Protein: 5.5 g	

High in: Magnesium • **A source of:** Dietary fiber

Pumpkin Spice Nut Bread

MAKES
12 SERVINGS

Natalie Carrier, Dietitian,
NB

- *Preparation time: 20 minutes / Cooking time: 50 to 60 minutes*
- *Preheat oven to 350°F (180°C)*
- *9-by 5-inch (2 L) loaf pan, lightly greased*

1 cup	all-purpose flour	250 mL
¾ cup	whole wheat flour	175 mL
2 tsp	ground allspice	10 mL
1½ tsp	baking powder	7 mL
1 tsp	baking soda	5 mL
½ tsp	salt	2 mL
1 tsp	ground cinnamon	5 mL
½ tsp	ground nutmeg	2 mL
½ tsp	ground ginger	2 mL
1 cup	canned pumpkin purée (not pie filling)	250 mL
¾ cup	packed brown sugar	175 mL
½ cup	vegetable oil	125 mL
2	eggs, lightly beaten	2
1 tsp	vanilla	5 mL
⅓ cup	water (approx.), divided	75 mL
½ cup	chopped pecans or walnuts	125 mL

This terrific recipe offers the benefits of pumpkin, as well as whole grains and nuts.

VARIATION
Use mini loaf pans to make 12 mini loaves. Bake at the same temperature for 25 minutes, or until a tester comes out clean. These are great for lunches or mid-morning snacks.

1. In a small bowl, combine all-purpose flour, whole wheat flour, allspice, baking powder, baking soda, salt, cinnamon, nutmeg and ginger.

2. In a large bowl, whisk together pumpkin, brown sugar and oil. Whisk in eggs, vanilla and half of the water. Fold in flour mixture (do not overmix). If batter is too thick, stir in the remaining water, a little at a time. Fold in pecans.

3. Spoon batter into prepared loaf pan and smooth top.

4. Bake in preheated oven for 50 to 60 minutes or until top is firm to the touch and a tester inserted in the center comes out clean. Let cool in pan for 10 minutes, then remove to a wire rack to cool completely.

❄ FREEZER FRIENDLY
✓ KID APPROVED

NUTRIENTS Per Serving		
Calories: 249	Carbohydrate: 29.8 g	Calcium: 50 mg
Fat: 13.5 g	Fiber: 2.5 g	Iron: 1.7 mg
Sodium: 256 mg	Protein: 3.8 g	
Very high in: Vitamin A • **A source of:** Dietary fiber		

Diabetes Food Choice Values Per Serving	
2	Carbohydrates
2½	Fats

Bannock

Diane May, Dietitian, SK

This Aboriginal favorite goes well with a hearty soup or stew. It tastes like tea biscuits, only much better. The children on our tasting panel gobbled them up, without even adding jam.

TIPS

When using margarine, choose a non-hydrogenated version to limit consumption of trans fats.

Use mashed potatoes with your usual milk and butter added.

If you score the top of the bannock into 12 portions with a sharp knife before baking, it is easier to cut after baking.

• **Preparation time: 20 minutes / Cooking time: 20 minutes**
• Preheat oven to 350°F (180°C)
• Baking sheet, lightly greased

1½ cups	all-purpose flour	375 mL
1 cup	whole wheat flour	250 mL
3 tbsp	granulated sugar	45 mL
2 tbsp	baking powder	25 mL
1 tsp	salt	5 mL
2 tbsp	margarine	25 mL
1 cup	leftover mashed potatoes	250 mL
1 cup	milk	250 mL

1. In a large bowl, combine all-purpose flour, whole wheat flour, sugar, baking powder and salt. Using a pastry cutter or two knives, cut in margarine until mixture resembles coarse crumbs. Stir in mashed potatoes and milk until a wet dough forms.

2. On a floured work surface, knead dough until smooth and elastic. Shape into a round about 1½ inches (4 cm) thick and place on prepared baking sheet. Prick the top with a fork.

3. Bake in preheated oven for about 20 minutes or until top is golden and a tester inserted in the center comes out clean. Let cool on baking sheet for 10 minutes, then remove to a wire rack to cool completely.

❄ FREEZER FRIENDLY
✓ KID APPROVED

SERVING IDEA: Serve with margarine or butter, Saskatoon berry jam (a real favorite in the west) or a slice of cheese. Delicious!

Diabetes Food Choice Values Per Serving

1½	Carbohydrates
½	Fat

NUTRIENTS Per Serving

Calories: 148	Carbohydrate: 27.6 g	Calcium: 99 mg
Fat: 2.7 g	Fiber: 1.9 g	Iron: 1.3 mg
Sodium: 378 mg	Protein: 4.0 g	

High in: Folate

Big-Batch Banana Blueberry Muffins

MAKES 24 MUFFINS (1 PER SERVING)

Jacqueline O'Keefe, NS

These tasty muffins are a great way to use up ripe bananas.

- *Preparation time: 20 minutes / Cooking time: 20 minutes*
- *Preheat oven to 350°F (180°C)*
- *Two 12-cup muffin tins, lightly greased or lined with paper cups*

3 cups	whole wheat flour	750 mL
3 cups	ground flaxseed	750 mL
2 cups	lightly packed brown sugar	500 mL
1 tbsp	baking powder	15 mL
1 tbsp	baking soda	15 mL
Pinch	salt	Pinch
3	eggs	3
3	ripe bananas, mashed (about 1 1/3 cups/325 mL)	3
1	jar (4 1/2 oz/128 mL) baby food prunes or unsweetened applesauce	1
2/3 cup	vegetable oil	150 mL
2 tsp	vanilla	10 mL
2 cups	fresh or frozen blueberries	500 mL

TIP
Ripe bananas can be thrown in the freezer, peel and all. To use, just thaw, peel and mash. You can also mash bananas and freeze in amounts appropriate for your recipes.

VARIATION
Substitute wheat germ or wheat bran for the ground flaxseed and chocolate chips for the blueberries. Children usually prefer the combination of wheat germ and chocolate chips.

1. In a large bowl, combine flour, flaxseed, brown sugar, baking powder, baking soda and salt.
2. In a very large bowl, combine eggs, bananas, prunes, oil and vanilla. Fold in flour mixture until just combined. Fold in blueberries.
3. Divide batter evenly among prepared muffin cups.
4. Bake in preheated oven for 20 minutes, rotating pans halfway through, or until tops are firm to the touch and a tester inserted in the center of a muffin comes out clean. Let cool in tin for 10 minutes, then remove to a wire rack to cool completely.

❄ FREEZER FRIENDLY
✓ KID APPROVED

NUTRIENTS Per Serving		
Calories: 226	Carbohydrate: 31.4 g	Calcium: 72 mg
Fat: 10.3 g	Fiber: 5.2 g	Iron: 1.4 mg
Sodium: 172 mg	Protein: 4.7 g	

Very high in: Magnesium • **High in:** Folate and dietary fiber

Diabetes Food Choice Values Per Serving	
2	Carbohydrates
2	Fats

Glenyss Turner, ON

Muffins are Glenyss's favorite morning snack when she's at work. She created this recipe to use whole wheat flour and less oil than other recipes.

Banana Applesauce Muffins

● **Preparation time: 10 minutes / Cooking time: 15 to 20 minutes**
● *Preheat oven to 400°F (200°C)*
● *12-cup muffin tin, lightly greased or lined with paper cups*

2 cups	whole wheat flour	500 mL
1 tbsp	baking powder	15 mL
1 tsp	baking soda	5 mL
½ tsp	salt	2 mL
3	ripe bananas, mashed (about 1⅓ cups/325 mL)	3
1	egg, lightly beaten	1
1 cup	unsweetened applesauce	250 mL
½ cup	granulated sugar	125 mL
¼ cup	vegetable oil	50 mL

1. In a large bowl, combine flour, baking powder, baking soda and salt.
2. In a medium bowl, combine bananas, egg, applesauce, sugar and oil. Stir into flour mixture until just combined.
3. Divide batter evenly among prepared muffin cups.
4. Bake in preheated oven for 15 to 20 minutes or until tops are firm to the touch and a tester inserted in the center of a muffin comes out clean. Let cool in tin for 10 minutes, then remove to a wire rack to cool completely.

❄️ **FREEZER FRIENDLY**
✓ **KID APPROVED**

Diabetes Food Choice Values Per Serving	
2	Carbohydrates
1	Fat

NUTRIENTS Per Serving		
Calories: 183	Carbohydrate: 32.3 g	Calcium: 45 mg
Fat: 5.4 g	Fiber: 3.2 g	Iron: 1.0 mg
Sodium: 283 mg	Protein: 3.6 g	

High in: Magnesium • **A source of:** Dietary fiber

Triple B Health Muffins

**MAKES 12 MUFFINS
(1 PER SERVING)**

Barbara Kajifasz, ON

- **Preparation time: 20 minutes / Cooking time: 20 to 25 minutes**
- *Preheat oven to 400°F (200°C)*
- *12-cup muffin tin, lightly greased or lined with paper cups*

These healthy muffins are a good choice for breakfast or a mid-morning snack.

1 cup	whole wheat flour	250 mL
1 cup	wheat bran or oat bran	250 mL
1 cup	fresh or frozen blueberries	250 mL
1 tsp	baking soda	5 mL
1 tsp	baking powder	5 mL
2	ripe bananas, mashed (about 1 cup/250 mL)	2
1	egg, lightly beaten	1
½ cup	granulated sugar	125 mL
½ cup	milk	125 mL
¼ cup	vegetable oil	50 mL
1 tsp	vanilla	5 mL

1. In a medium bowl, combine flour, wheat bran, blueberries, baking soda and baking powder.

2. In a large bowl, combine bananas, egg, sugar, milk, oil and vanilla. Fold in flour mixture until just combined.

3. Divide batter evenly among prepared muffin cups, filling each two-thirds full.

4. Bake in preheated oven for 20 to 25 minutes or until tops are firm to the touch and a tester inserted in the center of a muffin comes out clean. Let cool in tin for 10 minutes, then remove to a wire rack to cool completely.

❄ FREEZER FRIENDLY

NUTRIENTS Per Serving		
Calories: 152	Carbohydrate: 25.6 g	Calcium: 34 mg
Fat: 5.6 g	Fiber: 3.9 g	Iron: 1.1 mg
Sodium: 141 mg	Protein: 3.3 g	

High in: Magnesium • **A source of:** Dietary fiber

Diabetes Food Choice Values Per Serving	
1½	Carbohydrates
1	Fat

Pumpkin Bran Muffins

Lisa Vance, Dietitian, SK

Lisa's kids love these muffins, and even small children can help measure the ingredients. Since the batter is made ahead, it takes no time at all to bake these fresh for a special breakfast or coffee break. You can bake them all at once or scoop the batter as you need it.

TIPS

If you don't have buttermilk for a baking recipe, sour milk is a great substitute. Simply add 1 tbsp (15 mL) lemon juice or vinegar to each cup (250 mL) of regular milk. Let stand for 10 minutes before using.

You can substitute 1 cup (250 mL) natural bran for the bran cereal.

The batter will keep in the refrigerator for up to 1 week, so there's no need to bake the muffins all at once.

If you don't have leftover cooked pumpkin, you can use canned pumpkin purée (not pie filling).

- *Preparation time: 20 minutes / Cooking time: 15 to 20 minutes*
- *Two 12-cup muffin tins, lightly greased or lined with paper cups*

2 cups	bran cereal	500 mL
1 1/4 cups	all-purpose flour	300 mL
1 1/4 cups	whole wheat flour	300 mL
1 cup	raisins	250 mL
1/2 cup	sesame seeds	125 mL
1/2 cup	ground flaxseed	125 mL
1/4 cup	wheat germ	50 mL
2 1/2 tsp	baking soda	12 mL
1/2 tsp	salt	2 mL
2	eggs, lightly beaten	2
2 cups	buttermilk or sour milk	500 mL
1 1/2 cups	lightly packed brown sugar	375 mL
1 cup	mashed cooked pumpkin	250 mL
1/2 cup	vegetable oil	125 mL

1. In a large bowl, combine bran cereal, all-purpose flour, whole wheat flour, raisins, sesame seeds, flaxseed, wheat germ, baking soda and salt.

2. In a very large bowl, combine eggs, buttermilk, brown sugar, pumpkin and oil. Gradually fold in bran mixture until well combined. Bake immediately or cover and refrigerate for up to 1 week. Preheat oven to 400°F (200°C).

3. Scoop about 1/3 cup (75 mL) batter per muffin into prepared muffin cups.

4. Bake for 15 to 20 minutes or until tops are firm to the touch and a tester inserted in the center of a muffin comes out clean. Let cool in tins for 10 minutes, then remove to a wire rack to cool completely.

❄️ FREEZER FRIENDLY
✓ KID APPROVED

Diabetes Food Choice Values Per Serving	
2	Carbohydrates
1 1/2	Fats

NUTRIENTS Per Serving		
Calories: 216	Carbohydrate: 33.3 g	Calcium: 60 mg
Fat: 8.2 g	Fiber: 3.1 g	Iron: 1.9 mg
Sodium: 237 mg	Protein: 4.7 g	

High in: Vitamin A, folate and magnesium • **A source of:** Dietary fiber

Cheddar Corn Muffins
with Pumpkin Seeds (page 292)

Fruit Gazpacho (page 301)

Fiber-Power Biscotti (page 319)

Toffee Bars (page 322), Apricot Coconut Bars
(page 323) and Berry Cheesecake Bars (page 324)

Sweet Potato Muffins

MAKES 12 MUFFINS (1 PER SERVING)

Eileen Campbell

- *Preparation time: 15 minutes / Cooking time: 20 minutes*
- *Preheat oven to 400°F (200°C)*
- *12-cup muffin tin, lightly greased or lined with paper cups*

1 cup	quick-cooking rolled oats	250 mL
1 cup	buttermilk (approx.)	250 mL
½ cup	all-purpose flour	125 mL
½ cup	whole wheat flour	125 mL
¼ cup	granulated sugar	50 mL
1 tbsp	wheat germ	15 mL
1 tbsp	baking powder	15 mL
1 tsp	salt	5 mL
½ tsp	baking soda	2 mL
1 cup	mixed dried fruit	250 mL
1	egg, beaten	1
½ cup	grated sweet potato	125 mL
¼ cup	lightly packed brown sugar	50 mL
¼ cup	vegetable oil	50 mL
1 tsp	grated orange zest	5 mL

Start your day off well with one of these moist and delicious muffins.

TIP
For the mixed dried fruit, try raisins, blueberries, cherries and cranberries.

1. Place oatmeal in a large bowl and pour in buttermilk; stir to combine. Cover and let stand for 10 minutes.

2. Meanwhile, in a small bowl, combine all-purpose flour, whole wheat flour, granulated sugar, wheat germ, baking powder, salt and baking soda. Stir in dried fruit.

3. In another small bowl, combine egg, sweet potato, brown sugar, oil and orange zest. Stir into oatmeal mixture. Gradually fold in flour mixture until just moistened. If too stiff, add a little more buttermilk.

4. Divide batter evenly among prepared muffin cups, filling almost to the top (these muffins do not rise much).

5. Bake for 20 minutes or until a tester inserted in the center of a muffin comes out clean. Let cool in tin for 10 minutes, then remove to a wire rack to cool completely.

❄ **FREEZER FRIENDLY**

NUTRIENTS Per Serving		
Calories: 194	Carbohydrate: 32.7 g	Calcium: 88 mg
Fat: 6.0 g	Fiber: 2.4 g	Iron: 1.2 mg
Sodium: 352 mg	Protein: 4.1 g	
A source of: Dietary fiber		

Diabetes Food Choice Values Per Serving	
2	Carbohydrates
1	Fat

Donna Suerich, ON

The kids on our tasting panel loved these muffins made with chocolate chips, but adults may prefer them with dried fruit.

TIPS

If you choose to use dried fruit instead of chocolate chips, you will add nutrition and fiber to your muffins.

For the nuts, try walnuts, pecans or almonds.

Chocolate Chip Oatmeal Muffins

- **Preparation time: 10 minutes / Cooking time: 15 to 20 minutes**
- *Preheat oven to 400°F (200°C)*
- *12-cup muffin tin, lightly greased or lined with paper cups*

1 ½ cups	whole wheat flour	375 mL
½ cup	quick-cooking rolled oats	125 mL
¼ cup	ground flaxseed	50 mL
¼ cup	granulated sugar	50 mL
2 tsp	baking powder	10 mL
½ tsp	baking soda	2 mL
½ tsp	salt	2 mL
1	egg	1
1 cup	milk	250 mL
¼ cup	vegetable oil	50 mL
¼ cup	liquid honey	50 mL
½ cup	semisweet chocolate chips or dried fruit	125 mL
½ cup	chopped nuts (optional)	125 mL

1. In a large bowl, combine flour, oats, flaxseed, sugar, baking powder, baking soda and salt.
2. In a small bowl, whisk together egg, milk, oil and honey. Stir into flour mixture until just combined. Fold in chocolate chips and nuts (if using).
3. Divide batter evenly among prepared muffin cups.
4. Bake in preheated oven for 15 to 20 minutes or until tops are firm to the touch and a tester inserted in the center of a muffin comes out clean. Let cool in tin for 10 minutes, then remove to a wire rack to cool completely.

❄ FREEZER FRIENDLY
✓ KID APPROVED

Diabetes Food Choice Values Per Serving

2	Carbohydrates
1 ½	Fats

NUTRIENTS Per Serving

Calories: 210	Carbohydrate: 30 g	Calcium: 66 mg
Fat: 8.7 g	Fiber: 3.3 g	Iron: 1.2 mg
Sodium: 214 mg	Protein: 4.6 g	

High in: Magnesium • **A source of:** Dietary fiber

Orange Cranberry Muffins

MAKES 12 MUFFINS (1 PER SERVING)

Helen Haresign, Dietitian, ON

- **Preparation time: 15 minutes / Cooking time: 20 to 25 minutes**
- *Preheat oven to 375°F (190°C)*
- *12-cup muffin tin, lightly greased or lined with paper cups*

1½ cups	all-purpose flour	375 mL
¾ cup	granulated sugar	175 mL
2 tsp	baking powder	10 mL
1 tsp	baking soda	5 mL
1	whole navel orange	1
1	egg	1
½ cup	milk	125 mL
⅓ cup	vegetable oil	75 mL
1 cup	fresh cranberries (or frozen, thawed)	250 mL

1. In a large bowl, combine flour, sugar, baking powder and baking soda.
2. Cut off ends of orange, then cut into quarters, without peeling. Remove seeds.
3. In food processor, process orange (including peel), egg, milk and oil until blended. Stir into flour mixture until just moistened. Gently stir in cranberries.
4. Divide batter evenly among prepared muffin cups.
5. Bake in preheated oven for 20 to 25 minutes or until tops are firm to the touch and a tester inserted in the center of a muffin comes out clean. Let cool in tin for 10 minutes, then remove to a wire rack to cool completely.

 FREEZER FRIENDLY

These delicious fruit muffins are perfect with a cup of tea when you need a mid-afternoon boost — and they're a festive choice for the holiday season. It's hard to believe that you mix in the whole orange, but it makes the muffins so moist!

VARIATION
Substitute fresh or frozen blueberries for the cranberries.

NUTRIENTS Per Serving		
Calories: 180	Carbohydrate: 28.2 g	Calcium: 49 mg
Fat: 6.9 g	Fiber: 1.4 g	Iron: 0.9 mg
Sodium: 165 mg	Protein: 2.7 g	
High in: Folate		

Diabetes Food Choice Values Per Serving	
2	Carbohydrates
1	Fat

These muffins are great for lunch or dinner with soup and/or salad. Keep some on hand in the freezer and pop them out in the morning to thaw; by dinnertime, they'll be ready to serve with a slow-cooked soup.

TIP

This recipe also works well as a topping for a Mexican meat pie. Ladle your favorite chili into a casserole dish and spoon batter on top. Bake in a 350°F (180°C) oven for 35 to 45 minutes or until a tester inserted into the topping comes out clean. It is a great way to change your leftover chili into a brand-new dish.

Cheddar Corn Muffins with Pumpkin Seeds

- **Preparation time: 10 minutes / Cooking time: 25 to 30 minutes**
- *Preheat oven to 375°F (190°C)*
- *12-cup muffin tin, lightly greased or lined with paper cups*

1 cup	cornmeal	250 mL
1 cup	whole wheat flour	250 mL
1 cup	shredded sharp Cheddar cheese	250 mL
1 tsp	salt	5 mL
1 tsp	freshly ground black pepper	5 mL
½ tsp	baking soda	2 mL
3	eggs	3
1	can (10 oz/284 mL) creamed corn	1
1 cup	plain yogurt or buttermilk	250 mL
¼ cup	vegetable oil	50 mL
½ cup	raw green pumpkin seeds or sunflower seeds	125 mL
2 tbsp	chopped fresh parsley	25 mL

1. In a medium bowl, combine cornmeal, flour, cheese, salt, pepper and baking soda.
2. In a large bowl, whisk together eggs, creamed corn, yogurt and oil. Gradually fold in flour mixture until just combined. Stir in pumpkin seeds and parsley.
3. Divide batter evenly among prepared muffin cups.
4. Bake in preheated oven for 25 to 30 minutes or until tops are firm to the touch and a tester inserted in the center of a muffin comes out clean. Let cool in tin for 10 minutes, then remove to a wire rack to cool completely.

❄️ **FREEZER FRIENDLY**

SERVING IDEA: Dunk one of these muffins into a bowl of Chunky Southwest Vegetable Soup (page 120).

Diabetes Food Choice Values Per Serving	
1½	Carbohydrates
1	Meat & Alternatives
2	Fats

NUTRIENTS Per Serving		
Calories: 236	Carbohydrate: 23.8 g	Calcium: 121 mg
Fat: 12.4 g	Fiber: 2.7 g	Iron: 1.8 mg
Sodium: 410 mg	Protein: 9.2 g	

Very high in: Magnesium • **High in:** Folate and zinc
A source of: Dietary fiber

Savory Breakfast Muffins

MAKES 12 MUFFINS (1 PER SERVING)

Compass Group Canada

- **Preparation time: 10 minutes / Cooking time: 18 minutes**
- *Preheat oven to 375°F (190°C)*
- *12-cup muffin tin, lightly greased or lined with paper cups*

2 cups	whole wheat flour	500 mL
1 cup	all-purpose flour	250 mL
1 tbsp	baking powder	15 mL
½ tsp	baking soda	2 mL
½ tsp	freshly ground black pepper	2 mL
½ tsp	salt	2 mL
2 cups	buttermilk	500 mL
1 cup	egg whites or egg substitute (or 2 whole eggs)	250 mL
3 tbsp	vegetable oil	45 mL
2 cups	shredded nacho cheese blend	500 mL
1 cup	thinly sliced green onions	250 mL
1 cup	chopped cooked Canadian (back) bacon	250 mL
½ cup	diced red bell pepper	125 mL

1. In a very large bowl, combine whole wheat flour, all-purpose flour, baking powder, baking soda, pepper and salt.
2. In a large bowl, whisk together buttermilk, egg whites and oil. Stir in cheese, green onions, bacon and red pepper. Pour over flour mixture and stir until just moistened.
3. Divide batter evenly among prepared muffin cups (cups will be very full).
4. Bake in preheated oven for 18 minutes or until tops are firm to the touch and a tester inserted in the center of a muffin comes out clean. Let cool in tin for 10 minutes before removing. Serve warm.

❄ FREEZER FRIENDLY

These unusual but delicious savory muffins contain great-tasting breakfast ingredients such as Canadian bacon and cheese.

TIP
Regular bacon contains seven times more fat and three times more calories than back bacon. Back bacon is also lower in sodium. To reduce the sodium content of recipes containing bacon or ham, look for reduced-sodium products.

NUTRIENTS Per Serving		
Calories: 271	Carbohydrate: 26.9 g	Calcium: 230 mg
Fat: 11.8 g	Fiber: 3.1 g	Iron: 1.8 mg
Sodium: 624 mg	Protein: 15.7 g	

Very high in: Niacin • **High in:** Calcium, thiamine, riboflavin, folate and magnesium • **A source of:** Dietary fiber

Diabetes Food Choice Values Per Serving	
1½	Carbohydrates
1½	Meat & Alternatives
1	Fat

Desserts

We often enjoy a little taste of something sweet to end a meal or as an accompaniment to an afternoon tea or latte. Desserts need not all be high-calorie cakes, cookies, bars and squares. The desserts in this book, ranging from the smooth and light Lemon Blueberry Panna Cotta (page 299) to Best-Ever Chocolate Cookies (page 314), all have a healthy twist!

other dessert ideas

If you don't have time to make one of the tasty desserts in this book, here are a few ideas for a light ending to your meal:

- angel food cake with berries
- fresh cut fruit
- applesauce
- frozen yogurt pop
- frozen juice bar
- yogurt parfait with fresh fruit
- grilled fruit kebabs
- cantaloupe wedge with fruit ice
- lower-fat cookie
- fig bar
- pudding made with low-fat milk

Enjoying More Fruit

Not only is a juicy piece of fruit a healthful dessert, but fruit also makes a great addition to many meals, any time of the day. Here are some ideas for adding fruit to your menu:

- Make fruit smoothies with 2 to 3 different fruits. Bananas, berries and peaches or pears work well. See our smoothie recipes for more ideas (pages 86 to 88).
- Remember that ½ cup (125 mL) of 100% fruit juice counts as a serving of fruit.
- Add dried fruit to muffins, cookies and other baked goods.
- Make a fruit salad, containing at least 3 different fruits, at least once a week. Keep it in the fridge for between-meals snacks or to serve as part of your breakfast fare.
- Add a smattering of berries to whole-grain cereal or a green salad. Toss a few into muffin or pancake batter.
- Serve interesting fruit salsas with meat, fish and poultry. Try our Mango Mint Mojo (page 109) or Pineapple Salsa (page 105).
- Pack fruit as part of lunch. Peel and cut it up in advance and pack in a small plastic bag or container.

Oven Rack Placement

Placement of oven racks is important when baking to make sure products do not get too dark on top (if on the top shelf) or on the bottom (if on the lowest rack). The middle of the oven is usually best. If you need to bake several pans at once, you may want to rotate them from one rack to another partway through to ensure that all products bake evenly.

Be Sensible About Sugar

Although complete avoidance of sugar is not necessary, be careful not to fill up on sugary foods such as pop, candies, cakes and cookies, which may reduce your appetite for more nutritious choices. Eating too many calories contributes to weight gain, and too much carbohydrate in the form of sugar can make it difficult for those with diabetes to manage blood sugar levels. Moreover, there is a proven link between excess sugar and dental cavities. This can be of particular concern in young children. To identify how much sugar you're eating and feeding your family, look at the Nutrition Facts table on packaged food and the ingredient list when you're preparing a recipe.

is chocolate good for me?

Research is a great thing. It revealed that cocoa beans contain flavonoids, phytonutrients that may have health benefits. Dark chocolate contains the most flavonoids. Trouble is, we don't know precisely how much chocolate is needed to reap these benefits, or at what cost in calories and fat. As you chocolate fans wait for these important answers, recognize that most chocolate-containing foods are high in calories, fat and sugar; therefore, portions should be reasonable. Satisfy your chocolate cravings in a healthy way: add a few chocolate chips to a healthy muffin batter or melt a small square of dark chocolate as a dip for fresh berries. Unsweetened cocoa powder does not contain any fat or sugar, so stir a little bit into low-fat milk.

Baked Granola Apples

Eileen Campbell

This is a very speedy dessert that you can prepare and cook while making the rest of a meal.

TIPS

The best apples for baking are Spartan, Empire, Golden Delicious and Cortland, as they will keep their shape while cooking.

When using margarine, choose a non-hydrogenated version to limit consumption of trans fats.

Make this dessert on a night when the oven is already on for another recipe.

VARIATIONS

These also bake quickly in the microwave. Place on a microwave-safe plate and cover with microwave-safe plastic wrap. Cook on High for 2 to 3 minutes or until apples are tender.

Pears can be prepared the same way.

- *Preparation time: 2 minutes / Cooking time: 30 minutes*
- *Preheat oven to 350°F (180°C)*
- *9-inch (23 cm) glass pie plate, ungreased*

4	apples	4
¾ cup	low-fat granola	175 mL
2 tsp	margarine	10 mL
½ cup	low-fat plain yogurt	125 mL
1 tbsp	pure maple syrup	15 mL

1. Core apples, creating a large hollow. Firmly pack with granola and dot with margarine. Place on pie plate.
2. Bake, uncovered, in preheated oven for 30 minutes or until apples are tender.
3. Meanwhile, in a small bowl, combine yogurt and maple syrup; set aside.
4. Place each apple in a dessert bowl and garnish with maple-flavored yogurt.

 **✓ KID APPROVED**

Diabetes Food Choice Values Per Serving	
2	Carbohydrates
1	Fat

NUTRIENTS Per Serving		
Calories: 192	Carbohydrate: 36.9 g	Calcium: 88 mg
Fat: 4.1 g	Fiber: 3.6 g	Iron: 0.8 mg
Sodium: 82 mg	Protein: 3.8 g	
A source of: Dietary fiber		

Balsamic Strawberry Sauce

MAKES 8 SERVINGS

Eileen Campbell

This is the easiest dessert sauce ever! It works well with ripe berries but also offers a tasty solution for unripe berries that are lacking in color and taste. Delicious! You'll want to lick up every last drop.

Fruit is always a great choice for dessert. Serve this sauce hot over your favorite frozen yogurt or cold over yogurt.

• Preparation time: 5 minutes / Cooking time: 4 minutes

4 cups	sliced hulled strawberries	1 L
3 tbsp	granulated sugar	45 mL
¼ cup	balsamic vinegar	50 mL

1. In a medium saucepan, over medium heat, cook strawberries and sugar for 2 minutes or until sugar melts and starts to form a sauce. Add balsamic vinegar; cook for 2 minutes. Remove from heat.

2. Serve warm, or cover and refrigerate to serve cold.

 **KID APPROVED**

Grilled Fruit

One of the simplest desserts for barbecue night is grilled fruit. Once the main meal has been cooked, clean the grill to remove any residue. Cut fruit into long pieces or chunks and skewer. Grill for a few minutes on each side, just until heated through. Serve drizzled with honey or your favorite dessert sauce over frozen yogurt. Crowd pleasers are pineapple, mango, watermelon, apple and pear.

VARIATION

This well-known Italian sauce is traditionally served with a dash of freshly ground black pepper on top. It can also be prepared without cooking. An hour before serving, place sliced berries in a bowl and add sugar. Just before serving, add the balsamic vinegar.

NUTRIENTS Per Serving		
Calories: 53	Carbohydrate: 13.1 g	Calcium: 13 mg
Fat: 0.2 g	Fiber: 1.9 g	Iron: 0.3 mg
Sodium: 1 mg	Protein: 0.6 g	
Very high in: Vitamin C and riboflavin		

Diabetes Food Choice Values Per Serving	
1	Carbohydrate

Pears in Tosca Sauce

Eileen Campbell

You can't get simpler than this quick dessert made with canned pear halves. It tastes rich and decadent. Enjoy it on its own or with a scoop of fruit sorbet or frozen yogurt.

TIP

This is a pretty dessert to serve directly from the dish, so use a glass or ceramic baking dish rather than a metal pan.

VARIATION

Substitute a combination of canned peaches and fresh or frozen raspberries for the pears. Serve with mango sorbet.

- *Preparation time: 10 minutes / Cooking time: 20 minutes*
- *Preheat oven to 350°F (180°C)*
- *8-inch (2 L) square glass baking dish, ungreased*

½ cup	sliced almonds	125 mL
⅓ cup	packed brown sugar	75 mL
⅓ cup	milk	75 mL
2 tbsp	unsalted butter	25 mL
1 tbsp	all-purpose flour	15 mL
1 tsp	vanilla	5 mL
1	can (28 oz/796 mL) pear halves, drained	1

1. In a small saucepan, over medium-high heat, combine almonds, brown sugar, milk, butter, flour and vanilla. Bring to a boil and cook until sauce thickens, about 5 minutes.

2. Place pears in baking dish and pour sauce over top.

3. Bake in preheated oven until browned on top, about 15 minutes.

✓ **KID APPROVED**

Diabetes Food Choice Values Per Serving

1½ Carbohydrates
1½ Fats

NUTRIENTS Per Serving		
Calories: 177	Carbohydrate: 25.3 g	Calcium: 52 mg
Fat: 8.2 g	Fiber: 2.1 g	Iron: 0.8 mg
Sodium: 16 mg	Protein: 2.6 g	
A source of: Dietary fiber		

Lemon Blueberry Panna Cotta

MAKES 8 SERVINGS

Eileen Campbell

- *Preparation time: 5 minutes / Standing time: 10 minutes / Cooking time: 5 minutes / Chilling time: 4 hours*
- *Eight ¾-cup (175 mL) custard cups or ramekins, sprayed with vegetable cooking spray*

1 cup	milk	250 mL
1 ½ tbsp	unflavored gelatin	22 mL
¾ cup	granulated sugar	175 mL
3 cups	evaporated milk	750 mL
1 tsp	grated lemon zest	5 mL
2 cups	fresh blueberries, divided	500 mL

This traditional Italian dessert means "cooked cream," and, indeed, the original is made with whipping cream. This version has the same silky texture but is a lighter end to a meal. It is a great make-ahead dessert, as it can be stored in the refrigerator for several days.

1. Pour milk into a small saucepan and sprinkle with gelatin; let stand for 10 minutes. Cook over medium-low heat, stirring constantly with a whisk, until gelatin dissolves, about 2 minutes. Increase heat to medium and add sugar. Continue whisking until sugar dissolves, about 2 minutes. Remove from heat. Stir in evaporated milk and lemon zest, stirring well to combine.

2. Divide mixture evenly among prepared custard cups and add 2 tbsp (25 mL) blueberries to each cup. Cover and refrigerate for at least 4 hours or overnight.

3. To serve, slide a knife around the edge of each cup to loosen the panna cotta. Invert onto a dessert plate and spoon 2 tbsp (25 mL) blueberries onto the side of each plate.

VARIATION

Vary the berries and the flavoring for a different taste: raspberries with grated orange zest; sliced strawberries with a splash of vanilla; diced mango with grated ginger. Ask your family to choose their favorites.

✓ KID APPROVED

NUTRIENTS Per Serving		
Calories: 219	Carbohydrate: 35.9 g	Calcium: 299 mg
Fat: 4.8 g	Fiber: 1.0 g	Iron: 0.4 mg
Sodium: 120 mg	Protein: 9.4 g	

Very high in: Calcium • **High in:** Riboflavin

Diabetes Food Choice Values Per Serving	
2	Carbohydrates
½	Fat

Dessert Nachos

Eileen Campbell

For a quick and festive dessert that children love, make a platter of these cinnamon-sugar tortilla chips with fruit salsa and low-fat yogurt for dipping. It won't last very long! A great way to enjoy fruit, yogurt and whole grains.

TIP

Pick fruits of your choice to make the 4 cups (1 L) salsa, or ask your children what they would like. Fresh or canned pineapple, fresh or frozen mango, fresh strawberries, kiwi, cantaloupe and watermelon all work well. Cut your chosen fruits into small dice and combine in a bowl.

• **Preparation time: 20 minutes / Cooking time: 4 to 5 minutes per batch**

• *Preheat oven to 450°F (230°C)*
• *Baking sheets, lightly greased*

½ cup	granulated sugar	125 mL
3 tbsp	ground cinnamon	45 mL
4	10-inch (25 cm) whole wheat flour tortillas	4
4 cups	fresh fruit salsa (see tip, at left)	1 L
2 cups	low-fat fruit-flavored yogurt	500 mL

1. On a large flat plate, mix sugar and cinnamon. Dip each tortilla in water. Shake off the excess and dip one side into the sugar and cinnamon mixture. Stack tortillas on top of each other as they are dipped. When completed, cut the stack into 8 triangular wedges.

2. Spread tortilla wedges in a single layer on prepared baking sheets, without overlapping, and bake in batches in preheated oven for 4 to 5 minutes per tray or until golden and crisp.

3. Place on a large platter with a bowl of fruit salsa and another of yogurt.

✓ **KID APPROVED**

Diabetes Food Choice Values Per Serving	
3	Carbohydrates

NUTRIENTS Per Serving		
Calories: 213	Carbohydrate: 50.8 g	Calcium: 126 mg
Fat: 1.6 g	Fiber: 4.3 g	Iron: 1.8 mg
Sodium: 173 mg	Protein: 5.5 g	

Very high in: Vitamin C • **High in:** Dietary fiber and magnesium

Fruit Gazpacho

Eileen Campbell

• Preparation time: 15 minutes / Chilling time: 1 hour

3 cups	finely diced fruit	750 mL
6 cups	tropical fruit juice	1.5 L
6	small scoops fruit sorbet (mango, raspberry or orange)	6
6	fresh mint sprigs (optional)	6

1. In a large bowl, combine diced fruit and fruit juice. Cover and refrigerate for at least 1 hour to allow flavor to develop.
2. Divide fruit gazpacho among 6 shallow bowls. Garnish each serving with a scoop of sorbet and a sprig of mint, if desired.

 **KID APPROVED**

This refreshing summer dessert is easy to make and has a stunning presentation. Have your family choose their favorite fruit, juice and sorbet every time you make it. Fruit is the ultimate healthy dessert, and this one is a crowd pleaser.

TIP

Pick fresh fruits of your family's choice to dice. Mango, pineapple, strawberries, whole blueberries, watermelon and kiwi all work well. Do not choose fruits that brown easily, such as apples, pears or bananas.

NUTRIENTS Per Serving		
Calories: 186	Carbohydrate: 44.9 g	Calcium: 33 mg
Fat: 0.2 g	Fiber: 1.6 g	Iron: 0.3 mg
Sodium: 12 mg	Protein: 0.6 g	
Very high in: Vitamin C • **High in:** Folate		

Diabetes Food Choice Values Per Serving

3	Carbohydrates

Patricia Chuey, Dietitian, BC

Serve this sweet and tart treat warm from the oven with a scoop of ice cream or frozen vanilla yogurt. Crisps are a great way to enjoy fruit and whole grains. Because this dessert is fairly high in fat, serve it only on special occasions.

TIP
Leftovers can be stored in an airtight container in the fridge for up to 3 days or in the freezer for up to 3 months.

VARIATION
When available, use fresh or frozen cranberries instead of dried.

Apple, Pear and Cranberry Crisp

- *Preparation time: 15 minutes / Cooking time: 30 to 45 minutes*
- *Preheat oven to 400°F (200°C)*
- *8-inch (2 L) square baking dish, lightly greased*

Topping

¾ cup	all-purpose flour	175 mL
¾ cup	packed brown sugar	175 mL
½ cup	old-fashioned rolled oats	125 mL
½ cup	cold butter	125 mL
3	apples, cored, peeled and sliced	3
2	pears, cored, peeled and sliced	2
¼ cup	dried cranberries	50 mL
1 tbsp	all-purpose flour	15 mL
1 tbsp	packed brown sugar	15 mL

1. *Prepare the topping:* In a medium bowl, combine flour, brown sugar and oats. Cut in butter until mixture resembles coarse meal.

2. Place apples, pears and cranberries in prepared baking dish. Sprinkle with flour and sugar and toss to coat. Top with oat mixture.

3. Bake in preheated oven for 30 to 45 minutes or until topping is golden and fruit is tender. Let cool for 5 minutes before serving.

❄ FREEZER FRIENDLY
✓ KID APPROVED

Diabetes Food Choice Values Per Serving	
3	Carbohydrates
2½	Fats

NUTRIENTS Per Serving		
Calories: 310	Carbohydrate: 50.1 g	Calcium: 33 mg
Fat: 12.2 g	Fiber: 2.8 g	Iron: 1.4 mg
Sodium: 92 mg	Protein: 2.6 g	
A source of: Dietary fiber		

Rhubarb Bread Pudding

MAKES 6 SERVINGS

Helen Haresign,
Dietitian, ON

- *Preparation time: 20 minutes / Standing time: 10 minutes / Cooking time: 40 to 45 minutes*
- *Preheat oven to 350°F (180°C)*
- *8-inch (2 L) square baking dish*

2 cups	chopped fresh or frozen rhubarb, thawed	500 mL
3 cups	torn stale white and whole wheat bread	750 mL
1	can (14 oz/385 mL) evaporated milk	1
2	eggs	2
¼ cup	granulated sugar	50 mL
1 tsp	vanilla	5 mL
1 tsp	ground cinnamon	5 mL
	Grated zest of 1 orange	

An interesting twist to an old favorite. Cold leftovers are good too!

TIP
Leftovers can be stored in an airtight container in the fridge for up to 3 days or in the freezer for up to 3 months.

VARIATION
Try making this pudding with another fruit, such as frozen berries or peaches.

1. Place rhubarb in prepared baking dish and cover with bread pieces.
2. In a medium bowl, beat evaporated milk, eggs, sugar, vanilla, cinnamon and orange zest. Pour over bread. Let stand for 10 minutes.
3. Bake in preheated oven for 40 to 45 minutes or until a tester inserted in the center comes out clean. Serve warm.

❄️ FREEZER FRIENDLY

NUTRIENTS Per Serving		
Calories: 175	Carbohydrate: 27.0 g	Calcium: 297 mg
Fat: 3.8 g	Fiber: 1.9 g	Iron: 1.1 mg
Sodium: 184 mg	Protein: 9.0 g	

Very high in: Calcium • **High in:** Riboflavin

Diabetes Food Choice Values Per Serving	
1½	Carbohydrates
½	Meat & Alternatives

Eileen Campbell

Rice pudding is a comfort-food favorite that never seems to go out of style. This version uses brown rice and is enhanced with spices, dried fruits and nuts.

TIPS

For 1 cup (250 mL) cooked brown rice, cook ⅓ cup (75 mL) rice with ⅔ cup (150 mL) water.

Freshly grated nutmeg has more aroma and flavor than ground. If you only have ground, it is fine to use it, but try grinding fresh sometime — you will really taste and smell the difference.

Indian-Style Rice Pudding

• **Preparation time: 10 minutes / Cooking time: 1 hour**
• *Preheat oven to 350°F (180°C)*
• *Glass baking dish with cover*
• *Baking sheet*

1 cup	cooked brown rice	250 mL
1	can (14 oz/398 mL) light coconut milk	1
3 cups	milk	750 mL
½ cup	raisins	125 mL
¼ cup	finely chopped almonds	50 mL
¼ cup	unsweetened shredded coconut	50 mL
¼ cup	granulated sugar	50 mL
½ tsp	ground cardamom	2 mL
1	cinnamon stick	1
½ tsp	grated nutmeg (see tip, at left)	2 mL

1. Place rice in baking dish. Add coconut milk, milk, raisins, almonds, coconut, sugar, cardamom and cinnamon stick. Cover, place dish on baking sheet and bake in preheated oven for 1 hour or until sauce has thickened.

2. Serve warm or chilled, sprinkled with nutmeg.

✓ **KID APPROVED**

Diabetes Food Choice Values Per Serving	
2	Carbohydrates
1½	Fats

NUTRIENTS Per Serving		
Calories: 208	Carbohydrate: 28.2 g	Calcium: 124 mg
Fat: 9.1 g	Fiber: 1.6 g	Iron: 0.6 mg
Sodium: 64 mg	Protein: 5.2 g	

Carrot Cake

**MAKES
20 SERVINGS**

Shefali Raja, Dietitian,
BC

- *Preparation time: 15 minutes / Cooking time: 30 to 35 minutes*
- *Preheat oven to 350°F (180°C)*
- *13- by 9-inch (3 L) baking pan, lightly greased*

¾ cup	all-purpose flour	175 mL
½ cup	whole wheat flour	125 mL
1¼ tsp	baking powder	6 mL
1¼ tsp	baking soda	6 mL
1 tsp	ground cinnamon	5 mL
½ tsp	salt	2 mL
3	eggs	3
½ cup	vegetable oil	125 mL
1 cup	lightly packed brown sugar	250 mL
2 tsp	vanilla	10 mL
2 cups	grated carrots	500 mL

*Kids love to snack
on this simple cake
without icing, and
it's a great way to
add more vegetables
to their menu. It
would make a healthy
addition to your
children's lunchboxes.*

VARIATION
Shefali sometimes
combines grated apples
with the carrots or only
uses apples.

1. In a small bowl, combine all-purpose flour, whole wheat flour, baking powder, baking soda, cinnamon and salt.

2. In a large bowl, beat eggs, oil, brown sugar and vanilla until well combined. Fold in dry ingredients. Stir in carrots. Pour into prepared pan.

3. Bake in preheated oven for 30 to 35 minutes or until a tester inserted in the center comes out clean. Let cool completely in pan on a wire rack. Cut cake into slices and lift servings out with a flat lifter.

 **FREEZER FRIENDLY**
✓ **KID APPROVED**

SERVING IDEA: Dust with icing sugar for a pretty presentation.

NUTRIENTS Per Serving		
Calories: 125	Carbohydrate: 15.8 g	Calcium: 26 mg
Fat: 6.3 g	Fiber: 0.8 g	Iron: 0.7 mg
Sodium: 174 mg	Protein: 1.9 g	
High in: Vitamin A		

Diabetes Food Choice Values Per Serving	
1	Carbohydrate
1	Fat

**MAKES
12 SERVINGS**

Janie Zwicker-Stolf, ON

*Serve this moist cake
for a morning or
afternoon coffee break.*

TIP
When using margarine,
choose a non-hydrogenated
version to limit
consumption of trans fats.

Cinnamon Streusel Coffee Cake

- **Preparation time: 20 minutes / Cooking time: 40 to 50 minutes**
- *Preheat oven to 350°F (180°C)*
- *10-inch (3 L) Bundt or 10-inch (4 L) tube pan, lightly greased and floured*

Streusel

½ cup	lightly packed brown sugar	125 mL
½ cup	finely chopped pecans (optional)	125 mL
1 tbsp	ground cinnamon	15 mL

Cake

1 cup	all-purpose flour	250 mL
1 cup	whole wheat flour	250 mL
1 tsp	baking powder	5 mL
¼ tsp	salt	1 mL
1 cup	low-fat or fat-free plain yogurt	250 mL
1 tsp	baking soda	5 mL
¾ cup	granulated sugar	175 mL
¾ cup	unsweetened applesauce	175 mL
¼ cup	margarine	50 mL
2	eggs	2
1 tsp	vanilla	5 mL

1. *Prepare the streusel:* In a small bowl, combine brown sugar, pecans (if using) and cinnamon. Set aside.
2. *Prepare the cake:* In a medium bowl, combine all-purpose flour, whole wheat flour, baking powder and salt. Set aside.
3. In another bowl, combine yogurt and baking soda. (Be prepared, yogurt will foam up!)
4. In a large bowl, using an electric mixer, cream sugar, applesauce and margarine until well mixed (it may look curdled). Beat in eggs, one at a time, then stir in vanilla. Stir in flour mixture alternately with yogurt, making 3 additions of flour and 2 of yogurt mixture.

5. Spoon half of the batter into prepared Bundt pan. Sprinkle with three-quarters of the streusel. Cover with remaining batter and sprinkle with remaining streusel. With the back of a small spoon, pat streusel lightly into batter (to prevent streusel from falling off when cake is inverted and removed from pan).

6. Bake in preheated oven for 40 to 50 minutes or until a tester inserted in the center comes out clean. Let cool on a wire rack for 10 minutes before removing from pan. Turn out onto rack to cool completely.

 FREEZER FRIENDLY

Sugars

- **Granulated sugar** (white sugar) is our table sugar and is the one most commonly used in recipes. White sugars will keep indefinitely if kept in an airtight container in a cool, dry place.
- **Superfine sugar** has a lighter texture than granulated and dissolves more quickly, making it an excellent choice for meringues, cakes and mousses and for sweetening beverages. It's also great for sprinkling. When used in cakes, the result is a fine crumb and a lighter texture. It may be labeled "fruit sugar" or "instant dissolving sugar."
- **Confectioner's (icing) sugar** contains 3% cornstarch and is excellent for making icing and candy and for sweetening whipped cream. Dust onto desserts for a restaurant-style presentation.
- **Brown sugar** consists of sugar crystals coated in a molasses syrup with natural flavor and color. When recipes call for brown sugar, use the sticky, damp kind, not raw brown sugar crystals. The lighter brown is used for baking, condiments and glazes; the darker for gingerbread, mincemeat, baked beans and other full-flavored foods. In some recipes, you can substitute 1 cup (250 mL) lightly packed brown sugar for 1 cup (250 mL) granulated sugar (but don't do this when making white cakes). Brown sugar hardens during storage when the moisture evaporates, so keep it in an airtight container in a cool, dry place. If it does dry out, add a slice of apple or fresh bread to the container.
- **Demerara sugar** is crystallized golden-brown sugar, which dissolves slowly. It is used in baking and to sweeten hot beverages.

NUTRIENTS Per Serving		
Calories: 217	Carbohydrate: 39.0 g	Calcium: 73.0 mg
Fat: 5.3 g	Fiber: 2.0 g	Iron: 1.4 mg
Sodium: 258 mg	Protein: 4.6 g	
A source of: Dietary fiber		

Diabetes Food Choice Values Per Serving	
2½	Carbohydrates
1	Fat

**MAKES
18 SERVINGS**

Beth Gould, Dietitian,
ON

*This coffee cake has
been made lower in fat
by using less butter, a
combination of whole
eggs and egg whites
and yogurt or light sour
cream. The resulting
taste is rich and delicious.
This is Beth's children's
favorite cake! It is a
little time-consuming
to make but would
be great for a special
dinner, served with
fresh berries on the side.*

Chocolate Chunk Coffee Cake

• **Preparation time: 30 minutes / Cooking time: 60 to 65 minutes**
• *Preheat oven to 350°F (180°C)*
• *10-inch (3 L) Bundt or 10-inch (4 L) tube pan, lightly greased and floured*

2 cups	all-purpose flour	500 mL
1 cup	whole wheat flour	250 mL
1½ tsp	baking powder	7 mL
¼ tsp	salt	1 mL
2 cups	plain yogurt or light sour cream	500 mL
1 tsp	baking soda	5 mL
2 oz	semisweet chocolate	60 g
2 oz	white chocolate	60 g
1¼ cups	granulated sugar	300 mL
½ cup	unsalted butter, at room temperature	125 mL
2	egg whites	2
2	whole eggs	2
2 tsp	vanilla	10 mL
⅓ cup	unsweetened cocoa powder	75 mL
¼ cup	water	50 mL

1. In a large bowl, using a fork, combine all-purpose flour, whole wheat flour, baking powder and salt until evenly blended. Set aside.

2. In a medium bowl, combine yogurt and baking soda. (Be prepared, yogurt will foam up!) Set aside.

3. Coarsely chop semisweet chocolate until pieces are about the size of chocolate chips. Repeat with white chocolate, keeping the two separate. Set aside.

4. In a large bowl, using an electric mixer, cream sugar and butter. Add egg whites and eggs, one at a time, beating well after each addition. Stir in vanilla. Stir in flour mixture alternately with yogurt mixture, making 3 additions of flour and 2 of yogurt.

5. To make the chocolate batter, sift cocoa powder into a medium bowl. Stir in water until a smooth paste forms. Stir in one-third of the white batter.

6. Add the white chocolate pieces to the chocolate batter and the semisweet chocolate pieces to the white batter.

7. Pour white batter into prepared Bundt pan, then pour chocolate batter on top. Using a spatula, swirl the two mixtures together to create a ribbon effect.

8. Bake in the lower third of preheated oven for 60 to 65 minutes or until a tester inserted in the center comes out clean. Let cool on a wire rack for 10 minutes before removing from pan. Turn out onto rack to cool completely.

FREEZER FRIENDLY

✓ **KID APPROVED**

Whipped Cream and Yogurt Topping
Barbara Selley, Dietitian, ON

This is Barbara's multipurpose dessert topping:

Beat ½ cup (125 mL) whipping (35%) cream until thick. Add 1 tbsp (15 mL) granulated sugar and ½ tsp (2 mL) vanilla; beat until stiff peaks form. Gently fold in ½ cup (125 mL) low-fat plain yogurt until thoroughly combined. Makes 1½ cups (375 mL).

Contains 88 calories and 7.4 g fat per ¼ cup (50 mL) serving; the same amount of whipped cream alone contains 103 calories and 11.0 g fat.

NUTRIENTS Per Serving		
Calories: 239	Carbohydrate: 36.2 g	Calcium: 73 mg
Fat: 8.7 g	Fiber: 1.9 g	Iron: 1.3 mg
Sodium: 161 mg	Protein: 5.4 g	
High in: Folate		

Diabetes Food Choice Values Per Serving	
2	Carbohydrates
2	Fats

Eileen Campbell

This tasty chocolate cake has Mexican flair. Cocoa powder adds a satisfying chocolate flavor. For a special treat, top with whipped cream spiked with cinnamon, or try the Whipped Cream and Yogurt Topping on page 309.

TIPS

If you don't have self-rising flour, substitute 1 cup (250 mL) all-purpose flour and add 1 1/2 tsp (7 mL) baking powder and 1/2 tsp (2 mL) salt.

If you prefer, use commercial liquid egg whites. You'll need about 3/4 cup (175 mL) for this recipe.

Chocolate Zucchini Cake

- *Preparation time: 10 minutes / Cooking time: 30 to 40 minutes*
- *Preheat oven to 350°F (180°C)*
- *8-inch (2 L) square baking pan, lightly greased*

1 cup	self-rising flour	250 mL
1/3 cup	unsweetened cocoa powder	75 mL
1 tsp	baking soda	5 mL
1 tsp	ground cinnamon	5 mL
6	egg whites	6
1 1/3 cups	firmly packed brown sugar	325 mL
1 cup	buttermilk	250 mL
2 tsp	vanilla	10 mL
1/4 tsp	almond extract	1 mL
2 cups	shredded zucchini	500 mL
	Confectioner's (icing) sugar (optional)	

1. In a small bowl, sift flour, cocoa powder, baking soda and cinnamon.

2. In a large bowl, beat egg whites, brown sugar, buttermilk, vanilla and almond extract until well blended. Fold in flour mixture until evenly moistened. Stir in zucchini. Pour batter into prepared pan.

3. Bake in preheated oven for 30 to 40 minutes or until center of cake springs back when lightly pressed and a tester inserted in the center comes out clean. Let cool on a wire rack for 10 minutes before removing from pan. Turn out onto rack to cool completely. Just before serving, dust with confectioner's sugar, if desired.

❄ FREEZER FRIENDLY
✓ KID APPROVED

Diabetes Food Choice Values Per Serving	
2	Carbohydrates

NUTRIENTS Per Serving		
Calories: 154	Carbohydrate: 34.8 g	Calcium: 88 mg
Fat: 0.6 g	Fiber: 1.5 g	Iron: 1.5 mg
Sodium: 295 mg	Protein: 3.9 g	

Chocolate Fondue

MAKES 6 SERVINGS

Dairy Farmers of
Canada

- **Preparation time: 3 minutes / Cooking time: 5 minutes**
- *Fondue pot*

8 oz	semisweet chocolate, chopped	250 g
½ cup	evaporated milk or whipping (35%) cream	125 mL
	A selection of chopped fruits for dipping (bananas, strawberries, apples, pears, etc.)	

1. In fondue pot, over low heat, heat chocolate and evaporated milk, stirring with a wooden spatula, until chocolate has melted, about 5 minutes. Place fondue pot over tabletop burner.
2. Arrange fruit in a serving dish and serve with fondue.

This simple dessert will encourage everyone in the family to eat more fruit (and the chocolate tastes great too)!

TIPS

Allow ½ cup (125 mL) fruit and 4 tbsp (60 mL) chocolate sauce per serving — the nutrient analysis is based on this!

This recipe is a little higher in fat than some of our other desserts, so save it for a special occasion.

VARIATION

For a milder chocolate flavor, replace the semisweet with milk chocolate. Children tend to prefer milk chocolate.

NUTRIENTS Per Serving		
Calories: 258	Carbohydrate: 38.3 g	Calcium: 77 mg
Fat: 10.5 g	Fiber: 4.2 g	Iron: 1.3 mg
Sodium: 25 mg	Protein: 3.7 g	

Very high in: Riboflavin • **High in:** Dietary fiber and magnesium

Diabetes Food Choice Values Per Serving	
2	Carbohydrates
2	Fats

Eileen Campbell

*These crêpes are easy
to make and very
versatile, as they can be
filled with your choice
of fruit and/or frozen
yogurt. The taste panel's
favorite filling was
vanilla frozen yogurt
and sliced strawberries.
Delicious!*

TIP
You can make the crêpes
the day before; wrap
them in plastic wrap and
refrigerate until ready to
use.

Chocolate Crêpes

• **Preparation time: 10 minutes / Cooking time: 15 minutes**
• *Sixteen 6-inch (15 cm) squares of parchment or waxed paper*

1 1/2 cups	all-purpose flour	375 mL
1/2 cup	unsweetened cocoa powder	125 mL
6 tbsp	confectioner's (icing) sugar	90 mL
Pinch	salt	Pinch
2	eggs	2
2 cups	milk	500 mL
2 tbsp	vegetable oil	25 mL
1/2 tsp	vanilla	2 mL

1. In a large bowl, sift flour, cocoa powder, sugar and salt.

2. In a medium bowl, whisk eggs, milk, oil and vanilla until
   blended. Add a little at a time to the flour mixture, whisking
   to dissolve lumps, until smooth. Cover and refrigerate for
   1 hour.

3. Heat a small skillet over medium heat and spray lightly
   with vegetable cooking spray. When skillet is hot, remove
   from heat and pour in 1/4 cup (50 mL) of the batter. Swirl
   skillet to spread batter evenly over the bottom. Return to
   heat and cook for 30 to 40 seconds, until bottom is light
   golden. Turn crêpe over and cook for about 15 seconds,
   until bottom is light golden. Remove from skillet. Repeat
   until all batter is used, stacking crêpes between squares
   of parchment or waxed paper to prevent them from
   sticking together.

❄ **FREEZER FRIENDLY**
✓ **KID APPROVED**

Diabetes Food Choice Values Per Serving	
1	Carbohydrate
1	Fat

NUTRIENTS Per Serving		
Calories: 107	Carbohydrate: 14.7 g	Calcium: 44 mg
Fat: 4.3 g	Fiber: 1.2 g	Iron: 1.0 mg
Sodium: 21 mg	Protein: 3.5 g	

Ginger Cookies

MAKES 30 COOKIES (1 PER SERVING)

Phyllis Levesque,
Dietitian, ON

A crisp, spicy cookie for those who like the flavor of gingerbread.

- *Preparation time: 20 to 30 minutes / Cooking time: 10 to 12 minutes*
- *Preheat oven to 350°F (180°C)*
- *Baking sheets, lightly greased or lined with parchment paper*

1¾ cups	all-purpose flour	425 mL
1½ tsp	baking powder	7 mL
1 tsp	ground ginger	5 mL
1 tsp	ground cinnamon	5 mL
½ tsp	baking soda	2 mL
½ tsp	salt	2 mL
¼ tsp	ground cloves	1 mL
1	egg	1
½ cup	granulated sugar	125 mL
½ cup	vegetable oil	125 mL
½ cup	fancy molasses	125 mL

1. In a small bowl, combine flour, baking powder, ginger, cinnamon, baking soda, salt and cloves.

2. In a medium bowl, whisk egg, sugar, oil and molasses until blended. Fold in flour mixture until a moist dough forms.

3. Shape dough into balls, using about 1 tbsp (15 mL) dough per cookie, and place 2 inches (5 cm) apart on prepared baking sheets.

4. Bake in preheated oven for 10 to 12 minutes or until lightly browned and crisp. Let cool on baking sheets on a wire rack for 5 minutes, then remove to rack to cool completely.

NUTRIENTS Per Serving		
Calories: 91	Carbohydrate: 13.3 g	Calcium: 21 mg
Fat: 3.9 g	Fiber: 0.3 g	Iron: 0.7 mg
Sodium: 79 mg	Protein: 1.0 g	

Diabetes Food Choice Values Per Serving

1	Carbohydrate
1	Fat

General Mills

Your family and friends will never know that bran cereal is one of the ingredients in these delicious crunchy cookies.

TIP

When using margarine, choose a non-hydrogenated version to limit consumption of trans fats.

Best-Ever Chocolate Cookies

> **• Preparation time: 15 minutes / Cooking time: 7 to 9 minutes**
> **• Preheat oven to 350°F (180°C)**
> **• Baking sheets, ungreased**

1 cup	all-purpose flour	250 mL
1/2 cup	unsweetened cocoa powder	125 mL
1 tsp	baking soda	5 mL
1/4 tsp	salt	1 mL
2	eggs	2
1 cup	margarine or butter, softened	250 mL
3/4 cup	packed brown sugar	175 mL
1 1/2 cups	quick-cooking rolled oats	375 mL
1 cup	bran cereal (not flakes)	250 mL
3/4 cup	white chocolate chips	175 mL

1. In a small bowl, sift flour, cocoa powder, baking soda and salt.
2. In a large bowl, beat eggs, margarine and brown sugar. Fold in flour mixture. Stir in oats, bran cereal and chocolate chips.
3. Drop dough by heaping tablespoonfuls (15 mL), about 2 inches (5 cm) apart, onto baking sheets.
4. Bake in preheated oven for 7 to 9 minutes or until just crisp. Let cool on baking sheets on a wire rack for 5 minutes, then remove to rack to cool completely.

✓ KID APPROVED

Diabetes Food Choice Values Per Serving	
1	Carbohydrate
1	Fat

NUTRIENTS Per Serving		
Calories: 103	Carbohydrate: 11.8 g	Calcium: 20 mg
Fat: 6.0 g	Fiber: 1.3 g	Iron: 0.7 mg
Sodium: 116 mg	Protein: 1.6 g	

Fruity Oatmeal Cookies

- *Preparation time: 10 minutes / Cooking time: 10 minutes*
- *Preheat oven to 350°F (180°C)*
- *Baking sheets, lightly greased or lined with parchment paper*

2 cups	old-fashioned rolled oats	500 mL
1¼ cups	whole wheat flour	300 mL
1 cup	semisweet chocolate chips	250 mL
1 cup	dried fruit	250 mL
¾ cup	ground flaxseed	175 mL
1 tsp	baking soda	5 mL
½ tsp	salt	2 mL
2	large bananas, mashed	2
¾ cup	liquid honey	175 mL
½ cup	margarine	125 mL

1. In a large bowl, combine oats, flour, chocolate chips, dried fruit, flaxseed, baking soda and salt.

2. In another large bowl, combine bananas, honey and margarine. Fold in oats mixture.

3. Drop dough by tablespoonfuls (15 mL), about 2 inches (5 cm) apart, onto prepared baking sheets. Flatten with a fork.

4. Bake in preheated oven for about 10 minutes or until lightly browned. Let cool on baking sheets on a wire rack for 5 minutes, then remove to rack to cool completely.

❄ FREEZER FRIENDLY
✔ KID APPROVED

MAKES 36 COOKIES (1 PER SERVING)

Eileen Campbell

These make a tasty, healthy snack any time of the day.

TIPS

When using margarine, choose a non-hydrogenated version to limit consumption of trans fats.

We tested these cookies with different dried fruits (raisins, chopped apricots, cranberries). All versions worked out well. A mixture would also work.

VARIATIONS

Replace the semisweet chocolate chips with white chocolate or butterscotch chips, or leave them out entirely for a fruitier cookie.

Try rice syrup or fancy molasses instead of honey.

NUTRIENTS Per Serving		
Calories: 133	Carbohydrate: 20.8 g	Calcium: 17 mg
Fat: 5.2 g	Fiber: 2.2 g	Iron: 0.8 mg
Sodium: 103 mg	Protein: 2.3 g	
A source of: Dietary fiber		

Diabetes Food Choice Values Per Serving	
1	Carbohydrate
1	Fat

Patricia Chuey, Dietitian,
BC

*These cookies, which
stay nice and soft,
make a great-tasting,
healthy treat for a
packed lunch or
after-school snack.*

Soft Apple Cinnamon Cookies

- **Preparation time: 15 minutes / Cooking time: 8 to 10 minutes**
- *Preheat oven to 400°F (200°C)*
- *Baking sheets, lightly greased or lined with parchment paper*

2 cups	all-purpose flour	500 mL
1 tbsp	ground cinnamon	15 mL
1 tsp	baking powder	5 mL
1/2 tsp	baking soda	2 mL
1/2 tsp	salt	2 mL
3	large apples (unpeeled), grated	3
1 cup	packed brown sugar	250 mL
2/3 cup	butter	150 mL
2	eggs	2
1/2 cup	sour milk or buttermilk	125 mL
2 cups	quick-cooking rolled oats	500 mL

1. In a small bowl, sift together flour, cinnamon, baking powder, baking soda and salt.

2. Sprinkle grated apples with 1/2 cup (125 mL) of the flour mixture.

3. In a large bowl, cream brown sugar and butter. Add eggs, one at a time, beating well after each addition. Add milk, then oats, and blend well. Fold in remaining flour mixture. Stir in apples.

4. Drop dough by tablespoonfuls (15 mL), about 2 inches (5 cm) apart, onto prepared baking sheets.

5. Bake in preheated oven for 8 to 10 minutes or until lightly browned. Let cool on baking sheets on a wire rack for 5 minutes, then remove to rack to cool completely.

❄ FREEZER FRIENDLY
✓ KID APPROVED

Diabetes Food Choice Values Per Serving	
1	Carbohydrate
1/2	Fat

NUTRIENTS Per Serving		
Calories: 85	Carbohydrate: 12.9 g	Calcium: 16 mg
Fat: 3.1 g	Fiber: 0.7 g	Iron: 0.6 mg
Sodium: 67 mg	Protein: 1.5 g	

Peanut Butter Flaxseed Cookies

MAKES 28 COOKIES (1 PER SERVING)

Patricia Chuey,
Dietitian, B.C.

Although these cookies appear rich, they contain wholesome ingredients and beat traditional coffee-shop fare by a long shot! Our taste panel said these were the best peanut butter cookies they had ever tasted.

- *Preparation time: 15 minutes / Cooking time: 8 to 10 minutes*
- *Preheat oven to 350°F (180°C)*
- *Baking sheets, lightly greased or lined with parchment paper*

1¼ cups	all-purpose flour	300 mL
½ cup	ground flaxseed	125 mL
1 tsp	baking soda	5 mL
Pinch	salt	Pinch
½ cup	granulated sugar	125 mL
½ cup	packed brown sugar	125 mL
½ cup	butter, softened	125 mL
1	egg	1
1 tsp	vanilla	5 mL
½ cup	creamy peanut butter	125 mL

1. In a small bowl, combine flour, flaxseed, baking soda and salt.

2. In a large bowl, cream granulated sugar, brown sugar and butter. Beat in egg and vanilla. Beat in peanut butter until smooth. Fold in flour mixture.

3. Shape dough into balls, using about 1 tbsp (15 mL) dough per cookie, and place 2 inches (5 cm) apart on prepared baking sheets. Using a fork, flatten cookies in a crisscross pattern.

4. Bake in preheated oven for 8 to 10 minutes or until lightly browned. Let cool on baking sheets on a wire rack for 5 minutes, then remove to rack to cool completely.

❄️ **FREEZER FRIENDLY**

✓ **KID APPROVED**

NUTRIENTS Per Serving		
Calories: 118	Carbohydrate: 13.2 g	Calcium: 15 mg
Fat: 6.7 g	Fiber: 1.0 g	Iron: 0.5 mg
Sodium: 94 mg	Protein: 2.4 g	

Diabetes Food Choice Values Per Serving	
1	Carbohydrate
1½	Fats

Kimberly Barber, AB

These cookies are great for a healthy snack, as they are made with whole grains that provide fiber and they are lower in sugar than typical cookies. During the taste tests, one person ate so many that other people did not get a chance to try them!

TIP
When using margarine, choose a non-hydrogenated version to limit consumption of trans fats.

Charlie and Emma's Favorite Carrot Cookies

• **Preparation time: 10 minutes / Cooking time: 10 to 15 minutes**

• *Preheat oven to 350°F (180°C)*
• *Baking sheets, lightly greased*

1 cup	whole wheat flour	250 mL
¾ cup	quick-cooking rolled oats	175 mL
½ cup	ground flaxseed	125 mL
1 tsp	ground cinnamon	5 mL
½ tsp	baking soda	2 mL
1	egg	1
¾ cup	lightly packed brown sugar	175 mL
½ cup	margarine	125 mL
1 tsp	vanilla	5 mL
1 cup	grated carrots	250 mL

1. In a medium bowl, combine flour, oats, flaxseed, cinnamon and baking soda.

2. In a large bowl, using an electric mixer, beat egg, brown sugar, margarine and vanilla until smooth. Fold in flour mixture. Stir in carrots.

3. Drop dough by heaping tablespoonfuls (15 mL), about 2 inches (5 cm) apart, onto prepared baking sheets.

4. Bake in preheated oven for 10 to 15 minutes or until lightly browned. Let cool on baking sheet on a wire rack for 5 minutes.

❄ FREEZER FRIENDLY
✓ KID APPROVED

Diabetes Food Choice Values Per Serving	
1	Carbohydrate
1	Fat

NUTRIENTS Per Serving		
Calories: 105	Carbohydrate: 13.5 g	Calcium: 21 mg
Fat: 5.3 g	Fiber: 1.7 g	Iron: 0.6 mg
Sodium: 86 mg	Protein: 1.9 g	

Fiber-Power Biscotti

MAKES 30 BISCOTTI (1 PER SERVING)

General Mills

- *Preparation time: 15 minutes / Cooking time: 60 to 65 minutes*
- *Preheat oven to 350°F (180°C)*
- *Baking sheets, lightly greased or lined with parchment paper*

2 cups	bran cereal, crushed	500 mL
1 ½ cups	all-purpose flour	375 mL
1 cup	granulated sugar	250 mL
¾ cup	quick-cooking rolled oats	175 mL
½ cup	sliced almonds	125 mL
½ cup	finely chopped dried apricots	125 mL
2 tsp	baking powder	10 mL
3	eggs, lightly beaten	3
1 tbsp	vegetable oil	15 mL
2 tsp	almond extract	10 mL
1 tsp	vanilla	5 mL

Biscotti are twice-baked cookies that are usually very crunchy and work well dipped in your favorite coffee beverage. These ones taste even better than the coffee-shop version, and they're full of fiber and other good-for-you ingredients. They were a huge hit with our tasting panel.

1. In a large bowl, combine bran cereal, flour, sugar, oats, almonds, apricots and baking powder.

2. In a small bowl, beat eggs, oil, almond extract and vanilla. Stir into bran cereal mixture until well blended (dough will be dry and crumbly).

3. Turn dough out onto a lightly floured surface and knead 10 to 15 times, until dough holds together. Divide dough in half and shape each half into a log about 8 inches (20 cm) long and 3 inches (7.5 cm) wide. Place on prepared baking sheets.

4. Bake in preheated oven for 30 minutes. Remove from oven and reduce oven temperature to 325°F (160°C). Remove logs from baking sheets and let cool on a wire rack for 10 minutes.

5. Using a serrated knife, cut each log into ½-inch (1 cm) thick slices. Return slices, cut side down, to baking sheets.

6. Bake for 15 minutes. Turn biscotti over and bake for 15 to 20 minutes or until light brown and crisp. Let cool on baking sheets on a wire rack for 5 minutes, then remove to rack to cool completely.

NUTRIENTS Per Serving		
Calories: 94	Carbohydrate: 18.0 g	Calcium: 32 mg
Fat: 2.1 g	Fiber: 2.5 g	Iron: 1.1 mg
Sodium: 44 mg	Protein: 2.4 g	
A source of: Dietary fiber		

Diabetes Food Choice Values Per Serving	
1	Carbohydrate
½	Fat

Shefali Raja, Dietitian,
BC

*These biscotti
are a favorite at
Christmastime, when
Shefali and her family
make many, many
cookies and package
them up for friends
and family.*

TIP

When using margarine,
choose a non-hydrogenated
version to limit
consumption of trans fats.

VARIATION

You can replace the orange
zest with 1 ½ tbsp (22 mL)
ground cardamom or
2 tbsp (25 mL) roasted
fennel seeds. To roast
seeds, place on a baking
sheet and bake in
preheated 350°F (180°C)
oven until they become
aromatic but not brown,
about 3 minutes.

Holiday Biscotti

- **Preparation time: 20 minutes / Cooking time: 50 to 55 minutes**
- *Preheat oven to 325°F (160°C)*
- *Baking sheets, lined with parchment paper*

2 ½ cups	all-purpose flour	625 mL
1 cup	slivered almonds or pistachios	250 mL
1 tbsp	grated orange zest	15 mL
1 tsp	baking powder	5 mL
½ tsp	salt	2 mL
2	eggs	2
¾ cup	granulated sugar	175 mL
½ cup	margarine	125 mL
2 tsp	vanilla or almond extract	10 mL

1. In a medium bowl, combine flour, almonds, orange zest, baking powder and salt.
2. In a large bowl, beat eggs, sugar, margarine and vanilla until slightly foamy. Fold in flour mixture.
3. Divide dough in half and shape each half into a log about 14 inches (35 cm) long and 2 inches (5 cm) wide. Place on prepared baking sheets. Smooth top and sides with clean hands.
4. Bake in preheated oven for 30 minutes. Remove from oven and reduce oven temperature to 275°F (140°C). Remove logs from baking sheets and let cool on a wire rack for 10 minutes.
5. Using a serrated knife, cut each log into ½-inch (1 cm) thick slices. Place slices upright on baking sheets.
6. Bake for 20 to 25 minutes or until golden and crisp. Let cool on baking sheets on a wire rack for 5 minutes, then remove to rack to cool completely.

Diabetes Food Choice Values Per Serving	
½	Carbohydrate
1	Fat

NUTRIENTS Per Serving		
Calories: 84	Carbohydrate: 10.5 g	Calcium: 14 mg
Fat: 4.0 g	Fiber: 0.6 g	Iron: 0.5 mg
Sodium: 70 mg	Protein: 1.7 g	

Almond Butter Cereal Squares

MAKES 16 SQUARES (1 PER SERVING)

Eileen Campbell

These squares are delicious! They're great as a breakfast bar or a mid-morning snack.

TIP
Brown rice syrup is available in the natural food section of your supermarket or from health food stores. If you cannot find it, use fancy molasses instead.

VARIATION
Instead of apricots, substitute another dried fruit. Raisins, cranberries, cherries, chopped pitted dates and figs all work well.

• **Preparation time: 15 minutes / Standing time: 30 minutes**
• *9-inch (2.5 L) square baking pan, lightly greased*

½ cup	crunchy almond butter	125 mL
½ cup	brown rice syrup	125 mL
½ cup	liquid honey	125 mL
1 tsp	vanilla	5 mL
1 cup	chopped dried apricots	250 mL
½ cup	sliced almonds	125 mL
¼ cup	sesame seeds	50 mL
¼ cup	ground flaxseed	50 mL
¼ cup	sunflower seeds	50 mL
2½ cups	high-fiber cereal, such as bran flakes	625 mL
1¼ cups	old-fashioned rolled oats	300 mL

1. In a large saucepan, over low heat, cook almond butter, rice syrup, honey and vanilla until blended. Add apricots, almonds, sesame seeds, flaxseed and sunflower seeds; mix well. Add cereal and oats; mix well.

2. Pour mixture into prepared pan. Press down with clean, damp hands to compact evenly. Let stand for 30 minutes, until firm, then cut into squares.

✓ **KID APPROVED**

NUTRIENTS Per Serving		
Calories: 234	Carbohydrate: 34.5 g	Calcium: 53 mg
Fat: 10.4 g	Fiber: 4.0 g	Iron: 2.1 mg
Sodium: 89 mg	Protein: 5.7 g	

Very high in: Magnesium • **High in:** Dietary fiber, iron and thiamine

Diabetes Food Choice Values Per Serving	
2	Carbohydrates
½	Meat & Alternatives
1½	Fats

Lisa Diamond, Dietitian, BC

This recipe has been handed down through Lisa's family. Lisa's mother used to make it without parchment paper, and there was always a panic to get the bars cooled and out of the pan before they glued themselves to the bottom. The moral of the story is, use parchment!

TIP
When using margarine, choose a non-hydrogenated version to limit consumption of trans fats.

VARIATION
You can substitute any kind of chip for the chocolate chips — white chocolate, butterscotch, peanut butter, etc. Dried fruit also tastes good.

Toffee Bars

• *Preparation time: 10 minutes / Cooking time: 25 minutes*
• *Preheat oven to 350°F (180°C)*
• *13- by 9-inch (3 L) baking pan, lined with parchment paper*

2 cups	quick-cooking rolled oats	500 mL
½ cup	lightly packed brown sugar	125 mL
⅓ cup	melted butter or margarine	75 mL
¼ cup	liquid honey or corn syrup	50 mL
1 ½ tsp	vanilla	7 mL
½ tsp	salt	2 mL
1 cup	semisweet chocolate chips	250 mL
½ cup	finely chopped nuts (pecans, walnuts, peanuts, etc.) or unsweetened shredded coconut	125 mL

1. In a large bowl, combine oats, brown sugar, butter, honey, vanilla and salt; mix thoroughly. Stir in chocolate chips and nuts until evenly mixed.

2. Pour mixture into prepared pan. Press down with clean, damp hands to compact evenly.

3. Bake in preheated oven for 25 minutes or until brown and crisp. Let cool in pan on a wire rack for 5 minutes. Remove from pan by lifting parchment and transfer to a cutting board. Remove parchment and cut into bars.

✓ **KID APPROVED**

Diabetes Food Choice Values Per Serving	
1 ½	Carbohydrates
2	Fats

NUTRIENTS Per Serving		
Calories: 177	Carbohydrate: 23.5 g	Calcium: 16 mg
Fat: 8.7 g	Fiber: 1.8 g	Iron: 1.0 mg
Sodium: 92 mg	Protein: 2.3 g	

Apricot Coconut Bars

MAKES 24 BARS (1 PER SERVING)

Lisa Diamond, Dietitian, BC

- *Preparation time: 20 minutes / Cooking time: 45 minutes*
- *Preheat oven to 350°F (180°C)*
- *13- by 9-inch (3 L) baking pan, greased*

2 cups	whole wheat flour	500 mL
1 1/2 cups	quick-cooking rolled oats	375 mL
1 1/3 cup	lightly packed brown sugar	325 mL
1/2 cup	oat bran	125 mL
1/2 cup	wheat bran	125 mL
1/2 tsp	baking soda	2 mL
1/2 cup	margarine or butter, softened	125 mL
1/2 cup	vegetable oil	125 mL
2 cups	chopped dried apricots	500 mL
1 1/2 cups	water	375 mL
1/2 cup	granulated sugar	125 mL
2 tbsp	all-purpose flour	25 mL
1 cup	unsweetened shredded coconut	250 mL

If you're looking for fiber, this is a great-tasting snack or dessert. But limit yourself to just one!

TIP
When using margarine, choose a non-hydrogenated version to limit consumption of trans fats.

VARIATION
Replace the apricots with your favorite dried fruit.

1. In a large bowl, combine flour, oats, brown sugar, oat bran, wheat bran and baking soda.

2. In a small bowl, combine margarine and oil. Stir into flour mixture until mixture resembles coarse crumbs. Reserve 1 cup (250 mL) crumb mixture. Press remaining crumb mixture into bottom of prepared pan. Set aside.

3. In a large saucepan, over medium high heat, combine apricots and water; bring to a boil. Reduce heat, cover and simmer for 5 minutes, until softened.

4. Meanwhile, combine sugar and flour. Stir into apricot mixture. Cook, stirring, for 1 minute or until thick. Stir in coconut.

5. Spread apricot mixture over crumbs in the pan and sprinkle evenly with reserved crumb mixture.

6. Bake for 35 minutes or until golden brown on top. Let cool completely in pan on a wire rack, then cut into bars.

❄ **FREEZER FRIENDLY**
✓ **KID APPROVED**

NUTRIENTS Per Serving		
Calories: 255	Carbohydrate: 38.0 g	Calcium: 27 mg
Fat: 11.6 g	Fiber: 3.9 g	Iron: 1.6 mg
Sodium: 86 mg	Protein: 3.6 g	

High in: Magnesium • **A source of:** Dietary fiber

Diabetes Food Choice Values Per Serving	
2	Carbohydrates
2 1/2	Fats

Eileen Campbell

These bars offer the decadent taste of cheesecake without all the calories. Enjoy after dinner or with afternoon tea.

TIPS

When lining the baking pan, make sure the foil extends 1 inch (2.5 cm) beyond the edge for easy removal.

We tested these bars with raspberries, blueberries and mixed berries. All versions tasted great.

VARIATION

If you prefer, replace the almond extract with vanilla and the orange zest with lemon.

Berry Cheesecake Bars

- *Preparation time: 20 minutes / Cooking time: 35 minutes*
- *Preheat oven to 350°F (180°C)*
- *13- by 9-inch (3 L) baking pan, lined with greased foil*

Crumb Mixture

1 cup	all-purpose flour	250 mL
1 cup	packed brown sugar	250 mL
½ cup	ground almonds	125 mL
¼ cup	melted butter	50 mL
2 tbsp	cold water	25 mL

Filling

2	eggs	2
1	egg white	1
1	package (8 oz/250 g) light cream cheese, softened	1
¾ cup	granulated sugar	175 mL
½ cup	low-fat plain yogurt	125 mL
1½ tsp	almond extract	7 mL
1 tsp	grated orange zest	5 mL
1½ cups	fresh or frozen berries (see tip, at left)	375 mL

1. *Prepare the crumb mixture:* In a medium bowl, combine flour, brown sugar, almonds, butter and water.

2. *Prepare the filling:* In a large bowl, using an electric mixer on high speed, beat eggs, egg white, cream cheese, sugar, yogurt, almond extract and orange zest until fluffy.

3. Press half of the crumb mixture into prepared pan. Pour in filling and spread evenly. Sprinkle with berries. Drop remaining crumb mixture by tablespoonfuls (15 mL) over berries. Using a knife, swirl filling, berries and crumb mixture.

4. Bake in preheated oven for 35 minutes or until a tester inserted in the center comes out clean. Let cool completely in pan on a wire rack. Remove from pan by lifting foil and transfer to a cutting board. Remove foil and cut into bars.

❄ **FREEZER FRIENDLY**
✓ **KID APPROVED**

Diabetes Food Choice Values Per Serving

2	Carbohydrates
1	Fat

NUTRIENTS Per Serving		
Calories: 163	Carbohydrate: 27.9 g	Calcium: 42 mg
Fat: 4.3 g	Fiber: 0.9 g	Iron: 1.0 mg
Sodium: 152 mg	Protein: 3.6 g	

Pink Strawberry Wiggles

MAKES 16 SERVINGS

Marion French, PEI

● *Preparation time: 10 minutes / Chilling time: 3 hours*

● *8-inch (2 L) square baking pan*

3 cups	pink or red fruit juice (such as grapefruit or cranberry-raspberry)	750 mL
4	envelopes (each ¼ oz/7 g) unflavored gelatin	4
2 tbsp	liquid honey (optional)	25 mL
1 cup	fat-free yogurt (strawberry- or raspberry-flavored)	250 mL

1. In a medium saucepan, heat juice to boiling.
2. In a large, heatproof bowl, whisk together gelatin and honey (if using; if not using honey, whisk 1 tbsp/15 mL cold water with gelatin). Gradually whisk in boiling juice, whisking until gelatin is dissolved. Gradually add yogurt, whisking until well combined. Pour into pan, cover and refrigerate until firm, about 3 hours.
3. Cut into squares and serve.

 **✓ KID APPROVED**

What a fun treat for kids (adults will enjoy them too)! Just the name makes you want to make them and eat them.

TIP
For fun, let kids choose a cookie cutter to make their own shapes.

VARIATION
Other colors of fruit juice can be used with an appropriate flavor of yogurt.

NUTRIENTS Per Serving		
Calories: 40	Carbohydrate: 7.9 g	Calcium: 26 mg
Fat: 0.0 g	Fiber: 0.0 g	Iron: 0.1 mg
Sodium: 21 mg	Protein: 2.2 g	

Diabetes Food Choice Values Per Serving

½ Carbohydrate

Chocolate Surprise Pudding Pops

• **Preparation time: 5 minutes / Freezing time: 6 hours**
• *Large ice pop molds*

1	large avocado, peeled and pitted	1
1	very ripe banana	1
½ cup	milk	125 mL
2 tbsp	unsweetened cocoa powder	25 mL
1 tbsp	liquid honey	15 mL
1 tsp	vanilla	5 mL

1. In blender, on high speed, blend avocado, banana, milk, cocoa powder, honey and vanilla until smooth.
2. Pour into molds and freeze until firm, about 6 hours or overnight.

❄ FREEZER FRIENDLY
✓ KID APPROVED

Healthy Frozen Pops
Doris Ouellet, QC

This great treat is healthier than store-bought Popsicles. Adapt the recipe to suit your family's preferences in fruit and yogurt. It is refreshing even with only yogurt in the mold. Everyone will ask for more!

Spoon low-fat vanilla yogurt into the bottom of ice pop molds. Add small pieces of chopped fruit (strawberry, blueberry, raspberry, mango, pineapple, etc.). Top with more yogurt. Freeze until firm, about 2 hours.

Diabetes Food Choice Values Per Serving	
1	Carbohydrate
2½	Fats

NUTRIENTS Per Serving		
Calories: 187	Carbohydrate: 19.8 g	Calcium: 49 mg
Fat: 12.7 g	Fiber: 5.1 g	Iron: 1.3 mg
Sodium: 21 mg	Protein: 3.3 g	

Very high in: Folate • **High in:** Dietary fiber, vitamin B$_6$ and magnesium

Fruit Frenzy Pops

**MAKES
16 SMALL POPS
(1 PER SERVING)**

**Anne-Christine Giguère,
Sabrina Tremblay and
Cindy Martel, QC**

- *Preparation time: 10 minutes / Freezing time: 6 hours*
- *Small ice pop molds*

1	very ripe banana	1
1 1/2 cups	bran cereal or bran flakes cereal	375 mL
1 cup	hulled strawberries	250 mL
10 oz	silken tofu	300 g
2 cups	low-fat plain yogurt	500 mL
3/4 cup	frozen orange juice concentrate (1/2 can)	175 mL

1. In food processor or blender, on low speed, purée banana, bran cereal and strawberries until smooth. Stir in tofu, yogurt and orange juice concentrate until well combined.
2. Pour into molds and freeze until firm, about 6 hours.

 **FREEZER FRIENDLY**
✓ **KID APPROVED**

These are a cool and tasty treat on a hot summer day. Invite the neighborhood kids over for a new taste sensation.

VARIATION
Vary the fruits used! Choose a mixture of berries or a combination of exotic fruits. You'll need about 1 1/2 cups (375 mL) total. Use a flavored tofu, such as almond, peach or banana. Use your favorite cereals. Be creative and don't be afraid to go wild with new combinations.

NUTRIENTS Per Serving		
Calories: 76	Carbohydrate: 13.9 g	Calcium: 70 mg
Fat: 1.2 g	Fiber: 1.1 g	Iron: 0.9 mg
Sodium: 63 mg	Protein: 3.5 g	
High in: Vitamin C and folate		

Diabetes Food Choice Values Per Serving	
1	Carbohydrate

About the Nutrient Analysis

Computer-assisted nutrient analysis of the recipes was performed by Info Access (1988) Inc., Don Mills, Ontario, using the Nutritional Accounting component of the CBORD Menu Management System. The nutrient database was the 2005 Canadian Nutrient File, supplemented when necessary with documented data from reliable sources.

The analysis was based on:

- imperial weights and measures (except for foods typically packaged and used in metric quantity);
- the larger number of servings (smaller portion) when there was a range;
- the smaller ingredient quantity when there was a range; and
- the first ingredient listed when there was a choice of ingredients.

Unless otherwise stated, recipes were analyzed using canola vegetable oil, non-hydrogenated margarine, 2% milk and 1% to 2% yogurt. Calculation of meat and poultry recipes assumed that only the lean portion, without skin, was eaten. Salt was included only when a specific amount was given. Optional ingredients and garnishes in unspecified amounts were not included in the calculations.

Nutrient Information on Recipes

- Nutrient values have been rounded to one decimal place, with the exception of those for sodium and calcium, which have been rounded to the nearest whole number.
- Good and excellent sources of vitamins (A, C, thiamin, riboflavin, niacin, B_6, folate, B_{12}) and minerals (calcium and iron) have been identified according to the criteria established for nutrition labelling ("2003 Guide to Food Labelling and Advertising," Canadian Food Inspection Agency).
- A serving that supplies 15% of the Daily Values (DV) for a vitamin or mineral (30% for vitamin C) is a good source of that nutrient. An excellent source must supply 25% of the DV (50% for vitamin C).
- A serving that provides at least 2 grams of dietary fiber is considered a moderate source. Servings that provide at least 4 grams are a high source, and those that provide at least 6 grams are a very high source ("2003 Guide to Food Labelling and Advertising").

Diabetes Food Choice Values

Diabetes Food Choice Values were assigned based on the Canadian Diabetes Association's "Beyond the Basics: Meal Planning for Healthy Eating, Diabetes Prevention and Management" system. Carbohydrate Choices assumed 15 grams of available carbohydrate per choice. Recipes containing vegetables assumed only 1 Vegetable per recipe; additional carbohydrate was included in the Carbohydrate Choice assignment. Meat and Alternatives Choices generally assumed 7 grams of protein and 3 to 5 grams of fat per choice, although the portion sizes and specific nutrient values of ingredients were also considered. Fat Choices were based on 5 grams of fat per assignment. Because there is an element of judgment in assigning choices, there may be more than one reasonable pattern for a recipe.

Index